A DAILY
GREEK
DEVOTIONAL

365 DEVOTIONS ON THE GREEK NEW TESTAMENT

EDITED BY
JARED M. AUGUST

A Daily Greek Devotional
Edited by Jared M. August
Copyright @ 2023

Published by Northeastern Baptist Press
        Post Office Box 4600
        Bennington, VT 05201

Cover design by Allie August and Leason Stiles
Paperback ISBN: 978-1-953331-26-7
Digital ISBN: 978-1-953331-25-0

A Daily Greek Devotional offers fresh insights and practical guidance for anyone seeking to regularly read the Greek New Testament. The contributors draw attention to features of grammar and syntax across the pages of the New Testament to strengthen readers' grasp of Greek and, even more, to cultivate deeper knowledge of God and worship. I recommend this book for pastors, seminarians, and other current and former Greek students.

Brian J. Tabb
Academic Dean and Professor of Biblical Studies
Bethlehem College and Seminary

Here we have a helpful tool which will assist pastors and students and teachers to keep using their Greek. It is especially helpful because it is short and pithy, which makes it user friendly. At the same time, readers are strengthened with reflections on the meaning of the text and the application for our lives today.

Thomas R. Schreiner
James Buchanan Harrison Professor of New Testament Interpretation
The Southern Baptist Theological Seminary

We as Greek students with our busy schedules just don't spend enough time in our Greek New Testaments. This book is a great way to solve this problem. A brief Greek passage, a word about context, then a helpful commentary along with parsing helps – what more could you ask for? I highly recommend this book for anyone wanting to spend more time applying their knowledge of Greek to the text of the New Testament.

David Alan Black
Senior Professor of New Testament and Greek (Retired)
Southeastern Baptist Theological Seminary

In an ideal world, those of us who read the New Testament in Greek, and who also read it devotionally, would do both on a daily basis. But it's not an ideal world, and most of us could use any help we can get. Thankfully, along comes *A Daily Greek Devotional*, which brings the Greek and the devotion together in easy, bite-size, daily offerings.

Constantine R. Campbell
Professor and Associate Research Director
Sydney College of Divinity

A Daily Greek Devotional is just plain fun to pick up. Depending on your experience with Greek in seminary, you may doubt me on that, but you won't if you take a look inside. First of all, the exegesis and applications are right on target, day after day. On top of that, it's a painless way to review valuable language skills that may be slipping a bit in your life. Given the combination of quick trips back to the classroom and great daily applications, you won't have to force yourself to get in it. You're going to love this!

James R. Lytle
President
Clarks Summit University

So often, after a student learns the Greek of the NT, the busyness of life and ministry choke out the need for daily practice in the language. This devotional helps fill that gap between seminary life and pastoral ministry with very do-able readings of the Greek NT. I especially appreciate the neat structure of each devotional, beginning with a Greek verse or two, followed by its overall context, before offering a brief exegetical commentary and parsing of key words. Packed with helpful insights into the grammar and syntax of that day's passage, I highly commend *A Daily Greek Devotional*—especially to those rusty in the Koine dialect who need a warm invitation back to the inspired language of the New Testament.

Cory M. Marsh
Professor of New Testament
Southern California Seminary

What a great resource! Dr. August has assembled an excellent team of evangelical scholars (37 in all) to complete this volume. This tool is sure to help you keep fresh in the Greek language and discover unique exegetical insights, all while studying the Bible devotionally. The table of contents also allows you to utilize it as a reference tool when preaching and teaching through these passages of Scripture. This also enables you to share the insights gleaned with your congregations, Bible studies, and small groups!

Paul D. Weaver
Associate Professor of Bible Exposition
Dallas Theological Seminary

Contents

PREFACE

T wo of the greatest needs for students of the Greek New Testament are motivation and daily practice. To build and maintain reading proficiency, students must see the practical difference made by knowing the language as they cultivate the habit of daily reading. *A Daily Greek Devotional* seeks to meet these needs. Each of the 365 devotions consists of a carefully selected passage, a sentence or two of context, and a brief paragraph of commentary. The goal has been to offer key devotional insights based primarily on the Greek grammar and syntax. Difficult vocabulary words are provided at the bottom of each page, along with verb parsings at the contributor's discretion.

It has been both a joy and an honor to labor alongside the contributors of this volume to bring it to fruition. These thirty-seven scholars—who come from a variety of evangelical traditions (Baptist, Presbyterian, Congregational, Evangelical Anglican, and non-denominational)—represent over two dozen colleges and seminaries. They all treasure the New Testament as the very Word of God, able to make one wise unto salvation. Many are Greek professors, some are pastors. More than a few have authored widely-respected commentaries on their passages. As one reads these devotions, it is clear that these contributors don't just care about Greek grammar; they care about Greek grammar *for a purpose*. That purpose is knowing and loving the God whose New Covenant revelation was penned in the Koine dialect some two thousand years ago.

This project would not have been possible were it not for the generous commitment on the part of the contributors. All royalties from *A Daily Greek Devotional* will be given to scholarship students pursing vocational ministry in New England. It would be remiss not to mention the editorial expertise and assistance of Randy Leedy as well as Ralph and Laurie Slater. This book is a far better product because of their work.

Our sincere hope and prayer is that these devotions may be both academically enriching and spiritually refreshing.

Jared M. August
Bennington, Vermont

ABBREVIATIONS

Category	Options	Abbreviations
Person	first, second, third	1 2 3
Number	singular, plural	S P
Tense-Form	present, aorist, imperfect, perfect, pluperfect, future	P A I R L F
Voice	active, middle, passive	A M P
Mood	indicative, imperative, subjunctive, optative, infinitive, participle	I M S O N P
Gender	masculine, feminine, neuter	M F N
Case	nominative, genitive, dative, accusative, vocative	N G D A V

²⁰ ταῦτα δὲ αὐτοῦ ἐνθυμηθέντος ἰδοὺ ἄγγελος κυρίου κατ᾽ ὄναρ ἐφάνη αὐτῷ λέγων· Ἰωσὴφ υἱὸς Δαυείδ, μὴ φοβηθῇς παραλαβεῖν Μαριὰμ τὴν γυναῖκά σου· τὸ γὰρ ἐν αὐτῇ γεννηθὲν ἐκ πνεύματός ἐστιν ἁγίου. ²¹ τέξεται δὲ υἱόν, καὶ καλέσεις τὸ ὄνομα αὐτοῦ Ἰησοῦν· αὐτὸς γὰρ σώσει τὸν λαὸν αὐτοῦ ἀπὸ τῶν ἁμαρτιῶν αὐτῶν.

Context:

In this passage, Matthew records the genealogy of Jesus, "the son of David, the son of Abraham" (1:1). He then describes Jesus' birth and the consistency of this event with OT expectations through the angel's interactions with Joseph (1:18–25).

Commentary:

In 1:20, the angel appears to Joseph and urges him not to fear (μὴ φοβηθῇς) to take Mary as his wife, and in 1:21, he commands Joseph to name (καλέσεις) the baby Jesus. Notice that both of these verbs function imperatively even though the first is a subjunctive, "you shall not be afraid," and the second is a future indicative, "you will call his name Jesus." Furthermore, the angel provides significant explanation as to why Joseph should obey through his use of the conjunction γάρ (*for* or *because*—a word Matthew uses more than 120x). Joseph is not to fear γάρ *what is conceived in Mary is from the Holy Spirit*; he is to name the child Jesus γάρ *he will save his people from their sins*. In both cases, the angel assures the anxious Joseph not only that Mary has been faithful to him, but also that the Lord has been faithful to his people in sending a Savior.

ἐνθυμηθέντος > APPMSG, as he considered ‖ ὄναρ > dream ‖ φοβηθῇς > 2SAPS, be [not] afraid ‖ παραλαβεῖν > AAN, to take ‖ γεννηθέν > APPNSN, conceived ‖ τέξεται > 3SFMI, will bear ‖ καλέσεις > 2SFAI, will call ‖ σώσει > 3SFAI, will save

Further Reading: Matthew 1:1–25
Jared M. August

¹⁴ ὁ δὲ ἐγερθεὶς παρέλαβεν τὸ παιδίον καὶ τὴν μητέρα αὐτοῦ νυκτὸς καὶ ἀνεχώρησεν εἰς Αἴγυπτον, ¹⁵ καὶ ἦν ἐκεῖ ἕως τῆς τελευτῆς Ἡρῴδου· ἵνα πληρωθῇ τὸ ῥηθὲν ὑπὸ κυρίου διὰ τοῦ προφήτου λέγοντος· ἐξ Αἰγύπτου ἐκάλεσα τὸν υἱόν μου.

CONTEXT:
Matthew 2:13-15 describes the account of Joseph fleeing with his family to Egypt as Herod sought to kill the infant Jesus (cf. 2:16-18).

COMMENTARY
In his Gospel, Matthew uses the verb πληρόω 14 times in reference to the "fulfillment" of the OT: 5x in reference to non-predictive OT historical accounts (2:15, 17; 13:14 [ἀναπληρόω], 35; 27:9), 4x in reference to generally anticipatory OT themes (2:23; 5:17; 26:54, 56), and 5x in reference to predictive OT prophecies (1:22; 4:14; 8:17; 12:17; 21:4). Matthew 2:15 is an instance where the Gospel author cites a non-Messianic OT passage, Hosea 11:1, which in its original context referred to the Lord's protection of the nation Israel: "When Israel was a child, I loved him. And out of Egypt I have called my son." Matthew, therefore, cites Hosea 11:1 and uses πληρωθῇ not to assert that Jesus "predictively fulfilled" a prophecy, but to articulate the reality that God consistently protected his Son, Israel in the OT, Jesus in the NT:

> Hosea 11:1—God protected his son, Israel, by leading the nation *out of* Egypt.
> Matthew 2:15—God protected his Son, Jesus, by leading his family *to* Egypt.

In an ironic twist, the place of safety is no longer the land of Israel, but the land of Egypt. The plans of our sovereign God cannot be thwarted by rogue nations or wicked rulers.

ἐγερθείς > APPMSN, arose || παρέλαβεν > 3SAAI, took || παιδίον > child || μητέρα > mother || νυκτός > night || ἀνεχώρησεν > 3SAAI, departed || Αἴγυπτον > Egypt || ἦν > 3SIAI, was, remained || τελευτῆς > death || Ἡρῴδου > of Herod || πληρωθῇ > 3SAPS, might be fulfilled || τὸ ῥηθέν > APPNSN, what was spoken || λέγοντος > PAPMSG, saying || ἐκάλεσα > 3SAAI, called

Further Reading: Matthew 2:13-18
Jared M. August

²³ καὶ ἐλθὼν κατῴκησεν εἰς πόλιν λεγομένην Ναζαρέτ· ὅπως πληρωθῇ τὸ ῥηθὲν διὰ τῶν προφητῶν ὅτι Ναζωραῖος κληθήσεται.

CONTEXT:

Matthew 2:19–23 summarizes the events after Herod's death and Joseph's return to the land of Israel with his family. This passage provides background information as to why Jesus grew up in Nazareth.

COMMENTARY:

If you search the OT for the statement, "He shall be called a Nazarene" (Ναζωραῖος κληθήσεται), you will not find it. How then, could Matthew assert, "So that what was spoken through the prophets might be fulfilled"? Some have suggested he may have alluded to: (1) Isaiah 4:3; 11:1 where a connection is made between the sound of the Hebrew word *nezer* ("branch") and "Nazarene"; (2) Judges 13:5, 7; 16:17 where a connection is made between Jesus and Samson as a "Nazirite to God"; and (3) Numbers 6:1–21, which describes the Nazirite vow. One intriguing alternative proposal, however, is that Matthew did not intend to cite any OT passage, but rather sought to develop the theme that the Messiah would come from a lowly background, a reality consistent with Jesus' upbringing in Nazareth (cf. Nathaniel's comment, "Can anything good come from Nazareth?" John 1:46, and Jesus' reputation as the "Nazarene," Matt 26:71; Mark 14:67; Luke 4:34). Favoring this option are the similarities between 2:23 and the other formula-citations where no OT passage is cited (5:17; 26:54, 56). Note how in 2:23 Matthew uses the plural τῶν προφητῶν rather than the singular τοῦ προφήτου, perhaps alluding to a theme from multiple prophets (e.g., Ps 22, 69; Zech 9–14; Isa 52–53). Additionally, although the participle λέγοντος ("saying") appears in all the formula-citations where an OT passage is cited to introduce the quotation, it does not appear in 2:23. In this way, the general OT anticipatory theme regarding a humble and lowly Messiah "might be fulfilled" (πληρωθῇ) by Jesus' upbringing in the humble and lowly Nazareth.

ἐλθών > AAPMSN, going ‖ κατῴκησεν > 3SAAI, lived ‖ πόλιν > city ‖ λεγομένην > PPPFSA, called ‖ Ναζαρέτ > Nazareth ‖ πληρωθῇ > 3SAPS, might be fulfilled ‖ τὸ ῥηθέν > APPNSN, what was spoken ‖ Ναζωραῖος > Nazarene ‖ κληθήσεται > 3SFPI, will be called

Further Reading: Matthew 2:19–23
Jared M. August

MATTHEW 4:19–22

¹⁹ καὶ λέγει αὐτοῖς· δεῦτε ὀπίσω μου, καὶ ποιήσω ὑμᾶς ἁλιεῖς ἀνθρώπων. ²⁰ οἱ δὲ εὐθέως ἀφέντες τὰ δίκτυα ἠκολούθησαν αὐτῷ. ²¹ καὶ προβὰς ἐκεῖθεν εἶδεν ἄλλους δύο ἀδελφούς, Ἰάκωβον τὸν τοῦ Ζεβεδαίου καὶ Ἰωάννην τὸν ἀδελφὸν αὐτοῦ, ἐν τῷ πλοίῳ μετὰ Ζεβεδαίου τοῦ πατρὸς αὐτῶν καταρτίζοντας τὰ δίκτυα αὐτῶν, καὶ ἐκάλεσεν αὐτούς. ²² οἱ δὲ εὐθέως ἀφέντες τὸ πλοῖον καὶ τὸν πατέρα αὐτῶν ἠκολούθησαν αὐτῷ.

CONTEXT:

In Matthew 4:18–22 Jesus calls his first disciples—all of whom were fishermen—to become fishers of men (ἁλιεῖς ἀνθρώπων). These disciples include Simon Peter, Andrew, James, and John.

COMMENTARY:

After Jesus calls Simon Peter and Andrew to follow him (4:19), they immediately leave all and follow (4:20). The same reaction is found with James and John (4:21–22). Notice the intentional repetition in this passage: οἱ δὲ εὐθέως ἀφέντες τὰ δίκτυα ἠκολούθησαν αὐτῷ (4:20) and οἱ δὲ εὐθέως ἀφέντες τὸ πλοῖον καὶ τὸν πατέρα αὐτῶν ἠκολούθησαν αὐτῷ (4:22). Both verses describe the disciples' identical, decisive response to "follow" (ἠκολούθησαν, aorist tense): "Immediately they left _____ and followed him." Simon Peter and Andrew left their nets; James and John left the boat and their father. In both cases, these disciples forsook all visible support to follow their Master. Are we willing to do the same?

λέγει > 3SPAI, said ‖ δεῦτε ὀπίσω μου > follow after me ‖ ποιήσω > 1SFAI, make ‖ ἁλιεῖς > fishers ‖ ἀφέντες > AAPMPN, leaving ‖ δίκτυα > nets ‖ ἠκολούθησαν > 3PAAI, followed ‖ προβάς > AAPMSN, going on ‖ ἐκεῖθεν > from there ‖ εἶδεν > 3SAAI, saw ‖ τὸν τοῦ Ζεβεδαίου > the son of Zebedee ‖ πλοίῳ > boat ‖ καταρτίζοντας > PAPMPA, mending ‖ ἐκάλεσεν > 3SAAI, called

Further Reading: Matthew 4:18–25
Jared M. August

JANUARY 5
MATTHEW 5:6

⁶μακάριοι οἱ πεινῶντες καὶ διψῶντες τὴν δικαιοσύνην, ὅτι αὐτοὶ χορτασθήσονται.

CONTEXT:
In Matthew 5:1–7:29, Matthew records Jesus' Sermon on the Mount. The first section (5:3–10) records a series of blessings known as the Beatitudes.

COMMENTARY:
Each of the Beatitudes is structured in the same manner: Jesus first makes a statement about those who are "blessed," "favored," or "happy" (Μακάριοι), he then uses the conjunction ὅτι and describes their reward. In Matthew 5:6, the blessed are *those who hunger and thirst for righteousness.* How are they blessed? *Because (ὅτι) they will be satisfied.* Notice how both participles (πεινῶντες and διψῶντες) are present and active, yet χορτασθήσονται is a future passive verb. When we hunger and thirst for righteousness, we can rest in the promise that we will be satisfied by our Savior.

οἱ πεινῶντες > PAPMPN, those who hunger ‖ διψῶντες > PAPMPN, thirst ‖ χορτασθήσονται > 3PFPI, will be satisfied

Further Reading: Matthew 5:3–12
Jared M. August

⁹ οὕτως οὖν προσεύχεσθε ὑμεῖς· Πάτερ ἡμῶν ὁ ἐν τοῖς οὐρανοῖς· ἁγιασθήτω τὸ ὄνομά σου· ¹⁰ ἐλθέτω ἡ βασιλεία σου· γενηθήτω τὸ θέλημά σου, ὡς ἐν οὐρανῷ καὶ ἐπὶ γῆς· ¹¹ τὸν ἄρτον ἡμῶν τὸν ἐπιούσιον δὸς ἡμῖν σήμερον· ¹² καὶ ἄφες ἡμῖν τὰ ὀφειλήματα ἡμῶν, ὡς καὶ ἡμεῖς ἀφήκαμεν τοῖς ὀφειλέταις ἡμῶν· ¹³ καὶ μὴ εἰσενέγκῃς ἡμᾶς εἰς πειρασμόν, ἀλλὰ ῥῦσαι ἡμᾶς ἀπὸ τοῦ πονηροῦ.

CONTEXT:
In Matthew 6:9–13, Jesus teaches the disciples how to pray.

COMMENTARY:
Notice the repeated use of aorist imperative verbs in this prayer: "Let your name be made holy" (ἁγιασθήτω), "let your kingdom come" (ἐλθέτω), "let your will be done" (γενηθήτω), "give us today our daily bread" (δός), "forgive us our debts" (ἄφες), "lead us not into temptation" (εἰσενέγκῃς, subjunctive with μή), and "deliver us from the evil one" (ῥῦσαι). These verbs illustrate a frequent way in which the imperative mood is used through the NT—not as a command or directive but as a request or plea directed toward God. In this way, Jesus is not teaching his disciples to demand the Father to act in a certain fashion but encouraging them to come before him with specific requests. What a great joy it is to have a God who knows our every need and hears all our prayers!

προσεύχεσθε > 2PPMM, pray || ἁγιασθήτω > 3SAPM, be made holy || ἐλθέτω > 3SAAM, come || γενηθήτω > 3SAPM, be done || ἐπιούσιον > daily || δός > 2SAAM, give || ἄφες > 2SAAM, forgive || ὀφειλήματα > debts || ἀφήκαμεν > 1PAAI, forgave || ὀφειλέταις > debtors || εἰσενέγκῃς > 2SAAS, lead || πειρασμόν > temptation || ῥῦσαι > 2SAMM, deliver

Further Reading: Luke 11:2–4
Jared M. August

JANUARY 7
MATTHEW 7:7–10

⁷ αἰτεῖτε καὶ δοθήσεται ὑμῖν, ζητεῖτε καὶ εὑρήσετε, κρούετε καὶ ἀνοιγήσεται ὑμῖν· ⁸ πᾶς γὰρ ὁ αἰτῶν λαμβάνει καὶ ὁ ζητῶν εὑρίσκει καὶ τῷ κρούοντι ἀνοιγήσεται. ⁹ ἢ τίς ἐστιν ἐξ ὑμῶν ἄνθρωπος, ὃν αἰτήσει ὁ υἱὸς αὐτοῦ ἄρτον, μὴ λίθον ἐπιδώσει αὐτῷ; ¹⁰ ἢ καὶ ἰχθὺν αἰτήσει, μὴ ὄφιν ἐπιδώσει αὐτῷ;

CONTEXT:
Jesus' Sermon on the Mount continues in Matthew 7:7–10 with Jesus' teaching about making requests to the Father: "Ask, seek, knock."

COMMENTARY:
Notice the three present active imperatives: "Ask" (αἰτεῖτε), "seek" (ζητεῖτε), and "knock" (κρούετε). Each is joined with a future verb that expresses a promise: "Ask and it will be given" (δοθήσεται), "seek and you will find" (εὑρήσετε), "knock and it will be opened" (ἀνοιγήσεται). Jesus' words are emphatic and might be paraphrased, "Ask and don't stop asking!" He provides two illustrations to demonstrate the goodness of the Father in answering prayer. If a son should ask for bread, would his father respond by giving him a stone? If a son should ask for a fish, would his father respond by giving him a snake? The use of μή in both these questions demands a negative answer, a resounding *No, of course not!* If an earthly father will give his son what he requests, how much more will our heavenly Father?

αἰτεῖτε > 2PPAM, ask || δοθήσεται > 3SFPI, will be given || ζητεῖτε > 2PPAM, seek || εὑρήσετε > 2PFAI, will find || κρούετε > 2PPAM, knock || ἀνοιγήσεται > 3SFPI, will be opened || ὁ αἰτῶν > PAPMSN, who asks || λαμβάνει > 3SPAI, receives || ὁ ζητῶν > PAPMSN, who seeks || εὑρίσκει > 3SPAI, finds || τῷ κρούοντι > PAPMSD, who knocks || ἐστιν > 3SPAI, is || αἰτήσει > 3SFAI, will ask || ἐπιδώσει > 3SFAI, will give || ἰχθύν > fish || ὄφιν > snake

Further Reading: Luke 11:9–13
Jared M. August

³ περὶ τοῦ υἱοῦ αὐτοῦ τοῦ γενομένου ἐκ σπέρματος Δαυὶδ κατὰ σάρκα,
⁴ τοῦ ὁρισθέντος υἱοῦ θεοῦ ἐν δυνάμει κατὰ πνεῦμα ἁγιωσύνης ἐξ
ἀναστάσεως νεκρῶν, Ἰησοῦ Χριστοῦ τοῦ κυρίου ἡμῶν.

CONTEXT:

At the very beginning of Romans, Paul introduces himself as an apostle (1:1) whose purpose is "to effect the obedience of faith among all the peoples on behalf of [Jesus'] name" (Rom 1:5).

COMMENTARY:

Jesus Christ both *is* the Son of God (περὶ τοῦ υἱοῦ αὐτοῦ) and is *appointed/declared* the Son of God (τοῦ ὁρισθέντος υἱοῦ θεοῦ). Notice that the phrase περὶ τοῦ υἱοῦ αὐτοῦ is not qualified in any way. He simply *is* the Son of God and always has been. Yet that phrase is explained with two substantival participles: τοῦ γενομένου and τοῦ ὁρισθέντος. With the former we learn that this eternal Son of God came into the world in a certain way, τοῦ γενομένου ἐκ σπέρματος Δαυίδ. Consequently, to come through the line of David means Jesus inherits an eternal dominion over all peoples and nations (2 Sam 7; Ps 2). Yet, he is specifically τοῦ ὁρισθέντος υἱοῦ θεοῦ ... ἐξ (cause or means) ἀναστάσεως νεκρῶν. That means he *claimed* his throne by virtue of the resurrection. For this reason, all peoples must now turn to him in obedience of faith: he is and always has been the Lord of all—a reality historically demonstrated through his birth and resurrection.

γενομένου > AMPMSG, the one born ‖ σπέρματος > seed, descendent ‖ ὁρισθέντος > APPMSG, the one determined, appointed, designated, declared

Further Reading: Romans 1:1–7 & Habakkuk 1–3
Nicholas G. Piotrowski

JANUARY 9
ROMANS 1:16–17

¹⁶ οὐ γὰρ ἐπαισχύνομαι τὸ εὐαγγέλιον, δύναμις γὰρ θεοῦ ἐστιν εἰς σωτηρίαν παντὶ τῷ πιστεύοντι, Ἰουδαίῳ τε πρῶτον καὶ Ἕλληνι. ¹⁷ δικαιοσύνη γὰρ θεοῦ ἐν αὐτῷ ἀποκαλύπτεται ἐκ πίστεως εἰς πίστιν, καθὼς γέγραπται· ὁ δὲ δίκαιος ἐκ πίστεως ζήσεται.

CONTEXT:
After introducing himself and summarizing the gospel he preaches (1:1–6), Paul tells the Roman Christians that he desires to visit them so that he may see the gospel bear fruit among them (1:11–13) as well as "among the rest of the peoples" of the world (1:13). With that Paul is prepared to lead into his thorough explanation of the gospel in 1:16–8:39.

COMMENTARY:
This is Paul's thesis statement; it encapsulates the theology of Romans *in nuce*. In the rest of the epistle Paul unpacks both how the gospel δύναμις ... θεοῦ ἐστιν εἰς σωτηρίαν παντὶ τῷ πιστεύοντι; as well as the means by which δικαιοσύνη ... θεοῦ ἐν αὐτῷ ἀποκαλύπτεται. And here he gives a hint on how his argument will unfold: ἐκ πίστεως εἰς πίστιν. Ἐκ is likely a preposition of source, meaning *from/out of* faith. And εἰς is a preposition of result, meaning *to generate* faith. Thus, it is God's faithfulness (namely to fulfill Habakkuk 2:4, cited at the end of verse 17) that will publicly demonstrate his righteousness (δικαιοσύνη γὰρ θεοῦ ἐν αὐτῷ ἀποκαλύπτεται), and in so doing provoke faith that will save sinners by creating an awareness of sin within them.

ἐπαισχύνομαι > 1SPMI, I am [not] ashamed ‖ ἀποκαλύπτεται > 3SPPI, it is revealed

Further Reading: Romans 1:8–17
Nicholas G. Piotrowski

⁵ κατὰ δὲ τὴν σκληρότητά σου καὶ ἀμετανόητον καρδίαν θησαυρίζεις σεαυτῷ ὀργὴν ἐν ἡμέρᾳ ὀργῆς καὶ ἀποκαλύψεως δικαιοκρισίας τοῦ θεοῦ.

CONTEXT:

Before Paul can proclaim how God's righteousness is revealed in the gospel, he first delineates how God's wrath is being revealed "against all ungodliness and unrighteousness of mankind" (1:18). Yet, he is patient toward sinners, desiring to lead them to repentance (2:4).

COMMENTARY:

God's patience, however, is not without limits. Because people refuse to repent (τὴν σκληρότητά σου καὶ ἀμετανόητον καρδίαν), a specific day is determined when the fullness of God's righteousness—in this case his righteous *judgment* (δικαιοκρισίας τοῦ θεοῦ)—will be revealed in wrath. This is not some generic day, as though to say "*a* day of wrath," but ἡμέρᾳ ὀργῆς is definite: "*the* day of wrath." The phrase is a genitive construction governed by Apollonius' Corollary, wherein two successive anarthrous nouns carry a definitive meaning. The result, therefore, is that Paul here speaks of a specific eschatologically determinative day. On that day the full measure of God's wrath—stored up over the ages—will be unimpeachably leveled against "all ungodliness and wickedness of men" (1:18). Until then, repentance is possible and deeply encouraged.

σκληρότητα > hardness, stubbornness ‖ ἀμετανόητον > unrepentant ‖ θησαυρίζεις > 2SPAI, you are storing up (cf. "treasure," Matt 6:19) ‖ ἀποκαλύψεως > revelation, unveiling ‖ δικαιοκρισίας > righteous judgment

Further Reading: Romans 2:1–16
Nicholas G. Piotrowski

²⁸ οὐ γὰρ ὁ ἐν τῷ φανερῷ Ἰουδαῖός ἐστιν οὐδὲ ἡ ἐν τῷ φανερῷ ἐν σαρκὶ περιτομή, ²⁹ ἀλλ᾽ ὁ ἐν τῷ κρυπτῷ Ἰουδαῖος, καὶ περιτομὴ καρδίας ἐν πνεύματι οὐ γράμματι, οὗ ὁ ἔπαινος οὐκ ἐξ ἀνθρώπων ἀλλ᾽ ἐκ τοῦ θεοῦ.

CONTEXT:
To the Jew who was already convinced of the sinfulness of the Gentiles, Paul has delivered the sobering truth that *everyone* is a sinner under God's judgment (2:1-16). Subsequently Paul will conclude that Jews and Greeks are "all under sin" (3:9), its power and its consequences.

COMMENTARY:
Paul now delivers this startling claim (though not unique to Rom 2, as he will go on in 9:6-33) that the principal mark of the people of God is not in some external reality, something visible like circumcision. Rather, the determining mark is invisible (ἐν τῷ κρυπτῷ)—a matter of the heart that God himself circumcises (περιτομὴ καρδίας). In making this point Paul employs a parallel: notice the similar constructs ὁ ἐν τῷ φανερῷ Ἰουδαῖος and ὁ ἐν τῷ κρυπτῷ Ἰουδαῖος. Such writing is poetically appealing, helps with memorization, and serves to drive home the contrast between competing ideas of what it means to be the people of God. In this way Paul is on his way to his boldest claim: λογιζόμεθα γὰρ δικαιοῦσθαι πίστει ἄνθρωπον χωρὶς ἔργων νόμου (3:28).

φανερῷ > visible, openly known ‖ **κρυπτῷ** > hidden, secret ‖ **γράμματι** > letter, writing ‖ **ἔπαινος** > praise, approval

Further Reading: Romans 2:17–29
Nicholas G. Piotrowski

²¹ νυνὶ δὲ χωρὶς νόμου δικαιοσύνη θεοῦ πεφανέρωται μαρτυρουμένη ὑπὸ τοῦ νόμου καὶ τῶν προφητῶν, ²² δικαιοσύνη δὲ θεοῦ διὰ πίστεως Ἰησοῦ Χριστοῦ εἰς πάντας τοὺς πιστεύοντας. οὐ γάρ ἐστιν διαστολή, ²³ πάντες γὰρ ἥμαρτον καὶ ὑστεροῦνται τῆς δόξης τοῦ θεοῦ.

CONTEXT:

After his lengthy treatise on the thoroughness of human sinfulness and the wrath of God against all sinners (1:18–3:20), Paul now turns to the good news of the revelation of God's righteousness in the gospel, as promised in 1:16–17.

COMMENTARY:

There are several genitives in these verses that force us to slow down: δικαιοσύνη θεοῦ, πίστεως Ἰησοῦ Χριστοῦ, and τῆς δόξης τοῦ θεοῦ. Yet it is the finite verb, πεφανέρωται, that should get our foremost attention. God's righteousness *has been manifested* (taking δικαιοσύνη θεοῦ as a possessive genitive). Was it hidden? Only now does it go public? Exactly! The phrase νυνὶ δέ demonstrates this historical shift. In the past (as in the days of Habakkuk, hence the quote in 1:17) God's judgment and salvation may have seemed dubious. *But now* the righteous character of God is on full display (even though it had always been μαρτυρουμένη ὑπὸ τοῦ νόμου καὶ τῶν προφητῶν) in Jesus' faithful act (πίστεως Ἰησοῦ Χριστοῦ is perhaps a subjective genitive) which he performs on behalf of all believers (πάντας τοὺς πιστεύοντας). And so, in Jesus' faithfulness—at the turn of the ages—God has demonstrated his righteousness, and this provokes sinners to faith in him.

πεφανέρωται > 3SRPI, has been made manifest ‖ διαστολή > a difference, a distinction ‖ ὑστεροῦνται > 3PPPI, lowered in status, made deficient, lack, brought up short

Further Reading: Romans 3:21–31
Nicholas G. Piotrowski

JANUARY 13
ROMANS 3:24-26

... ²⁴ δικαιούμενοι δωρεὰν τῇ αὐτοῦ χάριτι διὰ τῆς ἀπολυτρώσεως τῆς ἐν Χριστῷ Ἰησοῦ· ²⁵ ὃν προέθετο ὁ θεὸς ἱλαστήριον διὰ τῆς πίστεως ἐν τῷ αὐτοῦ αἵματι εἰς ἔνδειξιν τῆς δικαιοσύνης αὐτοῦ διὰ τὴν πάρεσιν τῶν προγεγονότων ἁμαρτημάτων ²⁶ ἐν τῇ ἀνοχῇ τοῦ θεοῦ, πρὸς τὴν ἔνδειξιν τῆς δικαιοσύνης αὐτοῦ ἐν τῷ νῦν καιρῷ, εἰς τὸ εἶναι αὐτὸν δίκαιον καὶ δικαιοῦντα τὸν ἐκ πίστεως Ἰησοῦ.

CONTEXT:
Paul has established in 3:21-23 that "the righteousness of God" is demonstrated through the faithfulness of Jesus Christ, which is effective for all believers. *What Jesus' unique act of faithfulness was*—and how it particularly unveils God's righteousness—now carries the discourse further.

COMMENTARY:
Again, there are a lot of exegetical issues to resolve here. But we can make good headway by noticing a beautiful shift in the use of the δικαιο- root. In 1:17 and in the previous verses 21-22 it was used as a noun referring to God's attribute of righteousness (as well as in v. 25, and as an adjective in v. 26). But in v. 24 it has a verbal use—God's act of declaring sinners righteous. How can God declare sinners righteous and himself still be righteous? Only because Jesus' blood serves as the propitiatory just recompense (ἱλαστήριον) for his people's sins. While God has always been righteous, it is only this public work of Jesus (προέθετο) that demonstrates or proves (ἔνδειξιν) God's righteousness ἐν τῷ νῦν καιρῷ. Thus Paul exults, εἰς τὸ εἶναι αὐτὸν δίκαιον καὶ δικαιοῦντα τὸν ἐκ πίστεως Ἰησοῦ!

δικαιούμενοι > PPPMPN, being justified ‖ δωρεάν > as a gift, without payment ‖ ἀπολυτρώσεως > release, redemption ‖ προέθετο > 3SAMI, set forth publicly ‖ ἔνδειξιν > demonstration, proof ‖ ἱλαστήριον > place of propitiation, means of expiation ‖ πάρεσιν > deliberate disregard, letting go unpunished ‖ προγεγονότων > RAPNPG, former ‖ ἀνοχῇ > forbearance, clemency ‖ δικαιοῦντα > PAPMSA, the one justifying, the one pronouncing as righteous

Further Reading: Romans 3:21-31
Nicholas G. Piotrowski

13

¹³ οὐ γὰρ διὰ νόμου ἡ ἐπαγγελία τῷ Ἀβραὰμ ἢ τῷ σπέρματι αὐτοῦ, τὸ κληρονόμον αὐτὸν εἶναι κόσμου, ἀλλὰ διὰ δικαιοσύνης πίστεως.

CONTEXT:

Abraham and David serve as Exhibits A and B of those justified by faith alone (4:1–12). Abraham, in particular, is the exemplar and type of all who are counted as righteous through their faith (4:11).

COMMENTARY:

Two very intriguing redemptive-historical motifs jump out of this one sentence: Abraham and his posterity were always promised *more than the land*, indeed the *whole world*; and such posterity is *ideologically* defined, not genetically defined. But the OT consistently speaks of *the land* as the *Jewish* inheritance. How, then, do Paul's words here make sense? For this sentence to help prove Paul's larger argument it cannot be a new theological development. The answer comes to us through the term τῷ σπέρματι. Before Abraham is promised "a seed" in Genesis 12:7, a theology of "the seed" had already been developing. In Genesis 3:15 a seed (LXX: σπέρματος) is promised to Eve who will reclaim the entire created order for God's purposes and humanity's destiny. The land of Israel, therefore, is a typological forecast of this larger creational promise, and Abraham's genetic seed is the means by which the Lord will eventually bless all peoples (Gen 12:3). Gentiles who act like Father Abraham by believing God's promises, therefore, are welcomed to join believing Israel in their cosmic inheritance.

σπέρματι > seed (singular or collective), posterity, offspring, descendants ‖ κληρονόμον > heir, inheritor, beneficiary

Further Reading: Romans 4:9–25 & Genesis 12–15
Nicholas G. Piotrowski

²³ οὐκ ἐγράφη δὲ δι᾽ αὐτὸν μόνον ὅτι ἐλογίσθη αὐτῷ ²⁴ ἀλλὰ καὶ δι᾽ ἡμᾶς, οἷς μέλλει λογίζεσθαι, τοῖς πιστεύουσιν ἐπὶ τὸν ἐγείραντα Ἰησοῦν τὸν κύριον ἡμῶν ἐκ νεκρῶν, ²⁵ ὃς παρεδόθη διὰ τὰ παραπτώματα ἡμῶν καὶ ἠγέρθη διὰ τὴν δικαίωσιν ἡμῶν.

CONTEXT:

Grace ultimately undergirds this program of justification by faith alone (4:16), seen in the way Abraham and Sarah were given a child when it was humanly impossible to conceive (4:18-19). Yet, while Abraham fully knew of the "deadness of Sarah's womb" (4:19), he remained fully convinced that God was able to do as he promised (4:21).

COMMENTARY:

In 3:24-26 we saw how God justifies believers based on Jesus' propitiatory self-sacrifice. Justification is, therefore, by grace alone through faith alone. The particular emphasis here is on the object of said faith. The participles τοῖς πιστεύουσιν and τὸν ἐγείραντα are both substantival: the former serving epexegetically for those to whom righteousness is credited (οἷς μέλλει λογίζεσθαι); the latter as the object of the verbal sense in the former. The righteous are *those who believe on or trust in* (τοῖς πιστεύουσιν) *the one who raised* (τὸν ἐγείραντα) Jesus from the dead. The implication is that Christians do not just believe in the reality of certain events; but trust specifically in *the God* who effects these things. As he was able to bring Sarah's womb to life, so too he brings Jesus back to life. Jesus' people, in turn, put their faith in *this* God. Thus (and in other ways) Jesus' resurrection contributes to our justification as much as his death does (καὶ ἠγέρθη διὰ τὴν δικαίωσιν ἡμῶν).

ἐλογίσθη > 3SAPI, it was reckoned, imputed, credited || λογίζεσθαι > PPN, to be reckoned, imputed, credited || παρεδόθη > 3SAPI, he was given over, delivered || παραπτώματα > violations of moral standards, sins

Further Reading: Romans 4:9-25
Nicholas G. Piotrowski

¹ δικαιωθέντες οὖν ἐκ πίστεως εἰρήνην ἔχομεν πρὸς τὸν θεὸν διὰ τοῦ κυρίου ἡμῶν Ἰησοῦ Χριστοῦ.

CONTEXT:

In 3:21–4:25 Paul has articulated and defended, through OT types and examples, how and why justification must be by faith alone.

COMMENTARY:

With the transitional conjunction οὖν the argument now pivots. Paul had told the Romans in 1:17 that they have χάρις ... καὶ εἰρήνη ἀπὸ θεοῦ πατρὸς ἡμῶν καὶ κυρίου Ἰησοῦ Χριστοῦ. Now we see how. The hypotactic clause δικαιωθέντες οὖν ἐκ πίστεως reviews the past several chapters of content and, in turn, grounds the rest of the sentence, εἰρήνην ἔχομεν πρὸς τὸν θεόν. Because believers are justified—declared righteous—the way is opened to have *peace* with God. Justification is, therefore, the logical precursor to reconciliation with God. Given the extensive discussion concerning the *wrath* of God in 1:18–3:20, Romans 5:1 appears to the reader as a glorious summit to the discourse so far. To people who know they are sinners under God's wrath, what could be more liberating and joy-inducing than to hear now εἰρήνην ἔχομεν πρὸς τὸν θεόν?

δικαιωθέντες > APPMPN, having been justified, pronounced righteous ‖ ἔχομεν > 1PPAI, have

Further Reading: Romans 5:1–11
Nicholas G. Piotrowski

¹⁷ εἰ γὰρ τῷ τοῦ ἑνὸς παραπτώματι ὁ θάνατος ἐβασίλευσεν διὰ τοῦ ἑνός, πολλῷ μᾶλλον οἱ τὴν περισσείαν τῆς χάριτος καὶ τῆς δωρεᾶς τῆς δικαιοσύνης λαμβάνοντες ἐν ζωῇ βασιλεύσουσιν διὰ τοῦ ἑνὸς Ἰησοῦ Χριστοῦ. ¹⁸ Ἄρα οὖν ὡς δι' ἑνὸς παραπτώματος εἰς πάντας ἀνθρώπους εἰς κατάκριμα, οὕτως καὶ δι' ἑνὸς δικαιώματος εἰς πάντας ἀνθρώπους εἰς δικαίωσιν ζωῆς.

CONTEXT:

But by *what logic* does the death and resurrection of one man reconcile believers to God and save them from his wrath (5:1–11)? The answer is: the same logic by which all those in Adam became guilty and inherited the wages of death (5:12–16): covenantal union with the one who represents them before God.

COMMENTARY:

Here is one of those cases where πᾶς/πᾶσα/πᾶν does not mean every person who ever lived (in fact it rarely does; the meanings of words are sharpened by the precision of the argument in which they are employed). Rather, Paul means all people *within specific groups*: πάντας ἀνθρώπους *in Adam* and πάντας ἀνθρώπους *in Christ*. In the former, death reigns/reigned through Adam (ὁ θάνατος ἐβασίλευσεν διὰ τοῦ ἑνός). But now, those who have received the grace and gift of righteousness/justification (οἱ ... τῆς δωρεᾶς τῆς δικαιοσύνης λαμβάνοντες) are the ones who reign "in life" (ἐν ζωῇ could be temporal—keeping with the eschatological thrust of 3:21–23—or causal or instrumental or even possessive) specifically through Jesus (βασιλεύσουσιν διὰ τοῦ ἑνὸς Ἰησοῦ Χριστοῦ). Thus, while all were at one time *in Adam*, only οἱ ... λαμβάνοντες grace and righteousness are *in Christ*. So while judgment comes to all those in Adam, the δικαίωσιν ζωῆς comes to, indeed, *all* those *in Christ*. In sum, this is a beautiful statement on the security of all those in Christ leading, therefore, to their assurance of salvation.

παραπτώματι > violation of a moral standard, sin ‖ ἐβασίλευσεν > 3SAAI, reigned ‖ περισσείαν > surplus, abundance ‖ δωρεᾶς > a free gift ‖ βασιλεύσουσιν > 3PFAI, reign ‖ κατάκριμα > condemnation ‖ δικαιώματος > righteousness ‖ δικαίωσιν > justification

Further Reading: Romans 5:12–21
Nicholas G. Piotrowski

⁵ εἰ γὰρ σύμφυτοι γεγόναμεν τῷ ὁμοιώματι τοῦ θανάτου αὐτοῦ, ἀλλὰ καὶ τῆς ἀναστάσεως ἐσόμεθα· ⁶ τοῦτο γινώσκοντες ὅτι ὁ παλαιὸς ἡμῶν ἄνθρωπος συνεσταυρώθη, ἵνα καταργηθῇ τὸ σῶμα τῆς ἁμαρτίας, τοῦ μηκέτι δουλεύειν ἡμᾶς τῇ ἁμαρτίᾳ· ⁷ ὁ γὰρ ἀποθανὼν δεδικαίωται ἀπὸ τῆς ἁμαρτίας.

CONTEXT:

Paul claimed in Romans 5:20 that the law served to increase trespasses, but as sin increased, grace abounded even more. In this section, Paul seeks to answer a possible question some might ask, "Should we continue in sin so that grace might abound?" (6:1).

COMMENTARY:

The first-class conditional sentence in 6:5 asserts for the sake of argument that the readers have been identified with the likeness of Christ's death. The context of 6:3-4 demonstrates that the condition is true since they had been buried with Christ in baptism. So ἀλλά here should be understood as "certainly," emphasizing that the Roman Christians would indeed be identified with the resurrection of Christ. The identification with the death and resurrection of Christ implies freedom from slavery to sin (6:6). Δεδικαίωται could refer either to the Christians being freed from the power of sin or acquitted from the charge of sin. Both senses are true theologically, but Paul's major emphasis here is that the believer's union with the death of Christ, instead of their own death, sets them free from the power of sin.

σύμφυτοι > identified with ǁ γεγόναμεν > 1PRAI, have been ǁ ὁμοίωμα > likeness ǁ ἐσόμεθα > 1PFMI, will be ǁ παλαιός > old ǁ συνεσταυρώθη > 3SAPI, was crucified with ǁ καταργηθῇ > 3SAPS, might be brought to nothing ǁ μηκέτι > no longer ǁ δουλεύειν > PAN, to be a slave ǁ ἀποθανών > AAPMSN, died ǁ δεδικαίωται > 3SRPI, has been set free

Further Reading: Romans 6:1-14
Charlie Ray III

²⁰ ὅτε γὰρ δοῦλοι ἦτε τῆς ἁμαρτίας, ἐλεύθεροι ἦτε τῇ δικαιοσύνῃ. ²¹ τίνα οὖν καρπὸν εἴχετε τότε; ἐφ' οἷς νῦν ἐπαισχύνεσθε, τὸ γὰρ τέλος ἐκείνων θάνατος. ²² νυνὶ δὲ ἐλευθερωθέντες ἀπὸ τῆς ἁμαρτίας δουλωθέντες δὲ τῷ θεῷ ἔχετε τὸν καρπὸν ὑμῶν εἰς ἁγιασμόν, τὸ δὲ τέλος ζωὴν αἰώνιον.

CONTEXT:

In Romans 6:15-23, Paul answers the question, "Should we sin because we are not under law but under grace?" (6:15). Paul's immediate response is "May it never be!" He argues that we will either be slaves to sin leading to death or Christians enslaved to obedience leading to righteousness.

COMMENTARY:

The conjunction γάρ in 6:20 builds on Paul's human analogy of slavery in 6:16-19. When the Roman Christians earlier "were slaves of sin" (δοῦλοι ἦτε τῆς ἁμαρτίας), their disobedience meant that they were "free in regard to righteousness" (ἐλεύθεροι ἦτε τῇ δικαιοσύνῃ). But this freedom led them to commit acts of which they should have been ashamed, acts that led to death. With his second use of νυνὶ δέ in Romans (3:21 and 6:22), Paul now moves from the rotten "fruit" (καρπόν) of slavery to sin to the righteous "fruit" (καρπόν) that comes from slavery to God, which is both sanctification and eternal life. To summarize, should the Roman church continue in sin because they were not under the law? Absolutely not! Paul asserts that they have been set free from the law so that they might become slaves to God, leading them to receive the gift of God, eternal life.

ἦτε > 2PIAI, were ‖ ἐλεύθεροι > free ‖ ἐπαισχύνεσθε > 2PPMI, you are ashamed ‖ ἐλευθερωθέντες > APPMPN, having been set free ‖ δουλωθέντες > APPMPN, having been enslaved ‖ ἁγιασμόν > sanctification

Further Reading: Romans 6:15-23
Charlie Ray III

³ ἄρα οὖν ζῶντος τοῦ ἀνδρὸς μοιχαλὶς χρηματίσει ἐὰν γένηται ἀνδρὶ ἑτέρῳ· ἐὰν δὲ ἀποθάνῃ ὁ ἀνήρ, ἐλευθέρα ἐστὶν ἀπὸ τοῦ νόμου, τοῦ μὴ εἶναι αὐτὴν μοιχαλίδα γενομένην ἀνδρὶ ἑτέρῳ. ⁴ ὥστε, ἀδελφοί μου, καὶ ὑμεῖς ἐθανατώθητε τῷ νόμῳ διὰ τοῦ σώματος τοῦ Χριστοῦ, εἰς τὸ γενέσθαι ὑμᾶς ἑτέρῳ, τῷ ἐκ νεκρῶν ἐγερθέντι, ἵνα καρποφορήσωμεν τῷ θεῷ.

CONTEXT:

After discussing the Christian's relationship to sin in Romans 6, Paul now moves to a discussion of the Christian's relationship to the law. In Romans 7:1-2, using the analogy of marriage, Paul argues that death releases one from the obligation of the law.

COMMENTARY:

With ἄρα οὖν ("accordingly"), Paul indicates that his assertion in 7:3-4 is the result of his argument in 7:2. Since only death releases a woman from her marital bond to her husband, if she unites with another man while her husband is living, she will be called an adulteress (μοιχαλίς). Yet if her husband dies, she does not commit adultery if she chooses to marry. Therefore (ὥστε), Paul concludes with the point of his analogy: the Christian has died to the law through the body of Christ. Εἰς τό + infinitive often indicates result, and here, the result of the believer's death is that he can now be joined to the one who was raised from the dead, in order to bear fruit for Christ. Therefore, freedom from the law is not for the purpose of indulging the flesh but for the purpose of being joined to Christ to bear fruit for God.

ἄρα οὖν > accordingly ‖ ζῶντος > PAPMSG, while living ‖ μοιχαλίς > adulteress ‖ χρηματίσει > 3SFAI, will be called ‖ γένηται > 3SAMS, should belong ‖ ἀποθάνῃ > 3SAAS, should die ‖ γενομένην > AMPFSA, belonging ‖ ἐλευθέρα > free ‖ ἐθανατώθητε > 2PAPI, were put to death ‖ γενέσθαι > AMN, to belong ‖ τῷ … ἐγερθέντι > APPMSD, the one having been raised ‖ καρποφορήσωμεν > 1PAAS, might bear fruit

Further Reading: Romans 7:1-6
Charlie Ray III

ROMANS 8:1–3

¹ οὐδὲν ἄρα νῦν κατάκριμα τοῖς ἐν Χριστῷ Ἰησοῦ. ² ὁ γὰρ νόμος τοῦ πνεύματος τῆς ζωῆς ἐν Χριστῷ Ἰησοῦ ἠλευθέρωσέν σε ἀπὸ τοῦ νόμου τῆς ἁμαρτίας καὶ τοῦ θανάτου. ³ Τὸ γὰρ ἀδύνατον τοῦ νόμου ἐν ᾧ ἠσθένει διὰ τῆς σαρκός, ὁ θεὸς τὸν ἑαυτοῦ υἱὸν πέμψας ἐν ὁμοιώματι σαρκὸς ἁμαρτίας καὶ περὶ ἁμαρτίας κατέκρινεν τὴν ἁμαρτίαν ἐν τῇ σαρκί.

CONTEXT:
Paul concluded his discussion of the law (Romans 7) with the claim that while he served the law of God with his mind, the law of sin was still at work in his flesh (7:15–20). Though free from the law, Paul still felt the pressure of sin.

COMMENTARY:
Romans 8:1 marks a shift in Paul's discussion to the victory that believers have in Christ. If Christians have died to the law in Christ yet still struggle with sin, in what state do they find themselves? Paul now claims that Christians are free from the condemnation of the law ἐν Χριστῷ Ἰησοῦ. With the conjunction γάρ, Paul introduces the grounds for this claim: Christians have been set free from the condemnation of the law by a different law, "the law of the Spirit of life" (ὁ … νόμος τοῦ πνεύματος τῆς ζωῆς). God accomplished in His Son what the Mosaic law could not do, so that now Christians are free from the condemnation (κατάκριμα) of the law, because God condemned (κατέκρινεν) sin in the flesh.

οὐδὲν ἄρα νῦν > "There is therefore now no …" || κατάκριμα > condemnation || ἠλευθέρωσεν > 3SAAI, has set free || ἀδύνατον > impossible || ἠσθένει > 3SIAI, weakened || πέμψας > AAPMSN, sending || ὁμοιώματι > likeness || κατέκρινεν > 3SAAI, condemned

Further Reading: Romans 8:1–11
Charlie Ray III

¹⁸ λογίζομαι γὰρ ὅτι οὐκ ἄξια τὰ παθήματα τοῦ νῦν καιροῦ πρὸς τὴν μέλλουσαν δόξαν ἀποκαλυφθῆναι εἰς ἡμᾶς. ¹⁹ ἡ γὰρ ἀποκαραδοκία τῆς κτίσεως τὴν ἀποκάλυψιν τῶν υἱῶν τοῦ θεοῦ ἀπεκδέχεται.

CONTEXT:

In Romans 8:12–17, Paul addresses the tension that Christians are children of God (8:15–17) yet still find themselves suffering in this present life (8:17). These verses help answer the question of how the adopted children of God might press forward even as creation groans and decays (8:21–22).

COMMENTARY:

Paul's encouragement in 8:18–19 is that Christians can press on amidst suffering because of the future hope they have in Christ. Paul contrasts the sufferings of the Christian in the present age (τὰ παθήματα τοῦ νῦν καιροῦ) to the coming glory (τὴν μέλλουσαν δόξαν) that is to be revealed. He concludes that there is no comparison. The predicate phrase οὐκ ἄξια ("are not worthy") is placed at the beginning of the clause in a clearly emphatic way. His point is that the coming glory to be revealed far outweighs the present sufferings. Even as Paul later describes the creation as groaning and suffering (8:22), he is clear that creation itself (a possible personification) eagerly expects the revealing of the sons of God (8:19). This assurance of our identity as "children of God" (τῶν υἱῶν τοῦ θεοῦ) enables us to confidently anticipate the restoration of all things.

λογίζομαι > 1SPMI, I consider || παθήματα > sufferings || μέλλουσαν > PAPFSA, about to || ἀποκαλυφθῆναι > APN, to be revealed || ἀποκαραδοκία > eager expectation || κτίσεως > creation || ἀποκάλυψιν > revelation || ἀπεκδέχεται > 3SPMI, awaits

Further Reading: Romans 8:18–25
Charlie Ray III

³⁷ ἀλλ' ἐν τούτοις πᾶσιν ὑπερνικῶμεν διὰ τοῦ ἀγαπήσαντος ἡμᾶς.
³⁸ πέπεισμαι γὰρ ὅτι οὔτε θάνατος οὔτε ζωὴ οὔτε ἄγγελοι οὔτε ἀρχαὶ οὔτε
ἐνεστῶτα οὔτε μέλλοντα οὔτε δυνάμεις ³⁹ οὔτε ὕψωμα οὔτε βάθος οὔτε τις
κτίσις ἑτέρα δυνήσεται ἡμᾶς χωρίσαι ἀπὸ τῆς ἀγάπης τοῦ θεοῦ τῆς ἐν
Χριστῷ Ἰησοῦ τῷ κυρίῳ ἡμῶν.

CONTEXT:

These verses form the climactic conclusion to Romans 8, answering the question posed by Paul: Will anything be able to separate the Christian from the love of Christ (8:35)? With τούτοις πᾶσιν, Paul refers back to worldly pressures that might seem to separate the Christian from the love of God, such as affliction, death, and persecution (8:35-36).

COMMENTARY:

Paul is again dealing with the tension between the believer's life on this earth, and the eternal realities that are true for the Christian. Paul just quoted Psalm 44:22, which refers to those who suffer in this life for the sake of God. The Psalm ends with a question, *Why does God hide His face?* and a plea, *Come to our help, O God* (44:24-26). Paul uses a word found only here in the NT (ὑπερνικάω) to indicate that Christians are those who completely overcome through the love of God. Therefore, Paul stands convinced (note the perfect tense, πέπεισμαι) that nothing is able to separate the Christian from the love of God. Paul concludes with a further explanation of the love demonstrated through Christ Jesus (8:37). Christians overcome great trials not necessarily because of their endurance, but because of the great love of God demonstrated in the obedience and sacrifice of Christ.

ὑπερνικῶμεν > 1PPAI, prevail completely || πέπεισμαι > 1SRPI, convinced || ἐνεστῶτα > RAPNPN, (things) present || ὕψωμα > height || βάθος > depth || κτίσις > created thing || δυνήσεται > 3SFMI, will be able || χωρίσαι > AAN, to separate

Further Reading: Romans 8:31-39
Charlie Ray III

⁶ οὐχ οἷον δὲ ὅτι ἐκπέπτωκεν ὁ λόγος τοῦ θεοῦ. οὐ γὰρ πάντες οἱ ἐξ Ἰσραὴλ οὗτοι Ἰσραήλ· ⁷ οὐδ᾽ ὅτι εἰσὶν σπέρμα Ἀβραὰμ πάντες τέκνα, ἀλλ᾽· ἐν Ἰσαὰκ κληθήσεταί σοι σπέρμα. ⁸ τοῦτ᾽ ἔστιν, οὐ τὰ τέκνα τῆς σαρκὸς ταῦτα τέκνα τοῦ θεοῦ ἀλλὰ τὰ τέκνα τῆς ἐπαγγελίας λογίζεται εἰς σπέρμα.

CONTEXT:

The background of this passage is the rejection of the Messiah by the Jews. Paul is making the case that descent from Abraham has never been a sufficient indicator of who belongs among the people of God.

COMMENTARY:

The phrase οὐχ οἷον δὲ ὅτι is idiomatic, and the first sentence in 9:6 can be translated as, "It is not as though the word of God has failed" (ESV). In light of the rejection of the Messiah by the Jews, Paul is emphasizing that God's promises remain true because inclusion in the people of Israel and natural descent from Abraham have never been sufficient grounds for membership in the people of God. Paul quotes from Genesis 21:12, where God promised Abraham that his offspring (σπέρμα) would be counted through Isaac, not Ishmael. Though physically descended from Abraham, Ishmael was not the child of the promise; Isaac was. So the rejection of the Messiah by the Jews of Paul's day did not indicate a failure on God's part. Instead, those who rejected the Messiah demonstrated that they were not children of the promise, not truly from Israel (9:6), unlike one who is "counted as offspring" (λογίζεται εἰς σπέρμα, 9:8).

οἷον > as though || ἐκπέπτωκεν > 3SRAI, failed || Ἰσαάκ > Isaac || κληθήσεται > 3SFPI, shall be called

Further Reading: Romans 9:1–12
Charlie Ray III

¹¹ λέγει γὰρ ἡ γραφή· πᾶς ὁ πιστεύων ἐπ' αὐτῷ οὐ καταισχυνθήσεται.
¹² οὐ γάρ ἐστιν διαστολὴ Ἰουδαίου τε καὶ Ἕλληνος, ὁ γὰρ αὐτὸς κύριος
πάντων, πλουτῶν εἰς πάντας τοὺς ἐπικαλουμένους αὐτόν· ¹³ πᾶς γὰρ ὃς ἂν
ἐπικαλέσηται τὸ ὄνομα κυρίου σωθήσεται.

CONTEXT:

Although Paul prayed for the salvation of the Jewish people (10:1), his
countrymen sought a righteousness that came from the law and not the
righteousness that comes from faith. In these verses, Paul provides the
scriptural basis for his claim that those who believe in Jesus and confess Him as
Lord will be made righteous (10:9–10).

COMMENTARY:

Paul's first line of argumentation comes from Isaiah 28:16 where all who trusted
in God's Cornerstone would not be put to shame. With his use of διαστολή, last
used in Romans 3:22, Paul refers back to a point already made in Romans: with
God, there is no distinction between Jew and Gentile in regard to salvation.
While the message may have come to the Jew first and then the Gentile, the
gospel is the power of salvation for all who believe (1:16). God is rich toward all
who call on His name. The blessings of God promised long ago to Abraham are
poured out richly on all who believe in Christ. Paul then appeals to Joel 2:32 (LXX
3:5), reminding his readers to whom he appeals here that, in the OT too,
salvation belonged to any who called on the name of the Lord.

καταισχυνθήσεται > 3SFPI, will be ashamed ǁ διαστολή > distinction ǁ
Ἕλληνος > Gentile ǁ πλουτῶν > PAPMSN, who is rich ǁ ἐπικαλέσηται > 3SAMS,
calls ǁ σωθήσεται > 3SFPI, will be saved

Further Reading: Romans 10:5–17
Charlie Ray III

ROMANS 11:7–8

⁷ τί οὖν; ὃ ἐπιζητεῖ Ἰσραήλ, τοῦτο οὐκ ἐπέτυχεν, ἡ δὲ ἐκλογὴ ἐπέτυχεν· οἱ δὲ λοιποὶ ἐπωρώθησαν, ⁸ καθὼς γέγραπται· ἔδωκεν αὐτοῖς ὁ θεὸς πνεῦμα κατανύξεως, ὀφθαλμοὺς τοῦ μὴ βλέπειν καὶ ὦτα τοῦ μὴ ἀκούειν, ἕως τῆς σήμερον ἡμέρας.

CONTEXT:

The question that frames this section is, "God hasn't rejected His people, has he?" (11:1). While many of the Jews had rejected the Messiah, Paul appeals to the OT to show that even in the midst of dire circumstances, God always preserves for Himself a remnant chosen by grace.

COMMENTARY:

Τί οὖν, or "what then?" invites the reader to draw an inference from what has come before. If God has not rejected His people Israel, and if there was in Paul's day a remnant chosen by grace, just like in Elijah's day, what can we conclude about the Jews of Paul's day? They had not obtained the grace they were seeking because they had been hardened. In 11:8, Paul alludes to Isaiah 29:10, where God hardened the hearts of the people as they rebelled against Him. But God is still faithful, and as the Jews rejected Christ, the gospel went forth to the Gentiles, so that the Jews might be provoked to jealousy and turn to Christ (11:11).

ἐπιζητεῖ > 3SPAI, seeks || ἐπέτυχεν > 3SAAI, obtain || ἐκλογή > elect || ἐπωρώθησαν > 3PAPI, were hardened || γέγραπται > 3SRPI, it is written || ἔδωκεν > 3SAAI, gave || κατανύξεως > of stupor

Further Reading: Romans 11:1–12
Charlie Ray III

ROMANS 11:25-27

²⁵ οὐ γὰρ θέλω ὑμᾶς ἀγνοεῖν, ἀδελφοί, τὸ μυστήριον τοῦτο, ἵνα μὴ ἦτε παρ' ἑαυτοῖς φρόνιμοι, ὅτι πώρωσις ἀπὸ μέρους τῷ Ἰσραὴλ γέγονεν ἄχρι οὗ τὸ πλήρωμα τῶν ἐθνῶν εἰσέλθῃ ²⁶ καὶ οὕτως πᾶς Ἰσραὴλ σωθήσεται, καθὼς γέγραπται· ἥξει ἐκ Σιὼν ὁ ῥυόμενος, ἀποστρέψει ἀσεβείας ἀπὸ Ἰακώβ. ²⁷ καὶ αὕτη αὐτοῖς ἡ παρ' ἐμοῦ διαθήκη, ὅταν ἀφέλωμαι τὰς ἁμαρτίας αὐτῶν.

CONTEXT:

Paul has just concluded his illustration of the branch from the wild olive tree being grafted into the cultivated olive tree. This illustration was given to the Gentiles in the church in Rome to encourage them not to be arrogant in their attitude toward the Jewish people.

COMMENTARY:

These verses are full of exegetical difficulties, so it is helpful to focus on the main point of the text and the flow of the entire section (chs. 9-11). Paul has been defending the faithfulness of God in the face of the rejection of the Messiah by the Jews and he has just encouraged the Gentiles not to become arrogant lest God cut them out of the tree as well. In 11:25, Paul tells the Gentiles that the hardening of Israel is not a complete hardening, but a hardening in part (ἀπὸ μέρους). God is still faithful to the promises that He has made, and He will not abandon His people. Paul quotes from Isaiah 59:20-21 to remind his readers that just as God in his covenant had promised a deliverer in Isaiah, He had now sent that deliverer in Jesus to call His people to Himself and to forgive their sins. Ultimately, God will save all of those who are His people, those who are a part of the true Israel (9:6) and who are the true descendants of Abraham (9:7).

ἀγνοεῖν > PAN, to be ignorant || φρόνιμοι > wise || πώρωσις > hardening || γέγονεν > 3SRAI, has come || πλήρωμα > fullness || εἰσέλθῃ > 3SAAS, should come || σωθήσεται > 3SFPI, will be saved || γέγραπται > 3SRPI, it is written || ἥξει > 3SFAI, will come || Σιών > Zion || ὁ ῥυόμενος > PMPMSN, the deliverer || ἀποστρέψει > 3SFAI, will turn away || ἀσεβείας > ungodliness || ἀφέλωμαι > 1SAMS, take away

Further Reading: Romans 11:25-36
Charlie Ray III

January 28
Romans 12:1

¹ παρακαλῶ οὖν ὑμᾶς, ἀδελφοί, διὰ τῶν οἰκτιρμῶν τοῦ θεοῦ παραστῆσαι τὰ σώματα ὑμῶν θυσίαν ζῶσαν ἁγίαν εὐάρεστον τῷ θεῷ, τὴν λογικὴν λατρείαν ὑμῶν.

CONTEXT:

Paul has just completed a lengthy discussion on the nature of the gospel message (chapters 1–11) in which he described how God brought sinners into a right relationship with himself through the death and resurrection of his son, Jesus. In Romans 12–16, Paul describes the appropriate response to God's work. Paul begins with a general response but later in the section, he considers implications relevant for the Roman church's specific needs and circumstances.

COMMENTARY:

God's plan of salvation is Good News! Paul's readers are ready to respond. Introduced by the inferential conjunction οὖν, much of the remainder of the book is devoted to instructing Christians how to live in light of God's work. Paul does not begin this "practical" section with an imperative command; rather, he uses a present tense verb (παρακαλῶ). This softened approach to commanding or instructing reflects the relational aspect of Christianity. Those given a great gift need not be commanded but will naturally desire to respond appropriately. The language that follows is that of sacrifice. Believers are "urged" to "offer" or "present" (παραστῆσαι) their "bodies" (τὰ σώματα) as a "sacrifice" (θυσίαν) to God. The word σώματα is likely a synecdoche for the believers' entire selves. The sacrifice metaphor utilizes the expected physical offering word for body (σώματα) but the predicate participle ζῶσαν and predicate adjectives ἁγίαν and εὐάρεστον, help extend this to a continual and complete commitment of one's entire being. God has blessed Christians with unimaginable riches in Christ. Our response to God is naturally to devote ourselves fully to him.

παρακαλῶ > 1SPAI, I urge || οἰκτιρμῶν > mercies || παραστῆσαι > AAN, to offer, present, dedicate || ζῶσαν > PAPFSA, alive, living || εὐάρεστον > pleasing, acceptable || λογικήν > genuine, reasonable || λατρείαν > worship

Further Reading: Romans 11:25–36
Joseph D. Fantin

ROMANS 12:2

² καὶ μὴ συσχηματίζεσθε τῷ αἰῶνι τούτῳ, ἀλλὰ μεταμορφοῦσθε τῇ ἀνακαινώσει τοῦ νοὸς εἰς τὸ δοκιμάζειν ὑμᾶς τί τὸ θέλημα τοῦ θεοῦ, τὸ ἀγαθὸν καὶ εὐάρεστον καὶ τέλειον.

CONTEXT:
Using sacrificial language, Paul has just "urged" his readers to devote themselves completely to God (12:1). He now instructs his readers on proper focus. This will lead to more specific instruction that will be helpful for the Romans' present circumstances.

COMMENTARY:
Paul now makes a contrast (ἀλλά) with two imperatives, one negative (μὴ συσχηματίζεσθε) and one positive (μεταμορφοῦσθε), to instruct his readers to resist non-godly influences of the age or world and to embrace renewing one's mind. The imperatives are both passive, indicating that there is a measure of permission commanded on the part of the believer. The agents of the passives are not identified (one would expect ὑπό + gen. to express agency) but it is clear that they are diametrically opposed to one another. The agent of the first (μὴ συσχηματίζεσθε) may simply be the world system which molds the unsuspecting person or it may be something more sinister. The agent of μεταμορφοῦσθε is likely God through one or more of his instruments, such as his word and/or the Holy Spirit. The means of transformation is "by the renewing" (dative of means) "of one's mind." As is common with body parts, the article modifying "mind" (τοῦ νοός) should be interpreted as a personal pronoun ("your"). The two words (συσχηματίζεσθε and μεταμορφοῦσθε) are fairly close in meaning. The implied agents and expected results of such activities are more important. The purpose of "being transformed" is expressed by the infinitive clause (εἰς τὸ δοκιμάζειν) which is the ability to discern God's will. Christians must avoid influences that are not godly and instead allow God to shape them. In this way, they will understand God's will for their lives.

συσχηματίζεσθε > 2PPPM, be [not] conformed || μεταμορφοῦσθε > 2PPPM, be transformed || τῇ ἀνακαινώσει > by the renewing || νοός > mind || δοκιμάζειν > PAN, may discern || εὐάρεστον > acceptable, pleasing || τέλειον > perfect, complete (i.e., having reached its end)

Further Reading: Romans 12:1–8
Joseph D. Fantin

⁴ καθάπερ γὰρ ἐν ἑνὶ σώματι πολλὰ μέλη ἔχομεν, τὰ δὲ μέλη πάντα οὐ τὴν αὐτὴν ἔχει πρᾶξιν, ⁵ οὕτως οἱ πολλοὶ ἓν σῶμά ἐσμεν ἐν Χριστῷ, τὸ δὲ καθ' εἷς ἀλλήλων μέλη.

CONTEXT:

Believers are to devote themselves entirely to God and allow him to mold them into what he desires (12:1-2). However, believers are not all intended to be identical. Verse 3 exhorts the readers to avoid considering themselves better than others. Christians are diverse with different gifts (12:6-8). In this passage, Paul begins to describe the diversity that will lead to his discussion of spiritual gifts. It also sets up Paul's future discussion regarding the way in which different types of people must live together (14:1-15:13).

COMMENTARY:

Paul begins to explain (γάρ) his previous statement about how believers should think of one another. He introduces a body metaphor (cf. 12:1, τὰ σώματα) to compare (καθάπερ) each individual's body (ἑνὶ σώματι) with the way (οὕτως) the church should function. Body parts do not have the same function. The pronoun αὐτήν is an identifying adjective modifying πρᾶξιν (same function). The present tense verbs (ἔχομεν, ἔχει, ἐσμεν) are gnomic, reflecting the familiar and universal nature of this metaphor. The Christians in the church, like parts of a human body, are interconnected or possibly dependent (εἷς ἀλλήλων). Unlike other uses of this metaphor in the ancient world, this body is ἐν Χριστῷ, a statement of unity or possibly more.

καθάπερ > just as || ἔχομεν > 1PPAI, we have || ἔχει > 3SPAI, [not] have || τὴν αὐτὴν ... πρᾶξιν > the same function || ἐσμεν > 1PPAI, we are

Further Reading: Romans 12:4-8; 1 Corinthians 12:12-30
Joseph D. Fantin

ROMANS 12:16-18

¹⁶ τὸ αὐτὸ εἰς ἀλλήλους φρονοῦντες, μὴ τὰ ὑψηλὰ φρονοῦντες ἀλλὰ τοῖς ταπεινοῖς συναπαγόμενοι. μὴ γίνεσθε φρόνιμοι παρ' ἑαυτοῖς. ¹⁷ μηδενὶ κακὸν ἀντὶ κακοῦ ἀποδιδόντες, προνοούμενοι καλὰ ἐνώπιον πάντων ἀνθρώπων· ¹⁸ εἰ δυνατὸν τὸ ἐξ ὑμῶν, μετὰ πάντων ἀνθρώπων εἰρηνεύοντες.

CONTEXT:

After describing the diversity of gifts among believers (12:3-8), Paul provides instructions that will help the readers live harmoniously within the church and with outsiders. In this brief section the focus is on humility and peaceful living.

COMMENTARY:

The participles in this passage are rare independent imperatival participles (see *GGBB*, 650-51). Romans 12 has the highest concentration of this usage in the NT (the first is found in 12:9). They are all present tense and thus emphasize the ongoing or continuous action of the commands. Verse 16 opens with an intensifying personal pronoun (τὸ αὐτό, the same [way]). The pronoun is accusative and functions as the object or goal of the commanding participle (φρονοῦντες). The phrase can be translated "be like minded" or "think the same way," emphasizing the notion of thinking about one another (εἰς ἀλλήλους) as equals. The conjunction ἀλλά contrasts two opposite attitudes, namely prohibiting pride (μὴ τὰ ὑψηλὰ φρονοῦντες) and encouraging humility (τοῖς ταπεινοῖς συναπαγόμενοι). The imperative mood is used once here to command the readers not to think themselves as wise (μὴ γίνεσθε φρόνιμοι παρ' ἑαυτοῖς). Finally, using a cognate verb (εἰρηνεύοντες [εἰρηνεύω]) of the familiar word for peace (εἰρήνη), the passage instructs the readers to do whatever is in their power to be at peace with everyone. Christians are to be humble, peaceful people in whatever context they find themselves.

τὸ αὐτὸ ... φρονοῦντες > PAPMPN, be like minded, live in harmony, think the same [way] || μὴ ... φρονοῦντες > PAPMPN, do not be ... [in mind] || ὑψηλά > arrogant, proud || τοῖς ταπεινοῖς > with the humble || συναπαγόμενοι > PPPMPN, associate || μὴ γίνεσθε > 2PPMM, do not be/become || φρόνιμοι > conceited || μηδενὶ ... ἀποδιδόντες > PAPMPN, do not repay anyone || ἀντί + genitive > for || προνοούμενοι > PMPMPN, consider, respect || εἰρηνεύοντες > PAPMPN, live in peace

Further Reading: Romans 12:9-21; 14:7-9

Joseph D. Fantin

⁸ μηδενὶ μηδὲν ὀφείλετε εἰ μὴ τὸ ἀλλήλους ἀγαπᾶν· ὁ γὰρ ἀγαπῶν τὸν ἕτερον νόμον πεπλήρωκεν.

CONTEXT:

Continuing his theme of maintaining peace, Paul has just completed encouraging his readers to obey civil authorities and pay taxes. He now returns to individual instruction. Paul picks up the theme and the command "to love" which he began in 12:9; however, here he strengthens the command to include obligation.

COMMENTARY:

Christians are commanded to "owe" (imperative, ὀφείλετε) μηδενὶ μηδέν. In other words, in the midst of a society that emphasizes reciprocity, believers are to pay their debts to others and not be under obligation. Obligation here is not simply financial but rather social, where debts could demand certain actions or allegiances from the debtor to the person owed. Paul then makes a striking exception (εἰ μή) that they are to "owe" love (τὸ ἀλλήλους ἀγαπᾶν, "to love one another"). The conjunction γάρ introduces the reason for the instruction "to love." The accusative τὸν ἕτερον (another) could be either the object of ὁ ... ἀγαπῶν (the one who loves another [person]) or it could modify νόμον (the one who loves another law). The former is preferable (Jewett, *Romans*, 807–8; Cranfield, *Romans 2*, 675–76) especially in light of the OT commandments listed in the next verse. In this way, "the one who loves another" (ὁ γὰρ ἀγαπῶν τὸν ἕτερον) has "fulfilled the law" (νόμον πεπλήρωκεν).

μηδενὶ μηδέν > nothing to anyone || ὀφείλετε > 2PPAM, owe || εἰ μή > except || ἀγαπᾶν > PAN, to love || ὁ ... ἀγαπῶν > PAPMSN, the one who loves || πεπλήρωκεν > 3SRAI, has fulfilled

Further Reading: Romans 12:9–16; 13:8–10
Joseph D. Fantin

[11] καὶ τοῦτο εἰδότες τὸν καιρόν, ὅτι ὥρα ἤδη ὑμᾶς ἐξ ὕπνου ἐγερθῆναι, νῦν γὰρ ἐγγύτερον ἡμῶν ἡ σωτηρία ἢ ὅτε ἐπιστεύσαμεν.

CONTEXT:

Paul has been discussing appropriate Christian living. His instruction has been specific yet applicable to many situations (12:1–13:10). He is about to transition to specific difficulties in the church itself (14:1–15:13). Before doing so, Roman 13:11 introduces a brief section (13:11–14) providing motivation to live as instructed.

COMMENTARY:

The meaning of καὶ τοῦτο is uncertain but likely serves to remind the reader of the previous section and moving on ("and this"). It may refer back to 13:8 but given the eschatological sense of the passage, it is likely going back to the beginning of the section (12:1–2). The perfect participle (εἰδότες) functions as a present tense as is always the case with οἶδα and is likely an adverbial participle of cause (*GGBB*, 631), "because we know ..." The conjunction ὅτι introduces the content of εἰδότες τὸν καιρόν. The accusative pronoun ὑμᾶς is the subject of the infinitive ἐγερθῆναι. In light of the time, believers are "to wake up from sleep." In other words, they are to be alert and ready. The reason for this readiness (γάρ) is that ἡμῶν ἡ σωτηρία ("our salvation"), that is, our final or eschatological salvation or glorification (not referring to whether a person is presently "saved") is nearer than (ἐγγύτερον [comparative form of ἐγγύς] ... ἢ ...) "when we believed." The verb ἐπιστεύσαμεν is an ingressive aorist emphasizing initial belief.

εἰδότες > RAPMPN, knowing, because we know || ὕπνου > sleep || ἐγερθῆναι > APN, to wake up || ἐγγύτερον > nearer || ἐπιστεύσαμεν > 1PAAI, we believed

Further Reading: Romans 13:8–14
Joseph D. Fantin

⁷ οὐδεὶς γὰρ ἡμῶν ἑαυτῷ ζῇ καὶ οὐδεὶς ἑαυτῷ ἀποθνῄσκει· ⁸ ἐάν τε γὰρ ζῶμεν, τῷ κυρίῳ ζῶμεν, ἐάν τε ἀποθνῄσκωμεν, τῷ κυρίῳ ἀποθνῄσκομεν. ἐάν τε οὖν ζῶμεν ἐάν τε ἀποθνῄσκωμεν, τοῦ κυρίου ἐσμέν.

CONTEXT:

For various reasons, believers have different convictions on some nonessential matters. Paul is concerned that these issues do not hinder the unity of the church. Up to this point, Paul's instruction has contributed to this desire but here he wishes to confront it directly. How are people with different convictions on such matters to get along and function constructively in one body? It is good to have convictions on these matters (14:5) but one should not judge his or her fellow believer (14:1–4). Instead, all should be thankful (14:6).

COMMENTARY:

The conjunction γάρ begins an explanation of why believers should not judge one another. The genitive pronoun ἡμῶν is partitive modifying οὐδείς. Thus, no one from among the Christian community "lives" (ζῇ) or "dies" (ἀποθνῄσκει) for themselves. These present tense verbs are gnomic and the combination likely suggests the comprehensive nature of the statement (Moo, *Romans*, 860). Verse 8 further explains (γάρ) the previous verse. Three third-class conditions likely suggest present general conditions here (see *GGBB*, 696–97). Note the identical forms for the indicative and subjunctive of the contract verb ζάω (ζῶμεν). The particle ἐάν makes it clear that the verb immediately following it is in the subjunctive form (the protasis of the conditional sentence). The four particles τε likely are a pair of "both … and" statements (Porter, *Idioms*, 216) (although "both" can remain untranslated) and/or they could suggest a tighter connection between these statements (Harvey, *Romans*, 333). The final clause concisely sums up this section. The verb ἐσμέν is stative. It is a simple statement of fact: τοῦ κυρίου ἐσμέν; it greatly encourages us.

ζῇ > 3SPAI, lives || ἀποθνῄσκει > 3SPAI, dies || ἐάν … ζῶμεν > 1PPAS, if we live (subjunctive demanded by ἐάν) || ζῶμεν > 1PPAI, live || ἐάν … ἀποθνῄσκωμεν > 1PPAS, if we die (subjunctive demanded by ἐάν) || ἀποθνῄσκομεν > 1PPAI, we die || ἐάν … ζῶμεν (second occurance) > 1PPAS, if we live (subjunctive demanded by ἐάν) || ἐάν … ἀποθνῄσκωμεν > 1PPAS, if we die (subjunctive demanded by ἐάν)|| ἐσμέν > 1PPAI, we are

Further Reading: Romans 6:1–23; 14:1–12
Joseph D. Fantin

¹⁹ ἄρα οὖν τὰ τῆς εἰρήνης διώκωμεν καὶ τὰ τῆς οἰκοδομῆς τῆς εἰς ἀλλήλους. ²⁰ μὴ ἕνεκεν βρώματος κατάλυε τὸ ἔργον τοῦ θεοῦ. πάντα μὲν καθαρά, ἀλλὰ κακὸν τῷ ἀνθρώπῳ τῷ διὰ προσκόμματος ἐσθίοντι.

CONTEXT:

Paul has just discussed how believers should have convictions but not judge one another (14:1-6, 10-13a). Further, they must not allow their convictions (specifically freedoms) to cause another to stumble (14:13b-18). Paul now adds a further consideration.

COMMENTARY:

The section opens with two inferential particles (ἄρα οὖν) and may suggest a slight emphatic nuance. However, this combination's rarity demands that we do not make too much of this. The two plural accusative articles (τά) have implied head nouns, "the [things]." The verb διώκωμεν is a hortatory subjunctive which is a self-command or encouragement aimed at the readers. They are actively (simple active) and continually (customary present) to pursue "the things of peace" and "the things that build up one another." Paul then gets specific. Food (βρώματος), which is the issue at hand but can represent anything that causes division, should not be used to "tear down (destroy) the work of God" (κατάλυε [imperative command] τὸ ἔργον τοῦ θεοῦ). These are strong words. Someone with a conviction that all foods are acceptable must see beyond this freedom and assure that his or her choice does not "tear down" or "destroy" God's work. Note the articular adjectival participle with an embedded prepositional phrase (τῷ διὰ προσκόμματος ἐσθίοντι) making it clear what the prepositional phrase modifies. Christians must not use their freedom to destroy God's work of peace by offending their brothers and sisters in their choice of what to eat. Instead, freedom should be used to build up fellow believers.

ἄρα οὖν > so then ‖ διώκωμεν > 1PPAS, let us pursue ‖ τῆς οἰκοδομῆς > the building up ‖ ἕνεκεν βρώματος > for the sake of, because of food ‖ μὴ ... κατάλυε > 2SPAM, do not destroy, tear down ‖ καθαρά > clean, acceptable ‖ διὰ προσκόμματος > with stumbling, with offense ‖ τῷ ... ἐσθίοντι > PAPMSD, who eats

Further Reading: Romans 14:13-15:6

Joseph D. Fantin

FEBRUARY 5
ROMANS 15:18-19

¹⁸ οὐ γὰρ τολμήσω τι λαλεῖν ὧν οὐ κατειργάσατο Χριστὸς δι' ἐμοῦ εἰς ὑπακοὴν ἐθνῶν, λόγῳ καὶ ἔργῳ, ¹⁹ ἐν δυνάμει σημείων καὶ τεράτων, ἐν δυνάμει πνεύματος θεοῦ· ὥστε με ἀπὸ Ἰερουσαλὴμ καὶ κύκλῳ μέχρι τοῦ Ἰλλυρικοῦ πεπληρωκέναι τὸ εὐαγγέλιον τοῦ Χριστοῦ.

CONTEXT:

After encouraging the church to focus on edifying one another (15:1–13), Paul turns to his own ministry and motivation. First and foremost, he is a minister of Christ.

COMMENTARY:

An inferential conjunction (γάρ) continues Paul's description of his perspective on his ministry. The negated future indicative (οὐ τολμήσω) is followed by a complementary infinitive (λαλεῖν). Paul may have used the future tense to emphasize that his attitude is not going to change. The little pronoun τι (anything) is first restricted by the following relative clause, "which Christ has not accomplished" (ὧν οὐ κατειργάσατο Χριστὸς) and then further restricted by the next two prepositional phrases (δι' ἐμοῦ εἰς ὑπακοὴν ἐθνῶν). Christ is so vital that Paul will only discuss Christ's ministry through him to the Gentiles. His ministry was supported by various supernatural signs and the Holy Spirit. This has resulted (ὥστε) in the saturation of the gospel from Jerusalem to around Illyricum. The perfect infinitive πεπληρωκέναι functions here like a perfect indicative. Paul began to preach at a point in the past and the results of this have continued at least through the time of his writing Romans. Given the prominence of Paul's role in the proclamation of the gospel, it is humbling to hear him speak of his complete dependence on Christ in the power of the Spirit [of God]—ἐν δυνάμει πνεύματος [θεοῦ]. Paul has done nothing. Christ is responsible for all.

οὐ ... τολμήσω > 1SFAI, I will not dare ‖ λαλεῖν > PAN, to speak ‖ οὐ κατειργάσατο > 3SAMI, has not accomplished ‖ εἰς ὑπακοήν > for the obedience ‖ τεράτων > wonders ‖ κύκλῳ > around ‖ μέχρι τοῦ Ἰλλυρικοῦ > as far as Illyricum ‖ πεπληρωκέναι > RAN, I have fully [preached]

Further Reading: Romans 15:14–21
Joseph D. Fantin

[30] παρακαλῶ δὲ ὑμᾶς [ἀδελφοί,] διὰ τοῦ κυρίου ἡμῶν Ἰησοῦ Χριστοῦ καὶ διὰ τῆς ἀγάπης τοῦ πνεύματος συναγωνίσασθαί μοι ἐν ταῖς προσευχαῖς ὑπὲρ ἐμοῦ πρὸς τὸν θεόν.

CONTEXT:
Paul now begins to conclude his letter by sharing with the church his plans and expressing his desire to visit the church in Rome.

COMMENTARY:
Paul appeals (παρακαλῶ) to the readers to pray for him (ἐν ταῖς προσευχαῖς ὑπὲρ ἐμοῦ) with familial terminology (ἀδελφοί [missing in two important manuscripts, P[46] (A.D. 200) and B (iv), but it fits Paul's style well]). Paul's appeal may involve some urgency supported by the two subsequent prepositional phrases indicating the authority of the request (διὰ τοῦ κυρίου ἡμῶν Ἰησοῦ Χριστοῦ) and the grounds of the request (διὰ τῆς ἀγάπης τοῦ πνεύματος) (Moo, *Romans*, 1084). Paul describes prayer as a joint effort between the Romans and himself. The verb expressed by the infinitive (συναγωνίσασθαί) is found only here in the NT. The prefix συν- often reflects association, "work or strive together." This verb may even include a nuance of "fighting" or "battle" in an athletic or military context (Jewett, *Romans*, 934; Thielman, *Romans*, 697). Paul understands his need for God and asks the Romans to join with him in the important activity of prayer. Prayer is not simply a religious function but is a vital active aspect of ministry.

παρακαλῶ > 1SPAI, I appeal to || συναγωνίσασθαι > AMN, work/strive together

Further Reading: Romans 15:22–33
Joseph D. Fantin

³ ἀσπάσασθε Πρίσκαν καὶ Ἀκύλαν τοὺς συνεργούς μου ἐν Χριστῷ Ἰησοῦ.

CONTEXT:
In the preceding chapters, Paul has described his gospel in detail and shared with the Romans his future plans. Paul now turns to his relationships. Paul sends greetings both to his friends in Rome and from those with him in Corinth.

COMMENTARY:
Ἀσπάσασθε is the first of many aorist imperatives of ἀσπάζομαι in this section (16:3-16). Although an imperative, the lexical form softens the nature of the command force. Concerning Πρίσκαν and Ἀκύλαν, it is difficult to know why the woman's name is listed first. Prisca may have had a higher social status and Aquila may have been a freed slave (see Longenecker, *Romans*, 1067). Whatever the reason, this is evidence that certain things overrode normal social gender considerations. They are both considered by Paul to be his τοὺς συνεργούς. This entire section emphasizes the importance of relationships in the church. Paul was busy and writing material was likely expensive. Nevertheless, he spent a significant amount of effort and space to connect personally with the church.

ἀσπάσασθε > 2PAMM, greet || Πρίσκαν > Prisca, Priscilla || Ἀκύλαν > Aquila || συνεργούς > coworkers

Further Reading: Romans 16:1–16
Joseph D. Fantin

²⁵ τῷ δὲ δυναμένῳ ὑμᾶς στηρίξαι κατὰ τὸ εὐαγγέλιόν μου καὶ τὸ κήρυγμα Ἰησοῦ Χριστοῦ, κατὰ ἀποκάλυψιν μυστηρίου χρόνοις αἰωνίοις σεσιγημένου, ²⁶ φανερωθέντος δὲ νῦν διά τε γραφῶν προφητικῶν κατ' ἐπιταγὴν τοῦ αἰωνίου θεοῦ εἰς ὑπακοὴν πίστεως εἰς πάντα τὰ ἔθνη γνωρισθέντος, ²⁷ μόνῳ σοφῷ θεῷ, διὰ Ἰησοῦ Χριστοῦ, ᾧ ἡ δόξα εἰς τοὺς αἰῶνας, ἀμήν.

CONTEXT:

This passage is a doxology and serves to summarize the book.

COMMENTARY:

Romans 16:25-27 is a single complex sentence that summarizes and concludes this epistle. Paul's gospel was given to him "according to the revelation of the mystery" (μυστηρίου). Three anarthrous adjectival participles modify this "mystery." First, the mystery is that "which had been kept secret (σεσιγημένου). Note that the article does not need to be explicit in prepositional phrases ("the revelation") nor its modifier ("the mystery") to express definiteness or identification. Second, the past mystery is now (νῦν) revealed (φανερωθέντος). Participles only have relative time if any. The aorist tense simply reflects that action has taken place. The adverb νῦν provides the present temporal frame. Third, the mystery's revelation is made known (γνωρισθέντος) to all the Gentiles (εἰς πάντα τὰ ἔθνη) for the purpose of bringing the Gentiles "to the obedience that comes from faith" (genitive of source; Harvey, *Romans*, 398)." Paul again uses a dative indirect object for God (θεῷ) to conclude his doxology to whom glory is directed forever (ᾧ ἡ δόξα εἰς τοὺς αἰῶνας).

τῷ ... δυναμένῳ > PMPMSD, to the one who is able || στηρίξαι > AAN, to establish || κήρυγμα > preaching || κατὰ ἀποκάλυψιν > according to the revelation || χρόνοις αἰωνίοις > for long ages [past] || σεσιγημένου > RPPNSG, which has been kept secret || φανερωθέντος > APPNSG, is revealed || προφητικῶν > prophetic || ἐπιταγήν > command || εἰς ὑπακοήν > to the obedience || γνωρισθέντος > APPNSG, is made known || σοφῷ > wise

Further Reading: Romans 1:1-7; 16:16-27

Joseph D. Fantin

¹ καταβάντος δὲ αὐτοῦ ἀπὸ τοῦ ὄρους ἠκολούθησαν αὐτῷ ὄχλοι πολλοί. ² καὶ ἰδοὺ λεπρὸς προσελθὼν προσεκύνει αὐτῷ λέγων· κύριε, ἐὰν θέλῃς δύνασαί με καθαρίσαι. ³ καὶ ἐκτείνας τὴν χεῖρα ἥψατο αὐτοῦ λέγων· θέλω, καθαρίσθητι· καὶ εὐθέως ἐκαθαρίσθη αὐτοῦ ἡ λέπρα. ⁴ καὶ λέγει αὐτῷ ὁ Ἰησοῦς· ὅρα μηδενὶ εἴπῃς, ἀλλ᾽ ὕπαγε σεαυτὸν δεῖξον τῷ ἱερεῖ καὶ προσένεγκον τὸ δῶρον ὃ προσέταξεν Μωϋσῆς, εἰς μαρτύριον αὐτοῖς.

CONTEXT:

In this portion of Matthew's gospel, chapters 8 and 9, Matthew presents several stories of Jesus' healing ministry. Throughout the brief narratives we find a consistent contrast between His concern for the poor and helpless of this world and the snide, heartless, legalistic reactions of the prevailing religious class of the time.

COMMENTARY:

A leper approaches Jesus and asks for a healing but couches his request in politely submissive terms. Viewing himself as unclean, he does not assume that Jesus will act: ἐὰν θέλῃς, "If you are willing ..." Jesus responds to the leper's request with a simple statement, "I am willing." Jesus' unqualified response of willingness shows the universality of his desire to seek the lost and the least and to give them abundant life. Jesus commands the leper to be cleansed—a passive imperative (καθαρίσθητι). The leper exercises a simple, childlike faith in Jesus' ability to heal him and thereby receives the healing passively from the Great Healer. Only God's son could miraculously heal his disease *and* in doing so also remove the stigma of being unclean.

προσεκύνει > 3SIAI, bowed down ‖ θέλῃς > 2SPAS, (if) you are willing ‖ καθαρίσθητι > 2SAPM, be cleansed! ‖ λέπρα > leprosy ‖ ἱερεῖ > priest ‖ δῶρον > offering

Further Reading: Mark 1:40–45; Luke 5:12–16

J. James Mancuso

FEBRUARY 10
MATTHEW 8:8-10

⁸ καὶ ἀποκριθεὶς ὁ ἑκατόνταρχος ἔφη· κύριε, οὐκ εἰμὶ ἱκανὸς ἵνα μου ὑπὸ τὴν στέγην εἰσέλθῃς, ἀλλὰ μόνον εἰπὲ λόγῳ, καὶ ἰαθήσεται ὁ παῖς μου. ⁹ καὶ γὰρ ἐγὼ ἄνθρωπός εἰμι ὑπὸ ἐξουσίαν, ἔχων ὑπ᾽ ἐμαυτὸν στρατιώτας, καὶ λέγω τούτῳ· πορεύθητι, καὶ πορεύεται, καὶ ἄλλῳ· ἔρχου, καὶ ἔρχεται, καὶ τῷ δούλῳ μου· ποίησον τοῦτο, καὶ ποιεῖ. ¹⁰ ἀκούσας δὲ ὁ Ἰησοῦς ἐθαύμασεν καὶ εἶπεν τοῖς ἀκολουθοῦσιν· ἀμὴν λέγω ὑμῖν, παρ᾽ οὐδενὶ τοσαύτην πίστιν ἐν τῷ Ἰσραὴλ εὗρον.

CONTEXT:

As Jesus is interacting with the people of his day, he encounters Jewish religious leaders whose strict adherence to the law has blinded them to the needs of those around them and God's compassion for them. In contrast, he finds profound, unquestioning faith in a Roman centurion, who perceives Jesus' power and authority—attributes important in the military—and ascribes divinity to him based on that. The Jewish religious leaders, obsessed over legal matters, completely missed both Jesus' miraculous divine power and his unconditional love for people.

COMMENTARY:

The centurion does not consider himself worthy (ἱκανός) of Jesus' presence. Note also, though, that he understands that Jesus' healing power is not limited by space or time, but rather that the healing power resides in His word (λόγῳ). Indeed, Jesus *is* the Word. The centurion also recognizes Jesus' authority (ἐξουσίαν) over human illness. By marveling over the Roman soldier's faith, Jesus turns the Jewish worldview upside down: religious leaders will find their destiny in hell whereas a heathen soldier finds favor with God.

ἑκατόνταρχος > centurion || στέγην > roof || εἰσέλθῃς > 2SAAS, you come || εἰπέ > 2SAAM, say || ἰαθήσεται > 3SFPI, healed || παῖς > servant boy || ἐξουσίαν > authority || στρατιώτας > soldiers || πορεύθητι > 2SAPM, go || ἔρχου > 2SPMM, go || ποίησον > 2SAAM, do || ἐθαύμασεν > 3SAAI, he marveled || εὗρον > 1SAAI, I have found

Further Reading: Matthew 8:5–13; Luke 7:2–10

J. James Mancuso

41

February 11
Matthew 9:35-36

³⁵ καὶ περιῆγεν ὁ Ἰησοῦς τὰς πόλεις πάσας καὶ τὰς κώμας διδάσκων ἐν ταῖς συναγωγαῖς αὐτῶν καὶ κηρύσσων τὸ εὐαγγέλιον τῆς βασιλείας καὶ θεραπεύων πᾶσαν νόσον καὶ πᾶσαν μαλακίαν. ³⁶ Ἰδὼν δὲ τοὺς ὄχλους ἐσπλαγχνίσθη περὶ αὐτῶν, ὅτι ἦσαν ἐσκυλμένοι καὶ ἐρριμμένοι ὡσεὶ πρόβατα μὴ ἔχοντα ποιμένα.

Context:

As Matthew wraps up this section of his gospel, he concludes with a summary statement about Jesus' healing ministry without giving any additional detailed stories of healings. The Church is commanded to carry on this ministry through evangelization, Christian education, and mercy ministries such as providing medical care and hospitals (e.g., Matt 28:19-20; Rom 12:8).

Commentary:

As He heals people, Jesus is also proclaiming the good news and teaching. He integrates these in his ministry to the lost, wanting to reclaim and restore fallen man. In verse 35, Matthew uses participles (διδάσκων, κηρύσσων, θεραπεύων) to describe the three activities that shaped His ministry. Jesus' compassion for the crowds is motivated by his perception of them being unable to rescue themselves. The Greek phrase μὴ ἔχοντα ποιμένα conveys the notion of sheep "lacking a shepherd," not merely that they were without one at the moment.

περιῆγεν > 3SIAI, went around ‖ κώμας > villages ‖ διδάσκων > PAPMSN, teaching ‖ κηρύσσων > PAPMSN, preaching ‖ θεραπεύων > PAPMSN, healing ‖ νόσον > disease ‖ μαλακίαν > affliction ‖ ἐσπλαγχνίσθη > 3SAPI, had compassion ‖ ἐσκυλμένοι > RPPMPN, harassed ‖ ἐρριμμένοι > RPPMPN, helpless, dispersed

Further Reading: Luke 10:2-3
J. James Mancuso

MATTHEW 10:19–20

¹⁹ ὅταν δὲ παραδῶσιν ὑμᾶς, μὴ μεριμνήσητε πῶς ἢ τί λαλήσητε· δοθήσεται γὰρ ὑμῖν ἐν ἐκείνῃ τῇ ὥρᾳ τί λαλήσητε· ²⁰ οὐ γὰρ ὑμεῖς ἐστε οἱ λαλοῦντες ἀλλὰ τὸ πνεῦμα τοῦ πατρὸς ὑμῶν τὸ λαλοῦν ἐν ὑμῖν.

CONTEXT:
Jesus is forewarning his disciples of troubles and difficult days to come; however, the warnings are paired with reassurances of His divine presence and aid. This passage presages the various persecutions that his disciples would face in the beginning of the church age after Jesus ascended into heaven.

COMMENTARY:
The disciples are commanded to μὴ μεριμνήσητε ("not be anxious") as in Matthew 6:25-34. In addition, with childlike faith they are to depend on the Father to give them utterance τὸ λαλοῦν ἐν ὑμῖν ("speaking through you"). Thus Jesus encourages their hearts in a statement that implies the Trinity: the words of the Father δοθήσεται ("will be given") in testimony about Jesus πῶς ἢ τί λαλήσητε ("how and what you are to say") by means of τὸ πνεῦμα ("the Holy Spirit").

παραδῶσιν > 3PAAS, they hand over ‖ μεριμνήσητε > 2PAAS, worry yourselves ‖ λαλήσητε > 2PAAS, might say ‖ δοθήσεται > 3SFPI, will be given ‖ λαλοῦντες > PAPMPN, speaking ‖ λαλοῦν > PAPNSN, speaking

Further Reading: Mark 13:9-13; Luke 21:12-17
J. James Mancuso

¹⁶ τίνι δὲ ὁμοιώσω τὴν γενεὰν ταύτην; ὁμοία ἐστὶν παιδίοις καθημένοις ἐν ταῖς ἀγοραῖς ἃ προσφωνοῦντα τοῖς ἑτέροις ¹⁷ λέγουσιν·

ηὐλήσαμεν ὑμῖν καὶ οὐκ ὠρχήσασθε,
ἐθρηνήσαμεν καὶ οὐκ ἐκόψασθε.

¹⁸ ἦλθεν γὰρ Ἰωάννης μήτε ἐσθίων μήτε πίνων, καὶ λέγουσιν· δαιμόνιον ἔχει. ¹⁹ ἦλθεν ὁ υἱὸς τοῦ ἀνθρώπου ἐσθίων καὶ πίνων, καὶ λέγουσιν· ἰδοὺ ἄνθρωπος φάγος καὶ οἰνοπότης, τελωνῶν φίλος καὶ ἁμαρτωλῶν. καὶ ἐδικαιώθη ἡ σοφία ἀπὸ τῶν ἔργων αὐτῆς.

CONTEXT:

Jesus protests the hypocrisy of a wicked generation who criticizes John the Baptist for his austere lifestyle and then condemns Jesus for his willingness to indulge those whom society deemed as sinful. In His assessment, these accusers cannot be placated by any particular behavior. Thus He reveals a heart issue: this perverse generation will criticize the Messiah and reject Him no matter what He does.

COMMENTARY:

John the Baptist came μήτε ἐσθίων μήτε πίνων ("neither eating nor drinking") whereas Jesus did both. Thus it cannot be that the actions themselves are inherently sinful. Rather, the heart's motivation, the context of the action, and the ultimate results of actions tell the real story. Jesus sums it up with ἐδικαιώθη ἡ σοφία ἀπὸ τῶν ἔργων αὐτῆς—the notion that wisdom is vindicated by her own outcomes. Only in retrospect can we judge motivations and see what has resulted from actions.

ὁμοιώσω > 1SFAI, shall I compare ‖ γενεάν > generation ‖ ἀγοραῖς > marketplace ‖ προσφωνοῦντα > PAPNPN, calling out ‖ ηὐλήσαμεν > 1PAAI, played the flute ‖ ὠρχήσασθε > 2PAMI, did [not] dance ‖ ἐθρηνήσαμεν > 1PAAI, sang a dirge ‖ ἐκόψασθε > 2PAMI, did [not] mourn ‖ ἐσθίων > PAPMSN, eating ‖ πίνων > PAPMSN, drinking ‖ φάγος > glutton ‖ οἰνοπότης > drunkard ‖ τελωνῶν > tax collectors ‖ φίλος > friend ‖ ἐδικαιώθη > 3SAPI, is vindicated

Further Reading: Luke 7:31-35

J. James Mancuso

MATTHEW 12:10, 13

¹⁰ καὶ ἰδοὺ ἄνθρωπος χεῖρα ἔχων ξηράν. καὶ ἐπηρώτησαν αὐτὸν λέγοντες·
εἰ ἔξεστιν τοῖς σάββασιν θεραπεῦσαι; ἵνα κατηγορήσωσιν αὐτοῦ. ... ¹³ τότε
λέγει τῷ ἀνθρώπῳ· ἔκτεινόν σου τὴν χεῖρα. καὶ ἐξέτεινεν καὶ
ἀπεκατεστάθη ὑγιὴς ὡς ἡ ἄλλη.

CONTEXT:

In Matthew 12:9–14, the Pharisees in the synagogue were looking for a way to
trap Jesus and destroy him.

COMMENTARY:

The Pharisee's zeal for the law had blinded them to the pain of a man in need of
having his hand restored to healthy use. He had a "dried up hand" (χεῖρα ἔχων
ξηράν), withered and useless, like the spiritual life of the Pharisees who were
unable to extend a helping hand to others. Jesus violates their sense of slavish
adherence to the law by boldly healing on the Sabbath. In retrospect, we are
able to clearly see the sinful hardheartedness of the Pharisees. We are tempted
to cluck our tongues and judge their spiritual blindness and rejection of Jesus
and the ministry of healing he extended to those around him. When we are
humble and teachable followers of Christ, we periodically examine our own
hearts honestly and we see our need to confess a Pharisaical spirit. We are all
tempted to judge others, ignore their need of healing, and set up rules that
others must obey to earn their salvation.

ξηράν > dried up || ἐπηρώτησαν > 3PAAI, asked || ἔξεστιν > 3SPAI, is it lawful ||
θεραπεῦσαι > AAN, to heal || κατηγορήσωσιν > 3PAAS, might accuse || ἔκτεινόν
> 2SAAM, stretch out || ἐξέτεινεν > 3SAAI, stretched out || ἀπεκατεστάθη >
3SAPI, it was restored || ὑγιὴς > healthy

Further Reading: Mark 3:1–6; Luke 6:6–11
J. James Mancuso

⁴⁹ οὕτως ἔσται ἐν τῇ συντελείᾳ τοῦ αἰῶνος· ἐξελεύσονται οἱ ἄγγελοι καὶ ἀφοριοῦσιν τοὺς πονηροὺς ἐκ μέσου τῶν δικαίων ⁵⁰ καὶ βαλοῦσιν αὐτοὺς εἰς τὴν κάμινον τοῦ πυρός· ἐκεῖ ἔσται ὁ κλαυθμὸς καὶ ὁ βρυγμὸς τῶν ὀδόντων.

CONTEXT:

In this chapter Jesus presents seven parables to illustrate the nature of the kingdom of heaven at the close of the age. In this final parable (13:47–50), Jesus uses the analogy of a fisherman's net to liken the sorting of good and bad fish after a net is drawn to the great division of all souls at the end of the world.

COMMENTARY:

In 13:49–50, Jesus clearly spells out the stark reality of dualism for his listeners. At the close of this age, the entirety of human souls is divided into two and only two groups—the *righteous* (τῶν δικαίων) and the *evil* (τοὺς πονηρούς)—those who are saved and inherit eternal life, and those who are doomed to perdition. Jesus confronts all who hear these words with the alarming truth that no third option is provided, nor does he offer the hope of a second chance after death.

ἔσται > 3SFMI, will be ‖ τῇ συντελείᾳ τοῦ αἰῶνος > the close of the age ‖ ἐξελεύσονται > 3PFMI, will come ‖ ἀφοριοῦσιν > 3PFAI, will separate ‖ βαλοῦσιν > 3PFAI, will throw ‖ κάμινον > furnace ‖ κλαυθμός > weeping ‖ βρυγμὸς τῶν ὀδόντων > gnashing of teeth

Further Reading: Revelation 20:11–15
J. James Mancuso

³⁴ καὶ διαπεράσαντες ἦλθον ἐπὶ τὴν γῆν εἰς Γεννησαρέτ. ³⁵ καὶ ἐπιγνόντες αὐτὸν οἱ ἄνδρες τοῦ τόπου ἐκείνου ἀπέστειλαν εἰς ὅλην τὴν περίχωρον ἐκείνην καὶ προσήνεγκαν αὐτῷ πάντας τοὺς κακῶς ἔχοντας ³⁶ καὶ παρεκάλουν αὐτὸν ἵνα μόνον ἅψωνται τοῦ κρασπέδου τοῦ ἱματίου αὐτοῦ· καὶ ὅσοι ἥψαντο διεσώθησαν.

CONTEXT:

In the gospels we often hear Jesus scolding the perverse generation for seeking after a sign. Note that in this passage the people of Gennesaret sought physical healing from disease. That 'sign' sufficed for them. We can credit these people who lived on the northwestern shore of the Sea of Galilee for having the faith to recognize Jesus as a miraculous healer sent from God and for their zeal in rounding up people in need of healing and bringing them to the healer.

COMMENTARY:

In verse 35 we read that the men of the region "recognized" (ἐπιγινώσκω) Him. We may marvel how they recognized his face, but more importantly they recognized his healing power and deity, and then they acted on that knowledge. Believing that healing power could come from just touching the fringe of garment of the Christ, they interrupted their own daily routines to physically bring needy people (πάντας τοὺς κακῶς ἔχοντας) to Him—an exemplary action for all followers of Christ.

διαπεράσαντες > AAPMPN, had crossed over || ἐπιγνόντες > AAPMPN, recognized || ἀπέστειλαν > 3PAAI, they sent word || περίχωρον > region || προσήνεγκαν > 3PAAI, (physically) brought || παρεκάλουν > 3PIAI, implored || ἅψωνται > 3PAMS, might touch || κρασπέδου > fringe (of a cloak) || ἥψαντο > 3PAMI, touched || διεσώθησαν > 3PAPI, were made well

Further Reading: Mark 6:53–56
J. James Mancuso

FEBRUARY 17
MATTHEW 15:18–20

¹⁸ τὰ δὲ ἐκπορευόμενα ἐκ τοῦ στόματος ἐκ τῆς καρδίας ἐξέρχεται, κἀκεῖνα κοινοῖ τὸν ἄνθρωπον. ¹⁹ ἐκ γὰρ τῆς καρδίας ἐξέρχονται διαλογισμοὶ πονηροί, φόνοι, μοιχεῖαι, πορνεῖαι, κλοπαί, ψευδομαρτυρίαι, βλασφημίαι. ²⁰ ταῦτά ἐστιν τὰ κοινοῦντα τὸν ἄνθρωπον, τὸ δὲ ἀνίπτοις χερσὶν φαγεῖν οὐ κοινοῖ τὸν ἄνθρωπον.

CONTEXT:
Here again in Matthew 15:15–20, Jesus turns the world of Judaic law upside down. Fearing being defiled by unclean food, the Jews of that day were bound by oppressive dietary restrictions. Jesus' baffling statement that their evil motives and actions were the true source of defilement met with great resistance.

COMMENTARY:
In 15:19–20, Jesus confounds even his disciples with a new perspective on what defiles a man. Jesus views men's souls from the vantage point of final judgment, as seen in the parables he had just told. From there He sees clearly that the wickedness of the human heart and its fruit of evil deeds are what will "defile" (κοινοῖ) a man and sentence him to hell. The consumption of prohibited food is of no significance. Quoting from Hosea 6:6, Jesus had just instructed them "I desire mercy, and not sacrifice." Much of human behavior is consumed with following rules and earning favor rather than with extending mercy to others. Jesus calls us to do the opposite.

τὰ ... ἐκπορευόμενα > PMPNPN, what comes || ἐξέρχεται > 3SPMI, proceeds || κἀκεῖνα > and these things || κοινοῖ > 3SPAI, defile || ἐξέρχονται > 3PPMI, proceed || διαλογισμοὶ πονηροί > evil thoughts || φόνοι > murders || μοιχεῖαι > adulteries || πορνεῖαι > sexual immoralities || κλοπαί > thefts || ψευδομαρτυρίαι > false witnesses || βλασφημίαι > slander || τὰ κοινοῦντα > PAPNPN, what defiles || ἀνίπτοις > unwashed || φαγεῖν > AAN, to eat

Further Reading: Mark 7:14–23
J. James Mancuso

²⁴ τότε ὁ Ἰησοῦς εἶπεν τοῖς μαθηταῖς αὐτοῦ· εἴ τις θέλει ὀπίσω μου ἐλθεῖν, ἀπαρνησάσθω ἑαυτὸν καὶ ἀράτω τὸν σταυρὸν αὐτοῦ καὶ ἀκολουθείτω μοι. ²⁵ ὃς γὰρ ἐὰν θέλῃ τὴν ψυχὴν αὐτοῦ σῶσαι ἀπολέσει αὐτήν· ὃς δ' ἂν ἀπολέσῃ τὴν ψυχὴν αὐτοῦ ἕνεκεν ἐμοῦ εὑρήσει αὐτήν.

CONTEXT:

Jesus builds on other concepts that he has recently presented to his disciples by pausing to forewarn them that following Him presents the challenge of denying oneself, which involves sacrifice and the loss of comfort, ease, and pleasure, in order to gain eternal life. Jesus places great value on the salvation of the soul in eternal glory and no value on transient, earthly treasure.

COMMENTARY:

Again Jesus calls for his disciples to follow him in a paradox: whoever loses his [earthly] life will gain [eternal] life. As with the other lessons he has just taught them in parables, he presents them with the need to radically shift their view of the world from pursuit of earthly gain, which will *certainly* be lost, to a life of service and mercy in pursuit of heavenly gain, which *cannot* be lost. Though this seems 'upside-down' to his hearers, nonetheless they can easily grasp that upon death, everyone does indeed lose all his earthly possessions.

ἀπαρνησάσθω > 3SAMM, let him deny || ἀράτω > 3SAAM, let him take up || σταυρόν > cross || ἀκολουθείτω > 3SPAM, let him follow || θέλῃ > 3SPAS, might desire || σῶσαι > AAN, to save || ἀπολέσει > 3SFAI, will lose || ἀπολέσῃ > 3SAAS, might lose || ἕνεκεν > for || εὑρήσει > 3SFAI, will find

Further Reading: Mark 8:34–38; Luke 9:23–26

J. James Mancuso

1 CORINTHIANS 1:10

¹⁰ παρακαλῶ δὲ ὑμᾶς, ἀδελφοί, διὰ τοῦ ὀνόματος τοῦ κυρίου ἡμῶν Ἰησοῦ Χριστοῦ, ἵνα τὸ αὐτὸ λέγητε πάντες καὶ μὴ ᾖ ἐν ὑμῖν σχίσματα, ἦτε δὲ κατηρτισμένοι ἐν τῷ αὐτῷ νοῒ καὶ ἐν τῇ αὐτῇ γνώμῃ.

CONTEXT:

Paul begins his letter to the church at Corinth in a typical pattern by indicating the sender and recipient (1:1–3) and then thanking God for the way he is blessing the church (1:4–9).

COMMENTARY:

In 1 Corinthians, Paul addresses a number of problems that had arisen in the church at Corinth. This verse begins the body of the letter and serves as the thesis statement for chapters 1–4; some have even understood it as the thesis statement for all of 1 Corinthians. Paul appeals to the brothers (in the vocative case) on the basis of (διά) their shared commitment to "our Lord," whom he identifies as "Jesus Christ." Paul expresses the content of his appeal in a ἵνα clause with three appeals in the subjunctive mood: (1) that you all say the same thing (i.e., they agree), (2) that there not be divisions, and (3) that you be united in the same mind and knowledge / thinking. A unique feature of this sentence is that αὐτός is used three times as an intensive adjective.

παρακαλῶ > 1SPAI, I appeal, exhort ‖ ὀνόματος > name ‖ λέγητε > 2PPAS, say, speak ‖ ᾖ > 3SPAS, there be ‖ σχίσματα > divisions ‖ ἦτε > 2PPAS, be ‖ κατηρτισμένοι > RPPMPN, united ‖ νοῒ > mind ‖ γνώμῃ > purpose, opinion, judgment

Further Reading: 1 Corinthians 1:11–17
Trent A. Rogers

February 20
1 Corinthians 2:3-5

³ κἀγὼ ἐν ἀσθενείᾳ καὶ ἐν φόβῳ καὶ ἐν τρόμῳ πολλῷ ἐγενόμην πρὸς ὑμᾶς, ⁴ καὶ ὁ λόγος μου καὶ τὸ κήρυγμά μου οὐκ ἐν πειθοῖς σοφίας λόγοις ἀλλ' ἐν ἀποδείξει πνεύματος καὶ δυνάμεως, ⁵ ἵνα ἡ πίστις ὑμῶν μὴ ᾖ ἐν σοφίᾳ ἀνθρώπων ἀλλ' ἐν δυνάμει θεοῦ.

Context:
As a part of his exhortation to unity in the church, Paul defends the nature of his ministry which had been criticized.

Commentary:
When Paul describes the manner of his presence with the Corinthians, we might expect him to list very positive nouns. Instead, Paul describes his ministry among them as weakness, fear, and much trembling (πολλῷ probably only governs τρόμῳ since ἀσθενείᾳ is feminine). The grammatical subject changes from "I" in verse 3 to "my word / speech and my message" in verse 4, and the contrast is stark. Whereas Paul is characterized by weakness, fear, and much trembling, his word/speech and message are (the verb "to be" is elided) not. Paul uses parallel phrases of ἐν + dative to describe the manner of his presence and the power of his message. Paul expresses the purpose of his manner of speech in a ἵνα clause.

ἀσθενείᾳ > weakness ‖ τρόμῳ > trembling ‖ ἐγενόμην > 1SAMI, was ‖ κήρυγμα > message ‖ πειθοῖς > persuasive ‖ ἀποδείξει > demonstration ‖ δυνάμεως > power ‖ ᾖ > 3SPAS, might [not] be

Further Reading: 1 Corinthians 2:1–5
Trent A. Rogers

⁵ τί οὖν ἐστιν Ἀπολλῶς; τί δέ ἐστιν Παῦλος; διάκονοι δι' ὧν ἐπιστεύσατε, καὶ ἑκάστῳ ὡς ὁ κύριος ἔδωκεν. ⁶ ἐγὼ ἐφύτευσα, Ἀπολλῶς ἐπότισεν, ἀλλὰ ὁ θεὸς ηὔξανεν.

CONTEXT:
Continuing his rebuke for the divisions in the church, Paul indicates that his readers are spiritual infants because they are dividing over merely human leaders.

COMMENTARY:
Paul asks two parallel rhetorical questions about the roles of Apollos and himself. He answers these rhetorical questions by curtailing their significance (they are [the verb "to be" is elided] merely servants) but indicating their effectiveness (through whom you believed). The credit belongs to the Lord who gave [the ministry] to each of them. With two correlative aorist indicative verbs, Paul describes his ministry and Apollos's ministry positively. But he contrasts (ἀλλα is adversative) them with the ultimate work of God. God's work of causing the increase (ηὔξανεν) is presented as a continuous activity through the imperfective aspect (by use of the imperfect tense).

τί > what? || διάκονοι > servants, ministers || ἐπιστεύσατε > 2PAAI, you believed || ἑκάστῳ > each || ἔδωκεν > 3SAAI, he gave || ἐφύτευσα > 1SAAI, I planted || ἐπότισεν > 3SAAI, he watered || ηὔξανεν > 3SIAI, he caused to grow

Further Reading: 1 Corinthians 3:8–15
Trent A. Rogers

1 CORINTHIANS 4:1

¹ οὕτως ἡμᾶς λογιζέσθω ἄνθρωπος ὡς ὑπηρέτας Χριστοῦ καὶ οἰκονόμους μυστηρίων θεοῦ.

CONTEXT:
Having corrected the Corinthians' incorrect divisions over Paul and Apollos, Paul instructs them about how they ought to think about these teachers.

COMMENTARY:
The subject of the imperative (λογιζέσθω) is the impersonal general noun, ἄνθρωπος (which is functionally equivalent to the indefinite pronoun τις in this context). The adverb οὕτως describes the manner in which someone ought to think about these teachers, in contrast to the Corinthians' missteps in chapter three. The comparative ὡς introduces the proper understanding of their roles as servants of Christ (either a possessive genitive meaning "servants belonging to Christ" or more likely an objective genitive meaning "those who serve Christ") and stewards of the mysteries (objective genitive) of God (probably genitive of source).

οὕτως > in this way || λογιζέσθω > 3SPMM, one should regard || ὑπηρέτας > servants || οἰκονόμους > stewards

Further Reading: 1 Corinthians 4:1–7
Trent A. Rogers

² καὶ ὑμεῖς πεφυσιωμένοι ἐστὲ καὶ οὐχὶ μᾶλλον ἐπενθήσατε, ἵνα ἀρθῇ ἐκ μέσου ὑμῶν ὁ τὸ ἔργον τοῦτο πράξας;

CONTEXT:

Chapter 4 concludes Paul's main refutation of divisions. Beginning in chapter 5, he addresses the issue of sexual immorality in the church.

COMMENTARY:

Instead of rebuking this sinful person, the Corinthians are proud. In place of a finite verb, Paul uses a periphrastic construction in which a form of "to be" is used with a participle. The second καί in the sentence is adversative and introduces a rebuttal of their behavior in the form of a rhetorical question that anticipates an affirmative answer. Their sorrow should result in removing the offender from their midst. Instead of naming the offender, Paul uses an adjectival participle substantivally in which the participle also takes a direct object (literally: the one having done this deed).

πεφυσιωμένοι > RPPMPN, puffed up, proud ‖ μᾶλλον > rather ‖ ἐπενθήσατε > 2PAAI, mourn ‖ ἀρθῇ > 3SAPS, be removed ‖ πράξας > AAPMSN, doing

Further Reading: 1 Corinthians 5:1–8

Trent A. Rogers

1 CORINTHIANS 6:11

¹¹ καὶ ταῦτά τινες ἦτε· ἀλλὰ ἀπελούσασθε, ἀλλὰ ἡγιάσθητε, ἀλλὰ ἐδικαιώθητε ἐν τῷ ὀνόματι τοῦ κυρίου Ἰησοῦ Χριστοῦ καὶ ἐν τῷ πνεύματι τοῦ θεοῦ ἡμῶν.

CONTEXT:
Paul's discussion about lawsuits among Christians leads him to a condemnation of evildoers (e.g., he condemns thieves, not the action of stealing). Paul affirms that the Corinthian Christians are different than the unrighteous listed in 6:10.

COMMENTARY:
Paul first acknowledges that at one time, some (τινες) of the Corinthian Christians were these things (i.e., the unrighteous people described in 6:9-10), but he strongly contrasts their previous state with their new reality through a series of ἀλλά clauses with passive verbs. Christians are in a new state because they were washed, sanctified, and justified. The agents of this work are the name of the Lord and the Spirit. The "name of the Lord" functions as a metonymy for the person; this is clarified by the appositive, "Jesus Christ." This verse highlights the new state of the Christian and the work of God in salvation.

ἦτε > 2PIAI, were ‖ ἀπελούσασθε > 2PAMI, you were washed (middle likely communicating a passive idea) ‖ ἡγιάσθητε > 2PAPI, you were sanctified ‖ ἐδικαιώθητε > 2PAPI, you were justified

Further Reading: 1 Corinthians 6:1–11
Trent A. Rogers

¹² πάντα μοι ἔξεστιν ἀλλ᾽ οὐ πάντα συμφέρει· πάντα μοι ἔξεστιν ἀλλ᾽ οὐκ ἐγὼ ἐξουσιασθήσομαι ὑπό τινος.

CONTEXT:

Paul shifts abruptly from a discussion of lawsuits to discussions about sexual immorality. He introduces this topic by quoting the Corinthians and qualifying their theology.

COMMENTARY:

Paul uses a grammatical feature, asyndeton (transitioning to a new sentence without the use of a conjunction or other connector), to move quickly and abruptly to a new topic. Most modern translations put quotation marks around a portion of these sentences. In the Greek text, there are no quotation marks, and the earliest manuscripts contain all capital letters with no punctuation. This means that labeling something as a quotation is an interpretation arising from the grammar and flow of the text. In both of these sentences, Paul begins with the same general statement about liberty that he follows with an adversative conjunction, ἀλλά. The clauses following the conjunctions qualify or refute the previous clause. It seems that the Corinthians were claiming that all things were permissible (ἔξεστιν; cf. 1 Cor 10:23), which Paul is seeking to restrain on account of commitments to holiness and love. Note that a neuter subject is sometimes viewed as a collective whole and takes a singular verb.

πάντα > everything, all things || ἔξεστιν > 3SPAI, they are lawful || συμφέρει > 3SPAI, they are beneficial || ἐξουσιασθήσομαι > 1SFPI, I will be mastered || τινος > anything (although grammatically, it could refer to someone)

Further Reading: 1 Corinthians 6:12–20
Trent A. Rogers

1 CORINTHIANS 7:2–3

² διὰ δὲ τὰς πορνείας ἕκαστος τὴν ἑαυτοῦ γυναῖκα ἐχέτω καὶ ἑκάστη τὸν ἴδιον ἄνδρα ἐχέτω. ³ τῇ γυναικὶ ὁ ἀνὴρ τὴν ὀφειλὴν ἀποδιδότω, ὁμοίως δὲ καὶ ἡ γυνὴ τῷ ἀνδρί.

CONTEXT:
In chapter 7, Paul begins to address the questions about which the Corinthians had written (7:1). He first quotes the Corinthians' position on marriage, and then he refutes it.

COMMENTARY:
The reason for Paul's endorsement of marriage (or perhaps, marital sexual relations, depending on the interpretation of ἔχω) is the existence of sexual immorality (English idiom tends to speak of "sexual immorality" in the singular). His use of the third-person imperative (ἐχέτω) with the subject ἕκαστος implies that the permission for marriage is universal. He clarifies the exclusivity of marriage with a singular subject (ἕκαστος), singular object (γυναῖκα), and singular possessive pronoun (ἑαυτοῦ). The permission for a man to have his wife is similarly extended to the woman to have her own husband. Paul further commands that the husband should give what is owed to his wife, and so the wife to her husband.

πορνείας > sexual immorality || ἕκαστος > each man || ἐχέτω > 3SPAM, let him/her have || ἴδιον > her own || ὀφειλήν > obligation || ἀποδιδότω > 3SPAM, let him give || ὁμοίως > likewise

Further Reading: 1 Corinthians 7:1–7
Trent A. Rogers

^{6} ἀλλ' ἡμῖν εἷς θεὸς ὁ πατὴρ
    ἐξ οὗ τὰ πάντα καὶ ἡμεῖς εἰς αὐτόν,
καὶ εἷς κύριος Ἰησοῦς Χριστὸς
    δι' οὗ τὰ πάντα καὶ ἡμεῖς δι' αὐτοῦ.

CONTEXT:

One of the questions the Corinthians asked concerned the permissibility or impermissibility of eating food that was sacrificed to idols. Paul first argues that there is only one God and therefore idols are nothing, but then he adds that love for a brother, not merely one's knowledge, must affect what a Christian does.

COMMENTARY:

In order to prove that idol-gods are not real, Paul cites a theological statement with which the Corinthians seem to agree, since he uses the first-person plural pronoun ἡμῖν ("for us"). This shared theological statement draws on the *Shema* (Deut 6:4) and revises it to include Christ. In each of the four lines, the verb "to be" is inferred. Lines one and two describe God the Father, and lines three and four describe Jesus Christ. Lines one and three are parallel affirmations of the one God and one Lord. Similarly, lines two and four are parallel affirmations about the work of God the Father and Christ, first in regard to all things (πάντα) and then in regard to the church (ἡμεῖς).

εἷς > one

Further Reading: 1 Corinthians 8:1–6
Trent A. Rogers

¹³ διόπερ εἰ βρῶμα σκανδαλίζει τὸν ἀδελφόν μου, οὐ μὴ φάγω κρέα εἰς τὸν αἰῶνα, ἵνα μὴ τὸν ἀδελφόν μου σκανδαλίσω.

CONTEXT:
Paul addresses the issue of food sacrificed to idols in three chapters (8–10). He concludes chapter 8 with a commitment to pursuing actions that do not harm other Christians. This commitment leads him to speak autobiographically, in chapter 9, about the voluntary withholding of his own rights for the purpose of the good of others.

COMMENTARY:
The conjunction διόπερ introduces a summary conclusion from Paul's preceding argumentation. His conclusion takes the form of a first-class condition in which the condition is assumed to be true for the sake of the argument. The grammatical subject of σκανδαλίζει is βρῶμα, which refers to the action of the knowledgeable Christian in eating specific foods. If that action of eating these foods makes a brother (i.e., another Christian) stumble, Paul's response is to forgo the action forever so that the brother does not stumble. For the first time in Paul's argument, he clarifies that the specific type of food in question is meat (κρέα), which accords with ancient sacrificial practices.

διόπερ > therefore || βρῶμα > food || σκανδαλίζει > 3SPAI, it causes to stumble || οὐ μή > not, never (emphatic negation) || φάγω > 1SAAS, I eat || κρέα > meats || ἵνα μή > lest, so that not || σκανδαλίσω > 1SAAS, I cause to stumble

Further Reading: 1 Corinthians 8:7–13
Trent A. Rogers

²⁴ οὐκ οἴδατε ὅτι οἱ ἐν σταδίῳ τρέχοντες πάντες μὲν τρέχουσιν, εἷς δὲ λαμβάνει τὸ βραβεῖον; οὕτως τρέχετε ἵνα καταλάβητε. ²⁵ πᾶς δὲ ὁ ἀγωνιζόμενος πάντα ἐγκρατεύεται, ἐκεῖνοι μὲν οὖν ἵνα φθαρτὸν στέφανον λάβωσιν, ἡμεῖς δὲ ἄφθαρτον.

CONTEXT:

In 1 Corinthians 9, Paul uses rhetorical questions and the imagery of a race to express the immeasurable value of the gospel and its blessings (9:23).

COMMENTARY:

Paul's intention here in 9:24–25 is to underscore the excellence of the gospel of Christ and the need to live in a manner worthy of this gospel. Notice Paul's use of the imperative "run" (τρέχετε). He uses a rhetorical question and the imagery of running a race to accentuate the difference between "all the runners who run in the race" (οἱ ἐν σταδίῳ τρέχοντες πάντες μὲν τρέχουσιν) and the particular "one who receives the prize" (εἷς ... λαμβάνει τὸ βραβεῖον) after running well. The prize is a definite award that is "received" or "won" (λαμβάνει). Paul then draws a striking contrast: those who run a literal race in this life do so for a "perishable wreath" (φθαρτὸν στέφανον), yet the believer who lives unto Christ does so for an "imperishable [one]" (ἄφθαρτον). Paul's exhortation, therefore, encompasses the hope that the one who devotes himself to finishing well "might obtain" (καταλάβητε) the prize of eternal life. The believer runs the race by developing piety and living in a manner worthy of the gospel, cultivated in communion with God.

οἴδατε > 2PRAI, you know || σταδίῳ > race || οἱ ... τρέχοντες > PAPMPN, the runners || τρέχουσιν > 3PPAI, run || λαμβάνει > 3SPAI, receives || βραβεῖον > prize || τρέχετε > 2PPAM, run! || καταλάβητε > 2PAAS, you might obtain [it] || ὁ ἀγωνιζόμενος > PAPMSN, athlete || ἐγκρατεύεται > 3SPMI, exercise self-control || φθαρτὸν στέφανον > perishable wreath || λάβωσιν > 3SAAS, they might receive || ἄφθαρτον > imperishable [one]

Further Reading: 1 Corinthians 9:1–23; Philippians 2:12–18; Hebrews 11:1–12:2
R. Vivian Pietsch

1 CORINTHIANS 10:23-24

²³ πάντα ἔξεστιν ἀλλ' οὐ πάντα συμφέρει· πάντα ἔξεστιν ἀλλ' οὐ πάντα οἰκοδομεῖ. ²⁴ μηδεὶς τὸ ἑαυτοῦ ζητείτω ἀλλὰ τὸ τοῦ ἑτέρου.

CONTEXT:

Paul continues his discourse from chapter 8 on the freedom experienced in the gospel of Christ and the believers' need to make sure that their Christian liberty does not become a stumbling block to the weak in the faith (1 Cor 8:9).

COMMENTARY:

When Paul states, "All things are lawful" (πάντα ἔξεστιν), he refers to the non-essentials of the faith, that which is included in Christian liberty. Here, Paul is bringing his readers' attention to the theological implications behind the liberty they enjoy in the gospel of Christ—the liberty found in and available through the person and work of Christ in his penal substitutionary atonement on the cross. Take note that the imperative command "let [no one] seek" (ζητείτω) comprises two elements indicated by the use of the contrasting conjunction ἀλλά: (1) "Let no one seek his own good" (μηδεὶς τὸ ἑαυτοῦ ζητείτω), (2) "but rather [seek] the good of his neighbor" (ἀλλὰ τὸ τοῦ ἑτέρου). This command is closely related to the second great commandment to "love your neighbor as yourself" (cf. Matt 22:37-40). Paul grounds his command in the principle of limitation. Although a thing may be preferable to some (available through Christian liberty), it must be limited if it is not spiritually beneficial or does not build up the character and faith of others. Rather than enjoying all liberty available in the gospel merely for the sake of liberty, believers are to build up one another (Gal 5:13-14); they are to be known by their love for one another, just as Jesus proclaimed, "By this all people will know that you are my disciples, if you have love for one another" (John 13:35). Believers must take care to love their neighbors well by desiring the good of their neighbor over their own good, seeking to edify and engender holiness in their neighbor.

ἔξεστιν > 3SPAI, is lawful ‖ συμφέρει > 3SPAI, is helpful ‖ οἰκοδομεῖ > 3SPAI, build up ‖ ζητείτω > 3SPAM, let [no one] seek

Further Reading: Matthew 22:34-40; John 13:31-35;
1 Corinthians 8:1-10:22; Galatians 5:1-15
R. Vivian Pietsch

³¹ εἴτε οὖν ἐσθίετε εἴτε πίνετε εἴτε τι ποιεῖτε, πάντα εἰς δόξαν θεοῦ ποιεῖτε. ³² ἀπρόσκοποι καὶ Ἰουδαίοις γίνεσθε καὶ Ἕλλησιν καὶ τῇ ἐκκλησίᾳ τοῦ θεοῦ, ³³ καθὼς κἀγὼ πάντα πᾶσιν ἀρέσκω μὴ ζητῶν τὸ ἐμαυτοῦ σύμφορον ἀλλὰ τὸ τῶν πολλῶν, ἵνα σωθῶσιν.

CONTEXT:

In 1 Corinthians 10, Paul reminds believers of the freedom found in the gospel which enables them to obey the law of Christ (having concern for neighbors), rather than adhere to the Law of Moses, as some thought was necessary for obedience (10:23–30).

COMMENTARY:

Continuing his discourse on obeying Christ's command to "love your neighbor as yourself" (cf. Matt 22:37–40), Paul exhorts believers with two imperatives: (1) "do all to the glory of God" (πάντα εἰς δόξαν θεοῦ ποιεῖτε) and (2) "give no offense" (γίνεσθε ἀπρόσκοποι). These commands add to Paul's earlier exhortation to ensure one acts in a manner that engenders spiritual maturity in others (1 Cor 10:23–24). Here, Paul draws attention to the need to be concerned with doing that which glorifies God—being blameless before and seeking the benefit of others (μὴ ζητῶν τὸ ἐμαυτοῦ σύμφορον, "not seeking my own advantage") for a specific purpose: "that they may be saved" (ἵνα σωθῶσιν). Notice here that God is the one who saves. The believer's ability to be blameless before others in no way ensures that others will be saved; for one is saved solely by the work of God. Believers, though, can be assured that God is at work saving his people and has provided faith in the hearts of many. Through the transformation of focus from self to God, believers begin the journey of progressive sanctification wrought by the Holy Spirit, whereby they are able to seek the good of and encourage spiritual maturity in others.

ἐσθίετε > 2PPAI, you eat || πίνετε > 2PPAI, you drink || ποιεῖτε > 2PPAI, you do || ποιεῖτε > 2PPAM, do! || ἀπρόσκοποι ... γίνεσθε > 2PPMM, give no offense! || ἀρέσκω > 1SPAI, I please || ζητῶν > PAPMSN, [not] seeking || σύμφορον > advantage || σωθῶσιν > 3PAPS, they might be saved

Further Reading: Matthew 22:34–40; Romans 14:13–23;
1 Corinthians 8:1–10:30; 1 Peter 4:11
R. Vivian Pietsch

1 CORINTHIANS 11:1

¹ μιμηταί μου γίνεσθε καθὼς κἀγὼ Χριστοῦ.

CONTEXT:

Paul concludes his argument of how believers should live with the principle of seeking the good of others above oneself so that they may be saved (1 Cor 10:23–33).

COMMENTARY:

Paul expresses the implication of the principle of self-sacrifice he introduced in the earlier discourse, namely that believers are to follow the example set by Paul just as he follows Christ (1 Cor 10:33). Notice the imperative, "Become imitators of me ..." (μιμηταί μου γίνεσθε). Here, Paul focuses on the significance of striving to follow in the footsteps of another to emulate their life. The command encompasses two elements: (1) "Become" or "be" (γίνεσθε), which indicates a continual action, and (2) "Imitators" (μιμηταί), which encompasses the moral imitation of the sacrifice of Christ—sacrificing one's desires and rights for the benefit of others (1 John 3:16). To imitate Paul is to imitate Christ; believers are to continually love their neighbor by seeking the good of their neighbor over experiencing the benefits of their own rights. The example of Christ's humbling himself on the cross demonstrates the love that believers should demonstrate toward each other (Matt 22:36–40; John 13:35; 1 John 5:2). The believers' capacity to imitate Paul (and Christ) results from the righteousness provided by Christ through his finished work on the cross; Christ fulfilled the Law, filled each believer with the Holy Spirit, and endowed righteousness to fulfill the Law of Love through the believers' union with Christ. Believers humble themselves and share the grace of the gospel from their consciousness of Christ's sacrifice and God's power as the impetus for salvation.

μιμηταί > imitators || γίνεσθε > 2PPMM, become, be!

Further reading: Matthew 22:36–40; 1 Corinthians 8:1–10:33;
John 13:33–35; 1 John 3:16; 4:7–5:5
R. Vivian Pietsch

1 CORINTHIANS 12:29-31

²⁹ μὴ πάντες ἀπόστολοι; μὴ πάντες προφῆται; μὴ πάντες διδάσκαλοι; μὴ πάντες δυνάμεις; ³⁰ μὴ πάντες χαρίσματα ἔχουσιν ἰαμάτων; μὴ πάντες γλώσσαις λαλοῦσιν; μὴ πάντες διερμηνεύουσιν; ³¹ ζηλοῦτε δὲ τὰ χαρίσματα τὰ μείζονα. Καὶ ἔτι καθ' ὑπερβολὴν ὁδὸν ὑμῖν δείκνυμι.

CONTEXT:
In 1 Corinthians 12, Paul addresses the gifts of the Spirit given to church members and how believers are to use their gifts interdependently (12:12-28).

COMMENTARY:
As Paul declares that members of the church body are united in Christ (1 Cor 12:12-14), he asserts that God has appointed gifts to some (12:4-11) so that the members may care for one another (12:15-27). Paul then poses several rhetorical questions, all negated by μή (which in a Greek question demands the answer, "No!"): "Are all apostles? Are all prophets? Are all teachers? Do all work miracles? Do all have gifts of healing? Do all speak in tongues? Do all interpret?" (12:29-30). In each case, Paul's assumed answer is "No!" Just as the members of a body all work together interdependently, Paul emphasizes that not all gifts are given to all people, but all gifts are given for the edification of the entire body. He commands believers to "earnestly desire" (ζηλοῦτε) the "greater gifts" (τὰ χαρίσματα τὰ μείζονα) that edify the body rather than the manifestation gifts which only serve the one person (14:19). This principle that gifts must be used to build up the body is seen in Paul's exhortation that there is a "still more excellent way" (ἔτι καθ' ὑπερβολὴν ὁδόν) of love (cf. chapter 13). Though the church holds various interpretations regarding the nuances of the continuation of these gifts, the underlying truth of the *charismata*—spiritual gifts endowed by the Holy Spirit to the body of Christ for the edification of the church—is, at a minimum, a theological absolute embraced by all true Christians (1 Cor 12:1-31; Eph 2:11-22). Notice that the baptism (indwelling) of the Spirit is not a gift denoted in this passage (1 Cor 12:13) but is a theological imperative related to the ontological nature of believers "in Christ" (1 Cor 15:21-23; Rom 15:12-21).

χαρίσματα ... ἰαμάτων > gifts of healing ‖ ἔχουσιν > 3PPAI, possess ‖ λαλοῦσιν > 3PPAI, speak ‖ διερμηνεύου > 3PPAI, interpret, translate ‖ ζηλοῦτε > 2PPAM, earnestly desire ‖ τὰ χαρίσματα τὰ μείζονα > the greater gifts ‖ καθ' ὑπερβολὴν ὁδόν > more excellent way ‖ δείκνυμι > 1SPAI, I will show

Further Reading: 1 Corinthians 12:1-28; 14:1; Ephesians 2:19-20

R. Vivian Pietsch

1 CORINTHIANS 14:20

²⁰ ἀδελφοί, μὴ παιδία γίνεσθε ταῖς φρεσὶν ἀλλὰ τῇ κακίᾳ νηπιάζετε, ταῖς δὲ φρεσὶν τέλειοι γίνεσθε.

CONTEXT:

Throughout 1 Corinthians, Paul uses the theme of maturity to encourage Christians to operate from a Christ-centered reasoning so that their hope in Christ may be emboldened as they walk through the trials and difficulties of life. Paul exhorts his audience to rightly desire the edification of one another rather than to seek personal glorification.

COMMENTARY:

Notice Paul's use of the vocative ἀδελφοί ("brothers [and sisters]") when addressing the audience. His use of this familial term shows pastoral care for the audience even as he proceeds with the stern command, "Do not be as little children" (μὴ παιδία γίνεσθε). Note that this imperative involves a continual response (present tense-form) and should be ever-present in believers' lives. Here, Paul reiterates the theme of immature reasoning from 13:11 ("When I was a child, I spoke as a child, I thought as a child, I reasoned as a child. When I became a man, I gave up childish ways"). Paul's subsequent commands to "be infants in evil" (τῇ κακίᾳ νηπιάζετε) and "be mature in your thinking" (ταῖς ... φρεσὶν τέλειοι γίνεσθε) provide clarity for the way a believer should reason. One who is not an infant in evil (i.e., one who is mature in evil) is driven by the progressively destructive patterns of sin, empowered by an evil cognitive framework (Ps 1:1). Conversely, as Christians, we are commanded to grow in the sapiential wisdom of Christ by leaving "the elementary doctrine of Christ and going on to maturity" (Heb 6:1; Ps 1:2–3; Ezra 7:10). We are to "have the mind of Christ" (1 Cor 2:16). As Christians are progressively sanctified and their wisdom of the doctrines of Scripture mature, their reasoning is driven by an innate framework through Scripture rather than the emotionally reactionary response of a child. As Christians, we grow in wisdom as our axioms are established in the doctrines of Scripture and we learn to apply a theological foundation to our daily lives.

γίνεσθε > 2PPMM, do [not] be! ‖ ταῖς φρεσίν > your thinking ‖ νηπιάζετε > 2PPAM, be as an infant! ‖ τέλειοι > mature, perfect ‖ γίνεσθε > 2PPMM, be!

Further Reading: Psalm 1; Hebrews 6; Ezra 7:10
Evan P. Pietsch

1 CORINTHIANS 15:1–2

¹ γνωρίζω δὲ ὑμῖν, ἀδελφοί, τὸ εὐαγγέλιον ὃ εὐηγγελισάμην ὑμῖν, ὃ καὶ παρελάβετε, ἐν ᾧ καὶ ἑστήκατε, ² δι' οὗ καὶ σῴζεσθε, τίνι λόγῳ εὐηγγελισάμην ὑμῖν εἰ κατέχετε, ἐκτὸς εἰ μὴ εἰκῇ ἐπιστεύσατε.

CONTEXT:

In 1 Corinthians 15, Paul uses the resurrection of Christ to establish the tangible hope and promise believers have through the gospel of Jesus Christ.

COMMENTARY:

Paul seeks to remind his audience continuously (γνωρίζω) of the implications of hearing the gospel. Notice the four verbs describing "the gospel" (τὸ εὐαγγέλιον), each of which follow a relative pronoun: ὃ εὐηγγελισάμην ("which I preached"), ὃ ... παρελάβετε ("which you received"), ἐν ᾧ ... ἑστήκατε ("in which you stand"), and δι' οὗ ... σῴζεσθε ("by which you are being saved"). Notice in particular the tense-form of each of these four verbs. The first two are aorist ("I preached" and "you received"), indicating a past event. The perfect tense-form of the third, ἑστήκατε ("you stand"), describes a state-of-being; it assures the believer that their condition has been genuinely and eternally impacted as an effectual result of the gospel message. The fourth, σῴζεσθε ("you are being saved"), is present, indicating the on-going nature of the believer's salvation through the gospel and work of Christ. Christians can rest in the assurance that they have been adopted into Christ for eternity and can equally be assured that their life will be a continual journey of progressive sanctification. The final clause ἐκτὸς εἰ μὴ εἰκῇ ἐπιστεύσατε ("unless you believed in vain") is reminiscent of Hebrews 4:1–7, which warns against not receiving the gospel message through faith.

γνωρίζω > 1SPAI, I remind ‖ εὐηγγελισάμην > 1SAMI, I preached ‖ παρελάβετε > 2PAAI, you received ‖ ἑστήκατε > 2PRAI, you stand ‖ σῴζεσθε > 2PPPI, you are being saved ‖ κατέχετε > 2PPAI, you hold fast ‖ ἐκτὸς εἰ μὴ εἰκῇ > unless in vain ‖ ἐπιστεύσατε > 2PAAI, you believed

Further Reading: 1 Corinthians 15:1–11; Romans 10:13–17; Hebrews 4:1–7

Evan P. Pietsch

²¹ ἐπειδὴ γὰρ δι' ἀνθρώπου θάνατος, καὶ δι' ἀνθρώπου ἀνάστασις νεκρῶν.
²² ὥσπερ γὰρ ἐν τῷ Ἀδὰμ πάντες ἀποθνήσκουσιν, οὕτως καὶ ἐν τῷ Χριστῷ πάντες ζῳοποιηθήσονται.

CONTEXT:

In 1 Corinthians 15:1-11, Paul uses the resurrection of Christ to establish the tangible hope and promise believers have through the gospel of Jesus Christ. 1 Corinthians 15:21-22 offers the theological truth concerning the ontological need for the resurrection of Christ and the redeeming work of Christ's redemption in response to the fall of humanity in Adam.

COMMENTARY:

Take note of Paul's use of "all" (πάντες) to describe the two states of human nature: "all in Adam" (ἐν τῷ Ἀδὰμ πάντες) and "all in Christ" (ἐν τῷ Χριστῷ πάντες). Paul's emphasis on the ontological reality of all humanity demonstrates the bifurcated nature of one's federal headship being either "in Adam" or "in Christ." Here we see the importance of teaching all believers that sin entered God's creation through the disobedience of Adam (Gen 3:16-17). Paul's thematic use of Adam should cause one to consider John 3:18, which indicates that all of humanity is inherently condemned under the punishment of death due to Adam's sin: "Whoever believes in him is not condemned, but whoever does not believe is condemned already, because he has not believed in the name of the only Son of God" (cf. Rom 6:23; apart from Christ, all will experience the cessation of life). Paul then demonstrates that Christ, the Second Adam, creates a new humanity through his greater headship. Though Christians will experience death through their humanity, they are promised resurrection and eternity with Christ because his resurrection satiated the wrath of God against those under Adam. Faith in Christ changes one's nature from being naturally under Adam's headship to being adopted under Christ's headship. Note that humanity has but one nature; the federal head will describe that nature.

ἐπειδή > since, as || ὥσπερ > just as || Ἀδάμ > Adam || ἀποθνήσκουσιν > 3PPAI, [all] die || ζῳοποιηθήσονται > 3PFPI, [all] will be made alive

Further Reading: Genesis 3:16-17; Romans 5:20-24; 1 Corinthians 15:42-50
Evan P. Pietsch

1 CORINTHIANS 15:51–52

⁵¹ ἰδοὺ μυστήριον ὑμῖν λέγω· πάντες οὐ κοιμηθησόμεθα, πάντες δὲ ἀλλαγησόμεθα, ⁵² ἐν ἀτόμῳ, ἐν ῥιπῇ ὀφθαλμοῦ, ἐν τῇ ἐσχάτῃ σάλπιγγι· σαλπίσει γὰρ καὶ οἱ νεκροὶ ἐγερθήσονται ἄφθαρτοι καὶ ἡμεῖς ἀλλαγησόμεθα.

CONTEXT:
The concluding verses of 1 Corinthians 15 constitute a paean of praise—a happy chant—and thanksgiving to God.

COMMENTARY:
Paul directs his audiences' attention to the means and object of the Christian hope, namely the bodily resurrection and eternal life with Christ. Though different interpretations regarding the nuances of eschatological details from this passage abound, the underlying truth of the *parousia*—that Christ will install the culmination of his eternal kingdom—is a theological absolute that all true Christians embrace. Notice the eschatological undertone in Paul's use of future verbs (κοιμηθησόμεθα, ἀλλαγησόμεθα, σαλπίσει, ἐγερθήσονται, and ἀλλαγησόμεθα) that indicates the definite and future culmination of Christ's eternal kingdom. Furthermore, note the passive voice of these verbs (other than σαλπίσει), which demonstrates the exclusivity of the Trinitarian work in a believer's resurrection and humanity's dependence on Christ as the founder and perfecter of their faith (Heb 12:2). It is the ultimacy of a believer's final redemption and glorification that emboldens the hope that "passes all understanding" (Phil 4:7).

μυστήριον > mystery || λέγω > 1SPAI, I tell || κοιμηθησόμεθα > 1PFPI, we will [not] sleep || ἀλλαγησόμεθα > 1PFPI, we will be changed || ἀτόμῳ > moment || ῥιπῇ ὀφθαλμοῦ > twinkling of an eye || ἐσχάτῃ σάλπιγγι > last trumpet || σαλπίσει > 3SFAI, the trumpet will sound || ἐγερθήσονται > 3PFPI, will be raised || ἄφθαρτοι > imperishable

Further Reading: Hebrews 12; Romans 8:18–25;
2 Corinthians 5:1–10; Philippians 1:21–26
Evan P. Pietsch

1 CORINTHIANS 16:22-23

²² εἴ τις οὐ φιλεῖ τὸν κύριον, ἤτω ἀνάθεμα. μαράνα θά. ²³ ἡ χάρις τοῦ κυρίου Ἰησοῦ μεθ᾽ ὑμῶν.

CONTEXT:

1 Corinthians 16:19–24 concludes Paul's letter to the Corinthian church. Even in Paul's closing salutations, we see his passion for practical theology as he provides one last exhortation and plea for all to examine themselves to ensure they have faith in Christ.

COMMENTARY:

In 1 Corinthians 16:22, Paul makes a strong statement concerning those who do not have a genuine love for Christ: "If anyone does not love the Lord ..." (εἴ τις οὐ φιλεῖ τὸν κύριον). Paul's use of the negated present active form of love (οὐ φιλεῖ) provides the audience with a phenomenological description of those outside of Christ: Their life will have a continual display of a rejection of God. The reader should consider Paul's discussion of the federal headship of Adam (15:22), which teaches that all who are not in Christ are naturally under the curse in Adam. Paul's use of the imperative ἤτω ἀνάθεμα ("let him be accursed"), therefore, is a reiteration that those who do not have genuine faith in Christ are already accursed under the effects of the inhered nature of sin (cf. John 3:18). Paul's use of the aorist form of the imperative θά (in the exclamation μαράνα θά, "Come, O Lord!") should be understood with his utmost reverence for the Lord in mind. Paul is not commanding the Lord to come; instead, he is petitioning that the Lord come soon (cf. 1 Cor 15:51–54). Believers should examine themselves continuously (2 Cor 13:5) to ensure they have a genuine faith in Christ, knowing that the second coming of Christ is an eschatological reality. Lastly, Paul's final exhortation, "The grace of the Lord Jesus be with you" (ἡ χάρις τοῦ κυρίου Ἰησοῦ μεθ᾽ ὑμῶν), has two purposes: (1) Paul desires that all have the gift of faith in Christ, and (2) Paul hopes that his audience will continuously live with the evidence of having been adopted into Christ (Matt 28:20; John 14:16–17).

φιλεῖ > 3SPAI, does [not] love || ἤτω > 3SPAM, let him be || ἀνάθεμα > accursed || μαράνα > O Lord || θά > 2SAAM, come!

Further Reading: 2 Corinthians 13:5,11–13, Romans 16:24–27;
Matthew 28:20; John 14:16–17
Evan P. Pietsch

¹³ τότε προσηνέχθησαν αὐτῷ παιδία ἵνα τὰς χεῖρας ἐπιθῇ αὐτοῖς καὶ προσεύξηται· οἱ δὲ μαθηταὶ ἐπετίμησαν αὐτοῖς. ¹⁴ ὁ δὲ Ἰησοῦς εἶπεν· ἄφετε τὰ παιδία καὶ μὴ κωλύετε αὐτὰ ἐλθεῖν πρός με, τῶν γὰρ τοιούτων ἐστὶν ἡ βασιλεία τῶν οὐρανῶν. ¹⁵ καὶ ἐπιθεὶς τὰς χεῖρας αὐτοῖς ἐπορεύθη ἐκεῖθεν.

CONTEXT:

After Jesus teaches a series of parables (18:10-35), he travels to Judea beyond the Jordan (19:1-2). In response to a question he receives from the Pharisees, he teaches about divorce (19:3-12). In 19:13-15, children are brought to Jesus for him to pray over.

COMMENTARY:

As "large crowds followed him" (19:2), "children" (παιδία) are brought to Jesus (19:13). The ἵνα clause introduces purpose marked by two subjunctive verbs: that Jesus "might place" (ἐπιθῇ) his hands on them and "pray" (προσεύξηται) for them. Given the crowds' purpose in following Jesus mentioned in 19:2—"he healed them there"—these children appear to be brought to Jesus for his miraculous healing hand (cf. Matt 9:18, 20), though perhaps they are brought only for general blessing (cf. Acts 6:6; 13:3). Either way, the disciples "rebuke" (ἐπετίμησαν) those who bring them, perhaps assuming Jesus has more pressing responsibilities. Jesus, however, will have none of this. In 19:14, he quickly rebukes his disciples and makes the intriguing statement: τῶν γὰρ τοιούτων ἐστὶν ἡ βασιλεία τῶν οὐρανῶν ("for the kingdom of heaven belongs to such as these"). It is not that the kingdom of heaven belongs *to these specific children*, but that it belongs *to those like them* (τῶν ... τοιούτων), lit. "of such a group." Jesus' point is that the kingdom of heaven belongs to those with simple, childlike faith who depend fully on Jesus for his blessing. This is directly contrasted in the following passage, 19:23-24, where "it is hard for a rich person enter the kingdom of heaven (τὴν βασιλείαν τῶν οὐρανῶν)."

προσηνέχθησαν > 3PAPI, were brought ‖ ἐπιθῇ > 3SAAS, might place ‖ προσεύξηται > 3SAMS, might pray ‖ ἐπετίμησαν > 3PAAI, rebuked ‖ εἶπεν > 3SAAI, said ‖ ἄφετε > 2PAAM, permit ‖ κωλύετε > 2PPAM, [do not] hinder ‖ ἐλθεῖν > AAN, to come ‖ ἐστίν > 3SPAI, is, belongs ‖ ἐπιθείς > AAPMSN, placing ‖ ἐπορεύθη > 3SAPI, went ‖ ἐκεῖθεν > from there

Further Reading: Luke 18:15-17

Jared M. August

MATTHEW 19:28

²⁸ ὁ δὲ Ἰησοῦς εἶπεν αὐτοῖς· ἀμὴν λέγω ὑμῖν ὅτι ὑμεῖς οἱ ἀκολουθήσαντές μοι ἐν τῇ παλιγγενεσίᾳ, ὅταν καθίσῃ ὁ υἱὸς τοῦ ἀνθρώπου ἐπὶ θρόνου δόξης αὐτοῦ, καθήσεσθε καὶ ὑμεῖς ἐπὶ δώδεκα θρόνους κρίνοντες τὰς δώδεκα φυλὰς τοῦ Ἰσραήλ.

CONTEXT:

When questioned by a young man, "Teacher, what good deed must I do to have eternal life?" (19:16), Jesus responds that he must sell all, give to the poor, and "follow me" (19:21). The result is that this man leaves "sorrowful, because he had great possessions" (19:22). Jesus then comments about the difficulty of the rich entering the kingdom of heaven (19:23–24) and Peter asks, "We have left everything and followed you. What then will we have?" (19:27). Jesus responds with today's verse, 19:28.

COMMENTARY:

The word παλιγγενεσίᾳ ("new world" or "regeneration") is used only here and in Titus 3:5 in the NT. Although both uses are distinct, they each do indicate a complete change and restoration. In Titus 3:4–5, "God our Savior ... saved us by the washing, *regeneration* (παλιγγενεσίας), and renewal of the Holy Spirit." In Matthew 19:28, the focus is on the eschatological restoration of the cosmos, an idea that is certainly related to the future messianic kingdom and new heavens and new earth (cf. 2 Pt 3:13; Rev 21:1–22:5). In the immediate context of this passage, Jesus brings together several terms to describe this future restoration: "eternal life" (ζωὴν αἰώνιον, Matt 19:16, 29), "kingdom of heaven" (ἡ βασιλεία τῶν οὐρανῶν, 19:12, 14, 23, 24), "treasure in heaven" (θησαυρὸν ἐν οὐρανοῖς, 19:21), "the life" (τὴν ζωήν, 19:17), and "new world" (παλιγγενεσίᾳ, 19:28). For those who follow (ἀκολουθήσαντες) Christ and ask, like Peter in 19:27, "What then will we have?" the answer is this same eschatological hope; we can anticipate eternal life, the kingdom of heaven, and a new world. This truly is "treasure in heaven" (19:21; cf. 6:20, 13:44).

εἶπεν > 3SAAI, said ‖ λέγω > 1SPAI, say ‖ οἱ ἀκολουθήσαντες > AAPMPN, who have followed ‖ παλιγγενεσίᾳ > new world, regeneration ‖ καθίσῃ > 3SAAS, will sit ‖ καθήσεσθε > 2PFMI, will sit ‖ κρίνοντες > PAPMPN, judging ‖ φυλάς > tribes

Further Reading: Matthew 19:25–30; Luke 22:28–30
Jared M. August

MARCH 13
MATTHEW 22:31–32

³¹ περὶ δὲ τῆς ἀναστάσεως τῶν νεκρῶν οὐκ ἀνέγνωτε τὸ ῥηθὲν ὑμῖν ὑπὸ τοῦ θεοῦ λέγοντος· ³² ἐγώ εἰμι ὁ θεὸς Ἀβραὰμ καὶ ὁ θεὸς Ἰσαὰκ καὶ ὁ θεὸς Ἰακώβ; οὐκ ἔστιν ὁ θεὸς νεκρῶν ἀλλὰ ζώντων.

CONTEXT:

In Matthew 22:23–33, the Sadducees—"who say there is no resurrection" (22:23)—try to refute Jesus by posing a question about marriage and the resurrection (22:28). Jesus responds with pointed clarity, "You are wrong because you do not know the Scriptures nor the power of God" (22:29).

COMMENTARY:

In 22:31, Jesus cites Exodus 3:6 from the LXX (omitting τοῦ πατρός σου for brevity) to make a specific point about the Lord's relationship to the patriarchs. Although Abraham, Isaac, and Jacob had physically died many years prior to the Lord appearing to Moses in Exodus 3, Jesus makes the point that these patriarchs are not "dead" (νεκρῶν) but "living" (ζώντων). This assertion appears to find its basis both linguistically and covenantally. Linguistically, the *present* tense εἰμί is used here ("I *am* the God of ..." not "I *was* the God of ..."). This is not to say that the present tense in and of itself necessarily demands that the patriarchs would be resurrected, but it is certainly consistent with the unconditional covenant made by the Lord to Abraham, Isaac, and Jacob. In this way, the patriarchs are characterized as the "living" (ζώντων), implying that somehow they lived on even after death to worship the Lord as they anticipated a bodily resurrection (cf. John 6:68; 11:25; Acts 13:38; Rom 6:23).

ἀνέγνωτε > 2PAAI, have you [not] read ‖ τὸ ῥηθέν > APPNSA, what was spoken ‖ λέγοντος > PAPMSG, saying ‖ εἰμί > 1SPAI, am ‖ ἔστιν > 3SPAI, is ‖ ζώντων > PAPMPG, living

Further Reading: Matthew 22:23–33
Jared M. August

MATTHEW 22:37–40

³⁷ ὁ δὲ ἔφη αὐτῷ· ἀγαπήσεις κύριον τὸν θεόν σου ἐν ὅλῃ τῇ καρδίᾳ σου καὶ ἐν ὅλῃ τῇ ψυχῇ σου καὶ ἐν ὅλῃ τῇ διανοίᾳ σου· ³⁸ αὕτη ἐστὶν ἡ μεγάλη καὶ πρώτη ἐντολή. ³⁹ δευτέρα δὲ ὁμοία αὐτῇ· ἀγαπήσεις τὸν πλησίον σου ὡς σεαυτόν. ⁴⁰ ἐν ταύταις ταῖς δυσὶν ἐντολαῖς ὅλος ὁ νόμος κρέμαται καὶ οἱ προφῆται.

CONTEXT:

In Matthew 22, a Pharisee who was a lawyer/legal expert (νομικός, 22:35) tries to trap Jesus by questioning him, "Teacher, which is the great commandment in the Law?" (22:36). Jesus' response is recorded in 22:37–40.

COMMENTARY:

Jesus responds to the Pharisee by citing Deuteronomy 6:5 and stating that this is "the great and first commandment" (22:38). He follows this up by citing Leviticus 19:18 as the second great commandment. In both cases, Jesus uses ἀγαπήσεις, a future verb that is used with imperatival force: "You *shall* love ..." These two commands impact both one's vertical relationship with God and one's horizontal relationship with other people. It is on these two commands that ὅλος ὁ νόμος ... καὶ οἱ προφῆται depend. Notice how ὁ νόμος and οἱ προφῆται, though certainly plural, are understood as a single entity with the use of the third-person singular κρέμαται ("depend"). In our modern terminology, it is as if Jesus says, "the whole Old Testament" is built on these two commands—loving God and loving one's neighbor.

ἔφη > 3SIAI, said ‖ ἀγαπήσεις > 2SFAI, shall love ‖ διανοίᾳ > mind ‖ ἐστίν > 3SPAI, is ‖ πλησίον > neighbor ‖ κρέμαται > 3SPPI, depend

Further Reading: Matthew 22:34–46
Jared M. August

MATTHEW 27:51–53

⁵¹ καὶ ἰδοὺ τὸ καταπέτασμα τοῦ ναοῦ ἐσχίσθη ἀπ' ἄνωθεν ἕως κάτω εἰς δύο καὶ ἡ γῆ ἐσείσθη καὶ αἱ πέτραι ἐσχίσθησαν, ⁵² καὶ τὰ μνημεῖα ἀνεῴχθησαν καὶ πολλὰ σώματα τῶν κεκοιμημένων ἁγίων ἠγέρθησαν, ⁵³ καὶ ἐξελθόντες ἐκ τῶν μνημείων μετὰ τὴν ἔγερσιν αὐτοῦ εἰσῆλθον εἰς τὴν ἁγίαν πόλιν καὶ ἐνεφανίσθησαν πολλοῖς.

CONTEXT:

In Matthew 27:51–53, the Gospel author records the events that occurred immediately after Jesus' death in 27:50. These truly extraordinary events include: (1) the curtain of the temple was torn, v. 51, (2) the earth shook, v. 51, (3) the rocks were split, v. 51, (4) the tombs were opened, v. 52, (5) those who died were raised, v. 52, and (6) the resurrected saints went into the city and appeared to many, v. 53.

COMMENTARY:

Καὶ ἰδού is used here to draw attention to the remarkable events, "And behold!" Notice the directional specificity indicated with the phrase ἀπ' ἄνωθεν ἕως κάτω ("from top to bottom," v. 51), surely indicating that this "tearing" or "splitting" (ἐσχίσθη) of the curtain was a supernatural and highly significant act of God. It appears most likely that these events described occurred simultaneously, perhaps all the result of this earthquake (ἡ γῆ ἐσείσθη, v. 51). It is only a couple days later when yet another "great earthquake" occurs, this time when the stone is rolled from the tomb and Jesus is resurrected (28:2). Having witnessed Jesus' death and the supernatural events surrounding it, the centurion responds with awe in 27:54, "Truly this was the Son of God!" May this be our response to our Savior's death as well.

καταπέτασμα > curtain ‖ ἐσχίσθη > 3SAPI, was split ‖ ἀπ' ἄνωθεν ἕως κάτω > from top to bottom ‖ ἐσείσθη > 3SAPI, shook ‖ πέτραι > rocks ‖ ἐσχίσθησαν > 3PAPI, were split ‖ ἀνεῴχθησαν > 3PAPI, were opened ‖ τῶν κεκοιμημένων > RPPMPG, who had fallen asleep ‖ ἠγέρθησαν > 3PAPI, were raised ‖ ἐξελθόντες > AAPMPN, coming out ‖ ἔγερσιν > resurrection ‖ εἰσῆλθον > 3PAAI, went in ‖ ἐνεφανίσθησαν > 3PAPI, appeared

Further Reading: Matthew 27:45–56
Jared M. August

MARCH 16
MATTHEW 28:18-20

¹⁸ καὶ προσελθὼν ὁ Ἰησοῦς ἐλάλησεν αὐτοῖς λέγων· ἐδόθη μοι πᾶσα ἐξουσία ἐν οὐρανῷ καὶ ἐπὶ γῆς. ¹⁹ πορευθέντες οὖν μαθητεύσατε πάντα τὰ ἔθνη βαπτίζοντες αὐτοὺς εἰς τὸ ὄνομα τοῦ πατρὸς καὶ τοῦ υἱοῦ καὶ τοῦ ἁγίου πνεύματος, ²⁰ διδάσκοντες αὐτοὺς τηρεῖν πάντα ὅσα ἐνετειλάμην ὑμῖν· καὶ ἰδοὺ ἐγὼ μεθ' ὑμῶν εἰμι πάσας τὰς ἡμέρας ἕως τῆς συντελείας τοῦ αἰῶνος.

CONTEXT:
In this familiar passage, often known as the Great Commission, the disciples meet Jesus on a mountain in Galilee (28:16). Here, Jesus provides final instructions.

COMMENTARY:
Notice that ἐδόθη is passive; Jesus *has been given all authority in heaven and on earth*. When was he given this authority? According to Matthew, it appears that it was given at his resurrection (cf. 28:1-10, 17). What, therefore, are the disciples to do? Notice that there is only one imperative in this passage; the disciples are to *make disciples* (μαθητεύσατε). Although the attendant circumstance participle πορευθέντες is often understood as a command (as is evident in English translations, "Go"), it is not the primary focus of this passage. In this way, the supporting participles (πορευθέντες, βαπτίζοντες, and διδάσκοντες) are the prerequisites or the means by which one might obey the command μαθητεύσατε. They are not the focus, yet they are still key to obedience. As his disciples seek to obey by making more disciples, Jesus concludes this passage with encouragement that he will always be with his followers *until the close of the age* (ἕως τῆς συντελείας τοῦ αἰῶνος).

ἐδόθη > 3SAPI, has been given ‖ πορευθέντες > APPMPN, having set out ‖ μαθητεύσατε > 2PAAM, make disciples ‖ βαπτίζοντες > PAPMPN, baptizing ‖ διδάσκοντες > PAPMPN, teaching ‖ τηρεῖν > PAN, to observe ‖ ἐνετειλάμην > 1SAMI, I commanded ‖ συντελείας > close, completion

Further Reading: Matthew 28:1-20
Jared M. August

March 17
2 Corinthians 1:10–11

¹⁰ ὃς ἐκ τηλικούτου θανάτου ἐρρύσατο ἡμᾶς καὶ ῥύσεται, εἰς ὃν ἠλπίκαμεν ὅτι καὶ ἔτι ῥύσεται, ¹¹ συνυπουργούντων καὶ ὑμῶν ὑπὲρ ἡμῶν τῇ δεήσει, ἵνα ἐκ πολλῶν προσώπων τὸ εἰς ἡμᾶς χάρισμα διὰ πολλῶν εὐχαριστηθῇ ὑπὲρ ἡμῶν.

CONTEXT:

Paul has just informed the Corinthians that he has recently been through some sort of harrowing persecution that he did not expect to survive. He put his confidence in God, though, whose deliverance practically amounted to raising him from the dead.

COMMENTARY:

In this past rescue (aorist tense), Paul sees as an assurance of future rescue, saying that he has settled a lasting, confident expectation (perfect tense of ἐλπίζω) of ongoing (ἔτι) rescues as well. The two occurrences of future ῥύσεται may indicate rescue in both the near and the more remote future; ἔτι ῥύσεται likely means *will keep on rescuing*. Paul then mentions two roles for the Corinthians: first, the genitive absolute participle expresses their help by urgent prayers, and then they give thanks for God's interventions. Προσώπων likely adopts God's perspective as he looks down on faces upturned in gratitude. Ἵνα indicates purpose; in this context dealing with ultimate outcomes it presents abundant (ἐκ πολλῶν προσώπων) thanks, not as an afterthought but as God's ultimate goal in doing good—gratitude to God is an ultimate end.

τηλικούτου > so great, such || ἐρρύσατο > 3SAMI, rescued (from severe danger) || ἠλπίκαμεν > 1PRAI, have hoped || συνυπουργούντων > PAPMPG, assisting together || δεήσει > (urgent) request || προσώπων > faces, or persons || χάρισμα > gift || εὐχαριστηθῇ > 3SAPS, may produce thanksgiving (lit. may be given thanks [for])

Further Reading: 2 Corinthians 1:1–11
Randy A. Leedy

²¹ ὁ δὲ βεβαιῶν ἡμᾶς σὺν ὑμῖν εἰς Χριστὸν καὶ χρίσας ἡμᾶς θεός, ²² ὁ καὶ σφραγισάμενος ἡμᾶς καὶ δοὺς τὸν ἀρραβῶνα τοῦ πνεύματος ἐν ταῖς καρδίαις ἡμῶν.

CONTEXT:
Paul's plans to visit Corinth had changed. Between the lines we detect an accusation by the Corinthians that Paul has vacillated, which he counters by stressing God's reliability and his status as God's servant. Whatever *God* promises is secure in Christ. The proper response is the Amen of acceptance and trust, even if God's dealings change our plans. All of this reflects God's work securing both Paul and the Corinthians together in Christ, so their accusation is unfounded.

COMMENTARY:
Paul is not the one to be counted on for perfect reliability; that domain belongs to God alone, and Paul includes the Corinthians as equal beneficiaries of that work. The pronoun ἡμᾶς at the beginning of v. 21 refers to Paul's team, distinct from ὑμῖν. In v. 22, ἡμᾶς certainly includes both Paul's team and the Corinthians; at the end of v. 21 it may refer, like the first, to Paul as one uniquely anointed. Or perhaps more likely, as in the following verse, ἡμᾶς may include the Corinthians. Σφραγισάμενος is middle voice: God has sealed us *for himself*. Ἀρραβών portrays the Spirit (genitive of apposition) as a down payment that pledges to complete the full transaction at the appropriate time. With such a priceless down payment, just try to imagine what is guaranteed to come!

βεβαιῶν > PAPMSN, establishing ‖ χρίσας > AAPMSN, having anointed ‖ σφραγισάμενος > AMPMSN, having sealed (for himself) ‖ δοὺς > AAPMSN, (from δίδωμι), having given ‖ ἀρραβῶνα > a pledge deposited to guarantee the completion of the full transaction

Further Reading: 2 Corinthians 1:12-24
Randy A. Leedy

⁴ ἐκ γὰρ πολλῆς θλίψεως καὶ συνοχῆς καρδίας ἔγραψα ὑμῖν διὰ πολλῶν δακρύων, οὐχ ἵνα λυπηθῆτε ἀλλὰ τὴν ἀγάπην ἵνα γνῶτε ἣν ἔχω περισσοτέρως εἰς ὑμᾶς.

CONTEXT:

In the preceding chapter, Paul began explaining his change of plans to visit Corinth, which had brought him under accusation of vacillation. Now he explains in more detail: he did not want to visit while the Corinthians were so resistant to him, lest he have to grieve them by dealing harshly. So instead, he expressed his severity in a letter (now apparently lost to us).

COMMENTARY:

Θλῖψις and συνοχή both express painful, confining pressure. Paul had felt, deep in his heart, no choice but to write severely, in spite of the painfulness to himself, as evidenced by his own tears. The highly unusual position of τὴν ἀγάπην before the conjunction (ἵνα) that introduces the clause within which that noun is the direct object indicates great emphasis and points up the contrast between grief (λυπηθῆτε) and love. The intent of Paul's severity was not to cause grief but to express great love! Περισσοτέρως is comparative, probably used with an elative sense (i.e., expressing a very high degree): the love for you which I have *so very deeply*. True spiritual leaders will seek grace and courage to follow Paul's example not to shy away from tough love when it is called for.

θλίψεως > affliction ‖ συνοχῆς > distress, anguish ‖ δακρύων > tears ‖ λυπηθῆτε > 2PAPS, you may be grieved ‖ γνῶτε > 2PAAI, you might know ‖ περισσοτέρως > more abundantly, so very abundantly

Further Reading: 2 Corinthians 2:1–13
Randy A. Leedy

¹⁷ οὐ γάρ ἐσμεν ὡς οἱ πολλοὶ καπηλεύοντες τὸν λόγον τοῦ θεοῦ, ἀλλ' ὡς ἐξ εἰλικρινείας, ἀλλ' ὡς ἐκ θεοῦ κατέναντι θεοῦ ἐν Χριστῷ λαλοῦμεν.

CONTEXT:

Rejoicing over the Corinthians' positive reception of his "severe letter," Paul reflects on Christ's triumphs through Paul's challenging ministry, which produces a pervading aroma (2:15) of the knowledge of God wherever he goes: to those perishing, the stench of death but to those being saved, a fragrance of life. He asserts his insufficiency for these things and goes on to express, in a negative vs. positive contrast, the central character of his work.

COMMENTARY:

English has directly adopted the Greek expression οἱ πολλοί ("hoi polloi"), meaning the common people, the majority, connoting a negative character. It is sobering that the majority of Christian preachers even in Paul's day were not godly ministers. Καπηλεύω was used of merchants who diluted their food or medical products while charging full price for them or who falsified claims about them to increase sales, sometimes not even knowing whether the product would help or harm the purchaser. Much of today's television preaching, for example, is of this character. Paul, by contrast, models truly godly ministry: taking care to be an accurate spokesman for God in Christ, under God's constant inspection (κατέναντι θεοῦ), and, by implication, subject to God's ultimate evaluation and judgment.

καπηλεύοντες > PAPMPN, peddling ‖ εἰλικρινείας > genuineness, sincerity ‖ κατέναντι > before, in the sight of

Further Reading: 2 Corinthians 2:14–3:6
Randy A. Leedy

¹⁷ ὁ δὲ κύριος τὸ πνεῦμά ἐστιν· οὗ δὲ τὸ πνεῦμα κυρίου, ἐλευθερία. ¹⁸ ἡμεῖς δὲ πάντες ἀνακεκαλυμμένῳ προσώπῳ τὴν δόξαν κυρίου κατοπτριζόμενοι τὴν αὐτὴν εἰκόνα μεταμορφούμεθα ἀπὸ δόξης εἰς δόξαν καθάπερ ἀπὸ κυρίου πνεύματος.

CONTEXT:

Beginning in v. 6, Paul reflects on the character of his New Covenant ministry, which features the Spirit rather than the letter of the law, and which grants life rather than demanding death. Even that Old Covenant was glorious, though, as evidenced in Moses' shining face, which he veiled so that the fading of that glory would not be visible. Paul's New Covenant ministry requires no veil; he is free to let the glory shine!

COMMENTARY:

Verse 17 declares that the Spirit of the New Covenant (v. 6) is the Lord Himself, likely referring to the intimacy of personal fellowship with Him unhindered by the law's demands. Ἐλευθερία, therefore, is not liberty to indulge the flesh (cf. Gal 5:13) but rather freedom from the law's condemnation, a freedom that enables not only Paul but all believers to behold our God with unveiled faces—or, possibly, to display with unveiled faces God's glory to others. Ἀπὸ δόξης εἰς δόξα likely refers to our being transformed, from the inside out (μεταμορφούμεθα), from the fading glory of the Old Covenant to the infinitely greater and lasting glory of the New. The law was never evil; those who obeyed sincerely enjoyed a certain glory in that experience. New Covenant glory by faith in Christ, though, immeasurably excels!

ἐλευθερία > liberty ‖ ἀνακεκαλυμμένῳ > RPPNSD, unveiled ‖ κατοπτριζόμενοι > PMPMPN, viewing as in a mirror, possibly reflecting ‖ εἰκόνα > image ‖ μεταμορφούμεθα > 1PPPI, are being transformed ‖ καθάπερ > just as

Further Reading: 2 Corinthians 3:7–18

Randy A. Leedy

⁵ οὐ γὰρ ἑαυτοὺς κηρύσσομεν ἀλλ' Ἰησοῦν Χριστὸν κύριον, ἑαυτοὺς δὲ δούλους ὑμῶν διὰ Ἰησοῦν.

CONTEXT:
Chapter three continues the discussion, delineating the spiritual integrity of Paul's ministry. The only hiding happening is not Paul's cloaking bad motives, but rather Satan's blinding the minds of the perishing to the truth of Paul's preaching of God's good news about Jesus Christ.

COMMENTARY:
Beware the self-exalting preacher! The placement of οὐ ἑαυτούς before the verb probably indicates emphasis: *not ourselves do we preach*. Paul kept his preaching focus fixed on Jesus Christ, proclaiming him to be κύριον: sovereign over all. The function of κύριον is predicate accusative: not *we preach the Lord Jesus Christ*, but *we preach Jesus Christ as Lord*. Paul puts himself and his team at the opposite end of social scale: slaves—first of Christ (since he is κύριος), but also of the Corinthian church. When a pastor is tempted to pity himself as his people's slave, better than convincing himself otherwise is to embrace that role in fellowship with Paul. He's no slave to their personal wishes, of course (Paul certainly was not!); he is, with the others (ἑαυτούς is plural), their slave διὰ Ἰησοῦν, as he pursues Christ's work in their lives.

κηρύσσομεν > 1PPAI, preach ǁ δούλους > slaves, owned by a master, with no rights of self-determination ǁ διά + accusative > for the sake of (not through, which would have a genitive object)

Further Reading: 2 Corinthians 4:1–12
Randy A. Leedy

2 CORINTHIANS 4:17

¹⁷ τὸ γὰρ παραυτίκα ἐλαφρὸν τῆς θλίψεως ἡμῶν καθ' ὑπερβολὴν εἰς ὑπερβολὴν αἰώνιον βάρος δόξης κατεργάζεται ἡμῖν.

CONTEXT:

Paul's recitation of the character of his ministry continues, now cataloging the various kinds of hardships that he endures and how God's resurrection power grants him overcoming grace. Verse 17 states the underlying conviction and actual experience that enable such endurance.

COMMENTARY:

Like Jesus often did, Paul speaks paradoxically of how unseen reality reverses what we see:

momentary	*light*	*affliction*
	—produces—	
eternal	*weight*	*of glory*

τὸ γὰρ παραυτίκα ἐλαφρὸν τῆς θλίψεως ἡμῶν reads, very literally, *the momentary* (stressing brevity—*temporary* is not brief enough) *lightness of our affliction*, the neuter substantive τὸ ἐλαφρόν expressing the abstract concept denoted by the adjective. Then, as if his word choices haven't made the comparison strong enough, Paul adds an indicator of extraordinary degree, καθ' ὑπερβολήν, *to the extreme*. The duration (*eternal*), the amount (*weight*), and the quality (*glory*) of heavenly joys completely dwarf those same aspects of earthly hardships. And then, further still, as though καθ' ὑπερβολήν were not strong enough language—when in fact it's the strongest available!—Paul adds the synonymous εἰς ὑπερβολήν to utterly burst all bounds of comparison. What a wordsmith Paul is! And what a future awaits God's faithful ones! Or *is* Paul speaking of the future? Nothing in the passage prevents us from taking him as expressing the joy that God pours into his heart right in the midst of his sufferings as God's faithful servant.

παραυτίκα > adv. used as adj., momentary ‖ ἐλαφρόν > light; τὸ ἐ. = lightness ‖ θλίψεως > affliction ‖ ὑπερβολήν > extremeness ‖ αἰώνιον > eternal ‖ βάρος > weight ‖ κατεργάζεται > 3SPMI, works out, produces

Further Reading: 2 Corinthians 4:13–18
Randy A. Leedy

⁹ διὸ καὶ φιλοτιμούμεθα, εἴτε ἐνδημοῦντες εἴτε ἐκδημοῦντες, εὐάρεστοι αὐτῷ εἶναι. ¹⁰ τοὺς γὰρ πάντας ἡμᾶς φανερωθῆναι δεῖ ἔμπροσθεν τοῦ βήματος τοῦ Χριστοῦ, ἵνα κομίσηται ἕκαστος τὰ διὰ τοῦ σώματος πρὸς ἃ ἔπραξεν, εἴτε ἀγαθὸν εἴτε φαῦλον.

CONTEXT:

Paul extends chapter four's discussion of his viewpoint on the suffering and glory of his ministry, focusing now on his desire to put off his mortal body and enter into life in the Lord's presence.

COMMENTARY:

Paul's use of strong affective language continues with φιλοτιμούμεθα, denoting intense desire to achieve. His goal to be well-pleasing to Christ is one that but a few today seem concerned over, as though the truth of our being accepted in the beloved (Eph 1:6) implies that our behavior could never displease God. Clearly Paul held no such view! Ἐν- and ἐκδημοῦντες denote presence or absence from one's home or other normal location. Though Paul remains on earth, he views heaven as home. But upon arrival, he (and we!) must stand at Christ's judgment seat, where every believer's actions will appear in their true character and be repaid accordingly. Aspiring to lifestyle and behavior that, by God's grace, pleases Christ will embolden our conscience, like Paul's, to anticipate that examination as a moment of joy to the glory of God.

φιλοτιμούμεθα > 1PPMI, earnestly aspire || εἴτε ... εἴτε > whether ... or || ἐνδημοῦντες > PAPMPN, being present (in one's normal place) || ἐκδημοῦντες > PAPMPN, being absent (from one's normal place) || εὐάρεστοι > well pleasing || φανερωθῆναι > APN, to be fully revealed || βήματος > judgment seat || κομίσηται > 3SAMS, receive (as payment) || ἔπραξεν > 3SAAI, he did or behaved || φαῦλον > bad, worthless

Further Reading: 2 Corinthians 5:1–10
Randy A. Leedy

MARCH 25
2 CORINTHIANS 5:14–15

¹⁴ ἡ γὰρ ἀγάπη τοῦ Χριστοῦ συνέχει ἡμᾶς, κρίναντας τοῦτο, ὅτι εἷς ὑπὲρ πάντων ἀπέθανεν, ἄρα οἱ πάντες ἀπέθανον· ¹⁵ καὶ ὑπὲρ πάντων ἀπέθανεν, ἵνα οἱ ζῶντες μηκέτι ἑαυτοῖς ζῶσιν ἀλλὰ τῷ ὑπὲρ αὐτῶν ἀποθανόντι καὶ ἐγερθέντι.

CONTEXT:

Paul continues explaining and defending himself, not to exalt himself but to provide the Corinthians with a defense to use against his detractors. His only agenda is the interests of God and of the people whom he serves in ministry (v. 13).

COMMENTARY:

Is this love that so controls Paul and drives his endurance Christ's own love operating within him (τοῦ Χριστοῦ as subjective genitive), or is Paul referring to his love for Christ (objective genitive)? Context informs our exegesis, as Paul goes on to refer to Christ's dying for all, which is of course the ultimate show of his love. But wait! Paul goes on further to say that the reason Christ died is so that believers may live not for themselves but for him. This is the believer's love for Christ, so the context supports both subjective and objective genitive. Daniel Wallace calls this the "plenary genitive": simultaneously subjective and objective. While I hesitate to list this as a normal genitive use, I do think that Paul intends both, pushing the language beyond normal bounds and counting on his careful reader to ask the right question and come to the correct two-fold answer. Christ's love first, then ours in response, just as John taught (1 John 4:19).

συνέχει > 3SPAI, controls, impels ‖ κρίναντας > AAPMPA, having concluded ‖ εἷς > one (not εἰς, into) ‖ ἄρα > therefore ‖ οἱ ζῶντες > PAPMPN, the ones living ‖ μηκέτι > no longer ‖ τῷ ... ἀποθανόντι > AAPMSD, to the one who died ‖ τῷ ... ἐγερθέντι > APPMSD, to the one who arose

Further Reading: 2 Corinthians 5:11–21
Randy A. Leedy

¹⁷ διὸ ἐξέλθατε ἐκ μέσου αὐτῶν καὶ ἀφορίσθητε, λέγει κύριος, καὶ ἀκαθάρτου μὴ ἅπτεσθε· κἀγὼ εἰσδέξομαι ὑμᾶς ¹⁸ καὶ ἔσομαι ὑμῖν εἰς πατέρα καὶ ὑμεῖς ἔσεσθέ μοι εἰς υἱοὺς καὶ θυγατέρας, λέγει κύριος παντοκράτωρ.

CONTEXT:
Having defended the integrity of his ministry, Paul goes on to plead with the Corinthians to reciprocate his deep commitment to them. Though his harsh letter had accomplished a great deal, apparently it did not win every heart to himself. The necessary flip side of pursuing the work of God for Paul is to break off any spiritual affinity with unbelievers and idolaters.

COMMENTARY:
Alluding to Exodus 29:45, Isaiah 52, and 2 Samuel 7, Paul commands his readers to establish definite boundaries (ἀφορίσθητε) to separate themselves from the idolatry of their culture. The imperative followed by a future indicative often, as here, implies a condition: *If you will come out and be separate, I will welcome you.* One's heart cannot be closer to God than it is far from the world. The motive, though, is not pharisaical: it is to enjoy full communion with God as his beloved child. Παντοκράτωρ conveys both encouragement and warning: God has all power to bless, but also all power to chasten! This passage calls for honest soul searching. What are our culture's idols? Our natural propensity is to be right in the middle (μέσος) of it. Only by firm self-denial will we be able to obey Paul's command to come out so that we can then enjoy the full experience of God's promise. The passage is intentionally confrontational. Let's not stumble; rather let's show Proverbs wisdom by loving and accepting this reproof!

ἐξέλθατε > 2PAAM, come out || μέσου > midst || ἀφορίσθητε > 2PAPM, separate yourselves || ἀκαθάρτου > unclean || ἅπτεσθε > 2PPMM, touch || εἰσδέξομαι > 1SFMI, I will welcome in || ἔσομαι ... εἰς > I will become || θυγατέρας > daughters || παντοκράτωρ > Almighty

Further Reading: 2 Corinthians 6:1–18
Randy A. Leedy

⁶ ἀλλ' ὁ παρακαλῶν τοὺς ταπεινοὺς παρεκάλεσεν ἡμᾶς ὁ Θεὸς ἐν τῇ παρουσίᾳ Τίτου, ⁷ οὐ μόνον δὲ ἐν τῇ παρουσίᾳ αὐτοῦ, ἀλλὰ καὶ ἐν τῇ παρακλήσει ᾗ παρεκλήθη ἐφ' ὑμῖν ...

CONTEXT:

Since we have God's promise of dwelling among his people (6:16), we should live holy lives (7:1). Paul defends the honorable character of his own ministry: "We have wronged no one, we have corrupted no one, we have taken advantage of no one" (7:2). Nevertheless, Paul had been discouraged by the Corinthians' critical response.

COMMENTARY:

In verse 6, "the one comforting the downcast" stands in apposition with "God" (ὁ Θεός). What an encouragement, that God actively comforts the discouraged! In his sovereignty, God often uses human representatives as his comforting agents. In this particular case, he comforted Paul by means of the arrival of Titus and the information he brought. In the phrase ἐν τῇ παρουσίᾳ Τίτου, the Τίτου is a subjective genitive—that is, Titus is the subject of the verbal idea of "coming." Highly emotive language flows throughout the remainder of the passage, as Titus informed Paul of the Corinthians' longing, sorrow, and zeal (7:7). Paul rejoiced that their sorrow did not lead to mere grief or regret but to genuine, life-changing repentance (7:9–11).

παρακαλῶν > PAPMSN, comforting ‖ ταπεινούς > downcast, lowly ‖ παρεκάλεσεν > 3SAAI, he comforted ‖ παρουσίᾳ > coming ‖ παρεκλήθη > 3SAPI, he was comforted

Further Reading: 2 Corinthians 7:2–9
Paul Hartog

2 CORINTHIANS 8:9

⁹ γινώσκετε γὰρ τὴν χάριν τοῦ Κυρίου ἡμῶν Ἰησοῦ Χριστοῦ, ὅτι δι’ ὑμᾶς ἐπτώχευσεν πλούσιος ὤν, ἵνα ὑμεῖς τῇ ἐκείνου πτωχείᾳ πλουτήσητε.

CONTEXT:

Chapter 8 reflects a shift in this epistle toward the topic of monetary giving. Paul cited the Macedonians as a worthy model of generosity (8:2) and Jesus Christ himself as the ultimate pattern of sacrificial giving (8:9). Based upon Christ's example, Paul encouraged the Corinthians to complete their unfulfilled intention of giving (8:11).

COMMENTARY:

In encouraging "grace giving" among the Corinthians, Paul summons the example of "the grace of our Lord Jesus Christ" (8:9), employing both a ὅτι clause and a ἵνα clause. The verb γινώσκετε is followed by a ὅτι clause of the content that is to be known. In a great and gracious exchange, Jesus Christ gave up the divine prerogatives of his pre-existent position in heaven: "though being rich" he became "poor" in his incarnation and resulting death (cf. Phil 2:5–9). The following ἵνα clause with the subjunctive (πλουτήσητε) then describes the purpose: "So that by his poverty you might become rich." God's own "inexpressible gift" (2 Cor 9:15) becomes our pattern for generous Christian giving.

γινώσκετε > 2PPAI, you know ‖ ἐπτώχευσεν > 3SAAI, he became poor ‖ πλούσιος > rich ‖ πτωχείᾳ > poverty ‖ πλουτήσητε > 2PAAS, you might become rich

Further Reading: 2 Corinthians 8:1–15
Paul Hartog

²² συνεπέμψαμεν δὲ αὐτοῖς τὸν ἀδελφὸν ἡμῶν, ὃν ἐδοκιμάσαμεν ἐν πολλοῖς πολλάκις σπουδαῖον ὄντα, νυνὶ δὲ πολὺ σπουδαιότερον πεποιθήσει πολλῇ τῇ εἰς ὑμᾶς.

CONTEXT:
Paul gratefully sent Titus, who deeply cared for the Corinthians (8:16). Titus would be joined by two others, one of whom would also accompany Paul as he transported church funds. Paul welcomed such accountability. "For we aim at what is honorable not only in the sight of the Lord but also in the sight of people" (8:21).

COMMENTARY:
Along with Titus (8:16) and a brother famous for his gospel preaching (8:18), Paul was also sending "our brother whom we have often proved to be diligent in many matters" (8:22). This passage illustrates the use of the epistolary aorist, in which events are described from the time perspective of the letter recipients looking backward from reception of the letter. Thus Paul described Titus with the aorist ἐξῆλθεν ("he went") (8:17), and he affirmed the commissioning of all three delegates with the aorist συνεπέμψαμεν ("we sent") (8:18, 22). The anonymous identities of the second and third members of this letter-bearing team remind us how God uses faithful laborers, even though they may "fly under the radar."

συνεπέμψαμεν > 1PAAI, we sent (epistolary aorist) ‖ ἐδοκιμάσαμεν > 1PAAI, we proved, tested ‖ πολλάκις > often, many times ‖ σπουδαῖον > diligent, earnest ‖ ὄντα > PAPMSA, being ‖ νυνί > now ‖ σπουδαιότερον > more diligent, more earnest ‖ πεποιθήσει > confidence

Further Reading: 2 Corinthians 8:16–25
Paul Hartog

2 CORINTHIANS 9:6-7

⁶ τοῦτο δέ, ὁ σπείρων φειδομένως φειδομένως καὶ θερίσει, καὶ ὁ σπείρων ἐπ' εὐλογίαις ἐπ' εὐλογίαις καὶ θερίσει. ⁷ ἕκαστος καθὼς προῄρηται τῇ καρδίᾳ, μὴ ἐκ λύπης ἢ ἐξ ἀνάγκης· ἱλαρὸν γὰρ δότην ἀγαπᾷ ὁ Θεός.

CONTEXT:

The apostle Paul alerted the Corinthians that he planned to send representatives to collect the funds they had previously promised (9:1-5). He used the occasion to share godly aphorisms (pithy truths of wisdom) concerning Christian giving (9:6-7). Christian giving meets the needs of saints and motivates thanksgiving to God (9:12).

COMMENTARY:

In verses 6 through 7, Paul peppers his readers with proverbial wisdom, drawing from allusions to Proverbs 22:8 LXX. "The one sowing sparingly will also reap sparingly." By contrast, "The one sowing generously will also reap generously." Paul uses the agricultural model of sowing and reaping for illustrative purposes elsewhere (cf. Gal 6:7-9). In this passage, Paul narrows from these general contrasts between stingy and generous sowing to focus upon individual responsibility: "Each one" (ἕκαστος) should give as he has determined in his heart, not in a reluctant or coerced manner (9:7). He ends the verse with a gnomic present, where the present tense is used to express a general maxim, that should motivate our giving: "God loves (ἀγαπᾷ, present tense) a cheerful giver."

σπείρων > PAPMSN, one sowing || φειδομένως > sparingly || θερίσει > 3SFAI, will reap || ἐπ' εὐλογίαις > bountifully || προῄρηται > 3SRMI, he has decided, he has determined || ἐκ λύπης > reluctantly (i.e., from reluctance) || ἀνάγκης > compulsion || ἱλαρόν > cheerful || δότην > giver || ἀγαπᾷ > 3SPAI, loves

Further Reading: 2 Corinthians 9:6-15
Paul Hartog

¹² οὐ γὰρ τολμῶμεν ἐνκρῖναι ἢ συνκρῖναι ἑαυτούς τισιν τῶν ἑαυτοὺς συνιστανόντων· ἀλλὰ αὐτοὶ ἐν ἑαυτοῖς ἑαυτοὺς μετροῦντες καὶ συνκρίνοντες ἑαυτοὺς ἑαυτοῖς οὐ συνιᾶσιν.

CONTEXT:
Paul reminded his readers that believers wield "divine power" in destroying arguments and opinions raised against the knowledge of God (10:1-6). He also defended his own ministry against naysayers who ridiculed his perceived lack of a commanding personal presence. In this context, Paul addressed the foolishness of personal comparisons (10:11–12).

COMMENTARY:
Verse 12 employs the negated verb τολμῶμεν ("we [do not] dare") followed by complementary infinitives. Such complementary infinitives complete (or complement) the thought of the main verb—in this instance, we do not dare "to classify" or "to compare" ourselves. Those who engage in such comparisons reveal their own lack of understanding. We must not measure ourselves by relative human standards, because only God's evaluation truly matters. God is sovereign over spheres of influence (10:13), and godly "boasting" (glorying) focuses solely in the Lord (10:17). It is easy to compare our ministries with those of others, leading either to a prideful sense of superiority or a despondent sense of inferiority—neither being a God-honoring perspective.

τολμῶμεν > 1PPAI, we dare || ἐνκρῖναι > AAN, to classify || συνκρῖναι > AAN, to compare || συνιστανόντων > PAPMPG, commending || μετροῦντες > PAPMPN, measuring || συνκρίνοντες > PAPMPN, comparing || συνιᾶσιν > 3PPAI, they [do not] understand

Further Reading: 2 Corinthians 10:1–18
Paul Hartog

2 CORINTHIANS 11:7

⁷ ἢ ἁμαρτίαν ἐποίησα ἐμαυτὸν ταπεινῶν ἵνα ὑμεῖς ὑψωθῆτε, ὅτι δωρεὰν τὸ τοῦ Θεοῦ εὐαγγέλιον εὐηγγελισάμην ὑμῖν;

CONTEXT:

Paul warned against so-called "super-apostles" (ESV, NIV) who proclaimed a variant Jesus and an aberrant gospel (11:1–6). They were actually "false apostles," although disguising themselves as "apostles of Christ" and "servants of righteousness" (11:13–15). Paul insinuates that these false teachers were in it for the money. By contrast, he refused to burden the Corinthians financially when ministering among them (11:9).

COMMENTARY:

According to Acts 18:1–3, Paul humbly toiled as a tentmaker while residing in Corinth. With a note of pointed rhetoric, Paul asked if he had committed a "sin" by such labor, because it (and the support of other churches, 11:8) had enabled him to preach the gospel without charging his hearers. Paul did not accept financial support from the Corinthians, although this transgressed the social conventions of the time and the expectations of most itinerant philosophers and teachers. Paul described his preaching with an anarthrous use (lacking an article) of the accusative δωρεάν. Elsewhere in his writings (Rom 3:24; Gal 2:21; 2 Thess 3:8) Paul similarly employed the anarthrous δωρεάν as an adverbial accusative, indicating the manner of action ("freely, without charge"). Such humble, unselfish service is worthy of our emulation.

ἐποίησα > 1SAAI, I committed ‖ ταπεινῶν > PAPMSN, humbling ‖ ὑψωθῆτε > 2PAPS, you might be exalted, you might be lifted up ‖ δωρεάν > freely, without charge ‖ εὐηγγελισάμην > 1SAMI, I preached, proclaimed

Further Reading: 2 Corinthians 11:1–15
Paul Hartog

APRIL 2
2 CORINTHIANS 11:21b–23

²¹ ... ἐν ᾧ δ' ἄν τις τολμᾷ, ἐν ἀφροσύνῃ λέγω, τολμῶ κἀγώ. ²² Ἑβραῖοί εἰσιν; κἀγώ. Ἰσραηλεῖταί εἰσιν; κἀγώ. σπέρμα Ἀβραάμ εἰσιν; κἀγώ. ²³ διάκονοι Χριστοῦ εἰσιν; παραφρονῶν λαλῶ, ὑπὲρ ἐγώ· ἐν κόποις περισσοτέρως, ἐν φυλακαῖς περισσοτέρως, ἐν πληγαῖς ὑπερβαλλόντως, ἐν θανάτοις πολλάκις.

CONTEXT:

Paul highlighted the irony of the Corinthian perspective. On the one hand, they looked down upon him from their high perch of self-importance (11:6–18). On the other hand, they allowed others to take advantage of them (11:20). Paul responded by recording his own ministerial resumé. Instead of successful achievements, however, he listed his many sufferings (11:22–33).

COMMENTARY:

The last word of verse 21 is an example of crasis (a contraction through the merging of vowel sounds): the merging of καί and ἐγώ into κἀγώ ("I also"). This same contraction (κἀγώ) then reappears three times in rapid succession in the following verse (11:22): "Are they Hebrews? So am I (κἀγώ). Are they Israelites? So am I (κἀγώ). Are they the seed of Abraham? So am I (κἀγώ)." The repetition heightens the back-and-forth succinctness of his rhetoric. The discussion then shifts from Paul's identity (as a Hebrew, an Israelite, and a descendant of Abraham) to his superior labors (ἐν κόποις περισσοτέρως) and a catalog of sufferings for the sake of the gospel (11:23–29). How different Paul's apostolic resumé appears, in contrast with today's "success syndrome"!

τολμᾷ > 3SPAS, might dare || ἀφροσύνη > foolishness || Ἑβραῖοι > Hebrews || Ἰσραηλεῖται > Israelites || διάκονοι > servants || παραφρονῶν > PAPMSN, being out of my mind, being deranged (lit. to be beside oneself) || κόποις > labors || περισσοτέρως > to a greater degree, all the more || πληγαῖς > beatings, plagues || ὑπερβαλλόντως > much more || πολλάκις > often

Further Reading: 2 Corinthians 11:16–33
Paul Hartog

2 CORINTHIANS 12:9

⁹ καὶ εἴρηκέν μοι Ἀρκεῖ σοι ἡ χάρις μου· ἡ γὰρ δύναμις ἐν ἀσθενείᾳ τελεῖται. Ἥδιστα οὖν μᾶλλον καυχήσομαι ἐν ταῖς ἀσθενείαις μου, ἵνα ἐπισκηνώσῃ ἐπ' ἐμὲ ἡ δύναμις τοῦ Χριστοῦ.

CONTEXT:
Paul continued his "boasting" by recounting a heavenly visit, probably his own (12:4). Such an amazing experience could have naturally led to conceit, but Paul was given "a thorn in the flesh" to check his pride. Interpreters have debated the nature of this "thorn," but Paul's focus was not upon its particular identity but upon God's all-sufficient grace.

COMMENTARY:
Verse 9 contains a good example of a possessive article, in the phrase ἡ γὰρ δύναμις. English translations invariably render the phrase as "for my power" rather than merely "for the power," and with good reason. (Some Greek manuscripts even add a μου into the phrase, making the possessive meaning explicit.) The phrase ἡ γὰρ δύναμις parallels the previous ἡ χάρις μου ("my grace"), which does employ the possessive μου. And the final clause of the verse explicitly refers to ἡ δύναμις τοῦ Χριστοῦ ("the power of Christ"), employing a possessive genitive in parallel fashion. In this manner, Christ's power is contrasted with Paul's own weaknesses (ταῖς ἀσθενείαις μου). All this reminds us that the Lord's grace is sufficient in our need, as *his* power is exhibited in *our* weaknesses.

εἴρηκεν > 3SRAI, he said ‖ ἀρκεῖ > 3SPAI, is sufficient ‖ ἀσθενείᾳ > weakness ‖ τελεῖται > 3SPPI, is made perfect ‖ ἥδιστα > most gladly, very gladly ‖ καυχήσομαι > 1SFMI, I will boast, I will glory ‖ ἀσθενείαις > weaknesses ‖ ἐπισκηνώσῃ > 3SAAS, may rest upon, may dwell upon

Further Reading: 2 Corinthians 12:1–10
Paul Hartog

2 CORINTHIANS 12:15

¹⁵ ἐγὼ δὲ ἥδιστα δαπανήσω καὶ ἐκδαπανηθήσομαι ὑπὲρ τῶν ψυχῶν ὑμῶν. εἰ περισσοτέρως ὑμᾶς ἀγαπῶν, ἧσσον ἀγαπῶμαι;

CONTEXT:

Paul defended his apostleship against the opposing "super-apostles" (12:11). "The signs of a [true] apostle were performed among you in all perseverance, with signs and wonders and miracles" (12:12). Paul planned to return to Corinth, where he hoped that he would not discover "discord, jealousy, angry outbursts, hostilities, defamations, malicious whispers, conceited swellings, and disturbances" (12:20).

COMMENTARY:

With a play on words, Paul exclaims his joy-filled approach to "spending" and "being spent" for the sake of the Corinthians. In doing so he pairs a future active verb (δαπανήσω) and a future passive verb (ἐκδαπανηθήσομαι), with the latter intensified by the prefix ἐκ-. In Greek literature, ἐκδαπανάω refers to being fully spent, exhausted, used up, as in the sacrifice of one's life. In a real sense, faithful Christian leaders not only spend their time and resources upon those whom they serve, they *themselves* are expended for the benefit of others. In chapter 8, Paul had already described the Macedonians as giving themselves (first to the Lord and then to Paul's missionary team), even prior to giving of their monetary resources (8:1–5). In ministry service, "self-donation" accompanies "donation."

ἥδιστα > most gladly, very gladly ‖ δαπανήσω > 1SFAI, I will spend ‖ ἐκδαπανηθήσομαι > 1SFPI, I will be spent out, I will be fully spent ‖ περισσοτέρως > more ‖ ἀγαπῶν > PAPMSN, loving ‖ ἧσσον > less ‖ ἀγαπῶμαι > 1SPPI, I am to be loved

Further Reading: 2 Corinthians 12:11–21
Paul Hartog

2 CORINTHIANS 13:8-9

⁸ οὐ γὰρ δυνάμεθά τι κατὰ τῆς ἀληθείας, ἀλλὰ ὑπὲρ τῆς ἀληθείας.
⁹ χαίρομεν γὰρ ὅταν ἡμεῖς ἀσθενῶμεν, ὑμεῖς δὲ δυνατοὶ ἦτε· τοῦτο καὶ εὐχόμεθα, τὴν ὑμῶν κατάρτισιν.

CONTEXT:

Paul summoned the Corinthians themselves as evidence of his apostolic ministry—"unless indeed you fail the test!" (13:5). He was not enamored with apparent success but was willing to appear weak for the sake of their benefit (13:9). He prayed that his readers would "do what is right" and would be restored to him (13:7-9).

COMMENTARY:

Verse 8 is a good example of how object noun cases affect prepositional meanings. Paul affirmed, "We are not able [to do] anything against the truth, but only for the truth." Κατά with the accusative means "on account of," while κατά with the genitive means "against." Paul was not asserting an inability to do anything "on account of the truth" (using the accusative), but quite the opposite—an inability to do anything "against the truth" (using the genitive). Then follows a contrast—but only "for the truth" (employing ὑπέρ with the genitive). The ensuing verse adds Paul's impetus for rejoicing (being weak while they were strong) and his motivation for prayer (that they would reach full maturity), highlighting the altruistic nature of his model ministry (13:9).

δυνάμεθα > 1PPMI, we are [not] able || χαίρομεν > 1PPAI, we rejoice || ἀσθενῶμεν > 1PPAS, we are weak || ἦτε > 2PPAS, you are || εὐχόμεθα > 1PPMI, we pray || κατάρτισιν > perfection, full maturity

Further Reading: 2 Corinthians 13:1-10
Paul Hartog

APRIL 6
MARK 1:14–15

¹⁴ μετὰ δὲ τὸ παραδοθῆναι τὸν Ἰωάννην ἦλθεν ὁ Ἰησοῦς εἰς τὴν Γαλιλαίαν κηρύσσων τὸ εὐαγγέλιον τοῦ θεοῦ ¹⁵ καὶ λέγων ὅτι Πεπλήρωται ὁ καιρὸς καὶ ἤγγικεν ἡ βασιλεία τοῦ θεοῦ, μετανοεῖτε καὶ πιστεύετε ἐν τῷ εὐαγγελίῳ.

CONTEXT:

These verses begin Jesus' public ministry in Galilee. With authority, Jesus announces that God's plan of redemption and restoration is here. God is bringing redemption to mankind through his Son.

COMMENTARY:

This verse and section of Mark's Gospel begins with a temporal phrase μετὰ δὲ τὸ παραδοθῆναι (μετὰ τό + infinitive) indicating John's arrest occurred prior to the action of the main verb (ἦλθεν, Jesus going into Galilee). John announced the need to repent (1:4), and the coming Messiah (1:7–8). Mark records that Jesus preaches the good news and even provides for the reader Jesus' words (direct discourse) using the conjunction ὅτι. It introduces the clausal complement to the participle λέγων, which functions as a participle of means. That is, Mark provides the means by which Jesus preaches the good news: by saying, "The time is fulfilled, the kingdom of God is close at hand; repent and believe in the good news."

παραδοθῆναι > APN, was arrested ‖ ἦλθεν > 3SAAI, came ‖ λέγων > PAPMSN, saying ‖ πεπλήρωται > 3SRPI, fulfilled ‖ μετανοεῖτε > 2PPAM, repent! ‖ πιστεύετε > 2PPAM, believe!

Further Reading: Mark 1:14–45
Wayne T. Slusser

APRIL 7

MARK 2:11–12

¹¹ σοὶ λέγω, ἔγειρε ἆρον τὸν κράβαττόν σου καὶ ὕπαγε εἰς τὸν οἶκόν σου.
¹² καὶ ἠγέρθη καὶ εὐθὺς ἄρας τὸν κράβαττον ἐξῆλθεν ἔμπροσθεν πάντων,
ὥστε ἐξίστασθαι πάντας καὶ δοξάζειν τὸν θεὸν λέγοντας ὅτι Οὕτως
οὐδέποτε εἴδομεν.

CONTEXT:
Mark narrates Jesus' healing of the paralyzed man. This continues Jesus' public
ministry, but not without controversy. There is a series of five controversies
through 3:6. It is Jesus' healing and forgiveness of sins that sparks interest from
the crowd and antagonistic responses from the religious leaders.

COMMENTARY:
Jesus commands the paralyzed man to "get up" (ἔγειρε), which demonstrates
that his desperate situation is not beyond Jesus' power. He came into the house
being carried; now he walks out carrying his own bed. Jesus' actions result (ὥστε
+ inf.) in the crowd's amazement and glorification of God. God is doing
something unique and unprecedented through his Son.

ἔγειρε > 2SPAM, get up! || κράβαττον > mat || ἠγέρθη > 3SAPI, he got up ||
ἐξῆλθεν > 3SAAI, he went out || ἐξίστασθαι > PMN, were amazed || οὐδέποτε >
never

Further Reading: Mark 2:1–22
Wayne T. Slusser

MARK 3:11–12

¹¹ καὶ τὰ πνεύματα τὰ ἀκάθαρτα, ὅταν αὐτὸν ἐθεώρουν, προσέπιπτον αὐτῷ καὶ ἔκραζον λέγοντες ὅτι Σὺ εἶ ὁ υἱὸς τοῦ θεοῦ. ¹² καὶ πολλὰ ἐπετίμα αὐτοῖς ἵνα μὴ αὐτὸν φανερὸν ποιήσωσιν.

CONTEXT:

Jesus continues his teaching ministry and attracts quite the crowd, even demons (3:7–12). The crowd wanted to both hear and touch him. Why such a crowd? What did they want?

COMMENTARY:

Who is Jesus? It is the unclean spirits that provide the clue. Look at their posture. The crowd "pressed toward" (ἐπιπίπτειν) Jesus to be healed; the demons however, fell before him (προσέπιπτον) to worship and acknowledge his divine sonship. Two different responses, one with enthusiasm and expectation of healing, and the other an acknowledgement of identity. The demons cried out emphatically "You, yourself are the Son of God" (σὺ εἶ ὁ υἱὸς τοῦ θεοῦ). It is the personal pronoun that serves as the subject (σύ) when two nominatives are used with a linking verb (εἶ), even if one of the nominatives has the article (ὁ υἱός). In this case, "the Son" serves as the predicate nominative.

ἀκάθαρτα > unclean ‖ ἐθεώρουν > 3PIAI, they saw ‖ ἔκραζον > 3PIAI, cried ‖ ἐπετίμα > 3SIAI, he warned ‖ ποιήσωσιν > 3PAAS, they might make

Further Reading: Mark 3:1–19
Wayne T. Slusser

APRIL 9
MARK 4:39–41

³⁹ καὶ διεγερθεὶς ἐπετίμησεν τῷ ἀνέμῳ καὶ εἶπεν τῇ θαλάσσῃ, Σιώπα, πεφίμωσο. καὶ ἐκόπασεν ὁ ἄνεμος καὶ ἐγένετο γαλήνη μεγάλη. ⁴⁰ καὶ εἶπεν αὐτοῖς, Τί δειλοί ἐστε; οὔπω ἔχετε πίστιν; ⁴¹ καὶ ἐφοβήθησαν φόβον μέγαν καὶ ἔλεγον πρὸς ἀλλήλους, Τίς ἄρα οὗτός ἐστιν ὅτι καὶ ὁ ἄνεμος καὶ ἡ θάλασσα ὑπακούει αὐτῷ;

CONTEXT:
This section (4:35–5:43) of Mark's Gospel demonstrates Jesus' authority over nature, demonic forces, disease, and even death. It is here (4:35–41) that Mark records Jesus' stilling of the storm to demonstrate his power over nature. The disciples respond to Jesus' power with fear; they were terrified, or awe-struck. They did not understand who was in the boat with them.

COMMENTARY:
It is interesting that although the disciples have spent quite a bit of time with Jesus, in this episode Mark records an unusual response. Jesus first rebukes (ἐπετίμησεν) the wind, an aorist tense-form verb providing the reader with background information. Then Jesus quiets (σιώπα) and silences (πεφίμωσο) the sea. The sea responds to his command, and it continues in the state of being silenced, a perfect tense-form of the verb. Only Jesus can do this! Hence, the disciples' response of fear—who silences the sea? To show the significance of their fear, Mark uses a cognate accusative, both the verbal and noun form of the same root word ("feared a great fear," ἐφοβήθησαν φόβον μέγαν). The sea is under the Master's command.

ἀνέμῳ > wind ‖ πεφίμωσο > 2SRPM, [you] be silenced! ‖ γαλήνη > calm ‖ δειλοί > afraid ‖ ἐφοβήθησαν > 3PAPI, they feared ‖ ὑπακούει > 3SPAI, it obeys

Further Reading: Mark 5:1–10
Wayne T. Slusser

MARK 5:35–36

³⁵ ἔτι αὐτοῦ λαλοῦντος ἔρχονται ἀπὸ τοῦ ἀρχισυναγώγου λέγοντες ὅτι Ἡ θυγάτηρ σου ἀπέθανεν; τί ἔτι σκύλλεις τὸν διδάσκαλον; ³⁶ ὁ δὲ Ἰησοῦς παρακούσας τὸν λόγον λαλούμενον λέγει τῷ ἀρχισυναγώγῳ, Μὴ φοβοῦ, μόνον πίστευε.

CONTEXT:

This section (5:21–43) is where Mark places two stories together (the healing of Jairus' daughter and the woman with an issue of blood) to illustrate the power of Jesus and the faith of seemingly hopeless people. In both stories, Jesus' healing touch brings about restoration and wholeness to those affected.

COMMENTARY:

Jairus the ruler is desperate (5:21–24) and falls at Jesus' feet because his daughter is sick. Due to the ruler's position within the town, to fall down before Jesus is a significant and daring act of respect and worship, thereby indicating a desperate situation. Mark records an interruption in the narrative through the healing of a woman with an issue of blood (5:25–34). However good this may be, now (5:35) the ruler's daughter is dead. The focus however shifts, it is no longer on Jesus, rather it is on those desperate people who came from the house of the ruler of the synagogue. Mark helps the reader know Jesus' speech (5:35) is less prominent using a genitive absolute (αὐτοῦ λαλοῦντος, pronoun and anarthrous participle in the genitive case). The point was for Jairus to believe, not fear. You can believe in what circumstances allow or believe in God who intervenes in those circumstances.

λαλοῦντος > PAPMSG, speaking ‖ θυγάτηρ > daughter ‖ σκύλλεις > 2SPAI, bother ‖ ἀρχισυναγώγῳ > ruler of synagogue ‖ πίστευε > 2SPAM, believe!

Further Reading: Mark 5:21–43
Wayne T. Slusser

APRIL 11

MARK 6:48–50

⁴⁸ καὶ ἰδὼν αὐτοὺς βασανιζομένους ἐν τῷ ἐλαύνειν, ἦν γὰρ ὁ ἄνεμος ἐναντίος αὐτοῖς, περὶ τετάρτην φυλακὴν τῆς νυκτὸς ἔρχεται πρὸς αὐτοὺς περιπατῶν ἐπὶ τῆς θαλάσσης καὶ ἤθελεν παρελθεῖν αὐτούς. ⁴⁹ οἱ δὲ ἰδόντες αὐτὸν ἐπὶ τῆς θαλάσσης περιπατοῦντα ἔδοξαν ὅτι φάντασμά ἐστιν, καὶ ἀνέκραξαν· ⁵⁰ πάντες γὰρ αὐτὸν εἶδον καὶ ἐταράχθησαν. ὁ δὲ εὐθὺς ἐλάλησεν μετ’ αὐτῶν, καὶ λέγει αὐτοῖς· θαρσεῖτε, ἐγώ εἰμι· μὴ φοβεῖσθε.

CONTEXT:

This section (6:45–56) is similar to the stilling of the storm (4:35–41). However, previously there was an emphasis on divine speech and here there is an emphasis on divine presence. Jesus came to the disciples while they were at sea (6:48). Both occasions demonstrate the inability of the disciples to understand Jesus' identity and therefore experience fear and amazement.

COMMENTARY:

After feeding the 5,000, Jesus went to the hills to pray and sent his disciples out into the boat to cross the lake and go to Bethsaida. *After seeing* (ἰδών, aorist temporal ptc.) the disciples struggle to row the boat, he went to them. Jesus walked on water. *After seeing* (ἰδόντες, aorist temporal ptc.) Jesus walking on the lake, they thought he was a ghost, for what human walks on water? These temporal participles describe actions antecedent to the time of the main verbs (ἔρχεται, ἤθελεν, and ἔδοξαν, respectively). Jesus' response, "Have courage, it's me; don't be afraid" (θαρσεῖτε, ἐγώ εἰμι, μὴ φοβεῖσθε) identifies him as God (ἐγώ εἰμι).

βασανιζομένους > PMPMPA, straining || ἐλαύνειν > PAN, to row || φυλακήν > watch || φάντασμα > ghost || ἐταράχθησαν > 3PAPI, they were terrified || θαρσεῖτε > 2PPAM, have courage!

Further Reading: Mark 6:45–56
Wayne T. Slusser

APRIL 12

MARK 7:37

³⁷ καὶ ὑπερπερισσῶς ἐξεπλήσσοντο λέγοντες, Καλῶς πάντα πεποίηκεν, καὶ τοὺς κωφοὺς ποιεῖ ἀκούειν καὶ τοὺς ἀλάλους λαλεῖν.

CONTEXT:

This section (7:24–37) returns to Gentile territory where Jesus is in another healing situation. He intervened in two situations, the Syrophoenician woman (7:24–30) and the deaf and mute man (7:31–37). There is faith, there is healing, and there is hearing.

COMMENTARY:

Jesus enters the region of Decapolis (a Gentile region) where some people bring him a deaf and mute person. They requested a healing from Jesus, saying, "We beg you, lay your hand on him" (7:32). Jesus indeed touches the man, and he is healed (7:34–35). He speaks plainly. Jesus makes the deaf *to hear* (ἀκούειν) and *to speak* (λαλεῖν), complementary infinitives serving to complete the thought of the main verb, ποιεῖ. Jesus restores; *he makes all things well* (καλῶς πάντα πεποίηκεν). What Jesus touches results in a state of being fine, good, or excellent (καλῶς ... πεποίηκεν)! The crowd responds with *extreme astonishment* (ὑπερπερισσῶς ἐξεπλήσσοντο).

ὑπερπερισσῶς > extremely, beyond measure ‖ ἐξεπλήσσοντο > 3PIPI, they were astonished ‖ καλῶς > well ‖ κωφούς > deaf ‖ ἀλάλους > mute

Further Reading: Mark 7:24–37
Wayne T. Slusser

APRIL 13

MARK 8:33–34

³³ ὁ δὲ ἐπιστραφεὶς καὶ ἰδὼν τοὺς μαθητὰς αὐτοῦ ἐπετίμησεν Πέτρῳ καὶ λέγει, Ὕπαγε ὀπίσω μου, Σατανᾶ, ὅτι οὐ φρονεῖς τὰ τοῦ θεοῦ ἀλλὰ τὰ τῶν ἀνθρώπων. ³⁴ Καὶ προσκαλεσάμενος τὸν ὄχλον σὺν τοῖς μαθηταῖς αὐτοῦ εἶπεν αὐτοῖς, Εἴ τις θέλει ὀπίσω μου ἀκολουθεῖν, ἀπαρνησάσθω ἑαυτὸν καὶ ἀράτω τὸν σταυρὸν αὐτοῦ καὶ ἀκολουθείτω μοι.

CONTEXT:

In this passage (8:27–9:1) the disciples attempt to identify Jesus. Prior to this Jesus had been proclaiming a message and performing miracles. Now Jesus' teaching specifically turns toward his disciples in order to teach them his role as the suffering Messiah and their role in cross-bearing discipleship.

COMMENTARY:

Jesus asked his disciples who people identify him as, and after several answers Peter responded that Jesus was the Messiah (8:27–29). Jesus then taught his disciples that it was necessary for him to suffer, be rejected, and be killed—but that he would rise from the dead after three days. His words were plain, clear to understand (8:30–32). Peter, however, stepped up and began to censure Jesus because a rejected Messiah is incompatible with Jewish conviction and hope. Jesus rebuked Peter and commanded him to assume the position of a follower, *behind* (ὀπίσω, 8:33) him rather than *beside* (προσλαβόμενος, 8:32) him. Jesus continues to state the importance of both the position and sacrifice of a follower, that is behind me (ὀπίσω μου) and he must deny himself and take up his cross (ἀπαρνησάσθω ἑαυτὸν καὶ ἀράτω τὸν σταυρὸν αὐτοῦ). The disciple of Jesus is to follow loyally, daily, and to be in agreement with/behave in accordance with his master. This is found in the present imperative (ἀκολουθείτω, 8:34).

ἐπιστραφείς > APPMSN, turning around ‖ ὕπαγε > 2SPAM, get ‖ ὀπίσω > behind ‖ προσκαλεσάμενος > AMPMSN, summoned ‖ ἀπαρνησάσθω > 3SAMM, let him deny

Further Reading: Mark 8:27–9:1
Wayne T. Slusser

103

MARK 9:35–37

³⁵ καὶ καθίσας ἐφώνησεν τοὺς δώδεκα καὶ λέγει αὐτοῖς, Εἴ τις θέλει πρῶτος εἶναι, ἔσται πάντων ἔσχατος καὶ πάντων διάκονος. ³⁶ καὶ λαβὼν παιδίον ἔστησεν αὐτὸ ἐν μέσῳ αὐτῶν καὶ ἐναγκαλισάμενος αὐτὸ εἶπεν αὐτοῖς, ³⁷ Ὃς ἂν ἓν τῶν τοιούτων παιδίων δέξηται ἐπὶ τῷ ὀνόματί μου, ἐμὲ δέχεται· καὶ ὃς ἂν ἐμὲ δέχηται, οὐκ ἐμὲ δέχεται ἀλλὰ τὸν ἀποστείλαντά με.

CONTEXT:

This passage (9:30–37) is part of a larger context (9:30–50). It demonstrates Jesus' mission in light of the journey to Jerusalem. The focus continues from chapter eight on teaching the disciples and giving them characteristics of Christ followers.

COMMENTARY:

Jesus predicts his death for a second time (9:31) and the disciples did not understand and were afraid to ask him. This announcement of suffering did not fit in the disciples' view of Messiah. While traveling through Galilee, the disciples were arguing about *who is the greatest*. They were preoccupied with precedence, rank, and honor—important characteristics within the culture. To illustrate, Jesus uses two different words with similar meanings, "take." Since it is important to be last and not first/prominent, Jesus *took* (λαβών) *a child ... and hugged it* (ἐναγκαλισάμενος). The child represented the insignificant in society, quite different from today. For Jesus to hug a child would have been considered taboo, to hug a child was reserved for mothers and servants, not men. Jesus' challenge, therefore, for his disciples was to *take/welcome* (δέξηται) the insignificant in society; break social and societal norms and *welcome/accept* others of lower status. Jesus is asking his loyal followers (cf. 8:33–34) no longer to seek positions of prestige (9:34) but now to engage society as table-waiters (διάκονος), which is acceptable only for servants. Willingly to care for others is to give importance to the unimportant.

ἐφώνησεν > 3SAAI, he called || παιδίον > child || πρῶτος > first, prominent || ἐναγκαλισάμενος > AMPMSN, hugging, taking [him] in his arms || δέξηται > 3SPMS, he [shall] welcome

Further Reading: Mark 9:30–50
Wayne T. Slusser

MARK 10:43–45

⁴³ οὐχ οὕτως δέ ἐστιν ἐν ὑμῖν, ἀλλ᾽ ὃς ἂν θέλῃ μέγας γενέσθαι ἐν ὑμῖν ἔσται ὑμῶν διάκονος, ⁴⁴ καὶ ὃς ἂν θέλῃ ἐν ὑμῖν εἶναι πρῶτος ἔσται πάντων δοῦλος; ⁴⁵ καὶ γὰρ ὁ υἱὸς τοῦ ἀνθρώπου οὐκ ἦλθεν διακονηθῆναι ἀλλὰ διακονῆσαι καὶ δοῦναι τὴν ψυχὴν αὐτοῦ λύτρον ἀντὶ πολλῶν.

CONTEXT:

This passage (10:32-45) is Jesus' third prediction of his death. The disciples exhibit pride, with a "what's in it for me attitude," and Jesus teaches what it means to have a sacrificial and self-giving heart as a disciple. Jesus models true servant leadership in front of his disciples while they vie for positions of power and prestige.

COMMENTARY:

Jesus, for a third time predicts his death (10:32-34). The disciples are following Jesus all the way to Jerusalem. However, two disciples ask of Jesus what Jesus himself cannot grant to them; "to sit on his right and left in glory" (10:35-37). What do they want? They want positions of honor and glory—they are seeking positions that quite frankly do not belong to them. Jesus' response is to teach them to serve others, not take advantage of others to get what they want. The world practices leadership from a position of dominance, authority, abusive power and coercion. "Not so of you," says Jesus. Jesus proceeds to redefine greatness (10:43-45). If you want to be *great* (μέγας), you *serve* (διάκονος); if you want to be *first* or *most prominent* (πρῶτος), you *must* become the least of society (δοῦλος). The future tense-form of the verb ἔσται functions imperatively—indicating the force by which a disciple ought to live daily—as a slave. Jesus models this expectation for his disciples as he came *to serve and to give his life* (διακονῆσαι καὶ δοῦναι, inf. of purpose) for others. According to Jesus' teaching and example, only by service does one become great!

διάκονος > servant ‖ **πρῶτος** > first ‖ **δοῦλος** > slave ‖ **ἦλθεν** > 3SAAI, he came ‖ **διακονηθῆναι** > APN, to be served ‖ **διακονῆσαι** > AAN, to serve ‖ **δοῦναι** > AAN, to give

Further Reading: Mark 10:32-45
Wayne T. Slusser

GALATIANS 1:6-7

⁶ θαυμάζω ὅτι οὕτως ταχέως μετατίθεσθε ἀπὸ τοῦ καλέσαντος ὑμᾶς ἐν χάριτι Χριστοῦ εἰς ἕτερον εὐαγγέλιον,⁷ ὃ οὐκ ἔστιν ἄλλο· εἰ μή τινές εἰσιν οἱ ταράσσοντες ὑμᾶς καὶ θέλοντες μεταστρέψαι τὸ εὐαγγέλιον τοῦ Χριστοῦ.

CONTEXT:

Galatians follows a typical format for a first-century Greco-Roman epistle, which would include a salutation or greeting, commendation, body, exhortation, and conclusion. However, this Pauline letter is the only one that does not contain a commendation of its readers—an obvious omission reflecting the urgency Paul felt about warning the Galatian believers of the serious consequences of abandoning the central doctrine of justification by faith alone.

COMMENTARY:

Paul was amazed that the Galatians were so quickly deserting (μετατίθεσθε) the gospel—this same word described military desertion, which was punishable by death. Paul's use of this verb in the middle voice indicated that the Galatian believers were willingly abandoning grace to pursue the legalism taught by the false teachers. The phrase χάριτι Χριστοῦ (grace of Christ) refers to God's free and sovereign act in granting salvation through the death and resurrection of Christ—totally apart from any human work or merit. The word *grace* is in the dative case—a dative of means—showing that the means by which we are called is the grace of Christ. By adding the law to the gospel of Christ, the false teachers were perverting the good news and effectively destroying grace, turning the message of God's undeserved favor toward sinners into the opposite idea of earned and merited favor.

θαυμάζω > 1SPAI, am astonished || ταχέως > quickly || μετατίθεσθε > 2PPMI, are deserting || καλέσαντος > AAPMSG, having called || ἔστιν > 3SPAI, is || εἰσιν > 3PPAI, are || ταράσσοντες > PAPMPN, are troubling || θέλοντες > PAPMPN, are desiring || μεταστρέψαι > AAN, to pervert, to distort

Further Reading: Galatians 1:1-10
Candi Finch

GALATIANS 2:15–16

¹⁵ ἡμεῖς φύσει Ἰουδαῖοι καὶ οὐκ ἐξ ἐθνῶν ἁμαρτωλοί, ¹⁶ εἰδότες δὲ ὅτι οὐ δικαιοῦται ἄνθρωπος ἐξ ἔργων νόμου ἐὰν μὴ διὰ πίστεως Ἰησοῦ Χριστοῦ, καὶ ἡμεῖς εἰς Χριστὸν Ἰησοῦν ἐπιστεύσαμεν, ἵνα δικαιωθῶμεν ἐκ πίστεως Χριστοῦ καὶ οὐκ ἐξ ἔργων νόμου, ὅτι ἐξ ἔργων νόμου οὐ δικαιωθήσεται πᾶσα σάρξ.

CONTEXT:
The second half of chapter 1 contains a lengthy autobiographical section where Paul defends his apostleship and describes his conversion (1:11–24). Then he outlines his visit to the Jerusalem Council (see Acts 15), where it is established that a person does not need to be circumcised in order to become a Christian (Gal 2:1–10). Paul also recounts his confrontation of Peter regarding Peter's hypocrisy for not eating with Gentiles (2:11–14).

COMMENTARY:
These verses contain the central idea of the letter. The contrasting conjunction δέ in verse 16 sets up Paul's argument for exactly how a person is justified before God. He asserts that both Jews and Gentiles are saved in the same way. The combination of the perfect participle εἰδότες with ὅτι signals that what follows is common knowledge: one is not justified by works of the law. Here the verb δικαιοῦται is in the present tense, indicating this is something that is always true. In fact, Paul sets up a grammatical play by using three different tenses of the verb *justified* just to settle any argument that would allow justification by works. A person is never *justified* by works (present tense) and will never be *justified* by such works (future tense). The only circumstance that has ever *justified* a person and made him righteous (aorist tense) is faith is Christ. All three uses of the verb are in the passive voice, showing that work of making someone righteous is God's work alone—we believe in Christ, and He alone justifies us.

φύσει > nature ‖ εἰδότες > RAPMPN, knowing ‖ δικαιοῦται > 3SPPI, is [not] justified ‖ ἐπιστεύσαμεν > 1PAAI, have believed ‖ δικαιωθῶμεν > 1PAPS, may be justified ‖ δικαιωθήσεται > 3SFPI, will be justified

Further Reading: Galatians 1:11–2:14
Candi Finch

APRIL 18
GALATIANS 2:19B–20

[19] ... Χριστῷ συνεσταύρωμαι· [20] ζῶ δὲ οὐκέτι ἐγώ, ζῇ δὲ ἐν ἐμοὶ Χριστός· ὃ δὲ νῦν ζῶ ἐν σαρκί, ἐν πίστει ζῶ τῇ τοῦ υἱοῦ τοῦ θεοῦ τοῦ ἀγαπήσαντός με καὶ παραδόντος ἑαυτὸν ὑπὲρ ἐμοῦ.

CONTEXT:
Paul continues the central argument of the letter by showing that believers have died to the law so that they can live for God. How senseless and crazy to go back to living under the yoke of the law when you have died to it! [Note that most translations start Gal 2:20 where today's text begins.]

COMMENTARY:
Paul and the Galatian believers had died to the law (v. 19). The funeral/death of the old self is powerfully illustrated with the use of word συνεσταύρωμαι in the perfect tense, suggesting that Paul was thinking of a completed event or state of being. When a person was convicted of a capital crime and executed, the law had no further claim on him. So too with the Christian who has died in Christ and risen to new life in Him; justice has been satisfied. A person who trusts in Christ for salvation receives victory over sin and death. Paul boldly proclaims, "I have been crucified with Christ; and I no longer live, but Christ lives in me" (vv. 19–20). Paul released the fantasy that he was somehow good or worthy in and of himself; he saw himself through God's eyes. He let go of his right to live his life his own way in order that Christ might live in him. When Paul let go, he was able to take hold of something much better—the life lived in faith in the Son of God.

συνεσταύρωμαι > 1SRPI, have been crucified with || ζῶ > 1SPAI, live || ζῇ > 3SPAI, lives || ἀγαπήσαντος > AAPMSG, having loved || παραδόντος > AAPMSG, having given up

Further Reading: Galatians 2:15–21
Candi Finch

GALATIANS 3:1–3

¹ ὦ ἀνόητοι Γαλάται, τίς ὑμᾶς ἐβάσκανεν, οἷς κατ' ὀφθαλμοὺς Ἰησοῦς Χριστὸς προεγράφη ἐσταυρωμένος; ² τοῦτο μόνον θέλω μαθεῖν ἀφ' ὑμῶν, ἐξ ἔργων νόμου τὸ πνεῦμα ἐλάβετε ἢ ἐξ ἀκοῆς πίστεως; ³ οὕτως ἀνόητοί ἐστε; ἐναρξάμενοι πνεύματι νῦν σαρκὶ ἐπιτελεῖσθε;

CONTEXT:
This section follows directly after Paul's declaration that Jews and Gentiles are saved by the same means, which is faith in the Lord Jesus. Chapter 3 begins with Paul's appeal to the Galatians' experience as proof of their salvation by faith and not by keeping works of the law.

COMMENTARY:
The emotive interjection ὦ displays the sorrow Paul feels because the Galatians had been deceived. He asks them a series of rhetorical questions designed to cause them to reflect on their own experience—Who has hypnotized you, before whose eyes Jesus Christ was vividly portrayed as crucified? (v. 1). Did you receive the Spirit by the works of the law or by hearing with faith? (v. 2). Are you so foolish, having begun by the spirit now are you perfected by flesh? (v. 3). Paul was not questioning whether or not the Galatians received the Spirit; he was simply asking them how they received the Spirit. Paul repeats the word ἀνόητοι (vv. 1, 3) showing how incredulous he was at how easily they had been duped. The notion that sinful, weak, fallen human nature could improve on the saving work of the Holy Spirit was ludicrous to Paul.

ὦ > O! || ἀνόητοι > foolish || Γαλάται > Galatians || ἐβάσκανεν > 3SAAI, has bewitched || προεγράφη > 3SAPI, was publicly portrayed || ἐσταυρωμένος > RPPMSN, having been crucified || θέλω > 1SPAI, wish || μαθεῖν > AAN, to learn || ἐλάβετε > 2PAAI, did receive || ἀκοῆς > hearing || ἐναρξάμενοι > AMPMPN, having begun || ἐπιτελεῖσθε > 2PPPI, are being perfected

Further Reading: Galatians 3:1–5
Candi Finch

GALATIANS 3:6–7

⁶ καθὼς Ἀβραὰμ ἐπίστευσεν τῷ θεῷ, καὶ ἐλογίσθη αὐτῷ εἰς δικαιοσύνην.
⁷ Γινώσκετε ἄρα ὅτι οἱ ἐκ πίστεως, οὗτοι υἱοί εἰσιν Ἀβραάμ.

CONTEXT:

After imploring the Galatians to remember how they became followers of Christ (by faith), Paul provides a powerful example for them to consider that even the Judaizers would have trouble refuting. Paul asks them to consider how Abraham, the first patriarch of the Jewish people, was justified.

COMMENTARY:

These verses are important if you have ever wondered, "How were people saved before Christ came to earth?" Paul uses the example of Abraham who (having lived long before God gave the law) was justified by faith alone (see Gen 15:6). The phrase υἱοὶ Ἀβραάμ refers to the truth that believing Jews and Gentiles are the true spiritual children of Abraham because they follow his example of faith (v. 7). The good news to Abraham (v. 8) was the news of salvation for all the nations. Salvation has always been by faith. So those who are of faith, whether Jew or Gentile, are blessed as Abraham. The OT predicted that Gentiles would receive the blessings of justification by faith, as did Abraham, and those blessings are poured out on all because of Christ.

ἐπίστευσεν > 3SAAI, believed ‖ ἐλογίσθη > 3SAPI, was reckoned ‖ γινώσκετε > 2PPAM, know ‖ εἰσιν > 3PPAI, are

Further Reading: Galatians 3:6–14
Candi Finch

GALATIANS 3:24

²⁴ ὥστε ὁ νόμος παιδαγωγὸς ἡμῶν γέγονεν εἰς Χριστόν, ἵνα ἐκ πίστεως δικαιωθῶμεν.

CONTEXT:
Paul continues making his case for justification by faith alone by turning to a discussion about the purpose of the law. If the law cannot save a person, why was it given?

COMMENTARY:
In Greek and Roman culture, the παιδαγωγός was a trustworthy slave entrusted with a supervisory role that involved protecting, guarding, instructing, correcting, and rebuking; he was given care over activities ranging from overseeing good hygiene to overseeing the studies of the child in his charge from his infancy to puberty. The role of the παιδαγωγός was not limited to, or even primarily focused on, formal education, and it would be an overstatement to consider the παιδαγωγός as a harsh warden or prison guard and an understatement to dismiss him as nothing more than a babysitter. The purpose for having the law as a custodian or guardian until Christ came was delineated with the ἵνα clause: so that we could be justified by faith. The aorist passive verb δικαιωθῶμεν conveys a forensic sense and brings to mind a picture of a judge who declares Christians as righteous when they accept Christ. Christ's death on the cross accomplished an open-and-shut case for any person willing to accept Him as Lord and Savior. The law was given to guide men and women to see their need of a Savior.

παιδαγωγός > custodian, guardian, tutor ‖ γέγονεν > 3SRAI, has become ‖ δικαιωθῶμεν > 1PAPS, we might be justified

Further Reading: Galatians 3:15–26
Candi Finch

GALATIANS 3:28

²⁸ οὐκ ἔνι Ἰουδαῖος οὐδὲ Ἕλλην, οὐκ ἔνι δοῦλος οὐδὲ ἐλεύθερος, οὐκ ἔνι ἄρσεν καὶ θῆλυ· πάντες γὰρ ὑμεῖς εἷς ἐστε ἐν Χριστῷ Ἰησοῦ.

CONTEXT:

Notice the shift from the first-person plural to the second-person in verse 26. Paul simply wanted to address the Galatians directly, and for the first time since 3:1–5, he does so. Galatians 3:28 is one of the most debated verses concerning the roles of women in the contemporary church. However, in order to gain a proper understanding of this verse, you must consider its context within the book of Galatians—it comes at the climax of Paul's discussion regarding salvation history. In other words, the text and context place this verse in the framework of soteriology or the doctrine of salvation. Paul is discussing the nature of salvation and not the proper social relationships of men and women in or out of the church and home.

COMMENTARY:

The emphatic form of the verb (ἔνι) is used to introduce each of the couplets in this verse. The origin of these three couplets has been a matter of considerable debate, but whatever your interpretation, the couplets together must be interpreted in light of the reason given for their negation, i.e., "for you are all one in Christ." Notice that πάντες is the word of inclusion, though its lexical meanings do not include "equal." The idea is unity in contrast to diversity—the common ground shared in Christ. Unity or oneness does not mean uniformity. Oneness does not mean equal in an unqualified sense; it usually connects different things that have something in common. In this case, what the Jew/Gentile, slave/free, and male/female have in common is a shared spiritual status before the Lord. Within God's household, all are in Christ. What it means to be one in Christ is that all people no matter their race, gender, or status are equal at the foot of the cross and enter into a relationship with God in the same way, through faith in Jesus Christ.

ἔνι > 3SPAI, there is || Ἕλλην > Greek || ἐλεύθερος > free || ἄρσεν > male || θῆλυ > female || ἐστε > 2PPAI, are

Further Reading: Galatians 3:26–4:7
Candi Finch

GALATIANS 5:16

¹⁶ λέγω δέ, πνεύματι περιπατεῖτε καὶ ἐπιθυμίαν σαρκὸς οὐ μὴ τελέσητε.

CONTEXT:

The final two chapters of Paul's epistle are a portrait of the Spirit-filled life, of the believer's implementation of the life of faith under the control and in the energy of the Holy Spirit. The Spirit-filled life thereby becomes a powerful testimony to the power of justification by faith.

COMMENTARY:

All believers have the presence of the indwelling Holy Spirit as the personal power for living to please God. The verbal tense of περιπατεῖτε indicates continuous action or a habitual lifestyle. Walking also implies progress; as a believer submits to the Spirit's control, responding in obedience to the simple commands of Scripture, he grows in his spiritual life. The σαρκός is not simply the physical body. It includes the mind, will, and emotions, which are all subject to sin, and refers in general to unredeemed humanity. The flesh opposes the work of the Spirit and leads believers toward sinful behavior that they would not otherwise be compelled to do. Believers have a choice—they can be led by the Spirit, which results in righteous behavior and spiritual attitudes (note the subjunctive used in emphatic negation [οὐ μὴ τελέσητε], which denies any possibility that one walking in the Spirit will be governed by carnality); or they can be led by the flesh, which can only produce unrighteous behavior and attitudes.

λέγω > 1SPAI, say ‖ περιπατεῖτε > 2PPAM, walk ‖ οὐ μὴ τελέσητε > 2PAAS, absolutely will not gratify

Further Reading: Galatians 5:1–26
Candi Finch

APRIL 24
GALATIANS 6:1-2

¹ ἀδελφοί, ἐὰν καὶ προλημφθῇ ἄνθρωπος ἔν τινι παραπτώματι, ὑμεῖς οἱ πνευματικοὶ καταρτίζετε τὸν τοιοῦτον ἐν πνεύματι πραΰτητος, σκοπῶν σεαυτόν, μὴ καὶ σὺ πειρασθῇς. ² ἀλλήλων τὰ βάρη βαστάζετε, καὶ οὕτως ἀναπληρώσετε τὸν νόμον τοῦ Χριστοῦ.

CONTEXT:

After discussing the role of freedom in the Christian life (5:1-15) and the life led by the Spirit versus the life led by the flesh (5:16-26), Paul moves to the final section of his letter. In this chapter he offers some concluding pastoral exhortations for the churches of Galatia, beginning with the importance of bearing the burdens of fellow believers.

COMMENTARY:

Paul uses the word προλημφθῇ, which may imply a person was actually seen committing sin, or that he was caught or overcome by the sin itself. Those believers who are walking in the Spirit, filled with the Spirit, and evidencing the fruit of the Spirit, are to help restore the one who has fallen into sin. The word καταρτίζετε, sometimes used metaphorically of settling disputes, has the sense of mending or repairing and was used of setting a broken bone or repairing a dislocated limb. Those who are spiritual are to help carry others' βάρη (extra heavy load), which here represent difficulties or problems that people have trouble handling. This is contrasted with the word φορτίον (load, v. 5), a word that has no connotation of extraordinary difficulty, which Paul instructs every person to carry on his own. The ministry of being a burden-bearer is one that requires diligence; the one who is spiritual must give heed to his own responsibilities and possible temptations while at the same time looking out for those who are struggling with sin or overwhelming burdens.

προλημφθῇ > 3SAPS, should be overcome || παραπτώματι > trespass || πνευματικοί > spiritual || καταρτίζετε > 2PPAM, restore || πραΰτητος > gentleness || σκοπῶν > PAPMSN, considering || πειρασθῇς > 2SAPS, be tempted || βάρη > burdens || βαστάζετε > 2PPAM, bear || ἀναπληρώσετε > 2PFAI, shall fulfill

Further Reading: Galatians 6:1-5
Candi Finch

GALATIANS 6:9

⁹ τὸ δὲ καλὸν ποιοῦντες μὴ ἐγκακῶμεν, καιρῷ γὰρ ἰδίῳ θερίσομεν μὴ ἐκλυόμενοι.

CONTEXT:

After exhorting believers to look out for each other, Paul turns to an agricultural example, applied metaphorically to the moral and spiritual realm, to show a biblical truth. For those tempted to give up or give in to sin, Paul concludes his letter with gentle encouragement.

COMMENTARY:

This verse offers a promise: in God's time, the proper time, the harvest or the benefits of doing good will come. The results are not up to us; they are in God's hand. καιρῷ is the appointed and suitable opportunity, referring to a distinct, fixed time period rather than occasional moments. Paul's point is that the believer's entire life provides the unique privilege by which one can serve others in Christ's name. We are just called to be obedient. The word ἐγκακῶμεν carries the idea of "giving in to evil" or "losing heart and becoming a coward." This weariness that Paul refers to is a kind of spiritual weariness that causes you to want give up on doing good and give in to sin. Paul understood this struggle so he wasn't writing to the Galatians as someone who was "holier than thou," who didn't understand the temptation or struggle. Paul faced his own struggle with doing good. In Romans 7:14–25 he talked about the spiritual battle that raged in his own life (and that rages in each of our lives), and he said in v. 19, "For the good that I want, I do not do, but I practice the very evil that I do not want."

ποιοῦντες > PAPMPN, doing ‖ ἐγκακῶμεν > 1PPAS, grow weary ‖ θερίσομεν > 1PFAI, will reap a harvest ‖ ἐκλυόμενοι > PPPMPN, giving up

Further Reading: Galatians 6:6–10
Candi Finch

... ¹⁷ ἵνα ὁ θεὸς τοῦ κυρίου ἡμῶν Ἰησοῦ Χριστοῦ, ὁ πατὴρ τῆς δόξης, δώῃ ὑμῖν πνεῦμα σοφίας καὶ ἀποκαλύψεως ἐν ἐπιγνώσει αὐτοῦ, ¹⁸ πεφωτισμένους τοὺς ὀφθαλμοὺς τῆς καρδίας ὑμῶν εἰς τὸ εἰδέναι ὑμᾶς τίς ἐστιν ἡ ἐλπὶς τῆς κλήσεως αὐτοῦ, τίς ὁ πλοῦτος τῆς δόξης τῆς κληρονομίας αὐτοῦ ἐν τοῖς ἁγίοις, ¹⁹ καὶ τί τὸ ὑπερβάλλον μέγεθος τῆς δυνάμεως αὐτοῦ εἰς ἡμᾶς τοὺς πιστεύοντας κατὰ τὴν ἐνέργειαν τοῦ κράτους τῆς ἰσχύος αὐτοῦ.

CONTEXT:
Paul constantly gives thanks to God for the Ephesians when he prays for them (Eph 1:16). The main content of Paul's request for the Ephesians is stated in verses 17 and 18.

COMMENTARY:
The first prayer request is alerted by ἵνα which is connected to the subjunctive δώῃ. The participle πεφωτισμένους is awkward grammatically, but it seems to also be a part of the prayer request, suggesting that Paul is praying for (1) πνεῦμα σοφίας, (2) ἀποκαλύψεως ἐν ἐπιγνώσει αὐτοῦ, and (3) πεφωτισμένους τοὺς ὀφθαλμοὺς τῆς καρδίας. The second prayer request is introduced by εἰς τό which is connected to the infinitive εἰδέναι. The content of the second prayer request is seen by the usage of three interrogative pronouns τίς ... τίς ... τί. Thus, Paul prays that the Ephesians would know (1) ἡ ἐλπὶς τῆς κλήσεως αὐτοῦ, (2) ὁ πλοῦτος τῆς δόξης τῆς κληρονομίας αὐτοῦ ἐν τοῖς ἁγίοις, and (3) τὸ ὑπερβάλλον μέγεθος τῆς δυνάμεως αὐτοῦ εἰς ἡμᾶς τοὺς πιστεύοντας. Paul's essential prayer is that the Ephesians believers might grow in the knowledge of our Savior Jesus Christ and realize the gospel hope and rewards they have. Surely this is something we all need continually to pray for ourselves and others.

δώῃ > 3SAAS, might give ‖ ἀποκαλύψεως > revelation ‖ ἐπιγνώσει > knowledge, recognition ‖ πεφωτισμένους > RPPMPA, having been enlightened, been given light to ‖ κλήσεως > calling ‖ πλοῦτος > riches, wealth ‖ κληρονομίας > inheritance ‖ ὑπερβάλλον > PAPNSN, to surpass ‖ μέγεθος > greatness ‖ ἐνέργειαν > working ‖ κράτους > power, might ‖ ἰσχύος > strength, power, might (two genitives together intensify by their similar meaning—ESV: "great might")

Further Reading: Ephesians 1:15–23
John Vo

EPHESIANS 2:8-9

⁸ τῇ γὰρ χάριτί ἐστε σεσῳσμένοι διὰ πίστεως· καὶ τοῦτο οὐκ ἐξ ὑμῶν, θεοῦ τὸ δῶρον· ⁹ οὐκ ἐξ ἔργων, ἵνα μή τις καυχήσηται.

CONTEXT:
Paul explains what life looks like before Christ and after salvation in Christ. The experience of passing from death unto life in Christ is accomplished only by God's grace.

COMMENTARY:
The explanatory γάρ looks back to the previous content (vv. 1-7, a single sentence in Greek) with a focus on grace, which was first introduced in a parenthetical comment in verse 5. The sole basis of salvation is χάριτι by means of πίστεως. In other words, the faith that people have is only obtained by God's grace, which is why salvation is described as θεοῦ τὸ δῶρον. Salvation being a gift from God entails that it is οὐκ ἐξ ἔργων so that humanity would not καυχήσηται. The beauty of salvation is that we are not able to obtain it ourselves, since if it were left up to us, we would fail miserably to obtain it. Thus, God gets all the glory for salvation because of his mercy and love (2:4).

σεσῳσμένοι > RPPMPN, have been saved ‖ δῶρον > gift, present ‖ καυχήσηται > 3SAMS, may [not] boast

Further Reading: Ephesians 2:1-10
John Vo

EPHESIANS 2:13

¹³ νυνὶ δὲ ἐν Χριστῷ Ἰησοῦ ὑμεῖς οἵ ποτε ὄντες μακρὰν ἐγενήθητε ἐγγὺς ἐν τῷ αἵματι τοῦ Χριστοῦ.

CONTEXT:

Ephesians 2:11–22 is the logical conclusion both theologically and practically for Jewish and Gentile Christians who have been saved in Christ. The ethnic hostility and separation between Jewish and Gentile Christians are abolished because of the work of Christ on the cross, making Gentiles now a part of God's people.

COMMENTARY:

The adversative phrase νυνὶ δέ provides a stark contrast to the previous place of Gentiles being separated from Christ (2:12). The phrase ἐν Χριστῷ should be understood in an incorporative sense describing the union Gentiles now have with Jews in Christ. Jesus as the Gentiles' representative has radically changed their status before God. The term μακράν describes the ethnic separation Gentiles, as exemplified by Ephesian believers, had toward Israel and thus being separated from God's covenant. However, through the means of τῷ αἵματι of Christ, Gentiles are brought ἐγγύς, demonstrating that in Christ all believing Gentiles can be incorporated. This verse demonstrates that ethnic hostility within the church should end between Jewish and Gentile Christians, and by extension all ethnic hostility, as all who are in Christ are part of the family of God.

νυνί > now, as it is ‖ μακράν > far (away) ‖ ἐγενήθητε > 2PAPI, brought [near]

Further Reading: Ephesians 2:11–13
John Vo

April 29
Ephesians 2:14–16

¹⁴ αὐτὸς γάρ ἐστιν ἡ εἰρήνη ἡμῶν, ὁ ποιήσας τὰ ἀμφότερα ἓν καὶ τὸ μεσότοιχον τοῦ φραγμοῦ λύσας, τὴν ἔχθραν ἐν τῇ σαρκὶ αὐτοῦ, ¹⁵ τὸν νόμον τῶν ἐντολῶν ἐν δόγμασιν καταργήσας, ἵνα τοὺς δύο κτίσῃ ἐν αὐτῷ εἰς ἕνα καινὸν ἄνθρωπον ποιῶν εἰρήνην ¹⁶ καὶ ἀποκαταλλάξῃ τοὺς ἀμφοτέρους ἐν ἑνὶ σώματι τῷ θεῷ διὰ τοῦ σταυροῦ, ἀποκτείνας τὴν ἔχθραν ἐν αὐτῷ.

CONTEXT:
Since both Jewish and Gentile Christians are in the family of God by of the blood of Christ, Jesus has broken down any sort of ethnic hostility that Jews may have against Gentiles. Jesus is the peace for both Jewish and Gentile Christians.

COMMENTARY:
The explanatory γάρ provides the reason why the blood of Christ has brought the Gentiles near, simply because Jesus is their peace. The peace is referring to the resolution of social and ethnic hostility between Jews and Gentiles, which no longer exists due to the fact that τὰ ἀμφότερα ἕν. The word ἔχθραν (2:14) is better seen as the direct object of καταργήσας expressing that, in Christ's flesh, the fleshly hostility between Jews and Gentiles was destroyed (see NASB). The primary emphasis of what Jesus abolishes in his flesh (τὸν νόμον τῶν ἐντολῶν ἐν δόγμασιν) is one of social and ethnic hostility. With the social and ethnic hostility gone, Christ, who is our peace, has created τοὺς δύο ... ἐν αὐτῷ εἰς ἕνα καινὸν ἄνθρωπον. What we see in this beautifully rich theological passage is how in Christ all tribes, tongues, and nations are brought into one family of God, breaking down any barriers for his glory and honor.

ἀμφότερα > both ǁ μεσότοιχον > dividing wall ǁ φραγμοῦ > fence, hedge, partition ǁ ἔχθραν > enmity, hostility ǁ δόγμασιν > ordinance, law, rule ǁ καταργήσας > AAPMSN, abolishing ǁ κτίσῃ > 3SAAS, he might create ǁ ἀποκαταλλάξῃ > 3SAAS, he might reconcile

Further Reading: Ephesians 2:17–18
John Vo

APRIL 30
EPHESIANS 2:17–18

¹⁷ καὶ ἐλθὼν εὐηγγελίσατο εἰρήνην ὑμῖν τοῖς μακρὰν καὶ εἰρήνην τοῖς ἐγγύς· ¹⁸ ὅτι δι' αὐτοῦ ἔχομεν τὴν προσαγωγὴν οἱ ἀμφότεροι ἐν ἑνὶ πνεύματι πρὸς τὸν πατέρα.

CONTEXT:
Paul continues his thought from 2:14 on the idea of Christ being the peace for both Jewish and Gentile Christians. It is because of Jesus' blood that both Jewish and Gentile Christians have access to the Father as they all have the indwelling of the Holy Spirit.

COMMENTARY:
The conjunction καί coordinates and continues the main thought of peace in 2:14. The language of far and near is used again to indicate the horizontal peace (social and ethnic peace) between Jews and Gentiles. In 2:16 the vertical reconciliation with God is emphasized, with 2:17 reminding again of the horizontal peace, which leads to 2:18 emphasizing what both Jews and Gentiles have because of their vertical and horizontal peace. The causal conjunction ὅτι provides the grounds for what the preaching of peace has accomplished, namely, that Jews and Gentiles both have the Holy Spirit (bringing them into one family) and both have access to the Father (bringing them into reconciliation with God). What a great gospel truth it is that all people who believe in Jesus are brought into one family and given a relationship with God the Father.

εὐηγγελίσατο > 3SAMI, preached, proclaimed ‖ μακράν > far (away) ‖ προσαγωγήν > access ‖ ἀμφότεροι > both

Further Reading: Ephesians 2:19–22
John Vo

EPHESIANS 3:6

⁶ εἶναι τὰ ἔθνη συγκληρονόμα καὶ σύσσωμα καὶ συμμέτοχα τῆς ἐπαγγελίας ἐν Χριστῷ Ἰησοῦ διὰ τοῦ εὐαγγελίου.

CONTEXT:
Paul explains in 3:1-13 the mystery, which is the fact that Gentiles are now fellow-heirs with the Jewish people of faith. This redemption of Gentiles has always been God's plan from the start, yet has now been revealed fully through Paul's apostolic ministry.

COMMENTARY:
Ephesians 3:1-7 is all one sentence in Greek with verse 2 being the true start of the idea conveyed in 3:2-7. Some translations have, "This mystery is ..." inserted at the beginning of 3:6 (see ESV), but such wording is not in the Greek and is used simply to clarify what is stated in 3:4, τῷ μυστηρίῳ τοῦ Χριστοῦ. This mystery is that Gentiles are συγκληρονόμα, σύσσωμα, and συμμέτοχα τῆς ἐπαγγελίας. The threefold description encapsulates that Gentiles receive many of the same benefits that Jewish Christians would enjoy. The διά expresses the means by which the Gentiles are able to receive the benefits, namely, *through the gospel*. All believers ought to rejoice in this truth, knowing that God had always planned to save all of humanity, not just those in ethnic Israel!

συγκληρονόμα > fellow heirs || σύσσωμα > of the same body || συμμέτοχα > sharing with, participants

Further Reading: Ephesians 3:1-7
John Vo

MAY 2
EPHESIANS 4:1–3

¹ παρακαλῶ οὖν ὑμᾶς ἐγὼ ὁ δέσμιος ἐν κυρίῳ ἀξίως περιπατῆσαι τῆς κλήσεως ἧς ἐκλήθητε, ² μετὰ πάσης ταπεινοφροσύνης καὶ πραΰτητος, μετὰ μακροθυμίας, ἀνεχόμενοι ἀλλήλων ἐν ἀγάπῃ, ³ σπουδάζοντες τηρεῖν τὴν ἑνότητα τοῦ πνεύματος ἐν τῷ συνδέσμῳ τῆς εἰρήνης.

CONTEXT:
Paul begins focusing on exhortation starting with Ephesians 4:1, having throughout chapters 4–6 several descriptions of what it means to live a life worthy of the gospel. The specific focus of these verses is on the practical actions and heart needed to have unity within the body of Christ.

COMMENTARY:
The οὖν is an inferential conjunction that connect the entire ethical section of chapters 4–6 with all of chapters 1–3, specifically chapter 2. The main verb, παρακαλῶ, is an appeal to the Ephesian believers *to walk* (περιπατῆσαι), a Jewish (and Greek) metaphor to describe how people are to live every day of their lives in every aspect of their lives. The communal qualities that the Jewish Christians and Gentile Christians are supposed to display to each other are: (1) ταπεινοφροσύνης, (2) πραΰτητος, (3) μακροθυμίας, and (4) ἀνεχόμενοι ἀλλήλων. These qualities ultimately result in the desire to maintain τὴν ἑνότητα τοῦ πνεύματος. In these few verses Paul exhorts believers who have different ethnic backgrounds, culture, upbringing, and traditions, to work through differences knowing that they are all saved by the same Savior. In the same manner, we today must realize that we ought to seek the qualities described in verse 2 so that we might have unity in Christ despite our various backgrounds and ethnicities.

δέσμιος > prisoner || **ἀξίως** > worthily || **κλήσεως** > calling || **ταπεινοφροσύνης** > humility, humble attitude || **πραΰτητος** > gentleness || **μακροθυμίας** > patience, forbearance || **ἀνεχόμενοι** > PMPMPN, bear with, endure || **σπουδάζοντες** > PAPMPN, be eager, make every effort || **ἑνότητα** > unity, oneness || **συνδέσμῳ** > bond

Further Reading: Ephesians 4:1–6
John Vo

EPHESIANS 5:1-2

¹ γίνεσθε οὖν μιμηταὶ τοῦ θεοῦ ὡς τέκνα ἀγαπητὰ ² καὶ περιπατεῖτε ἐν ἀγάπῃ, καθὼς καὶ ὁ Χριστὸς ἠγάπησεν ἡμᾶς καὶ παρέδωκεν ἑαυτὸν ὑπὲρ ἡμῶν προσφορὰν καὶ θυσίαν τῷ θεῷ εἰς ὀσμὴν εὐωδίας.

CONTEXT:

Ephesians 5:2 has the third *walk* command that began back in Ephesians 4:1 (see 2:2, 2:10, 4:17, 5:8, 5:15), indicating a new section for the command to live a life worthy of the gospel. The focus of this command is to be imitators of God and live a life of love like Christ lived.

COMMENTARY:

There are two commands here: (1) γίνεσθε μιμηταὶ τοῦ θεοῦ and (2) περιπατεῖτε ἐν ἀγάπῃ, which are connected by the coordinating conjunction καί. Verse 2 uses καθώς to compare Christ's sacrificial love with the kind of love Paul writes about. In other words, the love we must live is the same exact love Christ lived and showed to us. This type of love is further explained in verses 3–6, whereas verses 7–14 expand on what it means to be an imitator of God. As Paul calls on all believers to walk in a manner worthy of the gospel, it is no surprise that Paul exhorts us to imitate God's holiness and Christ's love.

γίνεσθε > 2PPMM, be ‖ περιπατεῖτε > 2PPAM, walk ‖ μιμηταί > imitators ‖ προσφοράν > offering ‖ ὀσμήν > fragrance ‖ εὐωδίας > aroma, sweet smell

Further Reading: Ephesians 5:1–14
John Vo

EPHESIANS 5:15–16

¹⁵ βλέπετε οὖν ἀκριβῶς πῶς περιπατεῖτε μὴ ὡς ἄσοφοι ἀλλ' ὡς σοφοί,
¹⁶ ἐξαγοραζόμενοι τὸν καιρόν, ὅτι αἱ ἡμέραι πονηραί εἰσιν.

CONTEXT:

This is the last *walk* exhortation that Paul uses with the Ephesian believers. The specific appeal broadens the scope of living a worthy life to living a wise life according to God's word.

COMMENTARY:

The adverb ἀκριβῶς could modify either βλέπετε or περιπατεῖτε. The more likely option is βλέπετε, as the exhortation is to use care to examine one's life to determine if the life lived is one that is wise or unwise. The participle ἐξαγοραζόμενοι is a participle of manner which expresses how a wise life is conducted by those who make the best use of their time in a God-honoring way. The conjunction ὅτι introduces a causal clause that provides the reason why they are to make the best use of their time by walking wisely in this world filled with evil. Wise living according to God's word goes hand in hand with a gospel filled life. The exhortation then is to know God's revealed will in His word (5:17), so that we might live wisely.

βλέπετε > 2PPAM, watch || ἀκριβῶς > carefully, accurately || περιπατεῖτε > 2PPAI, walk || ἄσοφοι > unwise || σοφοί > wise || ἐξαγοραζόμενοι > PMPMPN, making the most of, redeeming

Further Reading: Ephesians 5:15–21
John Vo

MAY 5

EPHESIANS 6:10-11

[10] τοῦ λοιποῦ, ἐνδυναμοῦσθε ἐν κυρίῳ καὶ ἐν τῷ κράτει τῆς ἰσχύος αὐτοῦ. [11] ἐνδύσασθε τὴν πανοπλίαν τοῦ θεοῦ πρὸς τὸ δύνασθαι ὑμᾶς στῆναι πρὸς τὰς μεθοδείας τοῦ διαβόλου.

CONTEXT:

Ephesians 6:10 is the final exhortation that Paul gives in this letter to the Ephesian church. What makes this exhortation particularly intriguing is that the command now changes from *walk* to *being strong, clothing oneself,* and *standing.*

COMMENTARY:

The phrase τοῦ λοιποῦ introduces the final exhortation section of Ephesians. The passive imperative ἐνδυναμοῦσθε governs the entire exhortation indicating the need to be strengthened by God's power to withstand the schemes of the devil. Verse 11 is an elaboration on the divine strength that is needed, namely, to have God's armor put on, which gives the ability for one *to stand* (στῆναι) against the schemes of the devil. In all the exhortations of Ephesians since chapter 4, there was an active appeal to *walk* focusing on one's daily living. This contrasts with the more passive action of *standing* in the power of God's strength. As Christians we must seek to actively live for God, knowing that it is only by God's strength that we can ultimately withstand the evils of the world.

τοῦ λοιποῦ > finally || ἐνδυναμοῦσθε > 2PPPM, to strengthen, become strong || κράτει > strength || ἰσχύος > might || ἐνδύσασθε > 2PAMM, put on || πανοπλίαν > full armor, whole armor || μεθοδείας > schemes, deceits

Further Reading: Ephesians 6:10-20
John Vo

¹καὶ ὅτε ἐγγίζουσιν εἰς Ἱεροσόλυμα εἰς Βηθφαγὴ καὶ Βηθανίαν πρὸς τὸ ὄρος τῶν ἐλαιῶν, ἀποστέλλει δύο τῶν μαθητῶν αὐτοῦ ... ¹¹Καὶ εἰσῆλθεν εἰς Ἱεροσόλυμα εἰς τὸ ἱερὸν καὶ περιβλεψάμενος πάντα, ὀψίας ἤδη οὔσης τῆς ὥρας, ἐξῆλθεν εἰς Βηθανίαν μετὰ τῶν δώδεκα.

CONTEXT:

In the previous section (chs. 8–10), Jesus has been "on the way" to Jerusalem, predicting his suffering and giving requirements for disciples (8:31*ff*; 9:31*ff*; 10:32*ff*). Now, in his climactic arrival, the King presents himself in Jerusalem and inspects his "house" (11:1–11, 17), the temple, leading to confrontation with and his condemnation of the hard-hearted nation (chs. 11–13).

COMMENTARY:

The use of the present tense form in v. 1, *they approached* (ἐγγίζουσιν), indicates a scene change in the narrative, whereas the two aorist tense forms in v. 11, *he entered / he departed* (εἰσῆλθεν/ ἐξῆλθεν), are the final events in the scene (11:1–11). Jesus' more specific destination in Jerusalem is *into the temple* [complex] (εἰς τὸ ἱερόν), a much larger area than the *sanctuary* (ναός) proper where the curtain will be torn (15:38). Note Mark's significant clue in v. 11 for Jesus' judgments, a brief temporal clause: *and after looking around at everything* (καὶ περιβλεψάμενος πάντα). Mark has six of the seven NT uses of this verb (cf. Lk 6:10), here with a direct object *all things* (πάντα). Jesus *departed*, but only after thoroughly inspecting the temple complex; he'll be back the next day to curse a tree and clean house. Does your temple and worship pass Christ's inspection?

ἐγγίζουσιν > 3PPAI, approach || ἐλαιῶν > olives || εἰσῆλθεν > 3SAAI, entered || περιβλεψάμενος > AMPMSN, looking around || ὀψίας > late || οὔσης > PAPFSG, being || ἐξῆλθεν > 3SAAI, departed

Further Reading: Mark 11:1–11; cf. περιβλέπω in 3:5, 34; 5:32; 9:8; 10:23
Jonathan Rinker

MAY 7
MARK 12:6-8

⁶ ἔτι ἕνα εἶχεν υἱὸν ἀγαπητόν· ἀπέστειλεν αὐτὸν ἔσχατον πρὸς αὐτοὺς λέγων ὅτι ἐντραπήσονται τὸν υἱόν μου. ⁷ ἐκεῖνοι δὲ οἱ γεωργοὶ πρὸς ἑαυτοὺς εἶπαν ὅτι οὗτός ἐστιν ὁ κληρονόμος· δεῦτε ἀποκτείνωμεν αὐτόν, καὶ ἡμῶν ἔσται ἡ κληρονομία. ⁸ καὶ λαβόντες ἀπέκτειναν αὐτὸν καὶ ἐξέβαλον αὐτὸν ἔξω τοῦ ἀμπελῶνος.

CONTEXT:

This final parable (12:1-12) illustrates the emphasis in chs. 11-13: Jesus' confrontation of the nation and their rejection. The nation's persistent wickedness is exposed in their abuse of the vineyard owner's slaves and their murder of his "beloved son."

COMMENTARY:

Notice what the parable's only recorded speeches highlight—*"They will respect my son,"* juxtaposed to *"Come. Let us kill him, and ours will be the inheritance."* The owner has one final slave to send, a *beloved son* (υἱὸν ἀγαπητόν), whom *he sent* (ἀπέστειλεν) while [he is] *saying* (λέγων), *"They will respect my son."* While the Father's large-hearted hope might sound insanely optimistic, it is eclipsed by the insanely evil Jewish leaders who play their part, *seeking to seize* [Jesus] *because they knew he told the parable against them* (12:12; cf. 4:11-12, 33-34). Be amazed at the Father's heart, as he sends his beloved Son, in contrast to the wicked heart of the Son's murderers.

ἐντραπήσονται > 3PFPI, will respect ‖ γεωργοί > tenant farmers ‖ κληρονόμος > heir ‖ δεῦτε > interj., Come! ‖ ἀποκτείνωμεν > 1PAAS, let us kill

Further Reading: Mark 4:1-34, 11:9-10, 12:10-12
Jonathan Rinker

MARK 12:35-37

³⁵ καὶ ἀποκριθεὶς ὁ Ἰησοῦς ἔλεγεν διδάσκων ἐν τῷ ἱερῷ· πῶς λέγουσιν οἱ γραμματεῖς ὅτι ὁ χριστὸς υἱὸς Δαυίδ ἐστιν; ³⁶ αὐτὸς Δαυὶδ εἶπεν ἐν τῷ πνεύματι τῷ ἁγίῳ· εἶπεν κύριος τῷ κυρίῳ μου· κάθου ἐκ δεξιῶν μου, ἕως ἂν θῶ τοὺς ἐχθρούς σου ὑποκάτω τῶν ποδῶν σου. ³⁷ αὐτὸς Δαυὶδ λέγει αὐτὸν κύριον, καὶ πόθεν αὐτοῦ ἐστιν υἱός; Καὶ ὁ πολὺς ὄχλος ἤκουεν αὐτοῦ ἡδέως.

CONTEXT:

Mark focuses Jesus' confrontation in Jerusalem on its location—the "temple" (11:11, 15, 27; 12:35, 41; 13:1); and, on his opponents—chief priests, scribes, and elders (11:27), Pharisees and Herodians (12:13), Sadducees (12:18), and one of the scribes (12:28). Jesus confounds each of their best attempts to trap him in a question and then asks his own question that pinpoints the primary issue: *Who is called Lord?*

COMMENTARY:

The participle *answering* (ἀποκριθείς) has no direct object, and it's often untranslated here. However, as it follows *No one dared any longer to question him* (12:34), the participle positions Jesus' question in 12:35–37 as his "answer" or response to the barrage of questions he faced. And, since the foil in Jesus' question is *the scribes* (οἱ γραμματεῖς, 12:35), his "answer" here is further connected to the previous dialogue with *one of the scribes* (εἷς τῶν γραμματέων, 12:28). That scribe agreed with Jesus that the greatest commandment is to wholly love the Lord, but he had yet to explicitly identify Jesus as "Lord." Thus, Jesus' use of Psalm 110:1 gets to the heart of Mark's central question: *Who is Jesus?* Answering this correctly is the difference between being *not far* from the kingdom and entering the kingdom. Do you love the *Lord* Jesus with all your heart?

ἀποκριθείς > APPMSN, answering || κάθου > 2SPMM, sit || δεξιῶν > as idiom, right side (i.e., place of honor) || θῶ > 1SAAS, place || ὑποκάτω > under || ποδῶν > feet || πόθεν > how || ἡδέως > gladly

Further Reading: Mark 12:28–44; 14:61–64; Acts 2:32–36
Jonathan Rinker

MAY 9
MARK 13:20-22

²⁰ καὶ εἰ μὴ ἐκολόβωσεν κύριος τὰς ἡμέρας, οὐκ ἂν ἐσώθη πᾶσα σάρξ·
ἀλλὰ διὰ τοὺς ἐκλεκτοὺς οὓς ἐξελέξατο ἐκολόβωσεν τὰς ἡμέρας.
²¹ Καὶ τότε ἐάν τις ὑμῖν εἴπῃ· ἴδε ὧδε ὁ χριστός, ἴδε ἐκεῖ, μὴ πιστεύετε·
²² ἐγερθήσονται γὰρ ψευδόχριστοι καὶ ψευδοπροφῆται καὶ δώσουσιν
σημεῖα καὶ τέρατα πρὸς τὸ ἀποπλανᾶν, εἰ δυνατόν, τοὺς ἐκλεκτούς.

CONTEXT:

Both major discourses in Mark concern the promised Kingdom of God—parables
on the Kingdom's character (ch. 4) and predictions of the King's coming (ch. 13).
The hortatory theme of ch. 13 is a call to be alert in light of coming judgments
and false messiahs before the Son of Man comes (13:5, 9, 23, 33, 35, 37).

COMMENTARY:

Note three different conditional statements and three uses of the term *elect*. A
second-class condition in v. 20 assumes the unreality of the protasis. *But* (ἀλλά),
instead of such a scenario where no one survives, the Lord shortens the days *for
the sake of the elect whom he elected*. A third-class condition begins v. 21,
presenting a future scenario and Jesus' command for such a situation: *Don't
believe* [it]. A first-class condition in v. 22 considers a potential—*to deceive, if* [it
was] *possible, the elect*. However, based on their status as "elect," such deception
is not possible. The future tribulation and deception (13:14–19) will be an
unprecedented threat to God's people, yet their election guarantees his mercy
and preservation of them. Likewise, your security is founded in God's gracious
choice.

ἐκολόβωσεν > 3SAAI, had [not] shortened ‖ ἐσώθη > 3SAPI, be saved ‖
ἐκλεκτούς > elect ‖ ἐξελέξατο > 3SAMI, elected ‖ ἐγερθήσονται > 3PFPI, will
appear ‖ δώσουσιν > 3PFAI, will produce ‖ τέρατα > wonders ‖ ἀποπλανᾶν >
PAN, deceive ‖ δυνατόν > possible

Further Reading: Mark 13:5, 9, 32–37; 14:37–38
Jonathan Rinker

MAY 10
MARK 14:8-9

⁸ ὃ ἔσχεν ἐποίησεν· προέλαβεν μυρίσαι τὸ σῶμά μου εἰς τὸν ἐνταφιασμόν. ⁹ ἀμὴν δὲ λέγω ὑμῖν, ὅπου ἐὰν κηρυχθῇ τὸ εὐαγγέλιον εἰς ὅλον τὸν κόσμον, καὶ ὃ ἐποίησεν αὕτη λαληθήσεται εἰς μνημόσυνον αὐτῆς.

CONTEXT:
Mark sets the scene of Jesus' passion with a literary "sandwich" (A¹-B-A²) showing two contrasting responses to Jesus. The murderous plotting of the chief priests and scribes (A¹, 14:1–2) and Judas's colluding betrayal (A², 14:10–11) is interrupted by the sacrificial love and spiritual insight of an unnamed woman who anoints Jesus (B, 14:3–9).

COMMENTARY:
Surprisingly, Jesus credits the woman with pre-burial anointing, making her the only one in Mark's narrative who has understood Jesus' three passion predictions. Even more amazing, Jesus looks beyond his burial to the global proclamation of the gospel. Such confidence is prefaced with the Hebraism *truly* (ἀμήν). In the NT, Jesus alone uses this term to assert boldly the guarantee of his own words. The final four of the thirteen uses in Mark appear in successive episodes (14:9, 18, 25, 30). The escalating trauma of Jesus' final hours is matched by his emphatic claim of controlling foreknowledge. Take heart; the certainty of God's plan is not based on the tranquility of your circumstances, but on the promise of his sovereign word.

ἔσχεν > 3SAAI, has ǁ προέλαβεν > 3SAAI, do ahead of time ǁ μυρίσαι > AAN, to anoint ǁ ἐνταφιασμόν > preparation for burial ǁ κηρυχθῇ > 3SAPS, shall be proclaimed ǁ λαληθήσεται > 3SFPI, will be told ǁ μνημόσυνον > remembrance

Further Reading: Mark 12:41–44, 14:1–11, 18, 25, 30; John 12:1–8
Jonathan Rinker

MARK 14:37-38

³⁷ καὶ ἔρχεται καὶ εὑρίσκει αὐτοὺς καθεύδοντας, καὶ λέγει τῷ Πέτρῳ· Σίμων, καθεύδεις; οὐκ ἴσχυσας μίαν ὥραν γρηγορῆσαι; ³⁸ γρηγορεῖτε καὶ προσεύχεσθε, ἵνα μὴ ἔλθητε εἰς πειρασμόν· τὸ μὲν πνεῦμα πρόθυμον ἡ δὲ σὰρξ ἀσθενής.

CONTEXT:

Peter declares that he's ready to die for Christ (14:31) but cannot even stay awake (14:37); the boastful spokesman (14:29-31) now doesn't know what to say (14:40) until he is again insistent, denying he knows Jesus (14:68-71). In contrast to Peter, Jesus is faithful—offering himself for them (14:22-24), watching and praying, resisting temptation (14:36), and telling the truth (14:62).

COMMENTARY:

The combination of *come, find, sleep* reminds us of the same trio in the warning at 13:36. Likewise, the verb *stay awake* (γρηγορεῖτε) is used three times there (13:34, 35, 37) and three times here (14:34, 37, 38). In 14:37-38, note its repetition on either side of the verse division: ... *to stay awake? Stay awake!* (γρηγορῆσαι; γρηγορεῖτε). This adjacent repetition, not found in Matthew 26 or Luke 22, recalls the same repetition across Mark 13:34-35: *He should stay awake; Stay awake!* (γρηγορῇ γρηγορεῖτε). The disciples' failure in the garden is viewed against the warnings of 13:33-37. Are you watching for Jesus?

καθεύδοντας > PAPMPA, sleeping || καθεύδεις > 2SPAI, sleeping || ἴσχυσας > 2SAAI, were able || γρηγορῆσαι > AAN, to watch || γρηγορεῖτε > 2PPAM, watch! || προσεύχεσθε > 2PPMM, pray || ἔλθητε > 2PAAS, enter || πειρασμόν > temptation || πρόθυμον > willing

Further Reading: Mark 13:33-37, 14:27-42
Jonathan Rinker

MAY 12
MARK 14:61-62

⁶¹ ὁ δὲ ἐσιώπα καὶ οὐκ ἀπεκρίνατο οὐδέν. πάλιν ὁ ἀρχιερεὺς ἐπηρώτα αὐτὸν καὶ λέγει αὐτῷ· σὺ εἶ ὁ χριστὸς ὁ υἱὸς τοῦ εὐλογητοῦ; ⁶² ὁ δὲ Ἰησοῦς εἶπεν· ἐγώ εἰμι, καὶ ὄψεσθε τὸν υἱὸν τοῦ ἀνθρώπου ἐκ δεξιῶν καθήμενον τῆς δυνάμεως καὶ ἐρχόμενον μετὰ τῶν νεφελῶν τοῦ οὐρανοῦ.

CONTEXT:

Mark 14:53-72 is another juicy literary sandwich, enclosed by Peter warming himself in the courtyard (14:54, 66-67). Ironically, while the Sanhedrin struggles to find consistent yet false witnesses (14:55-59), Peter consistently denies Jesus before the weak and Jesus clearly confesses himself as Christ before the powerful.

COMMENTARY:

When asked about his response to the false witnesses (14:60), Jesus was silent and *answered nothing at all* (note the double negative, οὐκ ... οὐδέν, in 14:61; cf. Isa 53:7). However, when asked if he is the Messiah, the Son of the Blessed (cf. 12:6), Jesus boldly responds "I am" (ἐγώ εἰμι), and quotes Psalm 110:1 and Daniel 7:13-14 (Mk 14:62). Thus, Jesus not only accepts the high priest's trap to claim he is Messiah, but also asserts that he will be vindicated. False witnesses said, "We heard him say ..." (14:58) but Jesus says, "You will see ..." Will you boldly witness for Christ with your confidence anchored in the Scriptures?

ἐσιώπα > 3SIAI, was silent || ἀπεκρίνατο > 3SAMI, answered || ἀρχιερεύς > high priest || ἐπηρώτα > 3SIAI, asked || εὐλογητοῦ > Blessed One || ὄψεσθε > 2PFMI, will see || δεξιῶν > as idiom, right side (i.e., place of honor) || καθήμενον > PMPMSA, sitting || νεφελῶν > clouds

Further Reading: Mark 14:53-72
Jonathan Rinker

MAY 13
MARK 15:37–39

³⁷ ὁ δὲ Ἰησοῦς ἀφεὶς φωνὴν μεγάλην ἐξέπνευσεν. ³⁸ Καὶ τὸ καταπέτασμα τοῦ ναοῦ ἐσχίσθη εἰς δύο ἀπ' ἄνωθεν ἕως κάτω. ³⁹ Ἰδὼν δὲ ὁ κεντυρίων ὁ παρεστηκὼς ἐξ ἐναντίας αὐτοῦ ὅτι οὕτως ἐξέπνευσεν εἶπεν· ἀληθῶς οὗτος ὁ ἄνθρωπος υἱὸς θεοῦ ἦν.

CONTEXT:

Mark's opening claim that Jesus is "the Son of God" (1:1) was soon affirmed by the divine voice after the heavens were torn apart (1:10–11). However, even though demons confessed Jesus' deity (5:7), the disciples struggled to grasp his identity (4:41), especially his necessary death (9:32). The first human to confess Mark's claim was, ironically, a centurion at the cross (15:39).

COMMENTARY:

By a double use of the verb ἐξέπνευσεν (he expired), Mark highlights two amazing responses to Jesus' death. First, a divine response: the supernatural tearing of the temple curtain (cf. heavens torn in 1:10–11) is placed in conjunction with Jesus' death by the καί that follows ἐξέπνευσεν (15:37–38). Second, a human response (ὁ κεντυρίων ... εἶπεν), prefaced by his (1) position: standing in front of Jesus, and his (2) observation: seeing ... that in this way he breathed his last. In other words, seeing Jesus' death on the Cross prompts this (3) confession: "Truly this man was the son of God." The adverb truly (ἀληθῶς) introduces the speaker's certain conclusion based on his observation (cf. 14:70). For Mark, the significance of this confession is not only from whom it first comes, a Roman centurion, but also where it first comes—it is by gazing at Jesus' passion that his divine identity is finally realized. Do you have an accurate view of Jesus—a cross-centered Christology that shapes your expectations as his follower?

ἀφείς > AAPMSN, uttering ‖ ἐξέπνευσεν > 3SAAI, breathed his last ‖ καταπέτασμα > curtain ‖ ναοῦ > sanctuary ‖ ἐσχίσθη > 3SAPI, was torn ‖ ἀπ' ἄνωθεν ἕως κάτω > from top to bottom ‖ ἰδών > AAPMSN, see ‖ κεντυρίων > centurion ‖ παρεστηκώς > RAPMSN, standing by ‖ ἐξ ἐναντίας > opposite, facing

Further Reading: Mark 15:33–41; cf. heavens torn (σχίζω) with the affirmation "You are my beloved Son" in 1:10–11.
Jonathan Rinker

MAY 14
MARK 15:46–47

⁴⁶ καὶ ἀγοράσας σινδόνα καθελὼν αὐτὸν ἐνείλησεν τῇ σινδόνι καὶ ἔθηκεν αὐτὸν ἐν μνημείῳ ὃ ἦν λελατομημένον ἐκ πέτρας καὶ προσεκύλισεν λίθον ἐπὶ τὴν θύραν τοῦ μνημείου. ⁴⁷ ἡ δὲ Μαρία ἡ Μαγδαληνὴ καὶ Μαρία ἡ Ἰωσῆτος ἐθεώρουν ποῦ τέθειται.

CONTEXT:
Judas betrays Jesus (14:10–11, 45), all leave him and flee at his arrest (14:50–52), Peter denies any association to him (14:66–72), and from the cross Jesus cries, *"My God! My God! Why have you forsaken me?"* (15:34). Surprisingly, a Sanhedrin member, Joseph, acts boldly to obtain and bury Jesus' corpse, while the women (15:40) are observing Jesus' death, burial, and empty tomb.

COMMENTARY:
A series of aorist verbs describe Joseph's very active Preparation Day evening before Sabbath (15:42): came boldly and asked (15:44), having bought, taken down, wrapped, placed (ἔθηκεν), and rolled (15:46). In contrast, the two tense forms in v. 47—an imperfect, they were watching (ἐθεώρουν), and a perfect, he was laid (τέθειται)—draw our attention to the watching of the eyewitnesses (cf. θεωρέω in 15:40, 47, and 16:4), and the resultant state of the corpse in the tomb, where they will return in about 36 hours to anoint him (16:1). A Sanhedrin member and women—God delights to use unlikely followers and imperfect witnesses in the advance of the Gospel.

ἀγοράσας > AAPMSN, having bought ‖ σινδόνα > linen cloth ‖ καθελών > AAPMSN, having taken down ‖ ἐνείλησεν > 3SAAI, wrapped in ‖ ἔθηκεν > 3SAAI, placed, laid ‖ λελατομημένον > RPPNSN, having been cut ‖ προσεκύλισεν > 3SAAI, rolled against ‖ θύραν > door ‖ μνημείου > tomb ‖ ἐθεώρουν > 3PIAI, were watching ‖ τέθειται > 3SRPI, was placed

Further Reading: Mark 15:40–47; cf. θεωρέω in 3:11; 5:15, 35; 12:41; cf. the perfect tense form of τίθημι in John 11:34 and 19:41.
Jonathan Rinker

MARK 16:6-8

⁶ ὁ δὲ λέγει αὐταῖς· μὴ ἐκθαμβεῖσθε· Ἰησοῦν ζητεῖτε τὸν Ναζαρηνὸν τὸν ἐσταυρωμένον· ἠγέρθη, οὐκ ἔστιν ὧδε· ἴδε ὁ τόπος ὅπου ἔθηκαν αὐτόν. ⁷ ἀλλὰ ὑπάγετε εἴπατε τοῖς μαθηταῖς αὐτοῦ καὶ τῷ Πέτρῳ ὅτι προάγει ὑμᾶς εἰς τὴν Γαλιλαίαν· ἐκεῖ αὐτὸν ὄψεσθε, καθὼς εἶπεν ὑμῖν. ⁸ Καὶ ἐξελθοῦσαι ἔφυγον ἀπὸ τοῦ μνημείου, εἶχεν γὰρ αὐτὰς τρόμος καὶ ἔκστασις· καὶ οὐδενὶ οὐδὲν εἶπαν· ἐφοβοῦντο γάρ.

CONTEXT:
Ironically, it is *unnamed* women who respond best to Jesus (5:21-43; 7:24-30; 12:41-44; 14:1-11). In the end, Mark's star witnesses to Jesus' death, burial, and empty tomb are the same *named* women (15:40, 47; 16:1).

COMMENTARY:
The response of the *young man, clothed in white* (cf. 16:5 and 9:3; 14:51-52), confronts the women's condition: *"Don't be alarmed!"* (μὴ ἐκθαμβεῖσθε), a verb found only in Mark (ἐκθαμβέω 4x; θαμβέω 3x). Contrasting adjacent verbs, *crucified raised* (ἐσταυρωμένον ἠγέρθη), a pairing not found in Matthew or Luke, accentuates the shock. The young man calls the women to see the vacant space, then commands them to say to Jesus' disciples *and to Peter* (καὶ τῷ Πέτρῳ)—a hint of Peter's restoration—that Jesus *is going ahead* (προάγει, cf. 10:32) of them to Galilee. In Mark's stunningly abrupt end, the women are in motion—*"going out, they fled"* (ἐξελθοῦσαι ἔφυγον)—and are described by three terms of emotion, drawing us to ponder our own response to the Resurrection. Do you believe and boldly tell others?

ἐκθαμβεῖσθε > 2PPPM, be [not] alarmed ‖ ἐσταυρωμένον > PPPMSA, was crucified ‖ ἠγέρθη > 3SAMI, he arose ‖ ἴδε > interj., look! ‖ ἔθηκαν > 3PAAI, laid ‖ εἴπατε > 2PAAM, tell! ‖ προάγει > 3SPAI, is going ahead of ‖ ὄψεσθε > 2PFMI, will see ‖ ἐξελθοῦσαι > AAPFPN, going out ‖ οὐδενὶ οὐδέν > nothing to anyone ‖ τρόμος > trembling ‖ ἔκστασις > astonishment ‖ ἐφοβοῦντο > 3PIMI, were afraid

Further Reading: Mark 16:1-8; φοβέω in Mark 4:41, 5:15, 33, 36,
6:20, 50, 9:6, 32, 10:32, 11:18, 32, 12:12, 16:8
Jonathan Rinker

PHILIPPIANS 1:1-2

¹ Παῦλος καὶ Τιμόθεος δοῦλοι Χριστοῦ Ἰησοῦ πᾶσιν τοῖς ἁγίοις ἐν Χριστῷ Ἰησοῦ τοῖς οὖσιν ἐν Φιλίπποις σὺν ἐπισκόποις καὶ διακόνοις, ² χάρις ὑμῖν καὶ εἰρήνη ἀπὸ θεοῦ πατρὸς ἡμῶν καὶ κυρίου Ἰησοῦ Χριστοῦ.

CONTEXT:

Paul begins his letter to the Philippians in verses 1 and 2.

COMMENTARY:

Paul begins his letter in his usual way, mentioning author, recipients, and a greeting. By the Hellenistic period the standard opening in the letters consisted of three components: the name of the sender (nominative case), the name of the addressee(s) (dative case), and the infinitive χαίρειν ('greeting'). Occasionally there were minor variations, including strengthening the greeting with a wish for good health (3 John 2). Although Paul's opening addresses are consistent with the letters of the period, they are far from being stereotyped introductions. He adapts his self-description and his credentials to the circumstances of each letter, employs phrases to describe his Christian readers, and pours Christian content into his greetings. Notice the use of δοῦλοι in the description of Paul and Timothy: "slaves of Christ Jesus." A δοῦλος was a person owned by a free person. In the OT, the *eved*, (regularly translated δοῦλος in the LXX) often indicates a special relationship with God in terms of possession (by God) and service (by the person). The term also was applied to those leaders who were mediators between God and His people, such as Joshua (Josh 24:30), David (2 Sam 7:8, 25, 29), and Moses (Ps 104:26; Mal 3:24). It is often used of the prophets as messengers of the Lord (Amos 3:7; Joel 3:2; Jonah 1:9; Zech 1:6; Jer 7:25; Ezek 38:17). In the NT the term can apply to Jesus (Phil 2:7) or to Christians (1 Pt 2:16; Acts 2:18; 4:29; Rev 10:7; 19:5).

οὖσιν > PAPMPD, are ‖ Φιλίπποις > Philippi ‖ ἐπισκόποις > overseers

Further Reading: Philippians 1:1-6
William C. Varner

PHILIPPIANS 1:9–11

⁹ καὶ τοῦτο προσεύχομαι, ἵνα ἡ ἀγάπη ὑμῶν ἔτι μᾶλλον καὶ μᾶλλον περισσεύῃ ἐν ἐπιγνώσει καὶ πάσῃ αἰσθήσει ¹⁰ εἰς τὸ δοκιμάζειν ὑμᾶς τὰ διαφέροντα, ἵνα ἦτε εἰλικρινεῖς καὶ ἀπρόσκοποι εἰς ἡμέραν Χριστοῦ, ¹¹ πεπληρωμένοι καρπὸν δικαιοσύνης τὸν διὰ Ἰησοῦ Χριστοῦ εἰς δόξαν καὶ ἔπαινον θεοῦ.

CONTEXT:
In Philippians 1:9–11, Paul concludes his introductory section to this letter.

COMMENTARY:
The final element in the introductory paragraph is also its climax. There had been an interruption in 1:7–8, so that instead of praying, Paul spoke directly to the church in the second-person with warmth and feeling. He now resumes that prayer by expressing the specific contents of his interceding for them. The prayer is an outward expression of those feelings he had just mentioned, although the opening "I pray" recalls his earlier reference to prayer in 1:4.

Καὶ τοῦτο προσεύχομαι,
A. ἵνα ἡ ἀγάπη ὑμῶν ἔτι μᾶλλον καὶ μᾶλλον περισσεύῃ ἐν ἐπιγνώσει καὶ πάσῃ αἰσθήσει
    B. εἰς τὸ δοκιμάζειν ὑμᾶς τὰ διαφέροντα,
A'. ἵνα ἦτε εἰλικρινεῖς καὶ ἀπρόσκοποι εἰς ἡμέραν Χριστοῦ,
    B'. πεπληρωμένοι καρπὸν δικαιοσύνης τὸν διὰ Ἰησοῦ Χριστοῦ εἰς δόξαν καὶ ἔπαινον θεοῦ.

Based on the two ἵνα clauses, there are two main requests (A A'). There are then two intended results of those requests if granted (B B'). The two content ἵνα clauses carry the mainline requests and the two subordinate clauses (εἰς τὸ ... and πεπληρωμένοι ...) elaborate the result of each request. Both subordinate BB' convey result. Paul probably uses different constructions in BB' because the first one better conveys that the purpose of discernment is that we can distinguish correctly the more excellent things, while the second conveys that the result of being pure and blameless is that we are filled with the fruit of righteousness.

προσεύχομαι > 1SPMI, pray || περισσεύῃ > 1SPAS, may abound || ἐπιγνώσει > knowledge || αἰσθήσει > discernment || δοκιμάζειν > PAN, approve || διαφέροντα > PAPNPA, excellent || ἦτε > 2PPAS, may be || εἰλικρινεῖς > pure || ἀπρόσκοποι > blameless || πεπληρωμένοι > RPPMPN, filled || ἔπαινον > praise

Further Reading: Philippians 1:7–14
William C. Varner

²⁷ μόνον ἀξίως τοῦ εὐαγγελίου τοῦ Χριστοῦ πολιτεύεσθε, ἵνα εἴτε ἐλθὼν καὶ ἰδὼν ὑμᾶς εἴτε ἀπὼν ἀκούω τὰ περὶ ὑμῶν, ὅτι στήκετε ἐν ἑνὶ πνεύματι, μιᾷ ψυχῇ συναθλοῦντες τῇ πίστει τοῦ εὐαγγελίου ²⁸ καὶ μὴ πτυρόμενοι ἐν μηδενὶ ὑπὸ τῶν ἀντικειμένων, ἥτις ἐστὶν αὐτοῖς ἔνδειξις ἀπωλείας, ὑμῶν δὲ σωτηρίας, καὶ τοῦτο ἀπὸ θεοῦ.

CONTEXT:

Paul exhorts his readers to live in a manner consistent with the gospel message in Philippians 1:27–28.

COMMENTARY:

Paul was a Roman citizen and so were his readers. He tried to live in a manner worthy of his citizenship and so must they. He had a still higher ambition, however, that he and they might live as "citizens worthy of the gospel of Christ." He fought as a good soldier, stood fast in the faith, and was in no way afraid of his adversaries. They should then follow his example, since they were engaged in the same conflict. To them it had been granted to believe and to suffer on the behalf of Christ. Their faith was not of themselves since it was the gift of God, so their suffering also was not self-chosen because it too was a gift of God. Notice the phrase τῇ πίστει τοῦ εὐαγγελίου. The genitive τοῦ εὐαγγελίου has been viewed as (1) objective; (2) subjective; and (3) apposition or epexegetical, "the faith which is the gospel." This third option is consistent with the earlier meaning of πίστις in 1:25 as "the body of faith."

πολιτεύεσθε > 2PPMM, live as a citizen || ἐλθών > AAPMSN, come || ἰδών, AAPMSN, see || ἀπών > PAPMSN, am absent || ἀκούω > 1SPAS, may hear || στήκετε > 2PPAI, are standing firm || συναθλοῦντες > PAPMPN, struggling side by side || πτυρόμενοι > PPPMPN, be frightened || ἀντικειμένων > PMPMPG, opponents || ἐστίν > 3SPAI, is || ἔνδειξις > proof || ἀπωλείας > destruction

Further Reading: Philippians 1:19–30
William C. Varner

MAY 19
PHILIPPIANS 2:1-2

¹ εἴ τις οὖν παράκλησις ἐν Χριστῷ, εἴ τι παραμύθιον ἀγάπης, εἴ τις κοινωνία πνεύματος, εἴ τις σπλάγχνα καὶ οἰκτιρμοί, ² πληρώσατέ μου τὴν χαρὰν ἵνα τὸ αὐτὸ φρονῆτε, τὴν αὐτὴν ἀγάπην ἔχοντες, σύμψυχοι, τὸ ἓν φρονοῦντες.

CONTEXT:
In Philippians 2:1-4, Paul expresses in one compound/complex sentence the same concern as the previous sentence unit (1:27-30).

COMMENTARY:
The similar imperative in both 1:27-30 and 2:1-4 is to be fervent in unity: *stand firm in one Spirit, striving together with one accord for the faith of the gospel* (1:27); *being like-minded, having the same love, being one in spirit and of one mind* (2:2). The first imperative emphasizes the need to remain united for the gospel in the face of opponents. This one focuses on the need to be one even with those who divide the church. Paul's concern is that we be one together so we can be able to endure suffering caused by those outside the body and also to heal any divisions caused by those inside the assembly.

παράκλησις > encouragement ‖ παραμύθιον > consolation ‖ κοινωνία > fellowship ‖ σπλάγχνα > affection ‖ οἰκτιρμοί > compassion ‖ πληρώσατε > 2PAAM, complete ‖ φρονῆτε > 2PPAS, might have the [same] mind ‖ ἔχοντες > PAPMPN, having ‖ σύμψυχοι > united in spirit, harmonious ‖ φρονοῦντες > PAPMPN, being of [one] mind

Further Reading: Philippians 2:1-11
William C. Varner

²⁵ ἀναγκαῖον δὲ ἡγησάμην Ἐπαφρόδιτον τὸν ἀδελφὸν καὶ συνεργὸν καὶ συστρατιώτην μου, ὑμῶν δὲ ἀπόστολον καὶ λειτουργὸν τῆς χρείας μου, πέμψαι πρὸς ὑμᾶς, ²⁶ ἐπειδὴ ἐπιποθῶν ἦν πάντας ὑμᾶς καὶ ἀδημονῶν, διότι ἠκούσατε ὅτι ἠσθένησεν.

CONTEXT:
In Philippians 2:19–30, Paul announces his desire to send Timothy (2:19–24) and Epaphroditus (2:25–30) to visit and minister to the believers at Philippi.

COMMENTARY:
Before Timothy sets out for Philippi, Epaphroditus, a messenger of the congregation who had been sent with a gift for Paul's need, is to return home immediately without waiting to learn the result of Paul's trial. The apostle focuses on this member of the Philippian church, not only in order to inform them of what has happened to their brother and to explain his return with the letter itself, but to offer them still another striking example of the self-giving service that was originally exemplified by the Savior (2:5–8). Thus, Paul provides still another godly example (in addition to Timothy) of the way the Philippians should imitate Christ in their selfless giving for others. Notice the use of ἀπόστολον to describe Epaphroditus. The non-technical sense of "messenger" rather than "apostle" (cf. 2 Cor 8:23) is better suited to the context, because Epaphroditus is described as the Philippians' ἀπόστολος.

ἀναγκαῖον > necessary || ἡγησάμην > 1SAMI, thought || Ἐπαφρόδιτον > Epaphroditus || συνεργόν > fellow worker || συστρατιώτην > fellow soldier || λειτουργόν > servant || πέμψαι > AAN, to send || ἐπειδή > for, since || ἐπιποθῶν > PAPMSN, longing || ἀδημονῶν > PAPMSN, distressed || διότι > because || ἠκούσατε > 2PAAI, heard || ἠσθένησεν > 3SAAI, became sick

Further Reading: Philippians 2:19–30
William C. Varner

MAY 21

PHILIPPIANS 3:8-9

⁸ ἀλλὰ μενοῦνγε καὶ ἡγοῦμαι πάντα ζημίαν εἶναι διὰ τὸ ὑπερέχον τῆς γνώσεως Χριστοῦ Ἰησοῦ τοῦ κυρίου μου, δι᾽ ὃν τὰ πάντα ἐζημιώθην, καὶ ἡγοῦμαι σκύβαλα, ἵνα Χριστὸν κερδήσω ⁹ καὶ εὑρεθῶ ἐν αὐτῷ, μὴ ἔχων ἐμὴν δικαιοσύνην τὴν ἐκ νόμου ἀλλὰ τὴν διὰ πίστεως Χριστοῦ, τὴν ἐκ θεοῦ δικαιοσύνην ἐπὶ τῇ πίστει.

CONTEXT:

In Philippians 3:7-11, Paul describes the total reorientation of his life because of his encounter with Jesus the Messiah.

COMMENTARY:

In this passage, Paul employs accounting terminology and antithetic parallelism as he emphasizes the total re-alignment of his pre-Christian world view. Paul states that his supreme goal is to know Christ fully (3:8, 10) and then expands this goal in terms of knowing the power of his resurrection as he participates in Christ's sufferings which every believer must experience (3:10-11). Employing analogies of dying and rising, Paul indicates that this deeper relationship with Jesus is to be continually conformed to His death. Although Paul looks forward to resurrection, here he is not clear if he expects martyrdom or some other kind of death. Also important to note is Paul's use of σκύβαλα, a *hapax legomenon* appearing in the LXX only at Sirach 27:4, for what he counts as loss. Some suggestions for translation have included "refuse, rubbish, dung, excrement." Lightfoot suggests that the plural refers to "the refuse or leavings of a feast, the food thrown away from the table." He adds that "the Judaizers spoke of themselves as banqueters seated at the Father's table, of Gentile Christians as dogs greedily snatching up the refuse meat which fell therefrom. Paul has reversed the image. The Judaizers are themselves the dogs (v. 2); the meats served to the sons of God are spiritual meats; the ordinances, which the formalists value so highly, are the mere refuse of the feast" (*Philippians*, 149). In either case, the σκύβαλα is food refuse, and Lightfoot's suggestion avoids the shocking figure of "crap." The translation "garbage" is adequate.

μενοῦνγε > rather ‖ ἡγοῦμαι > 1SPMI, count ‖ ζημίαν > loss ‖ εἶναι > PAN, to be ‖ ὑπερέχον > PAPNSA, surpassing ‖ ἐζημιώθην > 1SAPI, have suffered ‖ σκύβαλα > garbage ‖ κερδήσω > 1SAAS, might gain ‖ εὑρεθῶ > 1SAPS, be found ‖ ἔχων > PAPMSN, having

Further Reading: Philippians 3:7-11
William C. Varner

141

PHILIPPIANS 3:20-21

²⁰ ἡμῶν γὰρ τὸ πολίτευμα ἐν οὐρανοῖς ὑπάρχει, ἐξ οὗ καὶ σωτῆρα ἀπεκδεχόμεθα κύριον Ἰησοῦν Χριστόν, ²¹ ὃς μετασχηματίσει τὸ σῶμα τῆς ταπεινώσεως ἡμῶν σύμμορφον τῷ σώματι τῆς δόξης αὐτοῦ κατὰ τὴν ἐνέργειαν τοῦ δύνασθαι αὐτὸν καὶ ὑποτάξαι αὐτῷ τὰ πάντα.

CONTEXT:

In Philippians 3:17-21, Paul returns to his warning about false teachers (see 3:2-3), and his pattern again is one of comparison and contrast. Paul moves to plural rather than singular subjects so that the entire church is included. Some see a change of opponents, while others see a reference to the Jewish false teachers previously condemned, which is more probably the case. Paul describes these false teachers in very strong terms: enemies of the cross whose citizenship is only on earth rather than in heaven, and who do not have the same destiny as believers.

COMMENTARY:

An introductory statement sets the focus for these verses (3:17); Paul then describes the opponents (3:18-19); and he finally contrasts them with true believers (3:20-21). Notice the *hapax legomenon* in 3:20, τὸ πολίτευμα ("our citizenship"), which is the neuter nominative subject of ὑπάρχει. Lightfoot's classic explanation about this term with the appropriate Greco-Roman sources is still worthy of consideration. "This may mean either (1) 'the state, the constitution, to which as citizens we belong' ... or (2) 'the functions which as citizens we perform'... The singular points to the former meaning, which is also more frequent. In either case ἐξ οὗ 'whence' will refer not to πολίτευμα, but to οὐρανοῖς" (*Philippians*, 156). For the metaphor, see 1:27 and the concept of the city of Philippi as a Roman colony.

πολίτευμα > citizenship ‖ ὑπάρχει > 3SPAI, actually is ‖ ἀπεκδεχόμεθα > 1PPMI, await ‖ μετασχηματίσει > 3SFAI, will transform ‖ ταπεινώσεως > lowliness ‖ σύμμορφον > [to be] conformed ‖ ἐνέργειαν > power ‖ τοῦ δύνασθαι αὐτόν > PMN, of his ability/power ‖ ὑποτάξαι > AAN, to subject

Further Reading: Philippians 3:17-21
William C. Varner

MAY 23
PHILIPPIANS 4:1-3

¹ ὥστε, ἀδελφοί μου ἀγαπητοὶ καὶ ἐπιπόθητοι, χαρὰ καὶ στέφανός μου, οὕτως στήκετε ἐν κυρίῳ, ἀγαπητοί. ² Εὐοδίαν παρακαλῶ καὶ Συντύχην παρακαλῶ τὸ αὐτὸ φρονεῖν ἐν κυρίῳ. ³ ναὶ ἐρωτῶ καὶ σέ, γνήσιε σύζυγε, συλλαμβάνου αὐταῖς, αἵτινες ἐν τῷ εὐαγγελίῳ συνήθλησάν μοι μετὰ καὶ Κλήμεντος καὶ τῶν λοιπῶν συνεργῶν μου, ὧν τὰ ὀνόματα ἐν βίβλῳ ζωῆς.

CONTEXT:

In Philippians 4:1-3, Paul returns to specific exhortations supported by both positive and negative models.

COMMENTARY:

The exhortation to "stand firm" in 4:1 is surrounded by affectionate expressions of Paul's close relationship to the readers, echoing the letter's warm beginning (1:3-11). The second exhortation "to be of the same mind" is made to Euodia and Syntyche, two women who have leadership roles within the community. Since the same exhortation has also been given to the larger community (2:2), it is likely that their differences have the potential of leading to a wider division. The third exhortation is given to his "true comrade," who is asked to assist the women in settling their differences (4:3). Is this person named Syzygos or is he one of Paul's co-workers, such as Timothy or Luke or Epaphroditus? Given Luke's association with Philippi in Acts and his desire for anonymity in the same book, one wonders if he is the best candidate. Paul's intended audience could undoubtedly recognize the allusion, even if we cannot.

ἐπιπόθητοι > greatly longed for || στέφανος > crown || στήκετε > 2PPAM, stand firm || Εὐοδίαν > Euodia || παρακαλῶ > 1SPAI, exhort || Συντύχην > Syntyche || τὸ αὐτὸ φρονεῖν > PAN, agree || ἐρωτῶ > 1SPAI, ask || γνήσιε > true || σύζυγε > companion, Syzygos || συλλαμβάνου > 2SPMM, help || συνήθλησαν > 3PAAI, struggled side by side || Κλήμεντος > Clement || τῶν λοιπῶν > the rest || συνεργῶν > fellow workers

Further Reading: Philippians 4:1-7
William C. Varner

⁴ χαίρετε ἐν κυρίῳ πάντοτε· πάλιν ἐρῶ, χαίρετε. ⁵ τὸ ἐπιεικὲς ὑμῶν γνωσθήτω πᾶσιν ἀνθρώποις. ὁ κύριος ἐγγύς. ⁶ μηδὲν μεριμνᾶτε, ἀλλ' ἐν παντὶ τῇ προσευχῇ καὶ τῇ δεήσει μετὰ εὐχαριστίας τὰ αἰτήματα ὑμῶν γνωριζέσθω πρὸς τὸν θεόν. ⁷ καὶ ἡ εἰρήνη τοῦ θεοῦ ἡ ὑπερέχουσα πάντα νοῦν φρουρήσει τὰς καρδίας ὑμῶν καὶ τὰ νοήματα ὑμῶν ἐν Χριστῷ Ἰησοῦ.

CONTEXT:

There are two separate paragraphs of final exhortations—4:4-6 and 4:8-9b—more general than 4:2-3 but still appropriate for the Philippians. Each is concluded with a promise of peace (4:7, 9c). Here, we consider 4:4-7.

COMMENTARY:

The first set of exhortations (4:4-6) differs both from those that immediately precede them (4:2-3) and those that follow (4:8-9), being less specific than the words spoken directly to Euodia, to Syntyche, and to a "true syzygos." Here we find a miscellaneous collection of four independent exhortations ("rejoice," "let your gentleness be known," "do not worry," and "let your requests be made known to God") and one affirmation ("the Lord is near"). The exhortations are appropriate to the letter that has preceded them. Rejoicing is a note heard repeatedly (1:3, 25; 2:2, 17-18, 28-29; 3:1; 4:1, 4, 10). "Gentleness" is needed by a congregation threatened with possible conflict. The statement made in the midst of the exhortations ("the Lord is near") keeps before the reader the eschatological thrust of the letter. Prayer as an antidote to worry is a fitting word for a community undergoing opposition and suffering. The militant guarding of hearts recalls the guarding of a city (2 Cor 11:32), to guard from the inside as well as the outside.

χαίρετε > 2PPAM, rejoice ‖ ἐρῶ > 1SFAI, say ‖ ἐπιεικές > reasonableness ‖ γνωσθήτω > 3SAPM, let be known ‖ μεριμνᾶτε > 2PPAM, be [not] anxious ‖ δεήσει > supplication ‖ εὐχαριστίας > thanksgiving ‖ αἰτήματα > requests ‖ γνωριζέσθω > 3SPPM, let be made known ‖ ὑπερέχουσα > PAPFSN, surpasses ‖ φρουρήσει > 3SFAI, guard ‖ νοήματα > minds

Further Reading: Philippians 4:4-9
William C. Varner

PHILIPPIANS 4:10–13

[10] ἐχάρην δὲ ἐν κυρίῳ μεγάλως ὅτι ἤδη ποτὲ ἀνεθάλετε τὸ ὑπὲρ ἐμοῦ φρονεῖν, ἐφ' ᾧ καὶ ἐφρονεῖτε, ἠκαιρεῖσθε δέ. [11] οὐχ ὅτι καθ' ὑστέρησιν λέγω, ἐγὼ γὰρ ἔμαθον ἐν οἷς εἰμι αὐτάρκης εἶναι. [12] οἶδα καὶ ταπεινοῦσθαι, οἶδα καὶ περισσεύειν· ἐν παντὶ καὶ ἐν πᾶσιν μεμύημαι, καὶ χορτάζεσθαι καὶ πεινᾶν καὶ περισσεύειν καὶ ὑστερεῖσθαι· [13] πάντα ἰσχύω ἐν τῷ ἐνδυναμοῦντί με.

CONTEXT:
Paul expresses his gratitude to the Philippians for their kindness and generosity in 4:10–13.

COMMENTARY:
Paul turns finally to one of the main reasons for writing his letter: to express his gratitude to the Philippians for their generous gift sent through their apostle/messenger, Epaphroditus. In chapter two he has alluded to their kindness and expressed great affection for Epaphroditus, but he has not described the gift in detail until now. We might think that a note of thanks at the end of a letter may look like an afterthought, however, it appears to be a key reason for this letter. This has caused some scholars to suggest that 4:10–20 may have been a separate letter written by Paul soon after the arrival of Epaphroditus and Paul received the gift from the Philippians. This purely hypothetical solution, however, is to be rejected and has been by most recent scholars. There are better explanations for what some imagine as an irregularity.

ἐχάρην > 1SAPI, rejoiced || ἀνεθάλετε > 2PAAI, revived || φρονεῖν > PAN, concern || ἐφρονεῖτε > 2PIAI, were concerned || ἠκαιρεῖσθε > 2PIMI, had [no] opportunity || ὑστέρησιν > need || λέγω > 1SPAI, am speaking || ἔμαθον > 1SAAI, learned || εἰμι > 1SPAI, am || αὐτάρκης > content || εἶναι > PAN, to be || οἶδα > 1SRAI, know || ταπεινοῦσθαι > PPN, to be brought low || περισσεύειν > PAN, to abound || μεμύημαι > 1SRPI, learned the secret || χορτάζεσθαι > PPN, to be satisfied || πεινᾶν > PAN, to be hungry || περισσεύειν > PAN, to abound || ὑστερεῖσθαι > PPN, to lack || ἰσχύω > 1SPAI, can do || ἐνδυναμοῦντι > PAPMSN, who strengthens

Further Reading: Philippians 4:10–20
William C. Varner

COLOSSIANS 1:1-2

¹ Παῦλος ἀπόστολος χριστοῦ Ἰησοῦ διὰ θελήματος θεοῦ καὶ Τιμόθεος ὁ ἀδελφὸς ² τοῖς ἐν Κολοσσαῖς ἁγίοις καὶ πιστοῖς ἀδελφοῖς ἐν χριστῷ· χάρις ὑμῖν καὶ εἰρήνη ἀπὸ θεοῦ πατρὸς ἡμῶν.

CONTEXT:

Paul begins his epistle to the Colossians as he does his other letters, in the customary threefold Hellenistic letterform: the (1) sender(s), to the (2) recipients, with a (3) salutation. These opening salvos are an important but sometimes overlooked part of Paul's letters. Here, we'll focus on verse 2.

COMMENTARY:

After introducing himself and Timothy, Paul describes the recipients in Colossae as ἁγίοις καὶ πιστοῖς ἀδελφοῖς ἐν χριστῷ. Some scholars take ἁγίοις substantivally and translate the phrase "to the saints and faithful brethren in Christ," as in the NKJV. It seems preferable, however, to translate both ἁγίοις and πιστοῖς as adjectivally modifying ἀδελφοῖς since both are governed by τοῖς and joined by καί. If so, the translation would read, "to the holy and faithful brothers (and sisters) in Christ," an admirable description of character and commitment after which to pattern our own lives.

τοῖς ἐν Κολοσσαῖς > to those in Colossae

Further Reading: Colossians 1:1–8
Jeff Kimble

¹⁵ ὅς ἐστιν εἰκὼν τοῦ θεοῦ τοῦ ἀοράτου, πρωτότοκος πάσης κτίσεως· ¹⁶ ὅτι ἐν αὐτῷ ἐκτίσθη τὰ πάντα ἐν τοῖς οὐρανοῖς καὶ ἐπὶ τῆς γῆς, τὰ ὁρατὰ καὶ τὰ ἀόρατα, εἴτε θρόνοι εἴτε κυριότητες εἴτε ἀρχαὶ εἴτε ἐξουσίαι· τὰ πάντα δι᾽ αὐτοῦ καὶ εἰς αὐτὸν ἔκτισται.

CONTEXT:

This passage falls on the heels of Paul's affirmation that God rescued the Colossians from darkness and transferred them into the kingdom of the Son he loves and whose supremacy over all things Paul further describes beginning in 1:15. One phrase deserves special attention in Paul's initial description of Jesus: πρωτότοκος πάσης κτίσεως.

COMMENTARY:

Biblical authors use πρωτότοκος in one of two ways, either literally to mean the *first one born* or metaphorically to mean *preeminent*. Context determines which of the two senses authors intend. Here, Paul uses πρωτότοκος metaphorically to stress Christ's supremacy and uses the genitive modifiers πάσης κτίσεως (most likely objective genitives) to highlight the extent of his supremacy: *over all creation*. In contrast, Jehovah's Witnesses understand πρωτότοκος literally and take it to mean that God created Jesus before he created anything else and take πάσης κτίσεως as partitive genitives meaning that Jesus is *a part of* rather than *over all* creation. They see Jesus as the first being God created, namely, "the firstborn of all creation," (NWT) and not the preeminent, uncreated Lord of the universe. Contrary to what they claim, however, verse 16 affirms that all created things came into existence by Christ and through Christ, which means he cannot be one of those created things.

ἐστιν > 3SPAI, is ‖ ἀοράτου > invisible ‖ πρωτότοκος > firstborn ‖ ἐκτίσθη > 3SAPI, they (i.e., the set of all things) were created ‖ ὁρατά > visible ‖ κυριότητες > dominions ‖ ἔκτισται > 3SRPI, they (the set of all things) have been created

Further Reading: Colossians 1:15–20
Jeff Kimble

[22] νυνὶ δὲ ἀποκατήλλαξεν ἐν τῷ σώματι τῆς σαρκὸς αὐτοῦ διὰ τοῦ θανάτου παραστῆσαι ὑμᾶς ἁγίους καὶ ἀμώμους καὶ ἀνεγκλήτους κατενώπιον αὐτοῦ. [23] Εἴ γε ἐπιμένετε τῇ πίστει τεθεμελιωμένοι καὶ ἑδραῖοι καὶ μὴ μετακινούμενοι ἀπὸ τῆς ἐλπίδος τοῦ εὐαγγελίου οὗ ἠκούσατε, τοῦ κηρυχθέντος ἐν πάσῃ κτίσει τῇ ὑπὸ τὸν οὐρανόν, οὗ ἐγενόμην ἐγὼ Παῦλος διάκονος.

CONTEXT:

This passage concludes the "Christ hymn" begun in verse with 15 by emphasizing Christ's agency in reconciling the Colossians through his death. Whereas previously Paul focused on the vast scope of Christ's reconciling work (note τά πάντα, "all things" in v. 20; 7x in ch. 1), here he adjusts the lens to focus on the reconciliation of those once alienated from God so as to present them before Him holy and free of accusation (22)—but not without an important stipulation: to continue in the faith.

COMMENTARY:

As elsewhere in Paul's letters, a pattern of initiative and response occurs here: God's initiative through Christ in reconciling sinners to himself results in a call to stand fast in the hope of the gospel as its appropriate response. Verse 23, for instance, opens with εἴ γε, which introduces a first-class condition modifying the infinitive παραστῆσαι in verse 22 (notice, here that the result precedes the condition). The condition calls them to ἐπιμένετε τῇ πίστει, which could refer to their personal faith or the gospel itself. In either case, the condition to ἐπιμένετε τῇ πίστει τεθεμελιωμένοι, καὶ ἑδραῖοι καὶ μὴ μετακινούμενοι calls for a response to the initiative of God on their behalf. This reflects Paul's optimism that the hope of the gospel will take root in their hearts such that they will stand before God holy and blameless on that final day.

ἀποκατήλλαξεν > 3SAAI, he reconciled ‖ παραστῆσαι > AAN, to present ‖ ἀμώμους > blameless ‖ ἀνεγκλήτους > irreproachable ‖ κατενώπιον > before ‖ ἐπιμένετε > 2PPAI, you remain ‖ τεθεμελιωμένοι > RPPMPN, having been established ‖ ἑδραῖοι > steadfast ‖ μετακινούμενοι > PPPMPN, being moved ‖ κηρυχθέντος > APPNSG, proclaimed

Further Reading: Colossians 1:21–29
Jeff Kimble

COLOSSIANS 2:4–5

⁴ τοῦτο λέγω, ἵνα μηδεὶς ὑμᾶς παραλογίζηται ἐν πιθανολογίᾳ· ⁵ εἰ γὰρ καὶ τῇ σαρκὶ ἄπειμι, ἀλλὰ τῷ πνεύματι σὺν ὑμῖν εἰμί, χαίρων καὶ βλέπων ὑμῶν τὴν τάξιν καὶ τὸ στερέωμα τῆς εἰς χριστὸν πίστεως ὑμῶν.

CONTEXT:

In his labors for the church, Paul presents God's mystery in its fullness (1:25–26), namely, that in Christ the Gentiles have become joint heirs with the people of God through faith. Moreover, in 1:28, Paul expresses the goal of his preaching: to present everyone complete in Christ that they may be encouraged in heart, united in love, and safeguarded from error through the knowledge of Christ, "in whom are hidden all the treasures of wisdom and knowledge" (2:3).

COMMENTARY:

The phrase τοῦτο λέγω in verse 4 likely points back to Paul's remarks about the supremacy of Christ in the previous chapter. Here, he warns the Colossians not to be enticed by persuasive arguments that could undermine their allegiance to Christ. Pivoting off the sufficiency of the wisdom and knowledge found in Christ (v. 3), Paul raises this caution: τοῦτο λέγω, ἵνα μηδεὶς ὑμᾶς παραλογίζηται ἐν πιθανολογίᾳ. Notice the ἵνα clause; it is often used to denote either a purpose or a result. In this context, it likely denotes Paul's purpose: to prevent the Colossians from being deceived through specious and speculative arguments and, as he later asserts in verse 8, being captured "by hollow and deceptive philosophy." Paul concerns himself here with his audience's ongoing loyalty to Christ in both mind and heart, as he endeavors to shore up their confidence in Christ's sufficiency to establish them in the faith and to keep their lives well-ordered.

παραλογίζηται > 3SPPS, may deceive ‖ πιθανολογίᾳ > persuasive words, persuasive speech ‖ ἄπειμι > 1SPAI, I am absent ‖ τάξιν > good order (i.e., orderly conduct) ‖ στερέωμα > firmness

Further Reading: Colossians 2:1–7
Jeff Kimble

[16] μὴ οὖν τίς ὑμᾶς κρινέτω ἐν βρώσει καὶ ἐν πόσει ἢ ἐν μέρει ἑορτῆς ἢ νουμηνίας ἢ σαββάτων, [17] ἅ ἐστιν σκιὰ τῶν μελλόντων, τὸ δὲ σῶμα τοῦ χριστοῦ.

CONTEXT:

Previously in 2:8–15, Paul warned the Colossians against a pernicious philosophy, possibly related to some form of Jewish mysticism, and associated with cosmic powers and human practices that ultimately enslaved its adherents. Now, however, in light of Christ's exaltation as divine head over all spiritual powers and the Colossians' participation in his death and resurrection, they need not submit themselves to these forces or rituals or any spiritual evaluation based on them. From this they had been freed.

COMMENTARY:

With the opening οὖν, Paul shifts his attention to a critique of the practices associated with this false philosophy: ἐν βρώσει καὶ ἐν πόσει ἢ ἐν μέρει ἑορτῆς ἢ νουμηνίας ἢ σαββάτων. The first two practices (i.e., ἐν βρώσει καὶ ἐν πόσει) are probably datives of reference or respect and may refer to kosher food laws. The final three practices, ἑορτῆς ἢ νουμηνίας ἢ σαββάτων, when found together in the OT often refer to rituals associated with Jewish festal days. So it appears that these false teachers held some form of Torah observance as an essential marker of authentic faith. Here, Paul warns his readers that no one should be judged by this standard (Μὴ οὖν τίς ὑμᾶς κρινέτω ἐν βρώσει καὶ ἐν πόσει ἢ ἐν μέρει ἑορτῆς ἢ νουμηνίας ἢ σαββάτων). For Paul, such forms of Torah observance merely foreshadowed the reality that ultimately set them apart as people of God: *the sufficiency of life in Jesus the Messiah.* Any veneer of religious identity associated with these various Torah practices was superseded by their new identity in Him and by conforming their lives to Him. In verse 17, Paul contrasts the shadow (σκιά) of these so-called identity markers and their substance or reality (σῶμα), which is found solely in their relationship with Christ.

κρινέτω > 3SPAM, let him [not] judge || **βρώσει** > eating || **πόσει** > drinking || **ἐν μέρει** > in regard to || **ἑορτῆς** > festival or feast || **νουμηνίας** > new moon || **σκιά** > shadow || **μελλόντων** > PAPNPG, about to be

Further Reading: Colossians 2:8–15
Jeff Kimble

MAY 31
COLOSSIANS 3:1-2

¹ εἰ οὖν συνηγέρθητε τῷ χριστῷ, τὰ ἄνω ζητεῖτε, οὗ ὁ χριστός ἐστιν ἐν δεξιᾷ τοῦ θεοῦ καθήμενος· ² τὰ ἄνω φρονεῖτε μὴ τὰ ἐπὶ τῆς γῆς.

CONTEXT:

This passage begins a new unit in the letter that touches on the practical entailments of participating in Christ's death introduced in 2:20 and now here in 3:1 sharing in his resurrection. (Note the connection between the conditionals in these two passages.) In contrast to the false teachers who encouraged the worship of angels, Paul admonishes his audience to set their minds on things above, not where angels dwell, but where Christ is sitting—a thoroughly Christocentric orientation.

COMMENTARY:

Paul introduces this admonition with a first-class conditional statement Εἰ οὖν συνηγέρθητε τῷ χριστῷ (in which the protasis is assumed to be true) followed by an imperative τὰ ἄνω ζητεῖτε, which points to Christ as the true object of worship. Note that the article in τὰ ἄνω "nominalizes" the adverb so that it functions as a noun. Since Paul's audience shares in Christ's resurrection (the reality of their present situation), the called-for response entails seeking the things above and centering their lives on Christ, who sits in the place of preeminence and authority. Moreover, as Paul spells out in more detail later (see 3:5-10), this involves abandoning their former pagan life and embodying a new life fixed on and sustained by Christ.

συνηγέρθητε > 2PAPI, you were raised up with || τὰ ἄνω > the things above || ζητεῖτε > 2PPAM, you seek || ἐν δεξιᾷ > at the right hand || καθήμενος > PMPMSN, sitting || φρονεῖτε > 2PPAM, set your mind on

Further Reading: Colossians 3:1-10
Jeff Kimble

151

COLOSSIANS 3:12–13

¹² ἐνδύσασθε οὖν, ὡς ἐκλεκτοὶ τοῦ θεοῦ ἅγιοι καὶ ἠγαπημένοι, σπλάγχνα οἰκτειρμοῦ, χρηστότητα, ταπεινοφροσύνην, πραΰτητα, μακροθυμίαν· ¹³ ἀνεχόμενοι ἀλλήλων καὶ χαριζόμενοι ἑαυτοῖς ἐάν τις πρός τινα ἔχῃ μομφήν· καθὼς καὶ ὁ κύριος ἐχαρίσατο ὑμῖν, οὕτως καὶ ὑμεῖς.

CONTEXT:

This passage contrasts with 3:8–11, in which Paul admonishes the Colossians to put off "the old man and his practices" and all that entails. He now unpacks what it means to put on "the new man." Note that what Paul calls them to put on reflects their present status as chosen ones of God.

COMMENTARY:

In keeping with this new identity, Paul admonishes the Colossians to ἐνδύσασθε virtues that sustain love within the community. To head the virtue list, Paul asks them to put on σπλάγχνα οἰκτειρμοῦ, where the genitive likely functions in an attributive sense and thereby describes the noun. In verse 13, two participle phrases follow: "forbearing one another and forgiving each other" (ἀνεχόμενοι ἀλλήλων καὶ χαριζόμενοι ἑαυτοῖς), which modify the main clause beginning with ἐνδύσασθε. They also complete a third-class conditional statement where the protasis (the "if-clause") follows the apodosis (the "then-clause"). It's an unusual construction because the protasis usually comes first (ἐάν τις πρός τινα ἔχῃ μομφήν). But note how the preceding virtues (compassion, kindness, humility, meekness, and longsuffering) contribute to expressions of forgiveness and forbearance in the church. All together, these virtues are to adorn believers with garments of grace that encourage harmony among God's people.

ἐνδύσασθε > 2PAMM, put on ‖ ἐκλεκτοί > chosen, elect ‖ ἠγαπημένοι > RPPMPN, beloved ‖ σπλάγχνα > hearts ‖ οἰκτειρμοῦ > mercy, compassion ‖ χρηστότητα > kindness ‖ ταπεινοφροσύνην > humility ‖ πραΰτητα > gentleness ‖ μακροθυμίαν > longsuffering ‖ ἀνεχόμενοι > PMPMPN, forbearing ‖ χαριζόμενοι > PMPMPN, forgiving ‖ μομφήν > complaint ‖ ἐχαρίσατο > 3SAMI, has forgiven

Further Reading: Colossians 3:1–11; Galatians 5:22
Jeff Kimble

COLOSSIANS 3:16–17

^{16} ὁ λόγος τοῦ χριστοῦ ἐνοικείτω ἐν ὑμῖν πλουσίως, ἐν πάσῃ σοφίᾳ, διδάσκοντες καὶ νουθετοῦντες ἑαυτοὺς ψαλμοῖς, ὕμνοις, ᾠδαῖς πνευματικαῖς ἐν χάριτι ᾄδοντες ἐν ταῖς καρδίαις ὑμῶν τῷ θεῷ· ^{17} καὶ πᾶν ὅ τι ἐὰν ποιῆτε ἐν λόγῳ ἢ ἐν ἔργῳ, πάντα ἐν ὀνόματι κυρίου Ἰησοῦ εὐχαριστοῦντες τῷ θεῷ πατρὶ δι' αὐτοῦ.

CONTEXT:

The previous list of Christian virtues that Paul commends to these believers (see 3:12–15) focused primarily on traits that foster harmony in their lives together as a community marked by peace. So, Paul says, "Let the peace of Christ rule in your hearts," followed by an equally important imperative in verse 16, "Let the message of Christ dwell in your midst," or possibly "indwell you," depending on how one understands the phrase ἐν ὑμῖν.

COMMENTARY:

Most likely the phrase ἐν ὑμῖν, carries a corporate sense (i.e., let the message of Christ dwell *among you*) with the phrase ἐν πάσῃ σοφίᾳ modifying the two participles διδάσκοντες καὶ νουθετοῦντες, thus "teaching and admonishing in all wisdom." The three instrumental datives ψαλμοῖς, ὕμνοις, and ᾠδαῖς πνευματικαῖς express the means through which the teaching and admonishing take place. Note the close correlation between worship and instruction here. By means of the psalms, hymns, and spiritual songs sung in worship, we teach and admonish one another in the word of Christ. This is one way His word dwells among us. Not only in worship, but in everything we do (καὶ πᾶν ὅ τι ἐὰν ποιῆτε ἐν λόγῳ ἢ ἐν ἔργῳ) Paul admonishes believers to keep Christ central so that, in effect, worship encompasses every aspect of our lives.

ἐνοικείτω > 3SPAM, let dwell || πλουσίως > richly || διδάσκοντες > PAPMPN, teaching || νουθετοῦντες > PAPMPN, admonishing || ψαλμοῖς > psalms || ὕμνοις > hymns || ᾠδαῖς > songs || ᾄδοντες > PAPMPN, singing || ποιῆτε > 2PPAS, you should do || εὐχαριστοῦντες > PAPMPN, giving thanks

Further Reading: Colossians 3:12–17
Jeff Kimble

COLOSSIANS 4:2-4

² τῇ προσευχῇ προσκαρτερεῖτε, γρηγοροῦντες ἐν αὐτῇ ἐν εὐχαριστίᾳ,
³ προσευχόμενοι ἅμα καὶ περὶ ἡμῶν, ἵνα ὁ θεὸς ἀνοίξῃ ἡμῖν θύραν τοῦ
λόγου, λαλῆσαι τὸ μυστήριον τοῦ Χριστοῦ, δι' ὃ καὶ δέδεμαι, ⁴ ἵνα
φανερώσω αὐτὸ ὡς δεῖ με λαλῆσαι.

CONTEXT:
As Paul moves toward his closing remarks in 4:7-18, he ends the body of his
letter with two imperatives: τῇ προσευχῇ προσκαρτερεῖτε (v. 2) and ἐν σοφίᾳ
περιπατεῖτε (v. 5), with verses 2-4 focused on prayer and 5-6 focused on walking
wisely before outsiders. We'll give our attention to verses 2-4.

COMMENTARY:
Beginning with τῇ προσευχῇ ("in prayer"), the dative complement of the plural
imperative προσκαρτερεῖτε ("be devoted"), Paul admonishes the Colossian
church to a life of constant prayer, reminiscent of Jesus' words to "always pray
and not give up" (Lk 18:1). Paul likewise describes the way to approach such
prayer: γρηγοροῦντες ἐν αὐτῇ ἐν εὐχαριστίᾳ, literally, "watching in it with
thanksgiving." The circumstantial participle γρηγοροῦντες along with ἐν αὐτῇ
suggests that this call to "watchfulness" means that the Colossians should
demonstrate their devotion to prayer by guarding their time of prayer. Perhaps
it builds on the idea of watching for the coming of Christ or remaining vigilant
in a time of danger; note that it is an active participle. However one understands
γρηγοροῦντες, devotion to prayer was characteristic of the early church (Acts
2:42) and Paul hoped to see it observed, replicated, and guarded in his Gentile
congregations.

προσκαρτερεῖτε > 2PPAM, be devoted, continue || **γρηγοροῦντες** > PAPMPN,
watching, guarding || **εὐχαριστίᾳ** > thanksgiving || **προσευχόμενοι** > PMPMPN,
praying || **ἅμα**, together || **ἀνοίξῃ** > 3SAAS, may open || **λαλῆσαι** > AAN, to speak
|| **δέδεμαι** > 1SRPI, I have been bound || **φανερώσω** > 1SAAS, I may make clear

Further Reading: Colossians 4:2-6; Luke 18:1-8
Jeff Kimble

JUNE 4
COLOSSIANS 4:12-13

¹²ἀσπάζεται ὑμᾶς Ἐπαφρᾶς ὁ ἐξ ὑμῶν, δοῦλος χριστοῦ Ἰησοῦ, πάντοτε ἀγωνιζόμενος ὑπὲρ ὑμῶν ἐν ταῖς προσευχαῖς, ἵνα σταθῆτε τέλειοι καὶ πεπληροφορημένοι ἐν παντὶ θελήματι τοῦ θεοῦ. ¹³μαρτυρῶ γὰρ αὐτῷ ὅτι ἔχει πολὺν πόνον ὑπὲρ ὑμῶν καὶ τῶν ἐν Λαοδικίᾳ καὶ τῶν ἐν Ἱεραπόλει.

CONTEXT:
At the close of his epistles, Paul frequently extends greetings from his companions to the church, acknowledging their contribution to the gospel mission and their efforts on the church's behalf. He does this here as well. His present entourage of co-workers includes both Jews and Gentiles, which includes three members of the church in Colossae: Tychicus, Onesimus and Epaphras.

COMMENTARY:
Paul intends to send Tychicus and Onesimus back with an updated report on his circumstances (4:7-9). Epaphras, probably the founder of the church (1:7), sends his greeting as well (1:12). In his closing remarks, Paul highlights the pastoral care and intensity of Epaphras's prayers for them in the phrase πάντοτε ἀγωνιζόμενος ὑπὲρ ὑμῶν ἐν ταῖς προσευχαῖς. Paul uses the same word (i.e., ἀγωνιζόμενος) earlier in the letter (1:29) to describe his own efforts "to present everyone fully mature in Christ." The purpose of Epaphras's prayer, introduced by ἵνα (although some scholars hold that ἵνα may here focus more on content than purpose), echoes Paul's earlier emphasis: that these believers σταθῆτε τέλειοι καὶ πεπληροφορημένοι ἐν παντὶ θελήματι τοῦ θεοῦ. Here, as elsewhere, maturity in Christ tops the list of prayer concerns for the people of God—a concern Epaphras *strives in prayer* to see accomplished among the Colossians.

ἀσπάζεται > 3SPMI, greets ‖ Ἐπαφρᾶς > Epaphras ‖ ἀγωνιζόμενος > PMPMSN, striving ‖ σταθῆτε > 2PAPS, you might stand ‖ τέλειοι > complete, perfect, mature ‖ πεπληροφορημένοι > RPPMPN, fully assured ‖ μαρτυρῶ > 1SPAI, I bear witness ‖ πολὺν πόνον > much distress ‖ Λαοδικίᾳ > Laodicea ‖ Ἱεραπόλει > Hierapolis

Further Reading: Colossians 4:7-18
Jeff Kimble

...³ ἔδοξε κἀμοὶ παρηκολουθηκότι ἄνωθεν πᾶσιν ἀκριβῶς καθεξῆς σοι γράψαι, κράτιστε Θεόφιλε, ⁴ ἵνα ἐπιγνῷς περὶ ὧν κατηχήθης λόγων τὴν ἀσφάλειαν.

CONTEXT:

The prologue to Luke (1:1–4) is composed of a single sentence in the Greek text, and it is perhaps the strongest example of polished Greek literary style in the entire NT. Verses 1–2 form the protasis of this sentence, identifying the existence of other accounts of the gospel that were derived directly from the testimony of eyewitnesses, while verses 3–4 form the apodosis of the sentence.

COMMENTARY:

Luke identifies the target audience of his letter, likely a man of influence named *Theophilus*, and furnishes his own qualifications for writing the treatise in verse 3. Perhaps the most significant statement that is made in Luke's prologue is the statement of authorial intent given in verse 4. The subjunctive can be used to express purpose, and the statement ἵνα ἐπιγνῷς is used by the author to draw the reader's attention as to *why* he set out to write this magnificent Gospel; it was for the purpose of demonstrating the *certainty* of the events of Jesus Christ's life and ministry. We too can rest in the certainty of every word, action, and miracle recorded in the Gospel account. Following Luke's pattern, we should also endeavor to express the certainty of the Gospel to others.

ἔδοξε > 3SAAI, it seemed || **κἀμοί** > to me also || **παρηκολουθηκότι** > RAPMSD, having investigated || **ἄνωθεν** > from the beginning || **ἀκριβῶς** > carefully, accurately || **καθεξῆς** > in order || **κράτιστε** > most honorable || **Θεόφιλε** > Theophilus || **κατηχήθης** > 2SAPI, you have been taught || **ἀσφάλειαν** > certainty

Further Reading: Luke 1:1–4
Eric M. McConnell

³¹ καὶ ἰδοὺ συλλήμψῃ ἐν γαστρὶ καὶ τέξῃ υἱὸν καὶ καλέσεις τὸ ὄνομα αὐτοῦ Ἰησοῦν. ³² οὗτος ἔσται μέγας καὶ υἱὸς ὑψίστου κληθήσεται καὶ δώσει αὐτῷ κύριος ὁ θεὸς τὸν θρόνον Δαυὶδ τοῦ πατρὸς αὐτοῦ, ³³ καὶ βασιλεύσει ἐπὶ τὸν οἶκον Ἰακὼβ εἰς τοὺς αἰῶνας καὶ τῆς βασιλείας αὐτοῦ οὐκ ἔσται τέλος.

CONTEXT:

In this passage, the angel Gabriel is sent by God to bring a message concerning the birth of Jesus to Mary. This angelic announcement is unique to the Gospel of Luke.

COMMENTARY:

The angel's message to Mary contains multiple future tense verbs, most of which are predictive future. However, the angel's statement in verse 31— καλέσεις—is imperatival future, as Mary is instructed to name the child *Jesus*. The prophetic statements made by the angel are wide in scope. First, they deal immediately with Mary, speaking of the conception and birth of the child. Second, they deal with the character and exaltation of the Son, for example, οὗτος ἔσται μέγας. Third, the angel's announcement contained eschatological statements concerning the earthly reign of Jesus that will commence at his Second Coming, such as the promise *"the Lord God will give him the throne of David his father."* Just as Mary looked with faith to the fulfillment of these promises, we too can anticipate the fulfillment of the eschatological elements of the angel's announcement. *Maranatha!*

συλλήμψῃ > 2SFMI, you will conceive ‖ γαστρί > womb ‖ τέξῃ > 2SFMI, you will give birth ‖ ὑψίστου > most high ‖ δώσει > 3SFAI, he will give ‖ βασιλεύσει > 3SFAI, he will rule

Further Reading: Luke 1:26–38
Eric M. McConnell

LUKE 1:68–70

⁶⁸ εὐλογητὸς κύριος ὁ θεὸς τοῦ Ἰσραήλ,
   ὅτι ἐπεσκέψατο καὶ ἐποίησεν λύτρωσιν τῷ λαῷ αὐτοῦ,
⁶⁹ καὶ ἤγειρεν κέρας σωτηρίας ἡμῖν ἐν οἴκῳ Δαυὶδ παιδὸς αὐτοῦ,
⁷⁰ καθὼς ἐλάλησεν διὰ στόματος τῶν ἁγίων ἀπ᾽ αἰῶνος προφητῶν αὐτοῦ.

CONTEXT:

This passage records a prophecy from Zechariah (transl. Zacharias), the father of John the Baptist, that is often referred to as *the Benedictus*, its first Latin word. The contents of this prophecy reflect on the promises of God to his people, the prophetic ministry of John, and the redemptive work of the Messiah.

COMMENTARY:

No longer mute, Zacharias spoke a magnificent prophecy as he was filled with the Holy Spirit. Zacharias proclaimed, "*Blessed be the Lord God of Israel*," and he continued throughout his *Benedictus* listing reasons that God was to be praised. Verses 68–69 contain three aorist verbs that describe the work of God that was transpiring: ἐπεσκέψατο, ἐποίησεν, and ἤγειρεν. These verbs are modified by an adverbial clause in verse 70, which acknowledged that all of these things were happening καθὼς ἐλάλησεν, just as God spoke by the holy prophets of old. This prophecy demonstrates the value of believing and patiently waiting for God's promises; Zacharias had been anticipating God's covenant promises throughout his lifetime and now they were being fulfilled before his very eyes.

εὐλογητός > blessed, well spoken of ‖ ἐπεσκέψατο > 3SAMI, he has visited ‖ λύτρωσιν > redemption ‖ κέρας > horn ‖ παιδός > servant

Further Reading: Luke 1:67–79
Eric M. McConnell

JUNE 8
LUKE 3:15–16

¹⁵ προσδοκῶντος δὲ τοῦ λαοῦ καὶ διαλογιζομένων πάντων ἐν ταῖς καρδίαις αὐτῶν περὶ τοῦ Ἰωάννου, μήποτε αὐτὸς εἴη ὁ χριστός, ¹⁶ ἀπεκρίνατο λέγων πᾶσιν ὁ Ἰωάννης· ἐγὼ μὲν ὕδατι βαπτίζω ὑμᾶς· ἔρχεται δὲ ὁ ἰσχυρότερός μου, οὗ οὐκ εἰμὶ ἱκανὸς λῦσαι τὸν ἱμάντα τῶν ὑποδημάτων αὐτοῦ· αὐτὸς ὑμᾶς βαπτίσει ἐν πνεύματι ἁγίῳ καὶ πυρί.

CONTEXT:
Luke 3 details the ministry of John the Baptist, which included a baptism of repentance, as well as a call to live righteously. The content and delivery of his message was bold, and crowds of people came to him to be baptized.

COMMENTARY:
The verb εἴη in verse 15 is in the optative mood. While the optative may be used to express a desire or wish, the optative is used in this passage to express the possibility of something being true. Due to the overwhelming response to the ministry of John the Baptist, people began to wonder *whether or not he could be the Messiah*. When fielding this question, John did not hesitate to indicate that there was one coming who was far greater than himself. While John baptized with water, he described the greater work of the one coming after him by stating, αὐτὸς ὑμᾶς βαπτίσει ἐν πνεύματι ἁγίῳ καὶ πυρί. John's role was vital, but he was merely preparing the way for the Messiah for whom the people had been waiting.

προσδοκῶντος > PAPMSG, expecting ‖ διαλογιζομένων > PMPMPG, wondered, wondering, pondering ‖ εἴη > 3SPAO, might be ‖ ἱμάντα > strap ‖ ὑποδημάτων > sandals

Further Reading: Luke 3:1–22
Eric M. McConnell

159

²⁰ καὶ αὐτὸς ἐπάρας τοὺς ὀφθαλμοὺς αὐτοῦ εἰς τοὺς μαθητὰς αὐτοῦ ἔλεγεν, Μακάριοι οἱ πτωχοί, ὅτι ὑμετέρα ἐστὶν ἡ βασιλεία τοῦ θεοῦ.

CONTEXT:

Luke 6:20-49 closely mirrors the message given in the Sermon on the Mount, although these two messages were thought to have been given at different times during the earthly ministry of Christ. This passage is known as *The Beatitudes of Luke* or *Luke's Blessings and Woes.*

COMMENTARY:

Luke's beatitudes and woes are highly structured and balanced. The first portion, verses 20–23, contains four blessings (μακάριοι), while the second portion, verses 24–26, contains four woes (οὐαί). The blessings and woes are followed by a rationale for each blessing or woe. The first beatitude states, μακάριοι οἱ πτωχοί. At face value, this statement seems to defy logic. However, the reason that they are blessed is stated immediately afterwards; ὅτι ὑμετέρα ἐστὶν ἡ βασιλεία τοῦ θεοῦ. The ὅτι is used in this instance to introduce a dependent causal clause, and a similar structure is utilized throughout this passage. Luke's blessings and woes describe the epitome of Christlike living, along with the consequences that result from righteous and unrighteous living.

ἐπάρας > AAPMSN, lifting ‖ **μακάριοι** > blessed ‖ **πτωχοί** > poor ‖ **ὑμετέρα** > belonging to you

Further Reading: Luke 6:20–49
Eric M. McConnell

³⁷ καὶ ἰδοὺ γυνὴ ἥτις ἦν ἐν τῇ πόλει ἁμαρτωλός, καὶ ἐπιγνοῦσα ὅτι κατάκειται ἐν τῇ οἰκίᾳ τοῦ Φαρισαίου, κομίσασα ἀλάβαστρον μύρου ³⁸ καὶ στᾶσα ὀπίσω παρὰ τοὺς πόδας αὐτοῦ κλαίουσα τοῖς δάκρυσιν ἤρξατο βρέχειν τοὺς πόδας αὐτοῦ καὶ ταῖς θριξὶν τῆς κεφαλῆς αὐτῆς ἐξέμασσεν καὶ κατεφίλει τοὺς πόδας αὐτοῦ καὶ ἤλειφεν τῷ μύρῳ. ³⁹ ἰδὼν δὲ ὁ Φαρισαῖος ὁ καλέσας αὐτὸν εἶπεν ἐν ἑαυτῷ λέγων· οὗτος εἰ ἦν προφήτης, ἐγίνωσκεν ἂν τίς καὶ ποταπὴ ἡ γυνὴ ἥτις ἅπτεται αὐτοῦ, ὅτι ἁμαρτωλός ἐστιν.

CONTEXT:

In Luke 7, Simon the Pharisee hosts Jesus in his home. A woman enters the house to render an act of humble service to Jesus.

COMMENTARY:

When employed in narratives, ἰδού is used to engage the imagination of the reader, as if to say, *Picture this!* This exclamation is employed in 7:37 to draw the reader's attention to a woman who was *a sinner*. In perhaps the most tender act of service to Jesus that is recorded in the gospels, the actions of the woman are highlighted with the imperfect verbs ἐξέμασσεν, κατεφίλει, and ἤλειφεν. Taken aback, the Pharisee who was hosting Jesus began to reason within himself. His inward statement, οὗτος εἰ ἦν προφήτης, introduces a second-class condition, which in this instance, is a *presumed* contrary-to-fact statement. Simon the Pharisee was inwardly doubting Jesus' supernatural discernment, but he was about to have his very thoughts rebuked by the Lord's parable concerning two debtors. The conclusion of this narrative (7:48–50) maximizes the power and extent of Christ's forgiveness while repudiating the error of self-righteousness.

κατάκειται > 3SPMI, reclining to eat ‖ κομίσασα > AAPFSN, having brought ‖ ἀλάβαστρον > jar ‖ μύρου > fragrant ointment ‖ δάκρυσιν > tears ‖ βρέχειν > PAN, to wet ‖ θριξίν > hair ‖ ἐξέμασσεν > 3SIAI, was drying ‖ κατεφίλει > 3SIAI, was kissing ‖ ἤλειφεν > 3SIAI, was anointing ‖ ποταπή > of what sort

Further Reading: 7:36–50
Eric M. McConnell

⁴³ ἐξεπλήσσοντο δὲ πάντες ἐπὶ τῇ μεγαλειότητι τοῦ θεοῦ. Πάντων δὲ θαυμαζόντων ἐπὶ πᾶσιν οἷς ἐποίει εἶπεν πρὸς τοὺς μαθητὰς αὐτοῦ· ⁴⁴ θέσθε ὑμεῖς εἰς τὰ ὦτα ὑμῶν τοὺς λόγους τούτους· ὁ γὰρ υἱὸς τοῦ ἀνθρώπου μέλλει παραδίδοσθαι εἰς χεῖρας ἀνθρώπων. ⁴⁵ οἱ δὲ ἠγνόουν τὸ ῥῆμα τοῦτο καὶ ἦν παρακεκαλυμμένον ἀπ᾽ αὐτῶν ἵνα μὴ αἴσθωνται αὐτό, καὶ ἐφοβοῦντο ἐρωτῆσαι αὐτὸν περὶ τοῦ ῥήματος τούτου.

CONTEXT:

Luke 9:37–45 describes the deliverance of a demon-possessed child, a miracle that took place as Jesus was met by a crowd upon his descent from the Mount of Transfiguration. After admonishing the disciples for their failure to help the child, Jesus cast out the demon, healed the child, and presented him to his father.

COMMENTARY:

While the main events of the narrative are driven by the aorist active verb, the imperfect verb is used in verses 43–45 to highlight the inward thoughts of the disciples; reacting to the actions and words of Jesus, the disciples were *astonished* (v. 43), they *did not understand* (v. 45), and they *feared* (v. 45). While the apostles were still fixated on the miraculous deliverance of the demon-possessed child, Jesus charged his disciples to pay close attention to his words concerning the events that would lead to his death. Verse 45 demonstrates an abrupt change in the disciples' hearts and minds; they shifted from astonishment to confusion, which was coupled with their fearfulness to ask Jesus for an explanation. The thoughts of the disciples are utilized by the author to immerse the reader in the narrative in a vivid way, and it becomes clear to the reader that the disciples failed to let the words of Jesus *sink into their ears*.

ἐξεπλήσσοντο > 3PIPI, they were amazed || μεγαλειότης > grandeur, majesty || θαυμαζόντων > PAPMPG, marveling || θέσθε > 2PAMM, let sink || ὦτα > ears || παρακεκαλυμμένον > RPPNSN, hidden || αἴσθωνται > 3PAMS, might perceive || ἐρωτῆσαι > AAN, to ask

Further Reading: Luke 9:37–45
Eric M. McConnell

LUKE 10:19-20

¹⁹ ἰδοὺ δέδωκα ὑμῖν τὴν ἐξουσίαν τοῦ πατεῖν ἐπάνω ὄφεων καὶ σκορπίων, καὶ ἐπὶ πᾶσαν τὴν δύναμιν τοῦ ἐχθροῦ, καὶ οὐδὲν ὑμᾶς οὐ μὴ ἀδικήσῃ. ²⁰ πλὴν ἐν τούτῳ μὴ χαίρετε ὅτι τὰ πνεύματα ὑμῖν ὑποτάσσεται, χαίρετε δὲ ὅτι τὰ ὀνόματα ὑμῶν ἐγγέγραπται ἐν τοῖς οὐρανοῖς.

CONTEXT:

In Luke 10, Jesus commissioned seventy, in pairs of two, to proceed before his entrance to particular cities and places. He gave them instructions concerning their work, and he sent them out with authority.

COMMENTARY:

The seventy returned to the Lord, exclaiming with joy that the devils were subject to them, but Jesus turned their attention to a far greater blessing. He first acknowledged the authority that was given to them; in verse 19, Jesus described supernatural authority that the seventy possessed over the most harmful adversaries in both the physical and spiritual realms by stating καὶ οὐδὲν ὑμᾶς οὐ μὴ ἀδικήσῃ. Jesus used a prohibitive imperative, πλὴν ἐν τούτῳ μὴ χαίρετε, to turn the focus on the more important blessing; their temporary authority on earth could not be compared with the fact that their names were written in heaven. Heavenly inheritance always outweighs the temporary nature of earthly blessings and influence.

δέδωκα > 1SRAI, I have given ‖ πατεῖν > PAN, to walk ‖ ἐπάνω > on ‖ ὄφεων > snakes ‖ ἐχθροῦ > enemy ‖ πλὴν > yet, but, nevertheless, except ‖ ἐγγέγραπται > 3SRPI, it is written

Further Reading: Luke 10:1-20
Eric M. McConnell

JUNE 13
LUKE 10:36-37

³⁶ τίς τούτων τῶν τριῶν πλησίον δοκεῖ σοι γεγονέναι τοῦ ἐμπεσόντος εἰς τοὺς λῃστάς; ³⁷ ὁ δὲ εἶπεν· ὁ ποιήσας τὸ ἔλεος μετ' αὐτοῦ. εἶπεν δὲ αὐτῷ ὁ Ἰησοῦς· πορεύου καὶ σὺ ποίει ὁμοίως.

CONTEXT:

In this passage, a lawyer attempts to test Jesus by asking how one can obtain eternal life. Replying to Jesus' command to love God with all his being and his neighbor as himself, the lawyer tried to justify himself by asking *who* his neighbor was. Jesus responded with the parable of the Good Samaritan, which is unique to Luke's Gospel.

COMMENTARY:

In the parable, Jesus described the reaction from three individuals when encountering a man who was beaten by robbers and left to die; only one individual, the Samaritan, was willing to help him. The aid that was rendered by the Samaritan demonstrated extraordinary compassion for this stranger who was beaten and deserted. Jesus asked the lawyer which of the three was a neighbor to the victim of the robbers. The man did not refer to him as *the Samaritan*, as Jesus did; rather, he identified him as ὁ ποιήσας τὸ ἔλεος μετ' αὐτοῦ. Although the lawyer's identification could have been an aversion to uttering the term *Samaritan*, more likely this was a statement that emphasized the compassion displayed, which is the central theme of the parable. Jesus masterfully used the parable to rebut the lawyer's test, and the discussion ended with a simple call to action from Jesus, "Go and do likewise." If we wonder why Jesus is telling the lawyer to perform works in order to inherit eternal life, we need only to observe that Jesus is simply answering the lawyer's question precisely as he asked it, telling him what *he* must *do* to inherit eternal life.

πλησίον > neighbor ‖ γεγονέναι > RAN, to be ‖ ἐμπεσόντος > AAPMSG, fallen ‖ λῃστάς > robber

Further Reading: Luke 10:25-37
Eric M. McConnell

⁴⁰ ἡ δὲ Μάρθα περιεσπᾶτο περὶ πολλὴν διακονίαν· ἐπιστᾶσα δὲ εἶπεν· κύριε, οὐ μέλει σοι ὅτι ἡ ἀδελφή μου μόνην με κατέλιπεν διακονεῖν; εἰπὲ οὖν αὐτῇ ἵνα μοι συναντιλάβηται. ⁴¹ ἀποκριθεὶς δὲ εἶπεν αὐτῇ ὁ κύριος· Μάρθα Μάρθα, μεριμνᾷς καὶ θορυβάζῃ περὶ πολλά, ⁴² ἑνὸς δέ ἐστιν χρεία· Μαριὰμ γὰρ τὴν ἀγαθὴν μερίδα ἐξελέξατο ἥτις οὐκ ἀφαιρεθήσεται αὐτῆς.

CONTEXT:

In a pericope that is unique to Luke, Jesus visits Martha's home. While Martha was overwhelmed by the task of playing the host, her sister Mary sat at the feet of Jesus to listen to his teaching.

COMMENTARY:

While Martha was busy serving, she was bothered by a perceived neglect of responsibility on the part of her sister Mary. Martha confronted Jesus about this perceived injustice with an accusatory tone, marked by the question οὐ μέλει σοι. Martha followed her question with instructions for the Lord as to how he ought to have rectified the situation. Jesus replied by saying her name twice, Μάρθα Μάρθα; this double vocative was employed to draw her attention to the importance of the message that would follow. A contrast is made by Jesus; while Martha was anxious and troubled about *many things*, Mary chose the *one thing* that was both necessary and good. Martha was not rebuked for wanting to serve; instead, she was instructed that, rather than serving Jesus at that moment, it was needful for her to be fed by him.

περιεσπᾶτο > 3SIPI, was overburdened, distracted ‖ ἐπιστᾶσα > AAPFSN, standing near ‖ μέλει σοι > 3SPAI, you care ‖ κατέλιπεν > 3SAAI, left behind ‖ συναντιλάβηται > 3SAMS, help ‖ μεριμνᾷς > 2SPAI, you are anxious ‖ θορυβάζῃ > 2SPPI, you are troubled ‖ μερίδα > portion ‖ ἐξελέξατο > 3SAMI, she has chosen ‖ ἀφαιρεθήσεται > 3SFPI, it will [not] be taken away

Further Reading: Luke 10:38-42
Eric M. McConnell

... ³ μνημονεύοντες ὑμῶν τοῦ ἔργου τῆς πίστεως καὶ τοῦ κόπου τῆς ἀγάπης καὶ τῆς ὑπομονῆς τῆς ἐλπίδος τοῦ κυρίου ἡμῶν Ἰησοῦ Χριστοῦ ἔμπροσθεν τοῦ θεοῦ καὶ πατρὸς ἡμῶν.

CONTEXT:

Paul, in greeting the church at Thessalonica, is giving thanks to God for saving and building up the believers. In this thanksgiving to God, Paul gives evidences that those who heard the gospel became genuine Christians.

COMMENTARY:

Paul expresses some of these evidences of salvation by employing the genitive case. The noun in the genitive case usually modifies another noun. The words "work" (ἔργου), "labor" (κόπου), and "endurance" (ὑπομονῆς) are also in the genitive but as objects of the participle "remembering" (μνημονεύοντες). Verbs expressing remembrance often take an object in the genitive. Compare English, "to be mindful of ..." The word "genitive" was taken to mean "kind" or "type." In 1 Thessalonians 1:3, Paul uses three genitive constructions: *work of faith* (τοῦ ἔργου τῆς πίστεως), *labor of love* (τοῦ κόπου τῆς ἀγάπης), and *patience of the hope of our Lord Jesus Christ* (τῆς ὑπομονῆς τῆς ἐλπίδος τοῦ κυρίου ἡμῶν Ἰησοῦ Χριστοῦ). The general meanings of these genitive constructions are: a faith kind/type of work, a love kind/type of labor, and a hope (of our Lord Jesus Christ) kind/type of endurance. The more specific meaning may be understood as a subjective genitive, meaning that the genitive is similar to a subject in a sentence with the verb form of the noun that the genitive is modifying. The *faith that works* is not a dead faith, but an evidence of genuine saving faith. The same is true with the other genitives: a *love that labors*, and a *hope* (of our Lord Jesus Christ) *that endures*. These genitives furnish marks of a genuine Christian: the faith, love, and hope that genuine Christians possess. Paul, therefore, thanks God that his preaching in Thessalonica bore true fruit.

μνημονεύοντες > PAPMPN, remembering ‖ κόπου > labor, toil ‖ ὑπομονῆς > endurance, perseverance, patience

Further Reading: 1 Corinthians 13:1–7
Russell Fuller

1 THESSALONIANS 1:5

... ⁵ ὅτι τὸ εὐαγγέλιον ἡμῶν οὐκ ἐγενήθη εἰς ὑμᾶς ἐν λόγῳ μόνον ἀλλὰ καὶ ἐν δυνάμει καὶ ἐν πνεύματι ἁγίῳ καὶ ἐν πληροφορίᾳ πολλῇ, καθὼς οἴδατε οἷοι ἐγενήθημεν ἐν ὑμῖν δι' ὑμᾶς.

CONTEXT:

Paul begins his first epistle to the Thessalonians by thanking God for the reception of the gospel by the Thessalonians. Paul preached the gospel to them, and many came to saving faith in Christ Jesus.

COMMENTARY:

Clear communication often employs contrasts. A form of contrast that Paul and other writers of Scripture employ is the negative with the positive or the positive with the negative. Contrast is often indicated by adversative particles, such as δέ, πλήν, and even καί, but the king of adversative particles is ἀλλά. Paul, for instance, writes in a negative and positive contrast in 1 Corinthians 1:17, "For God did *not* send me to baptize, but to preach the gospel." The same is true in 1 Thessalonians 1:5 where Paul details how the gospel was received by the Thessalonians. First the negative, the gospel did not come to you in word only. The gospel did come to them in word but not word *only*. If the gospel comes in word only, the hearers will not be saved. *But* (ἀλλά) it also came effactually in power and in the Holy Spirit and in much assurance. The divine power by the Holy Spirit worked deeply in these converts—as seen in the marks of salvation mentioned in verses 3, 6–10—to produce the full assurance of their salvation. God's word must not be a mere academic pursuit; it must come in power, in the Holy Spirit, and in much assurance by faith (echoing Heb 11:1 and 2 Tim 1:7). We must know both God's word and experience the power of God's word in our daily lives.

ἐγενήθη > 3SAPI, came || πληροφορίᾳ > full assurance, confidence, fullness || οἷοι > relative pronoun expressing quality: which kind (quality) of men || ἐγενήθημεν > 1PAPI, proved to be

Further Reading: 1 Corinthians 2:1–5
Russell Fuller

1 THESSALONIANS 1:9–10

⁹ αὐτοὶ γὰρ περὶ ἡμῶν ἀπαγγέλλουσιν ὁποίαν εἴσοδον ἔσχομεν πρὸς ὑμᾶς, καὶ πῶς ἐπεστρέψατε πρὸς τὸν θεὸν ἀπὸ τῶν εἰδώλων δουλεύειν θεῷ ζῶντι καὶ ἀληθινῷ ¹⁰ καὶ ἀναμένειν τὸν υἱὸν αὐτοῦ ἐκ τῶν οὐρανῶν, ὃν ἤγειρεν ἐκ τῶν νεκρῶν, Ἰησοῦν τὸν ῥυόμενον ἡμᾶς ἐκ τῆς ὀργῆς τῆς ἐρχομένης.

CONTEXT:

In 1 Thessalonians 1, Paul rejoices that the gospel came to the Thessalonians believers in power and in the Holy Spirit and in full assurance. In 1 Thessalonians 1:8 Paul rejoices that their evangelism of the word of the Lord echoed forth from them in every place where their faith toward God had come (cf. 1 Cor 2:4–5; Phil 1:29).

COMMENTARY:

The other evangelical grace along with saving faith is repentance. God grants men saving faith and repentance unto life (Acts 11:18; 20:21; 2 Cor 7:10; 2 Tim 2:25). In 1 Thessalonians 1:8, Paul speaks of their saving faith, but now he speaks of their repentance unto life (1:9–10). The word that Paul uses for repentance means "to turn" (ἐπεστρέψατε). The more common word for repentance in the NT is μετανοέω, which means "to change the mind." Repentance in the NT is an entire change of mind about God, sin, Christ Jesus, and many other things. This changing of the mind is demonstrated in the act of turning away from sin and in the act of turning toward God, as 1 Thessalonians 1:9 states, "For they themselves declare what kind of entrance we had to you and how you turned to God from idols." The Greek verb "to turn," an aorist indicative active, presents the action as simply completed in past time. They had turned away from their sins, idolatry being the foundation of much of their sins. Repentance is not simply negative, a turning away from sin, but it is positive, a turning to God. The two infinitives in 1 Thessalonians 1:9–10 give the purpose or reason for their turning: *to serve* a living and true God and *to await* his Son from heaven. Both infinitives are in the present tense: to keep on serving a living and true God and to keep on awaiting his Son from heaven.

ὁποίαν > what kind of || εἴσοδον > entrance, reception || ἔσχομεν > 1PAAI, had || ἐπεστρέψατε > 2PAAI, turned || δουλεύειν > PAN, to serve || ἀναμένειν > PAN, to await || ῥυόμενον > PMPMSA, delivers

Further Reading: 2 Corinthians 7:8–12

Russell Fuller

... ⁴ ἀλλὰ καθὼς δεδοκιμάσμεθα ὑπὸ τοῦ θεοῦ πιστευθῆναι τὸ εὐαγγέλιον, οὕτως λαλοῦμεν, οὐχ ὡς ἀνθρώποις ἀρέσκοντες ἀλλὰ θεῷ τῷ δοκιμάζοντι τὰς καρδίας ἡμῶν.

CONTEXT:

Paul is still rejoicing that his preaching to the Thessalonians was not in vain. Paul was suffering persecution and was experiencing great conflict as he proclaimed Christ. Such suffering without any success would be beyond despair. Yet the gospel took root in the hearts of many, encouraging Paul and his associates. The suffering was worth it all.

COMMENTARY:

Paul is assuring his readers of his motives in preaching the gospel to them. Clearly, there were many charlatans then as now, inside and outside the church. In 1 Thessalonians 2:4, Paul states that he was δεδοκιμάσμεθα ("tested"—and so approved) by God to be entrusted with the gospel. In saying this, Paul uses a perfect verb. The perfect is a descriptive verbal form in Greek since it combines the completed action of the aorist with the present time. Paul's testing and approval by God was completed sometime in the past, and now Paul currently stands tested and approved by God to be entrusted with the gospel. Later in the verse, Paul describes God as continually in process of δοκιμάζοντι "testing and approving" (present participle) the hearts of all his ministers. Paul goes on to say that having been entrusted with the gospel, he must faithfully proclaim it without the temptation to please men. We must seek the approval of God, not of men, in proclaiming the gospel (cf. Gal 1:10). If we add human philosophy or good works to the gospel, we corrupt it and make the cross null and void (cf. 1 Cor 1:17, Gal 5:11). If we subtract from the gospel—such as by rejecting the messiahship or sonship of Jesus—we corrupt the gospel by denying it (cf. 1 John 2:22). If we seek man's approval or our own selfish desires for fame in preaching the gospel, we betray it.

δεδοκιμάσμεθα > 1PRPI, we have been tested, approved || πιστευθῆναι > APN, to be entrusted || ἀρέσκοντες > PAPMPN, pleasing || δοκιμάζοντι > PAPMSD, testing, proving

Further Reading: Galatians 1:10–12
Russell Fuller

¹³ καὶ διὰ τοῦτο καὶ ἡμεῖς εὐχαριστοῦμεν τῷ θεῷ ἀδιαλείπτως, ὅτι παραλαβόντες λόγον ἀκοῆς παρ' ἡμῶν τοῦ θεοῦ ἐδέξασθε οὐ λόγον ἀνθρώπων ἀλλὰ καθώς ἐστιν ἀληθῶς λόγον θεοῦ, ὃς καὶ ἐνεργεῖται ἐν ὑμῖν τοῖς πιστεύουσιν.

CONTEXT:

Paul asserts that his labor among the Thessalonians was not in vain. Even suffering severe persecution, the Thessalonians are advancing in the faith. Paul, therefore, rejoices as the gospel takes root in their lives. He assures them that his motives are pure and that he preaches the gospel not out of greed. Paul is willing to work day and night and to lose his life for the sake of the Thessalonians because they had received his gospel as the very word of God.

COMMENTARY:

To understand verbs and participles, watch for contrasts within a verse or passage. In 1 Thessalonians 2:13 there are present and aorist verbal forms. For the aorist forms—both the verb ἐδέξασθε ("to welcome, accept") and participle παραλαβόντες ("receive")—the kind of action expressed is completed action, without any notion of present results or ongoing action. The aorist participle's association with the aorist indicative verb requires the participle to be a past action: "Having received ... you accepted." In contrast, the present verbs and participle express action ongoing in some manner—they are in process and so not yet completed. God's word is currently and continually (or from time to time) ἐνεργεῖται ("working") in those that are currently and continually πιστεύουσιν ("believing"). Notice how the receiving/accepting of God's word for salvation is communicated by the aorist tense (ἐδέξασθε and παραλαβόντες)—these actions are *done, finished, completed*. However, the work of God's word in the believers is communicated by the present tense (ἐνεργεῖται and πιστεύουσιν)—these actions are *in process, continuing, ongoing*. For this, Paul and his co-workers Silvanus and Timothy are now in process of continually εὐχαριστοῦμεν ("giving thanks") to God under all difficulties.

εὐχαριστοῦμεν > 1PPAI, giving thanks || ἀδιαλείπτως > constantly || παραλαβόντες > AAPMPN, having received || ἐδέξασθε > 2PAMI, you received || ἐνεργεῖται > 3SPMI, works || πιστεύουσιν > PAPMPD, believing

Further Reading: Galatians 3:1–14
Russell Fuller

1 Thessalonians 3:10

... ¹⁰ νυκτὸς καὶ ἡμέρας ὑπερεκπερισσοῦ δεόμενοι εἰς τὸ ἰδεῖν ὑμῶν τὸ πρόσωπον καὶ καταρτίσαι τὰ ὑστερήματα τῆς πίστεως ὑμῶν;

CONTEXT:

In 1 Thessalonians 3, Paul describes his anxiety for the Thessalonian believers. Paul knew when he left them that they would go through severe persecution. He continually warned them about this when he was with them (3:4). Now Paul hears news from Timothy that their faith is growing in the Lord and their love for Paul is growing as well. Paul is elated. Paul thanks God for their growth in grace and prays earnestly for them.

COMMENTARY:

In 1 Thessalonians 3:10, Paul prays to see the Thessalonians' faces again (by traveling to them) to perfect what is lacking in their faith. The infinitives ἰδεῖν ("to see) and καταρτίσαι ("to perfect") are governed by the preposition εἰς and the neuter article τό. Infinitives preceded by εἰς τό usually express purpose or result. The literal rendering of the infinitives here is "to the seeing ... and perfecting." When smoothly rendered, this passage might read, "that we might see your face and perfect what is lacking in your faith." Both are aorist infinitives and therefore express a kind of action that is simply completed. These purpose clauses, connected with the present participle δεόμενοι ("praying") and the present verb of the preceding verse (δυνάμεθα, "to be able"), are future relative to the time of the participle. Paul desires to return to the Thessalonians as soon as possible. First, he desires to see the faces of those Thessalonian believers that he quickly grew to love. Second, he desires to perfect the deficiencies of their faith. The second infinitive (καταρτίσαι) has the root idea of "making fit or complete." With its direct object, "the things lacking or coming up short," the infinitive means to mend or complete. These new believers were coming up short or lacking in their faith. Paul desired to disciple them to complete what was lacking in their faith. Of course, the desire and prayer of experienced Christians is to have those things that are lacking in their faith completed.

ὑπερεκπερισσοῦ > extra abundantly || δεόμενοι > PMPMPN, praying, asking for out of need || ἰδεῖν > AAN, to see || καταρτίσαι > AAN, to complete, supply, perfect || ὑστερήματα > things lacking, deficiencies

Further Reading: 1 Peter 2:1–3
Russell Fuller

³ τοῦτο γάρ ἐστιν θέλημα τοῦ θεοῦ, ὁ ἁγιασμὸς ὑμῶν, ἀπέχεσθαι ὑμᾶς ἀπὸ τῆς πορνείας, ⁴ εἰδέναι ἕκαστον ὑμῶν τὸ ἑαυτοῦ σκεῦος κτᾶσθαι ἐν ἁγιασμῷ καὶ τιμῇ, ⁵ μὴ ἐν πάθει ἐπιθυμίας καθάπερ καὶ τὰ ἔθνη τὰ μὴ εἰδότα τὸν θεόν, ⁶ τὸ μὴ ὑπερβαίνειν καὶ πλεονεκτεῖν ἐν τῷ πράγματι τὸν ἀδελφὸν αὐτοῦ, διότι ἔκδικος κύριος περὶ πάντων τούτων, καθὼς καὶ προείπαμεν ὑμῖν καὶ διεμαρτυράμεθα.

CONTEXT:

Paul encourages the Thessalonian believers to walk in a manner that is pleasing to God (4:1). The Gentiles walked in immorality (cf. Eph 4:17-19)—even as the pagan religions promoted immorality as part of their worship. As Christians, the Thessalonian believers should now walk in holiness of life.

COMMENTARY:

Paul tells the Thessalonian believers that the will of God for Christians is their sanctification. To explain this sanctification, Paul uses three explanatory infinitives: ἀπέχεσθαι, εἰδέναι, and ὑπερβαίνειν. The first explanatory infinitive in 4:3 tells them to keep on ἀπέχεσθαι ("abstaining" or "holding off") from sexual immorality. The phrase may be translated, "to keep on holding off *himself* from sexual immorality." The second explanatory infinitive εἰδέναι ("to know"), connects closely with another infinitive, κτᾶσθαι ("to possess"). This may be translated, "to know how ... to keep on possessing for himself." The "vessel" (σκεῦος) is usually interpreted as one's own body or one's own spouse. Notice the positive/negative contrast between verses four and five, "in sanctification and honor, *not* in passion of lust." The third explanatory infinitive combines two infinitives, ὑπερβαίνειν ("to transgress") and πλεονεκτεῖν ("to have more" or "to take more"), in a single thought. They are not to keep on transgressing God's law concerning immorality. Verse 7 sums up the passage with a negative/positive contrast, "For God has not called us to impurity, *but* in sanctification." Believers must live in a manner that is pleasing to God. To claim to believe in Christ and to live immorally is a contradiction and a lie.

ἁγιασμός > sanctification || ἀπέχεσθαι > PMN, to abstain, hold off || εἰδέναι > RAN, to know || σκεῦος > vessel || κτᾶσθαι > PMN, to possess || ὑπερβαίνειν > PAN, to go beyond || πλεονεκτεῖν > PAN, to have more, to desire more, or take more, to covet || πράγματι > matter || ἔκδικος > avenger || προείπαμεν > 1PAAI, told beforehand || διεμαρτυράμεθα > 1PAMI, solemnly warned

Further Reading: Ephesians 4:17-24
Russell Fuller

¹⁴ εἰ γὰρ πιστεύομεν ὅτι Ἰησοῦς ἀπέθανεν καὶ ἀνέστη, οὕτως καὶ ὁ θεὸς τοὺς κοιμηθέντας διὰ τοῦ Ἰησοῦ ἄξει σὺν αὐτῷ.

CONTEXT:

The Thessalonian believers needed further instruction about Christ's second coming, an issue addressed in both letters to the Thessalonians. The second coming of Christ, the blessed hope of believers, is vital to Christian faith and practice. It is the final climax of Christian belief and history, and everyone who has this hope purifies himself now in anticipation of that great day (1 John 3:3).

COMMENTARY:

In 1 Thessalonians 4:14, Paul emphasizes the second coming for Christian doctrine. If we believe the gospel that Jesus died for our sins and was raised for our justification, then after we die God will have us return from heaven with Christ at his second coming. If we are still alive on earth when Christ returns, then we will be caught up with Christ in the sky without dying. To express this doctrine, Paul uses a conditional clause that assumes the reality of the condition: if *this* is true (and we assume it is for this statement), then *that* is true. This does not imply that every conditional of this type is necessarily true. This kind of conditional clause brings out the consequences or outcome of a statement if assumed as true. The meaning is therefore, "If (assuming that) we believe that Jesus died and was raised again, even so God will bring with him those who sleep through Jesus." Paul's condition assumes that we truly believe in the work of Christ. If genuine faith is true, the promise of God bringing with him those believers at the second coming of Christ is true. The entire conditional statement expresses a promise. If the condition is met, the outcome is certain. Let us comfort one another with these words.

πιστεύομεν > 1PPAI, believe ‖ ἀπέθανεν > 3SAAI, died ‖ ἀνέστη > 3SAAI, arose ‖ κοιμηθέντας > APPMPA, have fallen asleep ‖ ἄξει > 3SFAI, will lead, bring

Further Reading: 1 Thessalonians 4:15–5:11
Russell Fuller

1 THESSALONIANS 5:23

²³ αὐτὸς δὲ ὁ θεὸς τῆς εἰρήνης ἁγιάσαι ὑμᾶς ὁλοτελεῖς, καὶ ὁλόκληρον ὑμῶν τὸ πνεῦμα καὶ ἡ ψυχὴ καὶ τὸ σῶμα ἀμέμπτως ἐν τῇ παρουσίᾳ τοῦ κυρίου ἡμῶν Ἰησοῦ Χριστοῦ τηρηθείη.

CONTEXT:

In 1 Thessalonians 5:17, Paul had told the Thessalonian believers to pray without ceasing. Paul now in 5:23 demonstrates *how* he prays without ceasing. In particular, Paul prays that in obeying his teaching to avoid every form of evil (5:22), they may find the God of peace sanctifying them. This verse is essentially a prayer without the formal introduction that Paul is praying.

COMMENTARY:

In 1 Thessalonians 5:23, Paul uses an optative finite verbal form to express his prayer. Optative verbal forms occur 68 times in the NT, nine times in 1 and 2 Thessalonians. The word "optative" means wish or desire. Paul's prayers are often expressed in the optative. In fact, in 1 and 2 Thessalonians, Paul employs all nine optatives in expressing his desires and wishes in prayer. In 5:23 there are two optatives: ἁγιάσαι ("to sanctify") and τηρηθείη ("to be kept, guarded"). They are both aorist optatives, conveying a simple completed action, not an action in process as a present optative might convey (for example, that God would *keep on* sanctifying). Optatives are naturally future when they express desire or wishes: "May God sanctify you wholly." Paul here is praying for the Thessalonian believers that "the God of peace" (ὁ θεὸς τῆς εἰρήνης)—a favorite Pauline description of God—would sanctify them completely in all respects. This sanctification would set them apart to God by purifying their hearts to die more and more to sin and to live unto righteousness. Paul goes on to pray that God would keep or guard their "whole lot"—spirit (πνεῦμα), soul (ψυχή), and body (σῶμα)—without blame or censure from sin.

ἁγιάσαι > 3SAAO, may he make holy ‖ ὁλοτελεῖς > complete in all respects ‖ ὁλόκληρον > "whole lot," complete in all its parts ‖ ἀμέμπτως > blamelessly, without censure ‖ τηρηθείη > 3SAPO, may [they] be kept

Further Reading: Jude 20–25
Russell Fuller

^{27} ἐνορκίζω ὑμᾶς τὸν κύριον ἀναγνωσθῆναι τὴν ἐπιστολὴν πᾶσιν τοῖς ἀδελφοῖς.

CONTEXT:

In the next to last verse of 1 Thessalonians, Paul gives a last command to the Thessalonian believers that this epistle should be read to all the brethren.

COMMENTARY:

Although many of Paul's commands are directly expressed by imperative verbs (cf. 1 Thess 5:16–22), in 5:27 Paul's command is indirectly expressed by an infinitive. The command is indirect since it follows a verb of speaking, commanding, taking an oath, and so forth (ἐνορκίζω, "to put under oath"). By using this indirect construction, Paul puts a strong emphasis on the command itself. He does not simply command the letter to be read (ἀναγνωσθῆναι), but he puts the Thessalonian believers under oath that the command to read this letter might be performed. Taking an oath or putting someone under an oath is perhaps the strongest language possible since an oath puts the speaker under the direct inspection and judgment of God. This is a most solemn command: "I put you all under oath to God to have this letter read to all the brethren." Clearly, this is no ordinary letter. If this were an ordinary letter or epistle, a command to read it would seem out of place or out of bounds. Furthermore, this command is not limited to the brethren at Thessalonica. It is to be read by all the brethren. Paul knew this was no ordinary letter. It was prophetic, that is, breathed out by God (5:20); it is not the words of man, but the very words of God (2:13). Peter knew that Paul writings were inspired Scripture (2 Pt 3:16), so did Paul (1 Cor 2:13), and so should we.

ἐνορκίζω > 1SPAI, put [someone] under oath, adjure (this verb takes two objects "you" and "the Lord") ‖ ἀναγνωσθῆναι > APN, to be read

Further Reading: 2 Timothy 3:14–17
Russell Fuller

JUNE 25
2 THESSALONIANS 1:5–7

⁵ ἔνδειγμα τῆς δικαίας κρίσεως τοῦ θεοῦ εἰς τὸ καταξιωθῆναι ὑμᾶς τῆς βασιλείας τοῦ θεοῦ, ὑπὲρ ἧς καὶ πάσχετε, ⁶ εἴπερ δίκαιον παρὰ θεῷ ἀνταποδοῦναι τοῖς θλίβουσιν ὑμᾶς θλῖψιν ⁷ καὶ ὑμῖν τοῖς θλιβομένοις ἄνεσιν μεθ’ ἡμῶν, ἐν τῇ ἀποκαλύψει τοῦ κυρίου Ἰησοῦ ἀπ’ οὐρανοῦ μετ’ ἀγγέλων δυνάμεως αὐτοῦ.

CONTEXT:

Paul is writing a follow-up letter to the Thessalonian church, which was suffering persecution as addressed in his first letter. In so doing, Paul writes to a church that was sharing in the sufferings that Christ foretold (1 Thess 2:14–17, Matt 5:10). This passage comes after the typical greeting and prayer of Greco-Roman letters (1:1–4).

COMMENTARY:

Paul states his purpose for writing—to encourage the church to continue to endure suffering based on the expectation of God's retribution at Christ's second coming. Notice the use of the preposition εἰς, denoting an "extension toward, in the direction of, a specific place to be reached" (BDAG, 288). The kingdom of God is a goal to be reached, and that is a goal that God often chooses for his children by having us endure suffering. Also notice the use of ὑπέρ, describing the incarnational ministry of believers as they suffer for the sake of, and on behalf of, the kingdom of God. Last, there is the employment of the emphatic conditional εἴπερ ("since" or "if indeed"). F.F. Bruce notes about this word, "There is no implication of doubt where the righteousness of God is involved" (Bruce, *1 & 2 Thessalonians*, WBC, 149). This emphatic conditional points to the fact that God is indeed just and will repay.

ἔνδειγμα > evidence || καταξιωθῆναι > APN, to be considered worthy || ἀνταποδοῦναι > AAN, to repay || θλίβουσιν > PAPMPD, those oppressing || θλιβομένοις > PPPMPD, those who are oppressed || ἀποκαλύψει > revelation

Further Reading: Revelation 6:9–11
Donald C. McIntyre

176

2 THESSALONIANS 1:11–12

[11] εἰς ὃ καὶ προσευχόμεθα πάντοτε περὶ ὑμῶν, ἵνα ὑμᾶς ἀξιώσῃ τῆς κλήσεως ὁ θεὸς ἡμῶν καὶ πληρώσῃ πᾶσαν εὐδοκίαν ἀγαθωσύνης καὶ ἔργον πίστεως ἐν δυνάμει, [12] ὅπως ἐνδοξασθῇ τὸ ὄνομα τοῦ κυρίου ἡμῶν Ἰησοῦ ἐν ὑμῖν, καὶ ὑμεῖς ἐν αὐτῷ, κατὰ τὴν χάριν τοῦ θεοῦ ἡμῶν καὶ κυρίου Ἰησοῦ Χριστοῦ.

CONTEXT:

Paul continues his second letter to the persecuted Thessalonian church (cf. 1:5–8). This section of the letter is part of the exordium that began in v. 5 and continues through the end of the first chapter. As such, Paul seeks to establish rapport with his suffering audience.

COMMENTARY:

This passage contains Paul's prayer for the church of Thessalonica. Verbal aspect has drawn attention to how verbal forms can aid exegesis. When an author wished to draw attention to something, he would use a more "marked tense" to bring it to the foreground—either defined (present tense), or well-defined (perfect tense). There are only four verbs in this passage, three aorist (ἀξιώσῃ, πληρώσῃ, ἐνδοξασθῇ) and one present (προσευχόμεθα). Here, Paul draws attention to the fact that the most important thing he can do to bring about the two ancillary purposes (denoted by ἵνα and ὅπως) is to pray.

ἀξιώσῃ > 3SAAS, may be considered worthy ‖ πληρώσῃ > 3SAAS, may fulfill ‖ εὐδοκίαν > that which pleases ‖ ἀγαθωσύνης > for goodness ‖ ἐνδοξασθῇ > 3SAPS, may be glorified

Further Reading: Galatians 6:1–10
Donald C. McIntyre

JUNE 27
2 THESSALONIANS 2:1–3

¹ ἐρωτῶμεν δὲ ὑμᾶς, ἀδελφοί, ὑπὲρ τῆς παρουσίας τοῦ κυρίου ἡμῶν Ἰησοῦ Χριστοῦ καὶ ἡμῶν ἐπισυναγωγῆς ἐπ' αὐτὸν ² εἰς τὸ μὴ ταχέως σαλευθῆναι ὑμᾶς ἀπὸ τοῦ νοὸς μηδὲ θροεῖσθαι, μήτε διὰ πνεύματος μήτε διὰ λόγου μήτε δι' ἐπιστολῆς ὡς δι' ἡμῶν, ὡς ὅτι ἐνέστηκεν ἡ ἡμέρα τοῦ κυρίου· ³ Μή τις ὑμᾶς ἐξαπατήσῃ κατὰ μηδένα τρόπον. ὅτι ἐὰν μὴ ἔλθῃ ἡ ἀποστασία πρῶτον καὶ ἀποκαλυφθῇ ὁ ἄνθρωπος τῆς ἀνομίας, ὁ υἱὸς τῆς ἀπωλείας.

CONTEXT:

In 2 Thessalonians, Paul further expounds upon much of what he wrote in 1 Thessalonians. In 1 Thessalonians, the church was worried that the dead may not participate in the resurrection; 2 Thessalonians indicates that some were worried about the timing of the *parousia*.

COMMENTARY:

Using verbal aspect theory, one can identify the two main concerns of the text. First, the term ἐρωτῶμεν ("we ask") is foregrounded in present tense. Paul asks the brothers to "be not quickly incited," detailing how the Thessalonians might be incited—by a spirit, by a word, or by a letter. All these causes of turmoil are to be dismissed. Second, and more emphatically, Paul gives the foreground verb as the reason why they should not be alarmed: "as if that day of the Lord has come." Paul's point is that although the Lord will come, he has not come yet.

παρουσίας > coming ‖ ἐπισυναγωγῆς > gathering ‖ ταχέως > quickly ‖ σαλευθῆναι > APN, [not] to be shaken ‖ νοός > mind ‖ θροεῖσθαι > PPN, to be alarmed ‖ ἐπιστολῆς > letter, epistle ‖ ἐνέστηκεν > 3SRAI, has come ‖ ἐξαπατήσῃ > 3SAAS, let [no one] deceive ‖ τρόπον > way ‖ ἀποστασία > apostasy ‖ ἀνομίας > lawlessness ‖ ἀπωλείας > destruction

Further Reading: 1 Thessalonians 5:1–10
Donald C. McIntyre

JUNE 28
2 THESSALONIANS 2:5-7

⁵ οὐ μνημονεύετε ὅτι ἔτι ὢν πρὸς ὑμᾶς ταῦτα ἔλεγον ὑμῖν; ⁶ καὶ νῦν τὸ κατέχον οἴδατε εἰς τὸ ἀποκαλυφθῆναι αὐτὸν ἐν τῷ ἑαυτοῦ καιρῷ. ⁷ τὸ γὰρ μυστήριον ἤδη ἐνεργεῖται τῆς ἀνομίας· μόνον ὁ κατέχων ἄρτι ἕως ἐκ μέσου γένηται.

CONTEXT:

In 2 Thessalonians 2:5, Paul builds on his assertion of 2:1-4 that the Thessalonian church should not be worried about the time of the *parousia* since foretold prerequisites had not yet occurred.

COMMENTARY:

The conjunctions in this passage articulate three important realities. The first conjunction (ὅτι) points out what the Thessalonians should have remembered— Paul's teaching on this topic. Paul then uses two additional conjunctions (καί and γάρ) to introduce the main topics of his teaching. The first teaching on the end times by Paul was introduced with καί, a coordinating connection. The second is introduced by the logical conjunction γάρ which has a close continuity to the preceding thought. "The man of lawlessness" was being restrained, and would continue to be restrained, until the Restrainer is out of the way.

μνημονεύετε > 2PPAI, remember || τὸ κατέχον > PAPNSA, what is restraining || ἀποκαλυφθῆναι > APN, may be revealed || ἐνεργεῖται > 3SPMI, is at work || ἀνομίας > lawlessness || ὁ κατέχων > PAPMSN, who is restraining

Further Reading: Revelation 19:11-16
Donald C. McIntyre

2 THESSALONIANS 2:13–15

¹³ ἡμεῖς δὲ ὀφείλομεν εὐχαριστεῖν τῷ θεῷ πάντοτε περὶ ὑμῶν, ἀδελφοὶ ἠγαπημένοι ὑπὸ κυρίου, ὅτι εἵλατο ὑμᾶς ὁ θεὸς ἀπαρχὴν εἰς σωτηρίαν ἐν ἁγιασμῷ πνεύματος καὶ πίστει ἀληθείας, ¹⁴ εἰς ὃ καὶ ἐκάλεσεν ὑμᾶς διὰ τοῦ εὐαγγελίου ἡμῶν εἰς περιποίησιν δόξης τοῦ κυρίου ἡμῶν Ἰησοῦ Χριστοῦ. ¹⁵ Ἄρα οὖν, ἀδελφοί, στήκετε καὶ κρατεῖτε τὰς παραδόσεις ἃς ἐδιδάχθητε εἴτε διὰ λόγου εἴτε δι' ἐπιστολῆς ἡμῶν.

CONTEXT:

In this passage, Paul begins his letter's hortatory section built on the previous commands not to worry about the *parousia*.

COMMENTARY:

Paul begins this section in 2:13 by exemplifying his own practice of thanksgiving (foregrounded) because of the debt he owes to God for the Thessalonians' election. He affirms their calling in the gospel so that they might experience the glory of the Lord Jesus. Note that the two verbs describing God's acts in salvation (εἵλατο and ἐκάλεσεν) are backgrounded in the aorist: "he chose" and "he called." In v. 15, Paul combines the resultant conjunctions ἄρα and οὖν. F. F. Bruce notes that this construction is "peculiar to Paul in the NT" and should be considered emphatic (Bruce, *1 & 2 Thessalonians*, WBC, 192). Although verbal aspect is foregrounding Paul's prayer and the Thessalonian's actions, the two conjunctions highlight the proper result of the Thessalonian's election: the continuation and clinging to the gospel traditions they were taught after God chose and called them.

εἵλατο > 3SAMI, chose ‖ ἀπαρχήν > first fruits ‖ ἁγιασμῷ > holiness ‖ περιποίησιν > obtaining ‖ στήκετε > 2PPAM, continue, stand firm ‖ κρατεῖτε > 2PPAM, hold ‖ παραδόσεις > traditions ‖ ἐδιδάχθητε > 2PAPI, were taught ‖ ἐπιστολῆς > letter, epistle

Further Reading: 1 Corinthians 15:20–28
Donald C. McIntyre

JUNE 30
2 THESSALONIANS 3:1–3

¹ τὸ λοιπὸν προσεύχεσθε, ἀδελφοί, περὶ ἡμῶν, ἵνα ὁ λόγος τοῦ κυρίου τρέχῃ καὶ δοξάζηται καθὼς καὶ πρὸς ὑμᾶς, ² καὶ ἵνα ῥυσθῶμεν ἀπὸ τῶν ἀτόπων καὶ πονηρῶν ἀνθρώπων· οὐ γὰρ πάντων ἡ πίστις. ³ Πιστὸς δέ ἐστιν ὁ κύριος, ὃς στηρίξει ὑμᾶς καὶ φυλάξει ἀπὸ τοῦ πονηροῦ.

CONTEXT:
Paul continues to give directives to the Thessalonian church with a prayer request for himself and his associates.

COMMENTARY:
Paul requests prayer for himself and his associates followed by a succession of ἵνα clauses. His prayer request is first that the word of the Lord would "spread quickly" (τρέχῃ) and "be honored" (δοξάζηται) and second, that he and his associates "may be delivered" (ῥυσθῶμεν). Paul's prayer for safety is sequentially subordinated to the spread of the gospel and the honor that it deserves. He leaves no doubt as to his values—he values his mission over personal comfort and safety. He then encourages the Thessalonians by informing them that the deliverance they can count on is from the evil one (using a substantive adjective), not evil in general.

τὸ λοιπόν > finally ‖ προσεύχεσθε > 2PPMM, pray ‖ τρέχῃ > 3SPAS, may spread quickly ‖ ῥυσθῶμεν > 1PAPS, we may be delivered ‖ ἀτόπων > wicked, out of place, perverse ‖ στηρίξει > 3SFAI, will strengthen ‖ φυλάξει > 3SFAI, will guard, keep

Further Reading: 2 Corinthians 1:8–11
Donald C. McIntyre

2 Thessalonians 3:4–5

⁴ πεποίθαμεν δὲ ἐν κυρίῳ ἐφ' ὑμᾶς, ὅτι ἃ παραγγέλλομεν καὶ ποιεῖτε καὶ ποιήσετε. ⁵ Ὁ δὲ κύριος κατευθύναι ὑμῶν τὰς καρδίας εἰς τὴν ἀγάπην τοῦ θεοῦ καὶ εἰς τὴν ὑπομονὴν τοῦ Χριστοῦ.

CONTEXT:

In 2 Thessalonians 3:4–5, Paul comforts the Thessalonian church concerning their current state after requesting prayer for his own perilous status.

COMMENTARY:

In verse 4, we find the phrase ἃ παραγγέλλομεν ("the things that we commanded"), which includes all the previous verbal commands since chapter 2. Paul is emphatically certain that the Thessalonians are already doing these things (ποιεῖτε) and that they will continue to do these things (ποιήσετε)—that is, that they will continue clinging to the traditions (2:15) and praying (3:1). Paul then offers a prayer that the Lord would direct their hearts toward the essence of the gospel; the love of God (evidenced through the endurance of Christ), by which they would be able to fulfill these commands. The Thessalonians can receive this letter with joy and encouragement because, like Paul, they can be certain that the gospel will propel future obedience to these commands.

πεποίθαμεν > 1PRAI, have confidence ‖ κατευθύναι > 3SAAO, may direct ‖ ὑπομονήν > steadfastness

Further Reading: 2 Timothy 2:8–13
Donald C. McIntyre

2 THESSALONIANS 3:6–7

⁶ παραγγέλλομεν δὲ ὑμῖν, ἀδελφοί, ἐν ὀνόματι τοῦ κυρίου ἡμῶν Ἰησοῦ Χριστοῦ στέλλεσθαι ὑμᾶς ἀπὸ παντὸς ἀδελφοῦ ἀτάκτως περιπατοῦντος καὶ μὴ κατὰ τὴν παράδοσιν ἣν παρελάβοσαν παρ' ἡμῶν. ⁷ Αὐτοὶ γὰρ οἴδατε πῶς δεῖ μιμεῖσθαι ἡμᾶς, ὅτι οὐκ ἠτακτήσαμεν ἐν ὑμῖν ...

CONTEXT:

As Paul continues his imperative section of the letter, he moves to final exhortations which are particularly relevant for those with an over-realized eschatology. It is intriguing that v. 4 spoke of Paul's confidence in the Thessalonian obedience to the previous commands before he issues this additional command.

COMMENTARY:

Paul issues a new command with the conjunction δέ in v. 6. He makes this command emphatic by repeating the indicative παραγγέλλομεν (from v. 4) and making it the main verb of the sentence so that the actual command is found in the infinitive στέλλεσθαι ("we command you ... to avoid"). The Thessalonians are to avoid certain brothers who are "idly walking" (ἀτάκτως περιπατοῦντος). The reason for this is that the Thessalonians knew better because they had the example of the apostles (3:7). Paul commands the Thessalonians to avoid those who are being lazy as they know exactly how Christians ought to act through his example.

παραγγέλλομεν > 1PPAI, we command ‖ στέλλεσθαι > PMN, to avoid ‖ ἀτάκτως > idly ‖ παράδοσιν > tradition ‖ μιμεῖσθαι > PMN, imitate ‖ ἠτακτήσαμεν > 1SAAI, we were [not] idle

Further Reading: Acts 18:1–3
Donald C. McIntyre

2 THESSALONIANS 3:8-10

... ⁸ οὐδὲ δωρεὰν ἄρτον ἐφάγομεν παρά τινος, ἀλλ' ἐν κόπῳ καὶ μόχθῳ νυκτὸς καὶ ἡμέρας ἐργαζόμενοι πρὸς τὸ μὴ ἐπιβαρῆσαί τινα ὑμῶν· ⁹ οὐχ ὅτι οὐκ ἔχομεν ἐξουσίαν, ἀλλ' ἵνα ἑαυτοὺς τύπον δῶμεν ὑμῖν εἰς τὸ μιμεῖσθαι ἡμᾶς. ¹⁰ καὶ γὰρ ὅτε ἦμεν πρὸς ὑμᾶς, τοῦτο παρηγγέλλομεν ὑμῖν, ὅτι εἴ τις οὐ θέλει ἐργάζεσθαι μηδὲ ἐσθιέτω.

CONTEXT:

Paul has just commanded the Thessalonians to avoid idle people (3:6-7). His readers know how Christians should act based on Paul's own example, which he specified in 3:8-10.

COMMENTARY:

The first word in 3:8, οὐδέ, is a particle and conjunction showing a close relationship to the previous clause. Paul and company were not idle among the Thessalonians, nor was their food given to them. By contrast (ἀλλ'), it was earned through the team working night and day with toil and labor. The goal of that work (πρός) was that they would not be a burden. Though Paul and the team had the authority (present tense, defining a foreground usage) to accept a gift of bread, they refused it to set an example that they might be imitated (μιμεῖσθαι, present tense, defining a foreground usage). The example of Paul was to binding: one who refuses to work should be refused food by the church.

δωρεάν > freely || ἐφάγομεν > 1PAAI, eat || κόπῳ > hard work || μόχθῳ > toil || ἐπιβαρῆσαι >AAN, to burden || τύπον > example || δῶμεν > 1PAAS, may give || μιμεῖσθαι > PMN, would imitate || ἐσθιέτω > 3SPAM, let him [not] eat

Further Reading: Philippians 4:14-19
Donald C. McIntyre

¹¹ ἀκούομεν γάρ τινας περιπατοῦντας ἐν ὑμῖν ἀτάκτως μηδὲν ἐργαζομένους ἀλλὰ περιεργαζομένους· ¹² τοῖς δὲ τοιούτοις παραγγέλλομεν καὶ παρακαλοῦμεν ἐν κυρίῳ Ἰησοῦ Χριστῷ, ἵνα μετὰ ἡσυχίας ἐργαζόμενοι τὸν ἑαυτῶν ἄρτον ἐσθίωσιν. ¹³ Ὑμεῖς δέ, ἀδελφοί, μὴ ἐγκακήσητε καλοποιοῦντες.

CONTEXT:

In view of his detailed example of working to provide for himself despite his apostolic position, Paul concludes his letter with an emphatic new command to avoid idle brothers. Paul further reminds the Thessalonians that just as his command to work was in effect while he was present with them, it remains in force even in his absence.

COMMENTARY:

Paul concludes his letter acknowledging a poor report which he has heard that people are walking among them idly, not working, and instead being meddlesome busybodies. He repeats the word παραγγέλλομεν but softens it for the first time in his epistle through καὶ παρακαλοῦμεν (both present tense, defining foreground usage) repeating the command from his previous trip: *work to eat*. Paul does not wish to end on a sour note and encourages the faithful to continue in their obedience by not losing enthusiasm in doing good (backgrounded in aorist). With this conclusion, Paul has placed certain idle brothers on notice as he commands them to work and in so doing, adorn the gospel.

ἀτάκτως > idly ‖ περιεργαζομένους > PMPMPA, meddlesome busybodies ‖ ἡσυχίας > quietness ‖ ἐσθίωσιν > 3PPAS, might eat ‖ ἐγκακήσητε > 2PAAS, lose enthusiasm ‖ καλοποιοῦντες > PAPMPN, doing good

Further Reading: 1 Timothy 5:9–15
Donald C. McIntyre

LUKE 14:2-3

² καὶ ἰδοὺ ἄνθρωπός τις ἦν ὑδρωπικὸς ἔμπροσθεν αὐτοῦ. ³ καὶ ἀποκριθεὶς ὁ Ἰησοῦς εἶπεν πρὸς τοὺς νομικοὺς καὶ Φαρισαίους λέγων· ἔξεστιν τῷ σαββάτῳ θεραπεῦσαι ἢ οὔ;

CONTEXT:

This event occurred as Jesus was on His journey to Jerusalem (9:51-19:27). One recurrent theme in this section concerns the critique of the religious leaders against Jesus. This section highlights one of Jesus' verbal victories over the darkness of legalism by healing the man (14:4).

COMMENTARY:

Despite Jesus' teaching and honest demeanor, the religious leaders were seeking how they might accuse Him of breaking the law. This event occurred on a Sabbath day in the house of a prominent Pharisee (14:1). That the suffering man was planted by the religious leaders to find fault with Jesus is suggested by the word *behold* (ἰδού). Some English versions translate the verb ἀποκριθείς as "asked" (e.g., NIV, NRSV). However the Greek participle actually means "answered" (NASB, ESV, NKJV). The significance of this word choice is that it reveals that Jesus was answering an unstated question; namely, "Will you heal this man?" Jesus was always a step beyond his opponents.

ὑδρωπικός > one suffering from excess fluid ‖ νομικούς > lawyers ‖ ἔξεστιν > 3SPAI, is it lawful ‖ θεραπεῦσαι > AAN, to heal

Further Reading: Luke 14:1-6
Tim Miller

LUKE 15:29-30

²⁹ ὁ δὲ ἀποκριθεὶς εἶπεν τῷ πατρὶ αὐτοῦ· ἰδοὺ τοσαῦτα ἔτη δουλεύω σοι καὶ οὐδέποτε ἐντολήν σου παρῆλθον, καὶ ἐμοὶ οὐδέποτε ἔδωκας ἔριφον ἵνα μετὰ τῶν φίλων μου εὐφρανθῶ· ³⁰ ὅτε δὲ ὁ υἱός σου οὗτος ὁ καταφαγών σου τὸν βίον μετὰ πορνῶν ἦλθεν, ἔθυσας αὐτῷ τὸν σιτευτὸν μόσχον.

CONTEXT:

As Jesus headed toward Jerusalem, He instructed His disciples (14:25-19:27). The teaching of this section consists of parables concerning lost things (15:1-16:31; a sheep [15:1-7]; a coin [15:8-10]; and a son [15:11-31]). In each case, Jesus highlights the value of the lost thing and the proper response of joy one should have at the recovery of the lost thing.

COMMENTARY:

This statement comes at the end of the famous parable of the Prodigal Son. The younger son has returned, the father has thrown a party, and the older son has become embittered. The older brother's response highlights the relational dynamics of the family. First, the older brother says that he has been "slaving" (δουλεύω) for his father. This contrasts with the younger brother, who sought to return as a "house servant" (v. 19 [μισθίων]) but was restored to sonship. Second, the older brother calls the younger brother "this son of yours" (ὁ υἱός σου οὗτος). The demonstrative pronoun creates metaphorical distance, as does the fact that he uses the belabored "son of yours" instead of the more concise "my brother." Together, these indicate that the older brother no longer wants to consider the younger brother a relation.

τοσαῦτα > so many [years] || δουλεύω > 1SPAI, have slaved, served || οὐδέποτε > never || ἔριφον > goat || εὐφρανθῶ > 1SAPS, be glad || καταφαγών > AAPMSN, devouring || βίον > property || πορνῶν > prostitutes || ἔθυσας > 2SAAI, killed || σιτευτόν > fattened || μόσχον > calf

Further Reading: Luke 15:11-32
Tim Miller

LUKE 16:16–17

¹⁶ ὁ νόμος καὶ οἱ προφῆται μέχρι Ἰωάννου· ἀπὸ τότε ἡ βασιλεία τοῦ θεοῦ εὐαγγελίζεται καὶ πᾶς εἰς αὐτὴν βιάζεται. ¹⁷ εὐκοπώτερον δέ ἐστιν τὸν οὐρανὸν καὶ τὴν γῆν παρελθεῖν ἢ τοῦ νόμου μίαν κεραίαν πεσεῖν.

CONTEXT:

As Jesus journeyed toward Jerusalem (9:51–19:27), He taught his disciples. The broader section that includes this passage concerns Jesus' instruction in parables (15:1–16:31). Nevertheless, these verses are short pithy teachings, which add additional elements of what Jesus wanted His disciples to know.

COMMENTARY:

Jesus highlights the major epochal change with John the Baptist. His ministry began the proclamation of the Kingdom of God, and Jesus continued that proclamation. The last portion of verse 16 is highly debated, with the verb βιάζεται at the center of the debate. The verb could be middle or passive (they share the same form), and the connotation can be negative or positive. The following chart shows the options. The positive passive is the most likely option contextually and has some parallel uses (LXX Gen 33:11; Judg 19:7; cf. the related verb παραβιάζομαι in Luke 24:29; Acts 16:15).

	Middle	Passive
Positive	trying to enter it	being compelled to enter it
Negative	being violent against it	being forced into it

μέχρι > until ‖ βιάζεται > 3SPPI, be forced, compelled ‖ εὐκοπώτερον > easier ‖ παρελθεῖν > AAN, to pass away ‖ κεραίαν > stroke ‖ πεσεῖν > AAN, to fall, become void

Further Reading: Luke 16:1–18
Tim Miller

July 8
Luke 18:4-5

⁴ καὶ οὐκ ἤθελεν ἐπὶ χρόνον. μετὰ δὲ ταῦτα εἶπεν ἐν ἑαυτῷ· εἰ καὶ τὸν θεὸν οὐ φοβοῦμαι οὐδὲ ἄνθρωπον ἐντρέπομαι, ⁵ διά γε τὸ παρέχειν μοι κόπον τὴν χήραν ταύτην ἐκδικήσω αὐτήν, ἵνα μὴ εἰς τέλος ἐρχομένη ὑπωπιάζῃ με.

CONTEXT:
As Jesus journeyed to Jerusalem (9:51-19:27), He taught his disciples. This passage occurs in a series of teaching events which broadly focus on the Kingdom of God (17:1-19:27).

COMMENTARY:
Luke informs the reader that Jesus told this parable to encourage His disciples to persist in prayer (18:1). A widow was seeking justice, yet the judge sought to ignore the issue, hoping she would go away. Verse 4 includes a concessive conditional statement, "even though." In verse 5, the διά joins the articular infinitive to express grounds ("because"). The preposition (εἰς τέλος) could be taken with either ἐρχομένη (continually come) or ὑπωπιάζῃ (completely wear me out). That it goes with ἐρχομένη is suggested by the context, which stresses persistence in coming to God in prayer. The word picture is powerful, for εἰς τέλος implies that we should bring our prayers before God "to the end"; i.e., until it is answered. Jesus encouraged His disciples not to give up hope of answered prayer.

ἤθελεν > 3SIAI, he did [not] desire ‖ ἐντρέπομαι > 1SPPI, respect ‖ παρέχειν > PAI, give ‖ κόπον > hardship ‖ ἐκδικήσω > 1SFAI, will give justice ‖ ὑπωπιάζῃ > 3SPAS, may wear down

Further Reading: Luke 18:1-8
Tim Miller

189

⁹ εἶπεν δὲ πρὸς αὐτὸν ὁ Ἰησοῦς ὅτι σήμερον σωτηρία τῷ οἴκῳ τούτῳ ἐγένετο, καθότι καὶ αὐτὸς υἱὸς Ἀβραάμ ἐστιν· ¹⁰ ἦλθεν γὰρ ὁ υἱὸς τοῦ ἀνθρώπου ζητῆσαι καὶ σῶσαι τὸ ἀπολωλός.

CONTEXT:

Jesus was concluding His journey to Jerusalem (9:51–19:27). This passage, along with 19:11–27, provides a transition from Jesus' teaching toward the disciples to Jesus' acts in Jerusalem that would lead to His passion.

COMMENTARY:

As Jesus entered Jericho, Zacchaeus, a Jewish tax-collector, sought to see Jesus (vv. 2–4). Jesus graciously addresses Zacchaeus (vv. 5–6), who then repents of his sins (v. 8). Verse 9 highlights Jesus' public response to Zacchaeus's public repentance. It is important to see that the crowds were not pleased with Jesus' interaction with such a sinner (v. 7). Nevertheless, Jesus says that salvation has come to the house and that Zacchaeus is "also himself a son of Abraham." Jesus was not saying that Zacchaeus's Judaism was the cause of his salvation; instead, he seems to be challenging the unstated view that tax collectors cannot be genuine sons of Abraham. The use of καί is emphatic and adjunctive ("also"), and the use of αὐτός is emphatic ("himself"). The use of both terms, which are functionally unnecessary, draws significant attention to the Jewish identity of this tax collector. Zacchaeus, though rejected by the crowds, was a true spiritual Israelite (cf. Rom 9:8). Even tax collectors, if repentant, had a place among Jesus' disciples.

καθότι > because

Further Reading: Luke 19:1–10
Tim Miller

LUKE 20:13–15A

¹³ εἶπεν δὲ ὁ κύριος τοῦ ἀμπελῶνος· τί ποιήσω; πέμψω τὸν υἱόν μου τὸν ἀγαπητόν· ἴσως τοῦτον ἐντραπήσονται. ¹⁴ ἰδόντες δὲ αὐτὸν οἱ γεωργοὶ διελογίζοντο πρὸς ἀλλήλους λέγοντες· οὗτός ἐστιν ὁ κληρονόμος· ἀποκτείνωμεν αὐτόν, ἵνα ἡμῶν γένηται ἡ κληρονομία. ¹⁵ καὶ ἐκβαλόντες αὐτὸν ἔξω τοῦ ἀμπελῶνος ἀπέκτειναν.

CONTEXT:

Jesus had entered Jerusalem and was engaged in debate in the temple (19:45–21:38). Prior to this debate, Jesus entered Jerusalem on a colt (19:28–44) and cleansed the temple (19:45–46). In light of these actions, the religious leaders were questioning Jesus, looking for an opportunity to kill Him (19:47–20:8).

COMMENTARY:

Jesus was telling a parable to and about the religious leaders who were seeking to kill Him. The parable concerned a landowner who sought to receive fruit from the tenant farmers. Instead of providing the fruit, the tenant farmers rejected the first servant and beat the two servants who followed. The landowner deliberates with himself and says, "I will send my beloved son." The word that follows this statement (ἴσως) is often translated in English as "perhaps" ("perhaps they will respect him") but the Greek word likely means "probably" (cf. BDAG, 484; NKJV). Translating it this way highlights the irrational nature of the religious leader's actions. It is assumed that they would respond rightly to the beloved Son, but their actions are not motivated by reason as the following verses clearly indicate.

ἀμπελῶνος > vineyard ‖ ἴσως > probably ‖ ἐντραπήσονται > 3PFPI, will respect ‖ γεωργοί > farmers ‖ διελογίζοντο > 3PIMI, were discussing ‖ κληρονόμος > heir ‖ ἀποκτείνωμεν > 1PPAS, let us kill ‖ γένηται > 3SAMS, may be ‖ κληρονομία > inheritance ‖ ἀπέκτειναν > 3SAAI, killed

Further Reading: Luke 20:9–19
Tim Miller

JULY 11
LUKE 21:32–33

³² ἀμὴν λέγω ὑμῖν ὅτι οὐ μὴ παρέλθῃ ἡ γενεὰ αὕτη ἕως ἂν πάντα γένηται. ³³ ὁ οὐρανὸς καὶ ἡ γῆ παρελεύσονται, οἱ δὲ λόγοι μου οὐ μὴ παρελεύσονται.

CONTEXT:

Jesus was in Jerusalem where he entered triumphantly (19:28–44) and cleansed the temple (19:45–46). Since coming into Jerusalem, He had been engaged in controversy with the religious leaders (19:45–21:4). In this section, Jesus turned to His disciples, instructing them on the future of the temple and the world (21:5–36).

COMMENTARY:

In response to the disciples' questions concerning the end of the age (21:7), Jesus gave an extended answer. The end will be preceded by earthquakes, wars, and other great signs from heaven (21:10–11; 25–28). "But before all this," believers will be persecuted, betrayed, hated, and killed (21:12–19). Our passage, then, is challenging because Jesus says that "*this generation* will not pass away until all these things have happened." Of course, the group of people Jesus was speaking to have passed away. The key to unlock this puzzle is the lexical range of the word "generation" (γενεά). In Greek, the word could refer to a class of people rather than a people alive at a certain time. In this case, it refers to unfaithful Israel. In sum, Jesus was saying, the unfaithful people of Israel will not pass away until all this takes place.

παρέλθῃ > 3SAAS, pass away ‖ γενεά > generation ‖ παρελεύσονται > 3PFMI, will pass away

Further Reading: Luke 21:5–38
Tim Miller

LUKE 22:31-32

³¹ Σίμων Σίμων, ἰδοὺ ὁ σατανᾶς ἐξῃτήσατο ὑμᾶς τοῦ σινιάσαι ὡς τὸν σῖτον· ³² ἐγὼ δὲ ἐδεήθην περὶ σοῦ ἵνα μὴ ἐκλίπῃ ἡ πίστις σου· καὶ σύ ποτε ἐπιστρέψας στήρισον τοὺς ἀδελφούς σου.

CONTEXT:

With the commitment of Judas to betray Jesus (22:1–6), Luke's Gospel turns toward the passion of Christ. This passage occurs during the Last Supper (22:7–38). Preceding this warning, the disciples once more argue over who would have the greatest place in the kingdom (22:24–30).

COMMENTARY:

After expressing how greatness would be measured in the coming kingdom (22:24–30), Jesus here warned Peter that Satan "asked" (ἐξῃτήσατο) to sift Peter like wheat. Sifting separated wheat from chaff. The verb ἐξῃτήσατο is variously translated. The translation "asked" is common (NIV, CSB, NKJV), but is likely too weak, for the word refers to a request for which someone has a right (BDAG, 344). In light of this, some versions have "demanded" (ESV, NRSV), yet this seems too strong, for Satan cannot command God. The NASB strikes a helpful middle ground with "has demanded permission." Such a reading highlights the striking parallel with the book of Job, in which Satan "sifts" Job after receiving permission to do so.

ἐξῃτήσατο >3SAMI, demanded || σινιάσαι > AAN, to sift || σῖτον > wheat || ἐδεήθην > 1SAPI, I prayed, begged, petitioned || ἐκλίπῃ > 3SAAS, may [not] fail || ἐπιστρέψας > AAPMSN, having turned || στήρισον > 2SAAM, strengthen

Further Reading: Luke 22:24–34
Tim Miller

LUKE 23:44–45

⁴⁴ καὶ ἦν ἤδη ὡσεὶ ὥρα ἕκτη καὶ σκότος ἐγένετο ἐφ' ὅλην τὴν γῆν ἕως ὥρας ἐνάτης ⁴⁵ τοῦ ἡλίου ἐκλιπόντος, ἐσχίσθη δὲ τὸ καταπέτασμα τοῦ ναοῦ μέσον.

CONTEXT:

After being betrayed (22:47-53) and enduring trials with mocking and abuse (22:66–23:25), Jesus was crucified. This passage records his death and the events surrounding it.

COMMENTARY:

As Jesus ended His passion, two significant events took place. First, there was a darkness that covered the land from about noon until three. In Greek, the case of nouns indicating time is significant. Datives indicate point in time (e.g., "in the ninth hour"); accusatives indicate extent of time (e.g., "for three days"); and genitives indicate kind of time (or general designation of time). Here, the translation "around noon until three" is appropriate. The significance of the darkness is debated. It may highlight the death of the "light of the world" (Jn 8:12), but almost certainly puts into visual form the wrath of the Father.

ὡσεί > about, approximately ǁ ἕκτη > sixth ǁ ἐνάτης > ninth ǁ ἐκλιπόντος > AAPMSG, having failed ǁ ἐσχίσθη > 3SAPI, was split ǁ καταπέτασμα > curtain

Further Reading: Luke 23:44–49
Tim Miller

JULY 14

LUKE 24:11-12

¹¹ καὶ ἐφάνησαν ἐνώπιον αὐτῶν ὡσεὶ λῆρος τὰ ῥήματα ταῦτα, καὶ ἠπίστουν αὐταῖς. ¹² Ὁ δὲ Πέτρος ἀναστὰς ἔδραμεν ἐπὶ τὸ μνημεῖον καὶ παρακύψας βλέπει τὰ ὀθόνια μόνα, καὶ ἀπῆλθεν πρὸς ἑαυτὸν θαυμάζων τὸ γεγονός.

CONTEXT:

After being crucified and buried, Jesus rose from the dead. Multiple female followers of Jesus came to the tomb early in the morning to apply spices to the body, but Jesus was already raised and absent from the tomb (24:1-3). In His place, they found two angels who announced his resurrection (24:4-6).

COMMENTARY:

The women returned and informed the eleven disciples that Jesus was raised. But the disciples did not believe them. The Greek reads literally as "*these words appeared to them as nonsense.*" The use of the demonstrative pronoun focuses the narrative on the words. In response, the disciples "did not believe the women." Accordingly, Thomas should not be isolated as the "doubting disciple"! Nevertheless, Luke highlights the response of Peter, who ran to the tomb. This indicates that although he struggled to believe, there was a spark of faith and hope. In the Greek, the verb "saw" (βλέπει) is a historic present, which draws thematic attention to the linen cloth lying alone. It symbolized the fact that the body of Jesus had been raised. As Peter went away, having seen only the linen wrapping but no body, he is marveling "in himself" at the sight!

ἐφάνησαν > 3PAPI, seemed || ὡσεί > as || λῆρος > nonsense || ἠπίστουν >3PIAI, disbelieved || ἀναστάς > AAPMSN, having arisen || ἔδραμεν > 3SAAI, ran || παρακύψας > AAPMSN, bending over to look || ὀθόνια > wrapping || θαυμάζων > PAPMSN, marveling || τὸ γεγονός > RAPNSA, what had happened

Further Reading: Luke 24:1-12
Tim Miller

195

³ καθὼς παρεκάλεσά σε προσμεῖναι ἐν Ἐφέσῳ πορευόμενος εἰς Μακεδονίαν, ἵνα παραγγείλῃς τισὶν μὴ ἑτεροδιδασκαλεῖν ⁴ μηδὲ προσέχειν μύθοις καὶ γενεαλογίαις ἀπεράντοις, αἵτινες ἐκζητήσεις παρέχουσιν μᾶλλον ἢ οἰκονομίαν θεοῦ τὴν ἐν πίστει.

CONTEXT:

By the time 1 Timothy is penned, false teachers had gained an influential position in the church of Ephesus. That influence manifested itself in teaching that subtly moved the church from a focus on the sound teaching of Jesus (6:3) in the gospel (1:13-16; 2:4-6) to abstract disputes about genealogies (1:3-4), marriage (4:1-3), and the like (6:4-5). The situation was so dire that Paul moves immediately from greeting (1:2) to correction (1:3), skipping his traditional thanksgiving.

COMMENTARY:

The required steps for correction are outlined with three infinitives: (1) I urge you (Timothy) προσμεῖναι ("to remain") in Ephesus in order that you might command certain ones, (2) μὴ ἑτεροδιδασκαλεῖν ("not to teach contrary instruction"), nor allow them (3) προσέχειν ("to devote themselves") to myths and endless genealogies. Since each infinitive follows a verb that expresses speech: παρεκάλεσα ("I urge") and παραγγείλῃς ("you command"), these infinitives most likely are used to express indirect discourse. Sometime in the recent past, Paul told Timothy to remain in Ephesus. Sometime in the near future, Paul expects Timothy to command these certain ones to stop their teaching and devotion to myths and endless genealogies. Focusing on the term γενεαλογίαις ("genealogies") specifically, it is quite possible that the genealogies in view could have originated from the Bible. Irrespective of the origin, the false teachers used this material to promote speculation. By moving in this direction, they derailed the church from the promotion of a proper stewardship of God's gift of faith.

προσμεῖναι > AAN, to remain || Ἐφέσῳ > Ephesus || Μακεδονίαν > Macedonia || ἑτεροδιδασκαλεῖν > PAN, to give contrary instruction || προσέχειν > PAN, to give heed to || μύθοις > myths || γενεαλογίαις > genealogies || ἀπεράντοις > endless || ἐκζητήσεις > speculations || παρέχουσιν > 3PPAI, they bring about || οἰκονομίαν > stewardship

Further Reading: Titus 1:9-16
Thomas K. Dailey

¹⁵ πιστὸς ὁ λόγος καὶ πάσης ἀποδοχῆς ἄξιος, ὅτι Χριστὸς Ἰησοῦς ἦλθεν εἰς τὸν κόσμον ἁμαρτωλοὺς σῶσαι, ὧν πρῶτός εἰμι ἐγώ. ¹⁶ ἀλλὰ διὰ τοῦτο ἠλεήθην, ἵνα ἐν ἐμοὶ πρώτῳ ἐνδείξηται Χριστὸς Ἰησοῦς τὴν ἅπασαν μακροθυμίαν πρὸς ὑποτύπωσιν τῶν μελλόντων πιστεύειν ἐπ' αὐτῷ εἰς ζωὴν αἰώνιον.

CONTEXT:

The introductory statement, "the saying is faithful," is used five times in the Pastoral Epistles (1:15; 3:1; 4:9; 2 Tim 2:11; Titus 3:8). The statement is used by Paul like a meta-comment to emphasize that the idea is well-known and trusted. The difficulty in some of the other uses elsewhere concerns the question as to whether the saying precedes (anaphoric) or follows (cataphoric) the introductory statement.

COMMENTARY:

In this case, it appears that the following ὅτι clause supplies the content of the saying: Χριστὸς Ἰησοῦς ἦλθεν εἰς τὸν κόσμον ἁμαρτωλοὺς σῶσαι ("Christ Jesus came into the world to save sinners"). Rehearsing this statement moves Paul toward personal reflection. Among the sinners whom Jesus came to save, Paul saw himself as the leader of the pack: ὧν πρῶτός εἰμι ἐγώ ("among whom I am first"). In this terrible state, Paul was given mercy. Why he received that mercy is explained by the use of a ἵνα purpose clause. In the first instance, he received mercy for the purpose of making his life a demonstration of τὴν ἅπασαν μακροθυμίαν ("the fullness of [Jesus'] patience"). Paul's sinfulness was not sufficient to wear out divine forbearance. In the second instance, the mercy he received was for the purpose of providing an example of τῶν μελλόντων πιστεύειν ἐπ' αὐτῷ εἰς ζωὴν αἰώνιον ("those about to believe in him for eternal life"). If God could transform a person like Paul, then he is able to transform anyone who places his faith in Christ Jesus for eternal life.

ἀποδοχῆς > acceptance ‖ σῶσαι > AAN, to save ‖ ἠλεήθην > 1SAPI, I received mercy ‖ ἐνδείξηται > 3SAMS, might demonstrate ‖ μακροθυμίαν > patience ‖ ὑποτύπωσιν > a pattern ‖ μελλόντων > PAPMPG, about to ‖ πιστεύειν > PAN, to believe

Further Reading: Titus 3:3–8

Thomas K. Dailey

JULY 17
1 TIMOTHY 2:5-6

⁵ εἷς γὰρ θεός, εἷς καὶ μεσίτης θεοῦ καὶ ἀνθρώπων, ἄνθρωπος Χριστὸς Ἰησοῦς, ⁶ ὁ δοὺς ἑαυτὸν ἀντίλυτρον ὑπὲρ πάντων, τὸ μαρτύριον καιροῖς ἰδίοις.

CONTEXT:

The corrosive influence of the false teachers has led the church in Ephesus to lose focus on sound teaching, and this influence was distracting them from genuine worship. In order to recapture lost ground in the area of worship, Paul addresses some misguided emphases in corporate prayer.

COMMENTARY:

Paul insists that prayer be made for all people (2:1) because this pleases God (2:3) who desires all people to be saved (2:4). The postpositive γάρ ("for") provides further explanation as to why prayer should be made with all people in mind. First of all, there is only one God. The first use of εἷς ("one") draws our attention to the language of the OT and how Yahweh stood in contrast to the polytheistic forms of worship among the nations: "Hear, O Israel: The LORD our God, the LORD is one" (Deut 6:4). Second, this one God has worked through a singular mediator. The second use of εἷς draws our attention to a fundamental role of Jesus found in the NT: He is εἷς ... μεσίτης θεοῦ καὶ ἀνθρώπων ("the only mediator between God and men"). How can this be? In language that draws our attention back to the words of Jesus (Mark 10:45; Matt 20:28), it is because Christ Jesus is ὁ δοὺς ἑαυτὸν ἀντίλυτρον ὑπὲρ πάντων ("the one who gave himself as a ransom for all"). The universal scope of God's saving intentions ("prayer for all"; "desiring all to be saved"; "a ransom for all") finds resolution in the one God's one mediator, Christ Jesus.

μεσίτης > mediator || δούς > AAPMSN, [one who] gave || ἀντίλυτρον > a ransom || μαρτύριον > testimony

Further Reading: Acts 4:5-12
Thomas K. Dailey

1 TIMOTHY 2:11–12

¹¹ γυνὴ ἐν ἡσυχίᾳ μανθανέτω ἐν πάσῃ ὑποταγῇ· ¹² διδάσκειν δὲ γυναικὶ οὐκ ἐπιτρέπω οὐδὲ αὐθεντεῖν ἀνδρός, ἀλλ᾽ εἶναι ἐν ἡσυχίᾳ.

CONTEXT:
Admittedly, this is a controversial portion of the Pastoral Epistles; nevertheless, certain structural items are worthy of note.

COMMENTARY:
Verse 11 utilizes a third-person imperative γυνὴ ... μανθανέτω ("let a woman learn") which is flanked by two prepositional phrases that address the manner by which the woman should learn: ἐν ἡσυχίᾳ ("in quietness") and ἐν πάσῃ ὑποταγῇ ("in full submission"). Using a third-person imperative softens the bluntness or directness that would come from using a second-person imperative form. Combined with the anarthrous γυνή, the imperative is taken as a general, not specific, command. Verse 12 supports the initial imperative μανθανέτω by creating a negative-positive contrast. Although the main verb is an indicative, (οὐκ ἐπιτρέπω, "I do not permit"), when it is combined with the stamp of Paul's apostolic authority, it functions like a prohibition. The verb ἐπιτρέπω is often followed by a complementary infinitive. In verse 12, there are three infinitives filling that role—the first two do so negatively as part of the prohibition and the third does so positively to reinforce μανθανέτω. In effect, Paul prohibits the woman διδάσκειν ("to teach") and αὐθεντεῖν ἀνδρός ("to have authority over a man"). By contrast, (ἀλλά, "but"), Paul "permits" the woman εἶναι ("to be") a learner ἐν ἡσυχίᾳ ("in quietness"), a reiteration of the wording in verse 11. Quietness does not mean silence. Clearly the woman's voice was intended to be heard in corporate worship (1 Cor 11:5; Col 3:16). Quietness reflects the quiet disposition to receive the truth taught in corporate worship and is to be combined with a readiness to submit to the teaching that leads to godliness.

ἡσυχίᾳ > quietness ‖ μανθανέτω > 3SPAM, let ... learn ‖ ὑποταγῇ > submission ‖ διδάσκειν > PAN, to teach ‖ ἐπιτρέπω > 1SPAI, permit ‖ αὐθεντεῖν > PAN, to have authority over ‖ εἶναι > PAN, to be

Further Reading: Titus 2:3–5
Thomas K. Dailey

... ⁴ τοῦ ἰδίου οἴκου καλῶς προϊστάμενον, τέκνα ἔχοντα ἐν ὑποταγῇ, μετὰ πάσης σεμνότητος ⁵ (εἰ δέ τις τοῦ ἰδίου οἴκου προστῆναι οὐκ οἶδεν, πῶς ἐκκλησίας θεοῦ ἐπιμελήσεται;)

CONTEXT:

In 1 Timothy 3, Paul introduces the godly characteristics that should mark the leadership of the church. One of those characteristics is that an overseer must be able to manage his own home (v. 4).

COMMENTARY:

The relevance of this point is teased out by Paul in verse 5 with the use of a first-class condition (εἰ + an indicative verb in the protasis). To say that εἰ ... τις τοῦ ἰδίου οἴκου προστῆναι οὐκ οἶδεν ("if ... someone does not know [how] to manage his own house") is a first-class condition means that the condition is presented as true for the sake of the argument. Though such structural semantics are helpful, conditionals should also be analyzed in the way that explains how the protasis (the *if* clause) relates to the apodosis (the *then* clause). In this case the apodosis is a rhetorical question πῶς ἐκκλησίας θεοῦ ἐπιμελήσεται; ("how shall he take care of the house of God?"). The relationship of the two clauses is one of grounds and inference. A potential candidate for leadership in the church who is ineffectual in managing his own home is the basis (grounds) for Paul to question (draw an inference) whether such a candidate can take care of God's house. This is a healthy reminder that church leadership must not only pay attention to how they conduct their affairs before those in God's house, but also to how they do so at home.

προϊστάμενον > PMPMSA, manage ‖ ὑποταγῇ > subjection ‖ σεμνότητος > dignity ‖ προστῆναι > AAN, to manage ‖ οἶδεν > 3SRAI, knows ‖ ἐπιμελήσεται > 3SFMI, shall take care of

Further Reading: Titus 1:5–9
Thomas K. Dailey

JULY 20
1 TIMOTHY 3:14-15

¹⁴ ταῦτά σοι γράφω ἐλπίζων ἐλθεῖν πρὸς σὲ ἐν τάχει· ¹⁵ ἐὰν δὲ βραδύνω, ἵνα εἰδῇς πῶς δεῖ ἐν οἴκῳ θεοῦ ἀναστρέφεσθαι, ἥτις ἐστὶν ἐκκλησία θεοῦ ζῶντος, στῦλος καὶ ἑδραίωμα τῆς ἀληθείας.

CONTEXT:
To this point, the argument of 1 Timothy has covered several topics. From the corrections offered in light of false teachers (1:3-7, 19b-20) to acceptable prayer (2:1-4) to the behavior of men and women in corporate worship (2:8-10) to the character of overseers and deacons (3:1-13), Paul now provides an overriding purpose statement (marked by the ἵνα clause) that ties these seemingly unconnected topics together.

COMMENTARY:
Sharpening the focus of corporate behavior is Paul's intention. He uses three designations to describe the community of believers in Ephesus: ἐν οἴκῳ θεοῦ ("God's house"), ἐκκλησία θεοῦ ζῶντος ("the church of the living God"), and στῦλος καὶ ἑδραίωμα τῆς ἀληθείας ("the pillar and support of the truth"). The last pair of terms, consisting of (1) στῦλος, which is used 4x in the NT, and (2) ἑδραίωμα, which is a NT *hapax legomenon*, appear to be a hendiadys, an idiom where an author uses two terms to communicate a singular idea. God's house, namely the church of the living God, is described as the pillar supporting the truth. Subsequently, it appears that πῶς δεῖ ἐν οἴκῳ θεοῦ ἀναστρέφεσθαι ("how it is necessary to behave in God's house") highlights the need for Christian conduct to conform to a standard appropriate for corporate worship. If corporate behavior is inappropriate, like that of men carried away in anger (2:8) or like that of women without self-control (2:9), then the church ceases to support the truth it professes in the gospel.

ἐλπίζων > PAPMSN, hoping || ἐλθεῖν > AAN, to come || τάχει > soon || βραδύνω > 1SPAS, I may be delayed || εἰδῇς > 2SRAS, you may know || ἀναστρέφεσθαι > PMN, to behave || ζῶντος > PAPMSG, living || στῦλος > pillar || ἑδραίωμα > support, foundation

Further Reading: 1 Timothy 2:1-15
Thomas K. Dailey

¹⁶ ἔπεχε σεαυτῷ καὶ τῇ διδασκαλίᾳ, ἐπίμενε αὐτοῖς· τοῦτο γὰρ ποιῶν καὶ σεαυτὸν σώσεις καὶ τοὺς ἀκούοντάς σου.

CONTEXT:

Although this letter is written to Timothy, Paul's true child in the faith (1:2), up to this point the letter reads rather impersonally dealing with issues that are of churchwide concern. In this section (4:11–16), we begin to get a glimpse of Paul's relationship to Timothy through a series of personal, albeit forceful, exhortations.

COMMENTARY:

Paul's summary exhortation to Timothy is that he ἔπεχε ("pay close attention") to two items, indicated by datives functioning as direct objects: (1) σεαυτῷ ("to yourself") and (2) τῇ διδασκαλίᾳ ("to the teaching"). To give requisite attention to yourself involves Timothy's honest self-assessment. This is an opportunity for him to test the conformity of his affections with godly ends or, negatively, it provides the chance for him to uncover deceptive motivations in the hope that they may be corrected. To give requisite attention to the teaching is to align the content of his message with "the sound words of our Lord Jesus Christ" and that which "accords with godliness" (6:3). The adverbial participle ποιῶν ("doing") can be conditional or it can convey means. As conditional, if Timothy pays close attention, then he and his hearers will be saved. As means, by paying close attention, then he and his hearers will be saved. In this case the semantics of condition and means overlap significantly. Regarding the salvation involved, it may be helpful to provide a contrast. The false teachers were "depraved in mind" (6:5); they had not paid attention to themselves. Furthermore, their teaching was "deprived of the truth" (6:5); they had not paid attention to their teaching. Consequently, the false teachers could never be the condition or the instrument of salvation for themselves or their hearers.

ἔπεχε > 2SPAM, pay close attention to ‖ διδασκαλίᾳ > teaching ‖ ἐπίμενε > 2SPAM, persist in ‖ ποιῶν > PAPMSN, so doing ‖ σώσεις > 2SFAI, will save ‖ ἀκούοντας > PAPMPA, who hear

Further Reading: Titus 2:7–8
Thomas K. Dailey

1 TIMOTHY 5:3-4

³ χήρας τίμα τὰς ὄντως χήρας. ⁴ εἰ δέ τις χήρα τέκνα ἢ ἔκγονα ἔχει, μανθανέτωσαν πρῶτον τὸν ἴδιον οἶκον εὐσεβεῖν καὶ ἀμοιβὰς ἀποδιδόναι τοῖς προγόνοις· τοῦτο γάρ ἐστιν ἀπόδεκτον ἐνώπιον τοῦ θεοῦ.

CONTEXT:

The care of widows is an ethical indicator of those who mimic God's character (Ps 68:5; 146:9), and the abuse of widows is characteristic of the wicked (Ps 94:3-6; Job 24:21). When we turn to this section of 1 Timothy, we find that the concern for widows remains a constant obligation for God's people.

COMMENTARY:

Paul marks the introduction to the topic of widows by fronting the accusative χήρας ("widows"), and quickly qualifies the widows by the use of the term ὄντως ("truly"). The term ὄντως is related to the participle form of εἰμί (nom. ὤν, gen. ὄντος). It is traditionally classified as an adverb, but in this case it is functioning as an adjective. Paul calls the Ephesian church to express honor or care to widows who are true widows. The true widows of verse 3 are differentiated from another set of widows in verse 4, widows that have families. If it is the case that a widow has a family, then the family needs εὐσεβεῖν καὶ ἀμοιβὰς ἀποδιδόναι ("to show godliness and to render a return") to their widowed family member. The care of this class of widows should not fall on the church; it should be picked up by the extended family. To care for a widowed family member is a means to demonstrate godliness, to render what is acceptable to one's parents (or grandparents), and to express concern for those who are of special concern to God.

χήρας > widows || τίμα > 2SPAM, honor || ὄντως > truly || ἔκγονα > descendants || μανθανέτωσαν > 3PPAM, let them learn || εὐσεβεῖν > PAN, to show godliness || ἀμοιβάς > return || ἀποδιδόναι > PAN, to give || προγόνοις > parents || ἀπόδεκτον > acceptable

Further Reading: 1 Timothy 5:7-8; James 1:26-27
Thomas K. Dailey

JULY 23
1 TIMOTHY 5:24-25

²⁴ τινῶν ἀνθρώπων αἱ ἁμαρτίαι πρόδηλοί εἰσιν προάγουσαι εἰς κρίσιν, τισὶν δὲ καὶ ἐπακολουθοῦσιν· ²⁵ ὡσαύτως καὶ τὰ ἔργα τὰ καλὰ πρόδηλα, καὶ τὰ ἄλλως ἔχοντα κρυβῆναι οὐ δύνανται.

CONTEXT:

In 1 Timothy 5:22-25, Paul warns against the hasty appointment of elders because of the accidental possibility of mistakenly approving one who is ensnared by sin. To appoint such an elder can be to "share" (κοινώνει) in his sins (v. 22).

COMMENTARY:

The connection between someone's sin and his potential appointment as an elder is very difficult to work out practically, even though the principle that Paul articulates is simple. Some men sin in such a way that it is πρόδηλοι ("evident") and on that basis, it leads εἰς κρίσιν ("to judgment") or disqualification for consideration for the office of elder (taking the judgment as non-eschatological). On the other hand, there are some whose sins are not obvious, and knowledge of their sins only comes afterward ἐπακολουθοῦσιν ("they follow along later"). How does a church proceed in the circumstance where an individual appears qualified, but his ensnarement in sin is an unknown factor? If, as Paul says, their sin will be observable afterward, then his initial warning about being too hasty in the appointment of an elder must be heeded (5:22). In the place of haste, the church should allow for a sufficient amount of time to observe the character of the candidate so that these non-evident sins may surface. Of course, it is not an absolute guarantee that such sins will surface, but the church that follows this pattern will bypass obvious difficulties.

πρόδηλοι > evident || προάγουσαι > PAPFPN, going before || ἐπακολουθοῦσιν > 3PPAI, follow later || ὡσαύτως > likewise || πρόδηλα > evident || ἄλλως ἔχοντα > PAPNPN, being otherwise || κρυβῆναι > APN, be kept secret

Further Reading: 2 Timothy 2:22-26
Thomas K. Dailey

1 TIMOTHY 6:13-14

¹³ παραγγέλλω σοι ἐνώπιον τοῦ θεοῦ τοῦ ζῳογονοῦντος τὰ πάντα καὶ Χριστοῦ Ἰησοῦ τοῦ μαρτυρήσαντος ἐπὶ Ποντίου Πιλάτου τὴν καλὴν ὁμολογίαν, ¹⁴ τηρῆσαί σε τὴν ἐντολὴν ἄσπιλον ἀνεπίλημπτον μέχρι τῆς ἐπιφανείας τοῦ κυρίου ἡμῶν Ἰησοῦ Χριστοῦ.

CONTEXT:

Before closing the letter, Paul issues a series of final imperatives that should shape Timothy's internal motivations: flee greed's corruption! (v. 11a); pursue godly virtues! (v. 11b); fight the good fight of faith! (v. 12a); and take hold of eternal life! (v. 12b).

COMMENTARY:

In verses 13-14 Paul shifts to an indicative παραγγέλλω σοι ("I command [or, charge] you ...") in tandem with the infinitive clause τηρῆσαι σε τὴν ἐντολήν ("... you to keep the commandment"). The four imperatives, along with the indicative that functions like an imperative, are all delivered ἐνώπιον τοῦ θεοῦ ... καὶ Χριστοῦ Ἰησοῦ ("in the presence of God ... and Christ Jesus"). Initially, the invocation of these two Witnesses announces the seriousness of the charge that is being delegated to Timothy. Both Witnesses receive further description with adjectival participles. God is invoked as the one τοῦ ζῳογονοῦντος τὰ πάντα ("who gives life to all things") and Jesus is the one τοῦ μαρτυρήσαντος ἐπὶ Ποντίου Πιλάτου τὴν καλὴν ὁμολογίαν ("who testified the good confession before Pontius Pilate"). God, who sustains Timothy's life in his present difficult circumstances, and Jesus, who actually maintained the good confession in difficult circumstances, become the source and model for Timothy to overcome his circumstances and accomplish his mission.

παραγγέλλω > 1SPAI, command, charge || ζῳογονοῦντος > PAPMSG, who makes alive || μαρτυρήσαντος > AAPMSG, who testified || ὁμολογίαν > confession || τηρῆσαι > AAN, to keep || ἄσπιλον > without fault || ἀνεπίλημπτον > irreproachable || μέχρι > until || ἐπιφανείας > appearing

Further Reading: 1 John 3:19-24
Thomas K. Dailey

2 TIMOTHY 1:6

⁶ δι' ἣν αἰτίαν ἀναμιμνήσκω σε ἀναζωπυρεῖν τὸ χάρισμα τοῦ θεοῦ, ὅ ἐστιν ἐν σοὶ διὰ τῆς ἐπιθέσεως τῶν χειρῶν μου.

CONTEXT:

As Paul awaits his execution, he writes Timothy, encouraging him to come before winter (4:21). Just in case he doesn't make it in time, Paul shares his final instructions. The first chapter includes a reminder of Timothy's heritage, an encouragement not to be ashamed of Paul or the Gospel, and a call to continued faithfulness and loyalty.

COMMENTARY:

The word ἀναζωπυρεῖν has been translated in various ways. This is the only time the word is found in the NT. The NKJV translates the word as "stir up," while the NASB renders it "kindle afresh." Louw & Nida point out that some have translated the word as "keep alive" to avoid the idea that Timothy may have wavered in his earlier commitment to the gospel. The word is related to the process of stirring a fire to keep it alive. I remember growing up spending much time stirring a fire with a poker, dependent on wood stoves for warmth in the Colorado winters. A fire needs regular attention to keep it burning hot. So, Timothy needed constant attention to "stir up" God's gift.

αἰτίαν > reason || ἀναμιμνήσκω > 1SPAI, remind || ἀναζωπυρεῖν > PAN, to fan (see commentary for alternative glosses || χάρισμα > gift || ἐπιθέσεως > laying on

Further Reading: 2 Timothy 1:3-7
Mark H. Ballard

2 TIMOTHY 1:14

¹⁴ τὴν καλὴν παραθήκην φύλαξον διὰ πνεύματος ἁγίου τοῦ ἐνοικοῦντος ἐν ἡμῖν.

CONTEXT:
Following his greeting, Paul begins his letter to Timothy by expressing his thankfulness for his son in the faith. He expresses his desire to see Timothy again. He then reminds Timothy of his godly heritage and calls him to use the gift God has given him without fear, despite the perilous times in which both Paul and Timothy live. In the final paragraph of this chapter, Paul calls Timothy to remain faithful even as others have not.

COMMENTARY:
Notice the noun παραθήκην is found only three places in the NT: here, in 2 Timothy 1:12, and in 1 Timothy 6:20. It is translated as a "deposit" or something "placed alongside." In 1:12 the concept is that Paul had *entrusted* his life and ministry to Jesus. Here and in 1 Timothy 6:20 the focus is on what had been *deposited* with Timothy. In Timothy's case, Paul encouraged him to guard (φύλαξον) what the Lord (and Paul) *deposited* with him. In this text Paul adds how Timothy was to do so, διὰ πνεύματος ἁγίου τοῦ ἐνοικοῦντος ἐν ἡμῖν.

παραθήκην > deposit ‖ φύλαξον > 2SAAM, guard ‖ ἐνοικοῦντος > PAPNSG, dwells

Further Reading: 2 Timothy 1:8–18
Mark H. Ballard

2 TIMOTHY 2:2

... ² καὶ ἃ ἤκουσας παρ᾽ ἐμοῦ διὰ πολλῶν μαρτύρων, ταῦτα παράθου πιστοῖς ἀνθρώποις, οἵτινες ἱκανοὶ ἔσονται καὶ ἑτέρους διδάξαι.

CONTEXT:

Paul encourages Timothy to faithfulness in the midst of hardship. For Timothy to be faithful he must be strong in God's grace and he must look to the future by passing on the baton to others. Paul's encouragement includes looking to the examples of a soldier (2:3–4), an athlete (2:5), a farmer (2:6), Jesus (2:8), and Paul's own life (2:9–10).

COMMENTARY:

Notice that παράθου is the aorist imperative of παρατίθημι ("entrust"). This verb, παρατίθημι, is related to the noun παραθήκην ("deposit") used in 1:14 when Paul described the deposit the Lord (and Paul) has made in Timothy. The Apostle now commands Timothy to *deposit* what he had learned in the lives of "faithful men" (πιστοῖς ἀνθρώποις). These faithful men would then teach others, ensuring that the truth would continue to be passed from generation to generation. As Paul was nearing the end of his life, these instructions to Timothy were crucial for the truth to continue to impact others after Paul's departure.

ἤκουσας > 2SAAI, you heard ‖ παράθου > 2SAMM, entrust ‖ ἔσονται > 3PFMI, will be ‖ διδάξαι > AAN, to teach

Further Reading: 2 Timothy 2:1–13
Mark H. Ballard

¹⁶ τὰς δὲ βεβήλους κενοφωνίας περιΐστασο ἐπὶ πλεῖον γὰρ προκόψουσιν ἀσεβείας.

CONTEXT:

Twice in this paragraph (2:14–19) Paul warns Timothy of the dangers of unfruitful discussion. In verse 14, he charges Timothy to remind the Ephesians that they should not engage in useless arguments over words. In contrast, Timothy should be diligent to be approved by God by "rightly handling" or "cutting straight" (ὀρθοτομοῦντα) the Word of God (2:15) and by personally avoiding unfruitful disputes (2:16).

COMMENTARY:

Paul warns Timothy to avoid βεβήλους, *vile* or *profane talk*. He also warns him to avoid κενοφωνίας, *idle babblings* (NKJV). The word κενοφωνίας is found only here and in 1 Timothy 6:20. It may also be translated, *empty talk* or *empty chatter*. When combined, perhaps these words could be rendered *fruitless discussion*. While correcting and setting things in order in Ephesus, it was important for Timothy not only to avoid vile speech, but also to recognize and avoid *empty talk* and *fruitless discussion*. This encouragement is still necessary for the servant of God today.

βεβήλους > irreverent || κενοφωνίας > babble || περιΐστασο > 2SPMM, avoid || προκόψουσιν > 3PFAI, will lead || ἀσεβείας > ungodliness

Further Reading: 2 Timothy 2:14–19
Mark H. Ballard

²³ τὰς δὲ μωρὰς καὶ ἀπαιδεύτους ζητήσεις παραιτοῦ, εἰδὼς ὅτι γεννῶσι μάχας.

CONTEXT:

In the previous paragraph we noted that Paul warned Timothy to avoid (περιΐστασο) fruitless arguments and vile talk. Paul returns to the same concern in the final paragraph of this chapter. Not only was Timothy's life to be distinctly different from the false teachers of the day, but his speech was to be categorically different. He needed to act in wisdom and completely avoid certain discussions.

COMMENTARY:

Several noteworthy words are found in this verse. The main verb, παραιτοῦ, is a present imperative. Although the NKJV uses the English *avoid* when translating παραιτοῦ, the focus is likely stronger than a simple avoidance. Other options could include *refuse* (NASB) or even *have nothing to do with* (ESV). What is Timothy to have nothing to do with? He is strongly to avoid μωρὰς (*foolish or stupid*) and ἀπαιδεύτους (*uninstructed*) arguments. Why? Since Timothy *knows* (perfect participle εἰδὼς) that these types of arguments only generate μάχας (*contention, battles, strife*). Such arguments should be refused so as not to cause further division.

μωρὰς > foolish ‖ ἀπαιδεύτους > uninstructed ‖ ζητήσεις > disputes ‖ παραιτοῦ > 2SPMM, have nothing to do with ‖ εἰδὼς > RAPMSN, knowing ‖ γεννῶσι > 3PPAI, beget ‖ μάχας > quarrels

Further Reading: 2 Timothy 2:14–26
Mark H. Ballard

2 TIMOTHY 3:1

¹ τοῦτο δὲ γίνωσκε, ὅτι ἐν ἐσχάταις ἡμέραις ἐνστήσονται καιροὶ χαλεποί.

CONTEXT:

As difficult as the times were, Paul warned Timothy that in the last days things would be even more difficult (3:1). In verses 2–7, Paul explains the source of the difficulty (χαλεποί) by describing the anticipated behavior of people living in the time to come. He then compares the coming time to Moses' day and reminds Timothy of the folly of those who resisted Moses.

COMMENTARY:

There is debate regarding the time period to which Paul refers with the phrase ἐν ἐσχάταις ἡμέραις. Some assert that Paul refers to the entire church age as Peter did in his Acts 2 sermon. Others suggest that it refers to the conclusion of the last days, closer to the time of Jesus' return for His church. In considering the options, one should note the future verb ἐνστήσονται, "will come." Jesus once made an argument based on the tense of a word (Matt 22:32; cf. 5:18); following His example may settle the question at hand. Paul was warning Timothy that as difficult as things were in their day, more difficult and even fierce times were yet to come.

γίνωσκε > 2SPAM, understand ǁ ἐνστήσονται > 3PFMI, will come ǁ χαλεποί > difficult

Further Reading: 2 Timothy 3:1–9
Mark H. Ballard

2 TIMOTHY 3:16

¹⁶ πᾶσα γραφὴ θεόπνευστος καὶ ὠφέλιμος πρὸς διδασκαλίαν, πρὸς
ἐλεγμόν, πρὸς ἐπανόρθωσιν, πρὸς παιδείαν τὴν ἐν δικαιοσύνῃ ...

CONTEXT:

Having described the falling away of many in the last days, Paul contrasts
Timothy's condition by reminding him of his foundation. This foundation,
conveyed to Timothy by his mother and grandmother (2 Tim 1:5; 3:15), was
reinforced by Paul (2 Tim 3:10–11). However, neither Timothy's family nor Paul
was the foundation. Timothy's foundation was τὰ ἱερὰ γράμματα, which made
him wise unto salvation (3:15). Paul now turns to discuss both the origin of the
Scriptures and their impact (i.e., their direct action on us and their effects by
preaching or other means).

COMMENTARY:

The word θεόπνευστος is a *hapax legomenon* used only here in the NT. Some
translate the word as "inspired by God." However, the word "inspiration" may
have various meanings. A formal translation of the word likely conveys the best
understanding. This is a compound word, with θεός meaning *God*, and πνευ-
meaning to *breathe*. Thus, the translation *God-breathed* accurately conveys the
Apostle's intent. In other words, πᾶσα γραφή has its origin in God Himself. It is
truly *God's* Word. Since God cannot lie and knows all things, this speaks to both
the inerrancy and the sufficiency of Scripture, its entire truthfulness and
trustworthiness in every word.

θεόπνευστος > breathed by God || **ὠφέλιμος** > profitable || **διδασκαλίαν** >
teaching || **ἐλεγμόν** > reproof || **ἐπανόρθωσιν** > correction || **παιδείαν** >
training

Further Reading: 2 Timothy 3:1–17
Mark H. Ballard

AUGUST 1

2 TIMOTHY 3:17

... ¹⁷ ἵνα ἄρτιος ᾖ ὁ τοῦ θεοῦ ἄνθρωπος, πρὸς πᾶν ἔργον ἀγαθὸν ἐξηρτισμένος.

CONTEXT:
Grammatically, 2 Timothy 3:17 completes the thought Paul began in the previous verse. Yesterday we were reminded that God Himself is the origin of Scripture, thus it is inerrant. After establishing the *origin* of Scripture, the balance of verse 16 speaks to the *action* of Scripture. In today's verse, Paul writes Timothy about the *outcome* of Scripture.

COMMENTARY:
Second Timothy 3:17 begins with a ἵνα purpose clause and the subjunctive ᾖ (*he might be*) to indicate the importance of πᾶσα γραφή (3:16) in one's life. Notice ἐξηρτισμένος is a compound word—a perfect participle—formed from the adjective ἄρτιος (the second word in the verse, translated as *complete* or *equipped*) and the preposition ἐκ. The NKJV renders the shortened word as *complete,* and the compound word as *thoroughly equipped.* Other options could include *thoroughly furnished, completely adequate,* or *fully qualified.* When one understands the *origin* of Scripture and allows the Scripture's *action* to impact one's life, the *outcome* will be a person who is complete and fully qualified for πᾶν ἔργον ἀγαθόν.

ἄρτιος > complete || ᾖ > 3SPAS, may be || ἐξηρτισμένος > RPPMSN, being thoroughly equipped

Further Reading: 2 Timothy 3:10–17
Mark H. Ballard

² κήρυξον τὸν λόγον, ἐπίστηθι εὐκαίρως ἀκαίρως, ἔλεγξον, ἐπιτίμησον, παρακάλεσον, ἐν πάσῃ μακροθυμίᾳ καὶ διδαχῇ.

CONTEXT:

Paul's final written words to Timothy (indeed to anyone) are recorded in this chapter. While the later paragraphs focus on Paul's personal testimony, personal instructions, and personal greetings, the first paragraph (4:1–5) contains Paul's final commands for the young preacher.

COMMENTARY:

In just this one verse, Paul uses five aorist imperatives in rapid-fire succession: κήρυξον ... ἐπίστηθι ... ἔλεγξον ... ἐπιτίμησον ... παρακάλεσον. The first and primary imperative calls Timothy to *preach the Word* (κήρυξον τὸν λόγον). The preacher is not to be focused on finding unique ways to convey his own opinions. Neither is he to look to others, whether of the world or of the faith, for his message. His job is to *herald the Word* of God. Notice the context of the preceding paragraph. Since all Scripture is θεόπνευστος (3:16), the preacher is to act as God's herald by declaring His Word. He is to do so *in season* (εὐκαίρως, found only here and in Mark 14:11), and *out of season* (ἀκαίρως, a *hapax legomenon*).

κήρυξον > 2SAAM, preach || **ἐπίστηθι** > 2SAAM, be ready || **εὐκαίρως** > in season || **ἀκαίρως** > out of season || **ἔλεγξον** > 2SAAM, reprove || **ἐπιτίμησον** > 2SAAM, rebuke || **παρακάλεσον** > 2SAAM, exhort || **μακροθυμίᾳ** > patience || **διδαχῇ** > teaching

Further Reading: 2 Timothy 4:1–5
Mark H. Ballard

²² ὁ κύριος Ἰησοῦς Χριστὸς μετὰ τοῦ πνεύματός σου. ἡ χάρις μεθ᾽ ὑμῶν. ἀμήν.

CONTEXT:

In 2 Timothy 4:19, Paul asks Timothy to greet three close partners: Prisca, Aquila, and the household of Onesiphorus. He then gives a report on two who are not presently with him, Erastus and Trophimus (4:20). Paul emphasizes that time is of the essence for Timothy's travel plans and then sends greetings from four people by name, including "all the brethren" (4:21). He concludes the epistle with a double farewell, to which we now look.

COMMENTARY:

Notice two things. First, the Nestle-Aland text does not include Ἰησοῦς Χριστός, though these words are present in the Byzantine text (as above, for today's reading). Second, some might question the applicability of this epistle to the church at large since Timothy was the primary recipient. Notice, however, that Paul includes a double blessing: (1) Ὁ κύριος μετὰ τοῦ πνεύματός σου, and (2) ἡ χάρις μεθ᾽ ὑμῶν. The first is singular using the pronoun σου; the second is plural using the pronoun ὑμῶν. This plural pronoun ("you all") indicates that Paul likely intended the instructions for the entire church. Indeed, local churches today would greatly benefit from applying the message of this epistle.

Further Reading: 2 Timothy 4:19–22
Mark H. Ballard

JOHN 1:12–13

¹² ὅσοι δὲ ἔλαβον αὐτόν, ἔδωκεν αὐτοῖς ἐξουσίαν τέκνα θεοῦ γενέσθαι, τοῖς πιστεύουσιν εἰς τὸ ὄνομα αὐτοῦ, ¹³ οἳ οὐκ ἐξ αἱμάτων οὐδὲ ἐκ θελήματος σαρκὸς οὐδὲ ἐκ θελήματος ἀνδρὸς ἀλλ' ἐκ θεοῦ ἐγεννήθησαν.

CONTEXT:

John 1 introduces Jesus as the eternal "Word" (λόγος) who has now physically come into the world. Even though the world was made through him, the people of the world rejected him. What it means to receive Jesus is the theme of verses 12–13.

COMMENTARY:

These verses describe the miraculous transformation in the life of a person who receives Jesus. To receive Jesus begins by *believing in his name* (τοῖς πιστεύουσιν εἰς τὸ ὄνομα αὐτοῦ). Notice the two verbs that are used to articulate how this spiritual transformation is brought about by God. First, Jesus gives (ἔδωκεν) the right for someone to be become a child of God. Second, this new birth is not physical, but is a spiritual life from God (ἀλλ' ἐκ θεοῦ ἐγεννήθησαν).

ὅσοι > as many as || ἔλαβον > 3PAAI, received || ἔδωκεν > 3SAAI, he gave || γενέσθαι > AMN, to become || πιστεύουσιν > PAPMPD, believing || αἱμάτων > blood || ἐγεννήθησαν > 3PAPI, were born

Further Reading: John 1:1–51
Aaron Contino

JOHN 2:19-21

¹⁹ ἀπεκρίθη Ἰησοῦς καὶ εἶπεν αὐτοῖς· λύσατε τὸν ναὸν τοῦτον καὶ ἐν τρισὶν ἡμέραις ἐγερῶ αὐτόν. ²⁰ εἶπαν οὖν οἱ Ἰουδαῖοι· τεσσεράκοντα καὶ ἓξ ἔτεσιν οἰκοδομήθη ὁ ναὸς οὗτος, καὶ σὺ ἐν τρισὶν ἡμέραις ἐγερεῖς αὐτόν; ²¹ ἐκεῖνος δὲ ἔλεγεν περὶ τοῦ ναοῦ τοῦ σώματος αὐτοῦ.

CONTEXT:

After Jesus cleanses the temple, the Jews demand a sign to prove his authority. Jesus' response to them is both startling and perplexing.

COMMENTARY:

When the Jews asked Jesus for a sign to prove his authority, they were not expecting him to predict the destruction of their worship center. Jesus tells them that *this temple* (τὸν ναὸν τοῦτον) will be destroyed and raised again in three days. Their confusion is obvious and understandable. They ask how *this temple* (ὁ ναὸς οὗτος) could be raised in three days if it took forty-six years to build the first time! The use of these near demonstrative pronouns shows that what the Jews had in mind was not at all what Jesus had meant. Verse 21 reveals the startling and revolutionary conclusion that Jesus' own body was the temple that would be destroyed and resurrected in three days. This truth is the message we proclaim today that still transforms lives around the world.

λύσατε > 2PAAM, destroy || ἐγερῶ > 1SFAI, will raise || τεσσεράκοντα > forty || ἓξ > six || ἔτεσιν > years || ἐγερεῖς > 2SFAI, will raise || οἰκοδομήθη > 3SAPI, was built || σώματος > body

Further Reading: John 2:13–22
Aaron Contino

³¹ ὁ ἄνωθεν ἐρχόμενος ἐπάνω πάντων ἐστίν· ὁ ὢν ἐκ τῆς γῆς ἐκ τῆς γῆς ἐστιν καὶ ἐκ τῆς γῆς λαλεῖ. ὁ ἐκ τοῦ οὐρανοῦ ἐρχόμενος ἐπάνω πάντων ἐστίν.

CONTEXT:

In previous verses, John the Baptist is questioned concerning the identity of Jesus. In response, he speaks with humility as he exalts the deity and supremacy of Christ.

COMMENTARY:

In his defense, John contrasts Jesus with fallen human beings. People can exercise some authority, but it is limited since their origin is finite. However, Jesus is superior because of his origin and authority. He is from heaven *above* (ἄνωθεν) and is, as a result, above *all* (πάντων) in authority and power. John was used mightily by God, but he fully recognized and taught the supremacy of Christ and his authority over all creation. Like John, we should seek to submit to the authority of Jesus Christ in all things.

ἄνωθεν > from above || ἐρχόμενος > PMPMSN, coming || ἐπάνω > above || λαλεῖ > 3SPAI, speak

Further Reading: John 3:1–36
Aaron Contino

AUGUST 7

JOHN 4:41–42

⁴¹ καὶ πολλῷ πλείους ἐπίστευσαν διὰ τὸν λόγον αὐτοῦ, ⁴² τῇ τε γυναικὶ ἔλεγον ὅτι οὐκέτι διὰ τὴν σὴν λαλιὰν πιστεύομεν, αὐτοὶ γὰρ ἀκηκόαμεν καὶ οἴδαμεν ὅτι οὗτός ἐστιν ἀληθῶς ὁ σωτὴρ τοῦ κόσμου.

CONTEXT:

After her life-transforming encounter with Jesus, the Samaritan women returned to her community as a witness. Jesus was invited to stay there, where he taught and interacted with the Samaritans.

COMMENTARY:

When Jesus came to Sychar, many believed in him because of the Samaritan woman's testimony (v. 39). No doubt she was an effective witness! However, as the other Samaritans interacted with Jesus themselves, the reason for their belief changed. They tell her that *we believe* (πιστεύομεν) not simply because of her words, but because *we have heard* Jesus' words *ourselves* (αὐτοὶ ... ἀκηκόαμεν) and *we know* (οἴδαμεν) and are convinced of his identity and mission. Notice that the verbs ἀκηκόαμεν and οἴδαμεν are in the perfect form and therefore describe the state-of-being of the Samaritan believers. Sharing your experience with Jesus can be a powerful witness, but nothing is a substitute for people's hearing God's words themselves, straight from him (i.e., as the Spirit activates the power of Scripture in their hearts).

ἐπίστευσαν > 3PAAI, believed ‖ λαλιάν > speech ‖ πιστεύομεν > 1PPAI, believe ‖ ἀκηκόαμεν > 1PRAI, have heard ‖ οἴδαμεν > 1PRAI, know

Further Reading: John 4:1–45
Aaron Contino

219

¹⁸ διὰ τοῦτο οὖν μᾶλλον ἐζήτουν αὐτὸν οἱ Ἰουδαῖοι ἀποκτεῖναι, ὅτι οὐ μόνον ἔλυεν τὸ σάββατον, ἀλλὰ καὶ πατέρα ἴδιον ἔλεγεν τὸν θεὸν ἴσον ἑαυτὸν ποιῶν τῷ θεῷ.

CONTEXT:

After Jesus healed a paralyzed man on the Sabbath, he was questioned by some Jews. In responding to them, Jesus stated that he was equal with God (5:17).

COMMENTARY:

The narrator provides some intriguing details about the reason the Jews were seeking to kill Jesus. The narrative uses the subordinating conjunction ὅτι (*because*) to indicate that the Jews' first motivation was because Jesus was breaking the Sabbath. However, their true motivation is highlighted by two coordinating conjunctions. A major contrast is made using ἀλλά (*but*) combined with a logically ascensive καί (*even* or *also*) to show that the mounting opposition against Jesus was really because he was making himself equal to God. This deadly plot of the Jews against their own (Jn 1:11; 4:22; 11:50) is the means by which eternal salvation is offered to all.

ἐζήτουν > 3PIAI, were seeking ‖ ἀποκτεῖναι > AAN, to kill ‖ ἔλυεν > 3SIAI, was breaking ‖ σάββατον > Sabbath ‖ ἴσον > equal ‖ ποιῶν > PAPMSN, making

Further Reading: John 5:1–47
Aaron Contino

AUGUST 9
JOHN 6:19-20

¹⁹ ἐληλακότες οὖν ὡς σταδίους εἴκοσι πέντε ἢ τριάκοντα θεωροῦσιν τὸν Ἰησοῦν περιπατοῦντα ἐπὶ τῆς θαλάσσης καὶ ἐγγὺς τοῦ πλοίου γινόμενον, καὶ ἐφοβήθησαν. ²⁰ ὁ δὲ λέγει αὐτοῖς· ἐγώ εἰμι· μὴ φοβεῖσθε.

CONTEXT:
After Jesus feeds the five thousand (6:1-15), he withdraws to be alone while the disciples get into a boat to cross the sea.

COMMENTARY:
When the disciples see Jesus walking on the water, they respond with a momentary fear that dissipates once Jesus gets into the boat. Most intriguing are Jesus' words in response to the disciples. He says to them, ἐγώ εἰμι· μὴ φοβεῖσθε (It is I, do not be afraid!). Jesus' present imperative φοβεῖσθε is quite different from the disciples' aorist indicative ἐφοβήθησαν. In Jesus' presence their fear represents an unwarranted reaction to their immediate circumstances; but because Jesus is always with us (cf. Mt 28:20; Jn 14:17-20) they (and we) should never fear in any circumstance, least of all when his physical presence is replaced by the Spirit of truth. This call never to fear because of God's presence with his children is a challenge to us all.

ἐληλακότες > RAPMPN, having rowed ‖ σταδίους εἴκοσι πέντε ἢ τριάκοντα > three or four miles (lit. twenty-five or thirty stadia) ‖ θεωροῦσιν > 3PPAI, saw ‖ περιπατοῦντα > PAPMSA, walking ‖ ἐγγύς > near ‖ πλοίου > boat ‖ γινόμενον > PMPMSA, coming ‖ ἐφοβήθησαν > 3PAPI, were frightened ‖ φοβεῖσθε > 2PPPM, do [not] be afraid

Further Reading: John 6:1-18
Aaron Contino

²³ εἰ περιτομὴν λαμβάνει ἄνθρωπος ἐν σαββάτῳ ἵνα μὴ λυθῇ ὁ νόμος Μωϋσέως, ἐμοὶ χολᾶτε ὅτι ὅλον ἄνθρωπον ὑγιῆ ἐποίησα ἐν σαββάτῳ;

CONTEXT:

Jesus is teaching in the temple and the Jews question his authority. In response, Jesus reaffirms his deity and challenges the Jews not to judge by appearances.

COMMENTARY:

John uses a first-class condition in the form of a question to highlight the hypocrisy of the Jews. They are angry at Jesus because he healed a man's whole body on the Sabbath (perhaps the same man from John 5:18). In his question, Jesus points out the reality that the Jews would circumcise a man on the Sabbath to keep the law of Moses. In this way the Jews have a double standard when it comes to applying the law. Their hatred for Jesus has much more to do with his identity and teaching than with his Sabbath practices. May this verse serve as a reminder for us to recognize the authority of Jesus and be obedient to his perfect law, caring for the whole person.

λαμβάνει > 3SPAI, receives ‖ περιτομήν > circumcision ‖ λυθῇ > 3SAPS, may [not] be broken ‖ χολᾶτε > 2PPAI, are angry ‖ ὑγιῆ > sound, healthy ‖ ἐποίησα > 1SAAI, made

Further Reading: John 7:1–24
Aaron Contino

¹² πάλιν οὖν αὐτοῖς ἐλάλησεν ὁ Ἰησοῦς λέγων· ἐγώ εἰμι τὸ φῶς τοῦ κόσμου· ὁ ἀκολουθῶν ἐμοὶ οὐ μὴ περιπατήσῃ ἐν τῇ σκοτίᾳ, ἀλλ᾽ ἕξει τὸ φῶς τῆς ζωῆς.

CONTEXT:

In the context of this passage, Jesus was teaching the Jewish leaders during the Feast of Booths.

COMMENTARY:

In John 8:12, Jesus makes an emphatic point about those who follow him by using a double negative (οὐ μή). This is the strongest way to say "no" in Greek and is always paired with a subjunctive verb, the verb of potential. All who follow the Light of the World will walk (περιπατήσῃ), but their walk will *absolutely not* be in darkness (indicated by the double negative). Rather, their walk will be in the light, because they will have (ἕξει) the light of eternal life.

ἐλάλησεν > 3PAAI, spoke ‖ ἀκολουθῶν > PAPMSN, following ‖ περιπατήσῃ > 3SAAS, shall [not] walk ‖ ἕξει > 3SFAI, will have

Further Reading: John 8:12–30
Aaron Contino

³ ἀπεκρίθη Ἰησοῦς· οὔτε οὗτος ἥμαρτεν οὔτε οἱ γονεῖς αὐτοῦ, ἀλλ' ἵνα φανερωθῇ τὰ ἔργα τοῦ θεοῦ ἐν αὐτῷ.

CONTEXT:
Jesus and his disciples were walking by a man who had been blind all his life. This prompts the disciples to ask, "Rabbi, who sinned, this man or his parents, that he was born blind? (9:2).

COMMENTARY:
In reply, Jesus tells his disciples that the man's blindness was not caused by his sin nor by the sins of his parents. Instead, the man's blindness was to showcase the future works of God (φανερωθῇ τὰ ἔργα τοῦ θεοῦ). Note that φανερωθῇ is in the subjunctive mood. The specific work of God highlighted here is the total restoration of the blind man's sight. The realization of God's sovereignty and purposes in this verse is both startling and humbling as we seek to submit to his Lordship each day.

ἥμαρτεν > 3SAAI, sinned ‖ **γονεῖς** > parents ‖ **φανερωθῇ** > 3SAPS, might be revealed

Further Reading: John 9:1–40
Aaron Contino

¹⁶ ταῦτα οὐκ ἔγνωσαν αὐτοῦ οἱ μαθηταὶ τὸ πρῶτον, ἀλλ' ὅτε ἐδοξάσθη Ἰησοῦς τότε ἐμνήσθησαν ὅτι ταῦτα ἦν ἐπ' αὐτῷ γεγραμμένα καὶ ταῦτα ἐποίησαν αὐτῷ.

CONTEXT:
In the context of this passage, Jesus had just entered Jerusalem as the true King, riding on a donkey (cf. Zech 9:9).

COMMENTARY:
The disciples often failed to grasp the full meaning and significance of Jesus' ministry and teaching. Only after he had been glorified (note passive) did they begin to make some profound connections. This verse uses γεγραμμένα (*had been written*) to indicate how the disciples began to make these connections. They remembered (ἐμνήσθησαν) that many verses in the OT—such as Zechariah 9:9—pointed to the Messiah's identity and mission on earth. The disciples' experiences with Jesus were a fulfillment of what had been prophesied in the past. All of Scripture points to and finds its true object in the special revelation of Jesus Christ, the Son.

ἔγνωσαν > 3PAAI, did [not] understand ‖ ἐδοξάσθη > 3SAPI, was glorified ‖ ἐμνήσθησαν > 3PAPI, remembered ‖ γεγραμμένα > RPPNPN, written ‖ ἐποίησαν > 3PAAI, had done

Further Reading: John 12:12–19
Aaron Contino

... ⁹ ἀντεχόμενον τοῦ κατὰ τὴν διδαχὴν πιστοῦ λόγου, ἵνα δυνατὸς ᾖ καὶ παρακαλεῖν ἐν τῇ διδασκαλίᾳ τῇ ὑγιαινούσῃ καὶ τοὺς ἀντιλέγοντας ἐλέγχειν.

CONTEXT:
Since verse 6, Paul has been listing the important qualifications that Titus needs to observe when appointing elders for the churches on the island of Crete.

COMMENTARY:
The adjectival participle that begins this verse (ἀντεχόμενον modifying ἐπισκοπον in 1:7) together with its genitive direct object τοῦ ... πιστοῦ λόγου gives the climax of the list of elder qualifications. He is one *devoted to ... the faithful message*. What is this "message?" Paul clarifies with the prepositional phrase κατὰ τὴν διδαχήν. While διδαχήν can refer to teaching in general (2:7), this expression most likely refers to the teaching about Christ as passed down by the apostles (see 2:9). The need for such leaders is explained by two infinitives that complete the adverbial clause δυνατὸς ᾖ (*might be able*): first, *to encourage* (παρακαλεῖν) believers to walk *in this sound teaching* and second, *to reprove* (ἐλέγχειν) *those who contradict it*.

ἀντεχόμενον > PMPMSA, who is devoted to ‖ διδαχήν > teaching (the act of teaching what is taught) ‖ δυνατός > able ‖ ᾖ > 3SPAS, he might be ‖ παρακαλεῖν > PAN, to exhort ‖ διδασκαλίᾳ > teaching (that which is taught) ‖ ὑγιαινούσῃ > PAPFSD, sound ‖ ἀντιλέγοντας > PAPMPA, those who contradict ‖ ἐλέγχειν > PAN, to convict, reprove

Further Reading: Titus 1:5–9
Markus T. Klausli

... ^{11} οὓς δεῖ ἐπιστομίζειν, οἵτινες ὅλους οἴκους ἀνατρέπουσιν διδάσκοντες ἃ μὴ δεῖ αἰσχροῦ κέρδους χάριν.

CONTEXT:

Beginning in verse 10, Paul explains that the reason for selecting church leaders with strong teaching gifts is that they might protect the church from false teachers who muddle apostolic teaching and lead people away from the true gospel.

COMMENTARY:

Relative pronouns play an important role in this verse to describe the traits of the false teachers that will be encountered. First, the accusative plural οὓς at the beginning of verse 11 points back to their characteristics described in verse 10 (*whom* it is necessary to silence). Second, the masculine plural indefinite οἵτινες is used to describe the havoc caused in the churches by these kinds of people (*who* upset whole households). Finally, the neuter plural ἃ is used to encapsulate the wicked content of their teaching (by teaching *things* [that] ought not [to be taught]).

δεῖ > 3SPAI, it is necessary || ἐπιστομίζειν > PAN, to silence || ἀνατρέπουσιν > 3PPAI, upset || διδάσκοντες > PAPMPN, by teaching || αἰσχροῦ > shameful || κέρδους > gain, profit || χάριν + genitive > for the sake of

Further Reading: Titus 1:10–13a
Markus T. Klausli

¹⁶ θεὸν ὁμολογοῦσιν εἰδέναι, τοῖς δὲ ἔργοις ἀρνοῦνται, βδελυκτοὶ ὄντες καὶ ἀπειθεῖς καὶ πρὸς πᾶν ἔργον ἀγαθὸν ἀδόκιμοι.

CONTEXT:
Paul warns in the second half of chapter one against false teachings and teachers who can corrupt the church and lead it away from sound teaching.

COMMENTARY:
In verse 16 Paul gives his final and strongest statement against the false teachers plaguing the churches. In the second half of the verse he describes them as *abhorrent, disobedient, and unqualified for every good work.* The reason for this blistering assessment is their hypocritical character described in the opening clause. On the one hand they claim intimate knowledge of God: the infinitive εἰδέναι introduces indirect discourse that perhaps indicates their bold but unwarranted claim: "We know God." On the other hand (indicated by the contrastive δέ), Paul indicates that their pious profession is bogus. Using the dative of means τοῖς ... ἔργοις he explains why: their evil deeds indicate that they do not serve the God they claim to know.

ὁμολογοῦσιν > 3PPAI, they claim || εἰδέναι > RAN, to know || ἀρνοῦνται > 3PPMI, they deny || βδελυκτοί > abhorrent || ὄντες > PAPMPN, who are || ἀπειθεῖς > disobedient || ἀδόκιμοι > unqualified, unfit

Further Reading: Titus 1:13b–16
Markus T. Klausli

... ⁴ ἵνα σωφρονίζωσιν τὰς νέας φιλάνδρους εἶναι, φιλοτέκνους
⁵ σώφρονας ἁγνὰς οἰκουργοὺς ἀγαθάς, ὑποτασσομένας τοῖς ἰδίοις
ἀνδράσιν, ἵνα μὴ ὁ λόγος τοῦ θεοῦ βλασφημῆται. ⁶ τοὺς νεωτέρους
ὡσαύτως παρακάλει σωφρονεῖν.

CONTEXT:
The second chapter of Titus begins with a series of admonitions to various
groups in the congregation regarding how they ought to practice their Christian
faith in public. Paul begins with older men, then moves on to older women,
younger women (wives), young men, and finally slaves (2:9).

COMMENTARY:
There is nothing unique about Christianity in its admonition to its adherents to
live an upright and moral life. What makes Christianity distinct, however, is the
reason for pursuing this kind of walk as a follower of Jesus. In verses 2:4-10 Paul
uses four ἵνα clauses (2:4, 5, 8, 10) to teach us that practicing Christian virtue is
never intended as an end in itself but can have apologetic and even missional
purposes. For example, in 2:3-4 he explains that the holy behavior of older
women makes them fit to teach the *young women* how to live out the Christian
faith in their own families. In turn, the holy behavior of these wives and mothers
not only ensures a God-honoring home life but, in its own way, prevents
opponents from insinuating that the gospel corrupts the culture.

σωφρονίζωσιν > 3PPAS, they might encourage ‖ νέας > young women ‖
φιλάνδρους > loving (their) husbands ‖ εἶναι > PAN, to be ‖ φιλοτέκνους >
loving (their) children ‖ σώφρονας > self-controlled ‖ ἁγνάς > pure ‖
οἰκουργούς > carrying out household duties ‖ ὑποτασσομένας > PPPFPA, being
subject to ‖ βλασφημῆται > 3SPPS, might [not] be slandered ‖ παρακάλει >
2SPAI, exhort ‖ σωφρονεῖν > to be sensible

Further Reading: Titus 2:2-10
Markus T. Klausli

¹¹ ἐπεφάνη γὰρ ἡ χάρις τοῦ θεοῦ σωτήριος πᾶσιν ἀνθρώποις
¹² παιδεύουσα ἡμᾶς, ἵνα ἀρνησάμενοι τὴν ἀσέβειαν καὶ τὰς κοσμικὰς
ἐπιθυμίας σωφρόνως καὶ δικαίως καὶ εὐσεβῶς ζήσωμεν ἐν τῷ νῦν αἰῶνι,
¹³ προσδεχόμενοι τὴν μακαρίαν ἐλπίδα ...

CONTEXT:
In 2:1–10 Paul has surveyed the kind of behavior that should characterize the various members of a Christian household.

COMMENTARY:
The explanatory γάρ beginning 2:11 indicates that all righteous behavior should ultimately be intended as a worthy response to *God's grace* that *has* now *appeared.* The main component of this response is introduced in 2:12 by ἵνα (introducing the content of grace's teaching) and the subjunctive verb ζήσωμεν: *that we might live wisely, righteously, and godly in the present age.* Yet this positive action does not stand alone, as indicated by two accompanying adverbial participles. The attendant circumstance participle ἀρνησάμενοι that precedes the main verb indicates that a righteous life also consists of renouncing *impiety and worldly desires.* The contemporaneous time participle προσδεχόμενοι emphasizes the anticipatory attitude that should characterize all believers during this age: *while we wait for the blessed hope* of Christ's return.

ἐπεφάνη > 3SAPI, appeared || σωτήριος > bringing salvation || παιδεύουσα > PAPFSN, teaching || ἀρνησάμενοι > AMPMPN, we might renounce || ἀσέβειαν > impiety || κοσμικάς > worldly || ἐπιθυμίας > desires || σωφρόνως > showing self-control || δικαίως > uprightly || εὐσεβῶς > in a godly manner || ζήσωμεν > 1PAAS, we might live || προσδεχόμενοι > PMPMPN, while we wait for

Further Reading: Titus 2:11–14
Markus T. Klausli

AUGUST 19

TITUS 2:13B

¹³ ... καὶ ἐπιφάνειαν τῆς δόξης τοῦ μεγάλου θεοῦ καὶ σωτῆρος ἡμῶν Ἰησοῦ Χριστοῦ.

CONTEXT:
In 2:13a Paul indicates that one of the motivators of living as a Christian should be awaiting the return of the Lord Jesus Christ.

COMMENTARY:
Though the NT plainly teaches the divinity of Jesus, there are only a few places where he is expressly referred to as God, and this verse is one of them. The phrase τοῦ μεγάλου θεοῦ καὶ σωτῆρος ἡμῶν Ἰησοῦ Χριστοῦ is an example of Paul's writing that conforms to the Granville Sharp construction in which singular, personal, non-proper nouns joined together under one article refer to the same person (*GGBB*, 271–72). Here the nouns θεοῦ and σωτῆρος ἡμῶν both controlled by the article τοῦ are definitively used to refer to Ἰησοῦ Χριστοῦ. To the careful reader of Titus, however, this summary should not come as a surprise, as σωτήρ appears a number of times in the letter and is used alternatively for both God the Father and God the Son in three distinct places (see 1:3–4; 2:10, 13; 3:4–6).

ἐπιφάνειαν > (the) appearing ‖ σωτῆρος > savior

Further Reading: 2:11–14
Markus T. Klausli

231

... ⁵ οὐκ ἐξ ἔργων τῶν ἐν δικαιοσύνῃ ἃ ἐποιήσαμεν ἡμεῖς ἀλλὰ κατὰ τὸ αὐτοῦ ἔλεος ἔσωσεν ἡμᾶς διὰ λουτροῦ παλιγγενεσίας καὶ ἀνακαινώσεως πνεύματος ἁγίου.

CONTEXT:

Paul's exhortation to godly behavior continues in 3:1-2. Similar to 2:11-14, he also couches it in terms of a worthy response to God's saving acts that have now *appeared* (ἐπεφάνη) (3:4).

COMMENTARY:

In a book dedicated to encouraging Christian behavior, Titus 3:5 makes it clear that good works should never be viewed as a means to earning God's favor. This is indicated by the strong contrastive conjunction ἀλλά that makes a sharp distinction between what motivated God to save us (ἔσωσεν ἡμᾶς) and what did not. He did not save us *because we had done righteous works* that pleased him (οὐκ ἐξ ἔργων τῶν ἐν δικαιοσύνῃ ἃ ἐποιήσαμεν ἡμεῖς). Instead, it was his mercy directed toward our helpless condition that caused him to send the Holy Spirit to apply Christ's atoning sacrifice to our lives (3:5-6).

ἐποιήσαμεν > 1PAAI, we did ‖ ἔλεος > mercy ‖ ἔσωσεν > 3SAAI, he saved ‖ λουτροῦ > washing ‖ παλιγγενεσίας > rebirth ‖ ἀνακαινώσεως > renewal

Further Reading: Titus 3:1-7
Markus T. Klausli

... ⁶ ὅπως ἡ κοινωνία τῆς πίστεώς σου ἐνεργὴς γένηται ἐν ἐπιγνώσει παντὸς ἀγαθοῦ τοῦ ἐν ἡμῖν εἰς Χριστόν.

CONTEXT:
Paul opens his letter with greetings to Philemon and his household and expresses his thankfulness to God for him (vv. 1–5).

COMMENTARY:
In this key verse to the entire letter (v. 6), Paul reveals to Philemon the content of his prayer to God (ὅπως) before asking him to forgive his runaway slave, Onesimus, and release him into Paul's service for the gospel, now that he has become a Christian (vv. 8–20). His request is that ... *in knowing all the good which is in us for Christ's sake* (ἐν ἐπιγνώσει παντὸς ἀγαθοῦ τοῦ ἐν ἡμῖν εἰς Χριστόν), namely the releasing of Onesimus (see τον ἀγαθον, in v. 14), ἡ κοινωνία τῆς πίστεώς σου will become effective leading to the granting of the request. The meaning of this genitive phrase is challenging. The focus in verse 16 that this gracious act on Philemon's part should be related to Onesimus' now being a "brother" along with the appeal to his volition (see ἑκούσιον in v. 14) suggests that it be taken as a "Genitive of Production" (*GGBB*, 104–106; this interpretation follows D. Moo, *Colossians & Philemon*, 2008, 389–94). In other words, Paul wants Philemon to be motivated by none other than *the fellowship that comes from the faith (he shares with other believers)*.

κοινωνία > fellowship || ἐνεργής > effective, active || γένηται > 3SAMS, might become || ἐπιγνώσει > knowledge

Further Reading: Philemon 1–6
Markus T. Klausli

¹⁰ παρακαλῶ σε περὶ τοῦ ἐμοῦ τέκνου, ὃν ἐγέννησα ἐν τοῖς δεσμοῖς, Ὀνήσιμον, ¹¹ τόν ποτέ σοι ἄχρηστον νυνὶ δὲ καὶ σοὶ καὶ ἐμοὶ εὔχρηστον, ¹² ὃν ἀνέπεμψά σοι, αὐτόν, τοῦτ' ἔστιν τὰ ἐμὰ σπλάγχνα· ¹³ ὃν ἐγὼ ἐβουλόμην πρὸς ἐμαυτὸν κατέχειν, ἵνα ὑπὲρ σοῦ μοι διακονῇ ἐν τοῖς δεσμοῖς τοῦ εὐαγγελίου.

CONTEXT:

Paul makes his case in verses 8–9 for Philemon to grant his request based on their relationship rather than on his apostolic authority.

COMMENTARY:

In making his case that Philemon welcome home Onesimus and release him to serve Paul, Paul uses an entire row of accusative singular relative pronouns to describe what has happened to the runaway slave, all of which have τέκνου as their antecedent (v. 10). First, Paul has given Onesimus (spiritual) birth in prison (ὃν ἐγέννησα ἐν τοῖς δεσμοῖς). Second, Onesimus has gone from being *useless* to being *useful* (τὸν … ἄχρηστον νυνὶ δὲ … εὔχρηστον). Third, Onesimus has been sent by Paul to Philemon presumably carrying this letter (ὃν ἀνέπεμψά σοι). And fourth, Paul wishes to keep Onesimus so that he can help him with his ministry (ὃν ἐγὼ ἐβουλόμην πρὸς ἐμαυτὸν κατέχειν ἵνα … μοι διακονῇ ἐν τοῖς δεσμοῖς τοῦ εὐαγγελίου).

παρακαλῶ > 1SPAI, implore ‖ ἐγέννησα > 1SAAI, became the parent of ‖ δεσμοῖς > bonds, imprisonment ‖ Ὀνήσιμον > Onesimus ‖ ποτέ > formerly ‖ ἄχρηστον > useless ‖ εὔχρηστον > useful ‖ ἀνέπεμψα > 1SAAI, sent back ‖ [τουτ'] ἔστιν > 3SPAI, [that] is ‖ σπλάγχνα > beloved (lit. bowels) ‖ ἐβουλόμην > 1SIMI, wished ‖ ἐμαυτόν > myself ‖ κατέχειν > PAN, to keep ‖ διακονῇ > 3SPAS, he might serve

Further Reading: Philemon 8–13
Markus T. Klausli

¹⁷ εἰ οὖν με ἔχεις κοινωνόν, προσλαβοῦ αὐτὸν ὡς ἐμέ. ¹⁸ εἰ δέ τι ἠδίκησέν σε ἢ ὀφείλει, τοῦτο ἐμοὶ ἐλλόγα.

CONTEXT:

Having stated his request for Onesimus' acceptance (v. 13), Paul now turns his attention to encouraging Philemon to grant it (vv. 14–16).

COMMENTARY:

At the height of his argument to convince Philemon to free Onesimus, Paul makes use of two first-class conditional statements, as seen by the conjunction εἰ followed by indicative verbs in both the protasis (condition) and the apodosis (conclusion). Though both conditions appear to be true: (1) Philemon does have Paul as a partner (v. 17) and (2), it is likely that Onesimus has wronged Philemon by running away, the purpose of this construction is not simply to assert this fact. Instead, it is suggested the protasis be rendered "if and let us assume it's true for the sake of argument" rather than "since" (*GGBB*, 690-94). Taken this way, Philemon should consider that if either is true (and in this case both are), then the only logical thing would be to follow Paul's requests, namely, *receive Philemon as (Paul), and charge (Onesimus's debt) to (Paul's) account.*

ἔχεις > 2SPAI, you have ‖ κοινωνόν > partner ‖ προσλαβοῦ > 2SAMM, receive ‖ ἠδίκησεν > 3SAAI, he injured, caused damage, wronged ‖ ὀφείλει > 3SPAI, he owes ‖ ἐλλόγα > 2SPAM, charge to (my) account

Further Reading: 17–20
Markus T. Klausli

August 24
John 13:15–17

¹⁵ ὑπόδειγμα γὰρ ἔδωκα ὑμῖν ἵνα καθὼς ἐγὼ ἐποίησα ὑμῖν καὶ ὑμεῖς ποιῆτε. ¹⁶ ἀμὴν ἀμὴν λέγω ὑμῖν, οὐκ ἔστιν δοῦλος μείζων τοῦ κυρίου αὐτοῦ οὐδὲ ἀπόστολος μείζων τοῦ πέμψαντος αὐτόν. ¹⁷ εἰ ταῦτα οἴδατε, μακάριοί ἐστε ἐὰν ποιῆτε αὐτά.

CONTEXT:
In the opening scene of the prelude to the Upper Room Discourse (i.e., ch. 13), Jesus fulfills the role of a slave (δοῦλος) by washing the disciples' dirty feet. Then, after correcting Peter's impetuous request for a full bath, he addresses all the disciples regarding the significance of this foot-washing object lesson.

COMMENTARY:
Jesus explains to his disciples that he gave (ἔδωκα) them a pattern to follow with one another. By implication, this pattern is a gift in at least two different ways. First, the ἵνα purpose clause sets up a point/counterpoint construction with καθὼς ... καί, where the comparative adverb καθώς sets the standard for the disciples that they are to do "just as" Jesus did. In that sense, it is a gift of service. We see the second implied gift in the conditional sentence (v. 17) which is both a first-class condition (εἰ ταῦτα οἴδατε—only the protasis is expressed) combined with a third-class condition (μακάριοί ἐστε ἐὰν ποιῆτε αὐτά). This conditional construction reveals the "blessed" status (μακάριοί ἐστε) a person enjoys who commits himself to such necessary and menial forms of service for another. Thus, the same act of humble service is both a gift that blesses others and the means whereby the giver becomes blessed, demonstrating the truth that it is more blessed to give than to receive.

ὑπόδειγμα > an example, pattern ‖ ἔδωκα > 1SAAI, have given ‖ ποιῆτε > 2PPAS, should do ‖ τοῦ πέμψαντος > AAPMSG, the one who sent ‖ οἴδατε > 2PRAI, you know

Further Reading: John 13:1–17
Roger G. DePriest

¹ μὴ ταρασσέσθω ὑμῶν ἡ καρδία· πιστεύετε εἰς τὸν θεὸν καὶ εἰς ἐμὲ πιστεύετε. ² ἐν τῇ οἰκίᾳ τοῦ πατρός μου μοναὶ πολλαί εἰσιν· εἰ δὲ μή, εἶπον ἂν ὑμῖν ὅτι πορεύομαι ἑτοιμάσαι τόπον ὑμῖν;

CONTEXT:
Chapter 14 begins the Upper Room Discourse proper with Jesus comforting the troubled hearts of the disciples. Arguably, their hearts were troubled primarily by three prophetic statements Jesus had previously made (viz., someone's betrayal, another's denial, and his going away).

COMMENTARY:
The passive voice of ταρασσέσθω indicates there is something acting upon the disciples' hearts that is disturbing them deeply (see the context above). In eight words, Jesus encourages them with a statement that inverts back on itself (called a literary chiasm), which we might display as follows:

πιστεύετε

εἰς τὸν θεὸν

καὶ

εἰς ἐμὲ

πιστεύετε

Each use of πιστεύετε is ambiguous in form (imperative or indicative) but here we should probably understand it as imperative given the preceding imperative that opens the discourse (ταρασσέσθω). The emphasis falls upon the prepositional phrase εἰς ἐμέ as evidenced by (among other things) the emphatic personal pronoun, as well as Jesus' use of Jewish bridal imagery to reinforce his promise that he will come back and receive them unto himself.

ταρασσέσθω > 3SPPM, do [not] be troubled || ἑτοιμάσαι > AAN, to make ready || πιστεύετε > 2PPAM, trust! believe! or 2PPAI, you trust, believe || μοναί > dwelling places

Further Reading: John 14:1-24
Roger G. DePriest

¹ ἐγώ εἰμι ἡ ἄμπελος ἡ ἀληθινὴ καὶ ὁ πατήρ μου ὁ γεωργός ἐστιν. ² πᾶν κλῆμα ἐν ἐμοὶ μὴ φέρον καρπὸν αἴρει αὐτό, καὶ πᾶν τὸ καρπὸν φέρον καθαίρει αὐτὸ ἵνα καρπὸν πλείονα φέρῃ. ³ ἤδη ὑμεῖς καθαροί ἐστε διὰ τὸν λόγον ὃν λελάληκα ὑμῖν.

CONTEXT:
After the troubling news of Jesus' going away in chapter 13, followed by his comforting promise to come back for them (ch. 14), Jesus begins to instruct his disciples on the importance of abiding. In chapter 14, there are two significant uses of the noun μονή (abode, vv. 2, 23), whereas in chapter 15, there are eleven uses of its verbal cognate μένω (to abide, vv. 4, 5, 6, 7, 9, 10, 16).

COMMENTARY:
Although most translations render ἄμπελος as "vine," and κλῆμα as "branches," recent scholarship argues that by the time of John's writing, the two words primarily bore the respective senses of "vineyard" and "vine." For best viticultural practice, the farmer (γεωργός) both removes (αἴρει) the useless vines and prunes (καθαίρει) the fruit-bearing ones. According to 15:3, the same principle operates in spiritual viticulture, only the removing and pruning are accomplished διὰ τὸν λόγον (διά + accusative = causal), which Jesus "spoke" to them (λελάληκα, perfect tense = durative quality). Arguably, Judas and Peter, whose imminent failures were prophetically juxtaposed in chapter 13, serve as the respective examples here of removing and pruning. Judas did not abide in Jesus' vineyard when he went out into the night to do his evil deed, whereas Peter's pruning continues to the last chapter. God accomplished his spiritual viticulture with both men by the words Jesus spoke to them.

ἄμπελος > vineyard ‖ γεωργός > farmer ‖ πᾶν κλῆμα > every branch ‖ μὴ φέρον > PAPNSN, not producing ‖ αἴρει > 3SPAI, he removes ‖ καθαίρει > 3SPAI, he prunes ‖ φέρῃ > 3SPAS, it may produce ‖ λελάληκα > 1SRAI, I have spoken

Further Reading: John 15:1–17
Roger G. DePriest

³² ἰδοὺ ἔρχεται ὥρα καὶ ἐλήλυθεν ἵνα σκορπισθῆτε ἕκαστος εἰς τὰ ἴδια κἀμὲ μόνον ἀφῆτε· καὶ οὐκ εἰμὶ μόνος, ὅτι ὁ πατὴρ μετ' ἐμοῦ ἐστιν. ³³ ταῦτα λελάληκα ὑμῖν ἵνα ἐν ἐμοὶ εἰρήνην ἔχητε. ἐν τῷ κόσμῳ θλῖψιν ἔχετε· ἀλλὰ θαρσεῖτε, ἐγὼ νενίκηκα τὸν κόσμον.

CONTEXT:

As the Upper Room Discourse continues into chapter 16, Jesus picks up the notion from 13:33 of being with his disciples "a little while longer" and teases out themes from chapter 14, especially his promise to never forsake them. In addition, he also reprises the "in me" concept in chapter 15 and recasts the idea of the world hating his disciples as "tribulation in the world" (16:33).

COMMENTARY:

The combination of the perfect tense-form ἐλήλυθεν with the present tense-form ἔρχεται (futuristic present), connected by an ascensive καί, effectively functions to issue a warning to the disciples that a severe hour of testing has arrived. This time of testing will be so severe that (ἵνα, epexegetical) they will scatter, forsaking Jesus in the process. But in verse 33, Jesus uses another perfect tense-form, λελάληκα, (from λαλέω), whose stative aspect yields a durative reality. Thus, though the disciples may fail Jesus in this trial, he is essentially instructing them that they can find their way back and possess peace by reconsidering and abiding in his words. The evidence that they did precisely that is how they teased out the seminal truths Jesus taught in the Upper Room Discourse in their own NT epistles.

ἐλήλυθεν > 3SRAI, it is now come || σκορπισθῆτε > 2PAPS, you will be scattered || εἰς τὰ ἴδια > to his own home || ἀφῆτε > 2PAAS, you will leave || λελάληκα > 1SRAI, I have spoken || ἔχητε > 2PPAS, you may have || θαρσεῖτε > 2PPAM, take courage!

Further Reading: John 16:25–33
Roger G. DePriest

⁵ καὶ νῦν δόξασόν με σύ, πάτερ, παρὰ σεαυτῷ τῇ δόξῃ ᾗ εἶχον πρὸ τοῦ τὸν κόσμον εἶναι παρὰ σοί.

CONTEXT:

As chapter 13 opened by informing the reader that Jesus knew "his hour had come," so chapter 17 opens similarly—both chapters serving as literary brackets enclosing the Upper Room Discourse proper. In 17:1, Jesus lifts his eyes to heaven, prays to the Father (in the hearing of his disciples), and promptly acknowledges that "the hour has come" (ἐλήλυθεν ἡ ὥρα).

COMMENTARY:

Notice the double use of παρά plus a pronoun in the dative case (one reflexive, one personal). Together, these suggest that Jesus, in his preexistence, was at the Father's side (παρὰ σοί) enjoying the glory of his presence (παρὰ σεαυτῷ). Even though his "hour" involves excruciating suffering, he does not pray for a delay, but instead prays in harmony with God's unfolding providence, petitioning him to glorify him now (νῦν δόξασον). Thus, Jesus models for all his disciples that when one eagerly seeks to glorify God in all suffering—he can be assured that God's own presence is more than sufficient to carry him through even the most severe times of trial.

δόξασον > 2SAAM, glorify! || ᾗ > which || εἶχον > 1SIAI, I had || παρὰ σεαυτῷ > with your own presence || εἶναι > PAN, began to exist || παρὰ σοί > beside you

Further Reading: John 17:1–26
Roger G. DePriest

¹⁶ ὁ δὲ Πέτρος εἱστήκει πρὸς τῇ θύρᾳ ἔξω. ἐξῆλθεν οὖν ὁ μαθητὴς ὁ ἄλλος ὁ γνωστὸς τοῦ ἀρχιερέως καὶ εἶπεν τῇ θυρωρῷ καὶ εἰσήγαγεν τὸν Πέτρον.

CONTEXT:

With the Upper Room Discourse concluded, Jesus leads his disciples to a garden area to pray—an area Judas was privy to, who uses that knowledge to lead the Temple police there to arrest Jesus. The officials bind him and lead him away in custody, with Peter and John following at a distance.

COMMENTARY:

The pluperfect verb εἱστήκει puts Peter and Judas in background juxtaposition since the same verb was used earlier with reference to Judas in 18:5. That Peter positioned himself "before the door" (πρὸς τῇ θύρᾳ) yet "outside" (ἔξω) is an echo of chapter 10, where the good shepherd enters by the door (v. 2) and lays down his life for the sheep (v. 11). Moreover, the beloved disciple uses his connections to gain access for Peter into the courtyard by means of the gate, which the text describes in three rather matter-of-fact aorist verbs (ἐξῆλθεν ... εἶπεν ... εἰσήγαγεν). So, yes, that night Peter did indeed enter the courtyard legitimately (i.e., by its gate), but what is not so matter-of-fact is whether he will later enter the sheepfold properly (i.e., by its gate) and be willing to lay down his life for the sheep. Perhaps John wants his readers to ponder just how similar Peter's actions are to those of Judas.

εἱστήκει > 3SLAI, was standing there ‖ γνωστός > known ‖ τῇ θυρωρῷ > to the doorkeeper ‖ εἰσήγαγεν > 3SAAI, brought in

Further Reading: John 18:15–18; 25–27
Roger G. DePriest

AUGUST 30
JOHN 19:34–35

³⁴ ἀλλ' εἷς τῶν στρατιωτῶν λόγχῃ αὐτοῦ τὴν πλευρὰν ἔνυξεν, καὶ ἐξῆλθεν εὐθὺς αἷμα καὶ ὕδωρ. ³⁵ καὶ ὁ ἑωρακὼς μεμαρτύρηκεν, καὶ ἀληθινὴ αὐτοῦ ἐστιν ἡ μαρτυρία, καὶ ἐκεῖνος οἶδεν ὅτι ἀληθῆ λέγει, ἵνα καὶ ὑμεῖς πιστεύ[σ]ητε.

CONTEXT:

After the trial and brutal execution of Jesus, the soldiers commence breaking the legs of the condemned in order to hasten death and avoid violations of a fast-approaching Sabbath. Observing that Jesus was already dead, they refrained from doing so in his case, except for one presumably unconvinced soldier, who thrust his spear into Jesus' side.

COMMENTARY:

When the soldier pierced the side of Jesus so that "water and blood" (αἷμα καὶ ὕδωρ) "gushed out" (ἐξῆλθεν εὐθύς), the point is not the medical explanation for that phenomenon, but simply to establish the incontrovertible fact that Jesus really died while upon the cross. This is so important to John that he uses three stative verbs (i.e., all perfect tense-forms) that literarily place the eyewitness testimony in the forefront of the discourse (ἑωρακώς, μεμαρτύρηκεν, οἶδεν). The following purpose clause (ἵνα) explains its importance with a key verb with an original reading that may be either present subjunctive (πιστεύητε) or aorist subjunctive (πιστεύσητε), a difference in spelling of only one letter (viz., *sigma*). A possible difference between the two tense-forms may point to two different intended audiences/readers: (1) mainly believers whose faith is to be strengthened (present tense) or (2) mainly unbelievers who need to come to saving faith (aorist tense). Regardless of which is the original reading or which audience or readership is in view (or perhaps some other explanation), this passage emphasizes that a vital part of the Gospel message is that Jesus Christ truly died on the cross for sinners.

λόγχῃ αὐτοῦ > with his spear ‖ τὴν πλευράν > the side [i.e., his side] ‖ ἔνυξεν > 3SAAI, he pierced ‖ ἐξῆλθεν > 3SAAI, came out ‖ ἑωρακώς > RAPMSN, observing ‖ μεμαρτύρηκεν > 3SRAI, has testified [on record] ‖ οἶδεν > 3SRAI, he knows ‖ πιστεύ[σ]ητε > 2PPAS or 2PAAS, you would trust

Further Reading: John 19:31–37
Roger G. DePriest

242

JOHN 20:11–12

¹¹ Μαρία δὲ εἱστήκει πρὸς τῷ μνημείῳ ἔξω κλαίουσα. ὡς οὖν ἔκλαιεν, παρέκυψεν εἰς τὸ μνημεῖον ¹² καὶ θεωρεῖ δύο ἀγγέλους ἐν λευκοῖς καθεζομένους, ἕνα πρὸς τῇ κεφαλῇ καὶ ἕνα πρὸς τοῖς ποσίν, ὅπου ἔκειτο τὸ σῶμα τοῦ Ἰησοῦ.

CONTEXT:

Chapters 1–12 and 13–17 trace Jesus' public ministry and private ministry (respectively), with chapter 12 serving as the turning point, where Israel's leadership and most of its people reject him. Chapters 18–19 recount the passion of Jesus as he is executed as a criminal and hung upon a Roman cross and buried in a rich man's tomb.

COMMENTARY:

The stative verb, εἱστήκει (pluperfect) in verse 11, reveals background information that Mary had positioned herself so that she was "facing the tomb" (πρὸς τῷ μνημείῳ). The adverbial participle κλαίουσα and the imperfect ἔκλαιεν furnish yet more background. The progression of the next three verb tense-forms suggest that the prominence shifts to what Mary sees. We read that she stoops (παρέκυψεν, aorist) and sees (θεωρεῖ, present) two angels sitting (καθεζομένους, present participle), one positioned at the head and the other at the feet of where the body of Jesus had previously lain. This image recalls the Mercy Seat lid of the Ark of the Covenant which has two angels facing each other with their wings overarching the place where the blood of the atonement was applied. If this is the intended imagery, then surely the reader is to understand that the bruised and bloodied body of Jesus, as he suffered and died on the cross, was none other than The Mercy Seat where atonement for sinners was made (cf. Rom 3:24–25; Heb 9:11–12).

εἱστήκει > 3SLAI, was standing || κλαίουσα > PAPFSN, weeping || ἔκλαιεν > 3SIAI, she was weeping || παρέκυψεν > 3SAAI, she stooped down || θεωρεῖ > 3SPAI, she observes || ἔκειτο > 3SIMI, was lying || καθεζομένους > PMPMSA, sitting

Further Reading: John 20:1–18
Roger G. DePriest

²⁷ εἶτα λέγει τῷ Θωμᾷ Φέρε τὸν δάκτυλόν σου ὧδε καὶ ἴδε τὰς χεῖράς μου καὶ φέρε τὴν χεῖρά σου καὶ βάλε εἰς τὴν πλευράν μου, καὶ μὴ γίνου ἄπιστος ἀλλὰ πιστός. ²⁸ ἀπεκρίθη Θωμᾶς καὶ εἶπεν αὐτῷ Ὁ κύριός μου καὶ ὁ θεός μου.

CONTEXT:

All the disciples except Thomas are huddled in a room with the doors barred shut on Sunday night—the same Sunday Jesus appeared to Mary early on resurrection morning. One week later (the next Sunday), they gather again in the same place—this time with Thomas there—and Jesus appears in the room and greets them with the words, "Peace be with you."

COMMENTARY:

There are five imperatives in verse 27 with the first four operating as two coordinating pairs. Φέρε is the first in each pair and its present aspect suggests an eagerness by Jesus for Thomas to have an experience that verifies the reality that he is truly risen. But notice that the last imperative, γίνου (present tense), is modified by the negative adverb μή, a type of prohibition suggesting that one should stop something already at work. And what was already at work in Thomas was a *distrusting* (ἄπιστος) attitude toward his fellow apostles who were eyewitnesses of their risen Lord. The whole mission of the church will rely on *trusting* the faithful word of the apostles and not a personal, visionary experience. What Jesus' resurrection appearance does here is unify the apostolic band for the sake of his mission so that not just Thomas, but countless others can say by faith, as Thomas did by sight, Ὁ κύριός μου καὶ ὁ θεός μου.

εἶτα > then ‖ φέρε > 2SPAM, reach! ‖ τὸν δάκτυλόν σου > your finger ‖ ἴδε > 2SAAM, look here! ‖ βάλε > 2SAAM, thrust! ‖ τὴν πλευράν μου > my side ‖ γίνου > 2SPMM, do [not] be ‖ ἀπεκρίθη > 3SAPI, answered ‖ εἶπεν > 3SAAI, he said

Further Reading: John 20:1-18
Roger G. DePriest

JOHN 21:18-19

¹⁸ ἀμὴν ἀμὴν λέγω σοι, ὅτε ἦς νεώτερος, ἐζώννυες σεαυτὸν καὶ περιεπάτεις ὅπου ἤθελες ὅταν δὲ γηράσῃς, ἐκτενεῖς τὰς χεῖράς σου, καὶ ἄλλος σε ζώσει καὶ οἴσει ὅπου οὐ θέλεις. ¹⁹ τοῦτο δὲ εἶπεν σημαίνων ποίῳ θανάτῳ δοξάσει τὸν θεόν. καὶ τοῦτο εἰπὼν λέγει αὐτῷ Ἀκολούθει μοι.

CONTEXT:
Apart from the Prologue (1:1-18), the first and last chapters of John's Gospel mirror each other in several ways, not the least of which is Jesus' call, "Follow me" (Ἀκολούθει μοι), first to Philip (ch. 1), and then to Peter (ch. 21). But also in chapter 21, Jesus reinforces his call for Peter to follow with a second, more emphatic reiteration: "You, follow me" (σύ μοι ἀκολούθει).

COMMENTARY:
In verse 18, there are two adverbial conjunctions, ὅτε (used with indicative verbs) and ὅταν (used with subjunctive verbs), which serve as temporal markers. The subjunctive mood, which is the mood of possibility or potentiality, adds to the narrative tension. Peter, who previously said he would lay down his life for Jesus, but had failed miserably, led the Gospel author to juxtapose Peter and Judas in at least two passages. Here, John masterfully uses double-entendre by playing off the dual meanings of ζώννυμι (to fasten one's own belt {as in Peter dressing himself} / to fasten {as in another fastening Peter's hands to a cross}), allowing the Peter-Judas motif to reach resolution. Tenderly, Jesus encourages Peter that he will become a good shepherd by laying down his life for the sheep, which he will do because he obeyed and followed Jesus.

ἦς > 2SIAI, you were || νεώτερος > younger || ἐζώννυες > 2SIAI, you used to fasten || περιεπάτεις > 2SIAI, you were walking around || ἤθελες > 2SIAI, you were wanting || γηράσῃς > 2SAAS, you should grow old || ἐκτενεῖς > 2SFAI, you will stretch out || ζώσει > 3SFAI, he will fasten or he will dress || σημαίνων > PAPMSN, signifying || ποίῳ > what kind of || δοξάσει > 3SFAI, he will glorify || ἀκολούθει > 2SPAM, follow!

Further Reading: John 21:15–23
Roger G. DePriest

¹ πολυμερῶς καὶ πολυτρόπως πάλαι ὁ θεὸς λαλήσας τοῖς πατράσιν ἐν τοῖς προφήταις ² ἐπ' ἐσχάτου τῶν ἡμερῶν τούτων ἐλάλησεν ἡμῖν ἐν υἱῷ, ὃν ἔθηκεν κληρονόμον πάντων, δι' οὗ καὶ ἐποίησεν τοὺς αἰῶνας.

CONTEXT:

This is the beginning of the prologue to Hebrews. It introduces Jesus as God's final revelation. God "has spoken" his final word in his Son, Jesus.

COMMENTARY:

The full paragraph is 1:1–4 and the main verb is ἐλάλησεν, "has spoken," following the participle λαλήσας, "having spoken." Notice ὁ θεός is the subject of ἐλάλησεν which is modified by the participle λαλήσας. Ἐν before υἱῷ may be viewed as an instrumental preposition or, more likely, locative. The anarthrous use of the dative noun υἱῷ emphasizes the character and nature of the Son. Supplying "his" in the translation is an effort to make explicit what is implied in the construction. God's revelation through the OT prophets was piecemeal, preparatory, and progressive. God's revelation through the Son is personal and permanent.

πολυμερῶς > at many times || πολυτρόπως > in many ways || πάλαι > long ago || λαλήσας > AAPMSN, having spoken || ἐλάλησεν > 3SAAI, has spoken, spoke || ἔθηκεν > 3SAAI, appointed || κληρονόμον > heir || ἐποίησεν > 3SAAI, made, created

Further Reading: Hebrews 1:1–4
David L. Allen

³ ὃς ὢν ἀπαύγασμα τῆς δόξης καὶ χαρακτὴρ τῆς ὑποστάσεως αὐτοῦ, φέρων τε τὰ πάντα τῷ ῥήματι τῆς δυνάμεως αὐτοῦ, καθαρισμὸν τῶν ἁμαρτιῶν ποιησάμενος ἐκάθισεν ἐν δεξιᾷ τῆς μεγαλωσύνης ἐν ὑψηλοῖς.

CONTEXT:
Seven participial and relative clauses constitute vv. 2b–3 that further describe who the Son is and what he does.

COMMENTARY:
Verse 3 introduces the third relative clause modifying υἱῷ in v. 2. This third relative clause is introduced by ὅς, which is the subject of the final verb ἐκάθισεν, followed by three participial clauses, all modifying the final verb ἐκάθισεν at the end of the verse. Seven clauses summarize who the Son is in relation to the Father and what the Son does in relation to the universe, the eschaton, and human sin. Notice that the word order in six of these seven clauses is identical: SVO. But in the final clause, the word order shifts to OVS. Καθαρισμόν is fronted and is followed by a middle voice participle ποιησάμενος, "having made." This change is often missed by commentators and signals focus and emphasis. In fact, of the seven relative and participial clauses, the rest of Hebrews focuses on the atoning work of the Son as high priest, which is probably the reason for this unusual word order.

ἀπαύγασμα > radiance ‖ χαρακτήρ > exact imprint ‖ ὑποστάσεως > nature ‖ φέρων > PAPMSN, upholding ‖ καθαρισμόν > purification ‖ ποιησάμενος > AMPMSN, having made ‖ ἐκάθισεν > 3SAAI, sat down ‖ μεγαλωσύνης > majesty ‖ ὑψηλοῖς > high

Further Reading: Hebrews 1:1–14
David L. Allen

¹ διὰ τοῦτο δεῖ περισσοτέρως προσέχειν ἡμᾶς τοῖς ἀκουσθεῖσιν, μή ποτε παραρυῶμεν. ² εἰ γὰρ ὁ δι' ἀγγέλων λαληθεὶς λόγος ἐγένετο βέβαιος, καὶ πᾶσα παράβασις καὶ παρακοὴ ἔλαβεν ἔνδικον μισθαποδοσίαν, ³ πῶς ἡμεῖς ἐκφευξόμεθα τηλικαύτης ἀμελήσαντες σωτηρίας ...

CONTEXT:

Hebrews 2:1-4 is a hortatory paragraph following the two expository paragraphs, 1:1-4 and 1:5-14. It provides an exhortation based on the grounds of God's final revelation in the Son who made an atonement for sin and is now exalted to the right hand of God in heaven.

COMMENTARY:

Διὰ τοῦτο connects 1:1-14 with the exhortation to "pay close attention to what we have heard." The infinitive προσέχειν is the predicate complement of δεῖ, which is grammatically expanded by the subjunctive παραρυῶμεν (a NT *hapax*), a subordinate clause stating the purpose for the exhortation: "so we will not drift away." This is the first of five warning passages in Hebrews. Notice here that the content of the warning, i.e., the consequence, is not stated.

περισσοτέρως > much more || προσέχειν > PAN, to pay attention to || ἀκουσθεῖσιν > APPNPD, that which was heard || παραρυῶμεν > 1PAPS, drift away || λαληθείς > AAPMSN, declared || ἐγένετο > 3SAMI, proved || βέβαιος > inflexible || παράβασις > transgression || παρακοή > disobedience || ἔνδικον > just || μισθαποδοσίαν > retribution || ἐκφευξόμεθα > 1PFMI, will escape || τηλικαύτης > so great || ἀμελήσαντες > AAPMPN, neglect

Further Reading: Hebrews 2:1-9
David L. Allen

¹⁷ ὅθεν ὤφειλεν κατὰ πάντα τοῖς ἀδελφοῖς ὁμοιωθῆναι, ἵνα ἐλεήμων γένηται καὶ πιστὸς ἀρχιερεὺς τὰ πρὸς τὸν θεόν, εἰς τὸ ἱλάσκεσθαι τὰς ἁμαρτίας τοῦ λαοῦ.

CONTEXT:

This verse occurs in the context of Hebrews 2:10–19, which is further composed of two paragraphs: 2:10–13 and 2:14–18.

COMMENTARY:

Hebrews 2:16 begins with γάρ and has a two-fold function: 1) it introduces a summary conclusion of 2:10–15, and 2) it explains the reason for the incarnation in v. 14. The ὅθεν of v. 17 is an inferential conjunction playing multiple roles: 1) introducing a conclusion from v. 16; 2) introducing a further summary of 2:10–16; and 3) restating v. 14. The purpose of the incarnation is here stated to be εἰς τὸ ἱλάσκεσθαι τὰς ἁμαρτίας τοῦ λαοῦ, "to make propitiation for the sins of the people." ἱλάσκεσθαι is the infinitive of purpose expressing why it was necessary for Jesus to become man. There is some debate about whether this word group should be translated as "expiation," "propitiation," or "mercy seat." The latter two translations better express the meaning of the word. Here the ground is laid for the author's argument in the remainder of the letter: Jesus is our high priest who makes atonement for our sins.

ὤφειλεν > 3SIAI, had || ὁμοιωθῆναι > APN, to become like || ἐλεήμων > merciful || γένηται > 3SAMS, might become || ἱλάσκεσθαι > PMN, to propitiate

Further Reading: Hebrews 2:10–18
David L. Allen

¹ ὅθεν, ἀδελφοὶ ἅγιοι, κλήσεως ἐπουρανίου μέτοχοι, κατανοήσατε τὸν ἀπόστολον καὶ ἀρχιερέα τῆς ὁμολογίας ἡμῶν Ἰησοῦν.

CONTEXT:

Hebrews 3:1 is the introduction to the paragraph 3:1–6 and begins a new subsection in the letter. Whereas the previous paragraph, Hebrews 2:5–18, was expository in nature, this paragraph and in fact the entire section from 3:1–4:13 is hortatory in nature. The hortatory nature of 3:1–6 is signaled by the use of the imperative in 3:1 and the imperatival idea semantically encoded in the conditional clause of v. 6.

COMMENTARY:

The inferential conjunction ὅθεν, "therefore," indicates a conclusion drawn from 2:10–18, and provides the reason why the readers are to "consider Jesus." The hortatory nature of this paragraph is evidenced by the use of κατανοήσατε in v. 1, translated "consider." This imperatival verb will appear again in Hebrews 12:3, following the hortatory subjunction in 12:2 translated "let us run with endurance the race set before us." Its use in these two places signals something of an inclusio. The proper name Ἰησοῦν is placed clause final for emphasis. This is a common rhetorical technique of the author. Jesus is both ἀπόστολον καὶ ἀρχιερέα. The former connects back to Hebrews 1 where God has spoken his final word in Jesus the Son. The latter connects back to Hebrews 2 where Jesus is explicitly stated to be our high priest.

κλήσεως > calling || ἐπουρανίου > heavenly || μέτοχοι > share || κατανοήσατε > 2PAAM, consider

Further Reading: Hebrews 3:1–6
David L. Allen

¹² βλέπετε, ἀδελφοί, μήποτε ἔσται ἔν τινι ὑμῶν καρδία πονηρὰ ἀπιστίας ἐν τῷ ἀποστῆναι ἀπὸ θεοῦ ζῶντος, ¹³ ἀλλὰ παρακαλεῖτε ἑαυτοὺς καθ' ἑκάστην ἡμέραν, ἄχρις οὗ τὸ σήμερον καλεῖται, ἵνα μὴ σκληρυνθῇ τις ἐξ ὑμῶν ἀπάτῃ τῆς ἁμαρτίας.

CONTEXT:
Hebrews 3:12–19 is the final paragraph of chapter 3. It constitutes the author's application of the previous quotation in 3:7–11 and is primarily hortatory in genre.

COMMENTARY:
The author is comparing the situation of his present readers to the Exodus generation in the wilderness. Hebrews 3:12 is the continuation of the warning that was begun with the quotation from Psalm 95 in 3:7–11. The imperative βλέπετε, translated "see to it; beware," is further defined as μήποτε ἔσται ἔν τινι ὑμῶν καρδία πονηρὰ ἀπιστίας ἐν τῷ ἀποστῆναι ἀπὸ θεοῦ ζῶντος, "lest there be in any one of you an evil, unbelieving heart that turns away from the living God." The infinitive ἀποστῆναι, "turning away," gives commentators fits. No doubt the author had in mind Numbers 14:9 (LXX) where this same word is used. There, the sense of the word is "rebel," which best fits the Hebrew word used in the text. Interpreters should be careful in assigning the theological meaning of "apostasy" to this word (see Allen, *Hebrews*, NAC, 260–263).

βλέπετε > 2PPAM, beware, see to it ‖ ἔσται > 3SFMI, there will be ‖ ἀπιστίας > unbelieving ‖ ἀποστῆναι > AAN, falling away, turning away ‖ παρακαλεῖτε > 2PPAM, exhort, encourage ‖ σκληρυνθῇ > 3SAPS, may be hardened ‖ ἀπάτῃ > deceitfulness

Further Reading: Hebrews 3:7–19
David L. Allen

¹² ζῶν γὰρ ὁ λόγος τοῦ θεοῦ καὶ ἐνεργὴς καὶ τομώτερος ὑπὲρ πᾶσαν μάχαιραν δίστομον καὶ διϊκνούμενος ἄχρι μερισμοῦ ψυχῆς καὶ πνεύματος, ἁρμῶν τε καὶ μυελῶν, καὶ κριτικὸς ἐνθυμήσεων καὶ ἐννοιῶν καρδίας· ¹³ καὶ οὐκ ἔστιν κτίσις ἀφανὴς ἐνώπιον αὐτοῦ, πάντα δὲ γυμνὰ καὶ τετραχηλισμένα τοῖς ὀφθαλμοῖς αὐτοῦ, πρὸς ὃν ἡμῖν ὁ λόγος.

CONTEXT:

This short paragraph concludes the section begun in 4:1. It is the final paragraph in the first major section of Hebrews (1:5–4:13). Notice there is something of an inclusio formed with the prologue where Jesus is God's final word "spoken" to us. The use of γάρ ("for") indicates the reason for seeking to enter God's rest (4:1–10).

COMMENTARY:

There is an interpretive problem with this text. The issue is whether to interpret λόγος as a reference to the written word or Jesus as the living word. Since the Reformation, the tendency has been to choose the former interpretation. But the early Church Fathers almost always interpreted it as a reference to Jesus. Perhaps this is a case of "studied ambiguity" such that the author has left the matter ambiguous so as to suggest both possibilities. Whatever choice is made, it would seem the λόγος in v. 13 is best understood to be a reference to Jesus. All things are γυμνὰ καὶ τετραχηλισμένα τοῖς ὀφθαλμοῖς αὐτοῦ, "naked and laid bare before the eyes of *him*." Thus, the final clause, πρὸς ὃν ἡμῖν ὁ λόγος, would be something of a pun by the author such that the meaning is something like "we must give a word (account) to him who is himself the Word (of God), namely, Jesus."

ἐνεργής > active, effective || τομώτερος > sharper || δίστομον > double-edged || διϊκνούμενος > PMPMSN, piercing, penetrating || μερισμοῦ > division || ἁρμῶν > joints || μυελῶν > marrow || κριτικός > discerning || ἐνθυμήσεων > thoughts || ἐννοιῶν > intentions || ἀφανής > invisible || γυμνά > naked || τετραχηλισμένα > RPPMPN, exposed, laid bare

Further Reading: Hebrews 4:1–13
David L. Allen

¹⁶ προσερχώμεθα οὖν μετὰ παρρησίας τῷ θρόνῳ τῆς χάριτος, ἵνα λάβωμεν ἔλεος καὶ χάριν εὕρωμεν εἰς εὔκαιρον βοήθειαν.

CONTEXT:

Hebrews 4:14–16 is the opening paragraph of the second major division of Hebrews. The paragraph begins with ἔχοντες οὖν, "having therefore," and the only other place in the letter where this phrase is used is in 10:19 which begins the third and final division of the letter.

COMMENTARY:

Hebrews 4:14–16 is a hortatory paragraph based on the two hortatory subjunctives κρατῶμεν and προσερχώμεθα, "let us hold fast," and "let us draw near." Notice these identical hortatory subjunctives occur in Hebrews 10:22, 23 in reverse order. Likewise, the noun παρρησίας ("confidence") occurs in both paragraphs. That which we are exhorted to draw near to is τῷ θρόνῳ τῆς χάριτος, "the throne of grace." The ἵνα clause introduces the purpose for our drawing near: ἵνα λάβωμεν ἔλεος καὶ χάριν εὕρωμεν εἰς εὔκαιρον βοήθειαν: "that we may receive mercy and find grace for well-timed help." Notice the chiastic structure: λάβωμεν ἔλεος and χάριν εὕρωμεν, where the position of the subjunctive verbs and nouns are reversed (V-N – N-V).

προσερχώμεθα > 1PPMS, let us draw near ǁ λάβωμεν > 1PAAS, we may receive ǁ εὕρωμεν > 1PAAS, we may find ǁ εὔκαιρον > well-timed ǁ βοήθειαν > help

Further Reading: Hebrews 4:14–16
David L. Allen

253

... ⁸ καίπερ ὢν υἱός, ἔμαθεν ἀφ’ ὧν ἔπαθεν τὴν ὑπακοήν, ⁹ καὶ τελειωθεὶς ἐγένετο πᾶσιν τοῖς ὑπακούουσιν αὐτῷ αἴτιος σωτηρίας αἰωνίου.

CONTEXT:

Hebrews 5:1–10 is an expository paragraph unit introduced by the subordinating conjunction γάρ, which serves to introduce the grounds for the exhortation in 4:16. The purpose of this paragraph is to explain the contrast between the OT priesthood and that of Jesus.

COMMENTARY:

The conjunction καίπερ "although" modifies the participle ὢν and semantically encodes the concept of concession: "although being Son (of God), yet he learned obedience." To say that Jesus ἔπαθεν τὴν ὑπακοήν, "learned obedience," is to say that by virtue of his humanity, Jesus experienced suffering. This resulted in Jesus τελειωθεὶς, "having been made perfect," where the aorist participle is related to the main verb ἐγένετο, "he became." Commentators are divided over how to construe the final clause in v. 9. It could mean "he suffered and was perfected; as a result, he became the source of salvation." Others take it to mean something along the lines of "that as a result of having been perfected, he became the source of salvation."

καίπερ > although ‖ **ἔμαθεν** > 3SAAI, learned ‖ **ἔπαθεν** > 3SAAI, suffered ‖ **τελειωθεὶς** > APPMSN, perfected, brought to its goal ‖ **ἐγένετο** > 3SAMI, became ‖ **τοῖς ὑπακούουσιν** > PAPMPD, the ones obeying ‖ **αἴτιος** > source

Further Reading: Hebrews 5:1–10
David L. Allen

HEBREWS 5:11–14

¹¹ περὶ οὗ πολὺς ἡμῖν ὁ λόγος καὶ δυσερμήνευτος λέγειν, ἐπεὶ νωθροὶ γεγόνατε ταῖς ἀκοαῖς· ¹² καὶ γὰρ ὀφείλοντες εἶναι διδάσκαλοι διὰ τὸν χρόνον, πάλιν χρείαν ἔχετε τοῦ διδάσκειν ὑμᾶς τινὰ τὰ στοιχεῖα τῆς ἀρχῆς τῶν λογίων τοῦ θεοῦ, καὶ γεγόνατε χρείαν ἔχοντες γάλακτος, οὐ στερεᾶς τροφῆς. ¹³ πᾶς γὰρ ὁ μετέχων γάλακτος ἄπειρος λόγου δικαιοσύνης, νήπιος γάρ ἐστιν· ¹⁴ τελείων δέ ἐστιν ἡ στερεὰ τροφή, τῶν διὰ τὴν ἕξιν τὰ αἰσθητήρια γεγυμνασμένα ἐχόντων πρὸς διάκρισιν καλοῦ τε καὶ κακοῦ.

CONTEXT:

Hebrews 5:11–14 begins a new section that extends to 6:20. The paragraph divisions are 5:11–14, 6:1–8, 6:9–20. This section begins the third warning passage in Hebrews. This paragraph has as its theme spiritual maturity.

COMMENTARY:

Verse 11 is the topic sentence of the paragraph, identifying the problem of the readers: they have become spiritually hard of hearing in the sense that they need to listen and obey the word of God for spiritual growth. Verses 12 and 13 each introduces a new sentence beginning with the subordinate conjunction γάρ. Verse 14 begins with the conjunction δέ which semantically introduces a coordinate clause of greater semantic weight than the preceding clause. The passage is somewhat ambiguous about the nature of the immaturity. Are they immature because they have never progressed toward maturity or are they immature because they have regressed because of disobedience? The key point to notice is that the context of this paragraph is the issue of spiritual maturity, which will play a key hermeneutical role in the interpretation of the notoriously difficult warning in Hebrews 6:1–8.

δυσερμήνευτος > hard to explain || νωθροί > dull || γεγόνατε > 2PRAI, have become || ὀφείλοντες > PAPMPN, ought, be obligated || στοιχεῖα > principles || γάλακτος > milk || στερεᾶς τροφῆς > solid food || ὁ μετέχων > PAPMSN, the one partaking || ἄπειρος > unskilled || νήπιος > child || τελείων > mature || ἕξιν > practice || αἰσθητήρια > powers || γεγυμνασμένα > RPPNPA, trained, disciplined || διάκρισιν > discernment

Further Reading: Hebrews 5:11–6:8
David L. Allen

SEPTEMBER 13
HEBREWS 6:1-2

¹ διὸ ἀφέντες τὸν τῆς ἀρχῆς τοῦ Χριστοῦ λόγον ἐπὶ τὴν τελειότητα φερώμεθα, μὴ πάλιν θεμέλιον καταβαλλόμενοι μετανοίας ἀπὸ νεκρῶν ἔργων καὶ πίστεως ἐπὶ θεόν, ² βαπτισμῶν διδαχῆς ἐπιθέσεώς τε χειρῶν, ἀναστάσεώς τε νεκρῶν καὶ κρίματος αἰωνίου.

CONTEXT:

The writer has more to say about Jesus' Melchizedekian priesthood (5:10) but his audience isn't ready for it. First, they needed another exhortation (5:11–6:20; see his earlier two in 2:1–4 and 3:1–4:13). They needed to shake off their spiritual lethargy (5:11; 6:12), especially before it turned into something even more serious (6:4–6).

COMMENTARY:

In Hebrews 6:1–2, the author summarizes the teaching the audience wasn't yet ready to move beyond. In fact, he refers to the content in three ways: it's the "beginning or elementary (τῆς ἀρχῆς) word about the Messiah (τοῦ Χριστοῦ)" (v. 1a), "the foundation (θεμέλιον)" (v. 1b), and "instruction (διδαχῆς)" (v. 2). That is, they lack not only basic information but content that is straight from the OT (vv. 1b–2). Thus, "the perfection" (v. 1a, τὴν τελειότητα) the author wants his audience to reach is nothing less than a mature *understanding* of the Bible, specifically one that sees how it points to what Jesus has done and will do. To fail to see how the old covenant era anticipated the new, to fail to see how the Scriptures reach their τελειότητα in Messiah Jesus, is therefore not simply a hermeneutical failure, it's a *moral* failure too.

ἀφέντες > AAPMPN, having left off || τελειότητα > completeness, maturity, perfection || φερώμεθα > 1PPPS, let us move on || θεμέλιον > foundation || καταβαλλόμενοι > PMPMPN, laying down || μετανοίας > repentance || βαπτισμῶν > cleansings, baptisms || ἐπιθέσεως > laying on

Further Reading: Hebrews 6:3–12
Jared Compton

¹⁶ ἄνθρωποι γὰρ κατὰ τοῦ μείζονος ὀμνύουσιν, καὶ πάσης αὐτοῖς ἀντιλογίας πέρας εἰς βεβαίωσιν ὁ ὅρκος· ¹⁷ ἐν ᾧ περισσότερον βουλόμενος ὁ θεὸς ἐπιδεῖξαι τοῖς κληρονόμοις τῆς ἐπαγγελίας τὸ ἀμετάθετον τῆς βουλῆς αὐτοῦ ἐμεσίτευσεν ὅρκῳ, ¹⁸ ἵνα διὰ δύο πραγμάτων ἀμεταθέτων, ἐν οἷς ἀδύνατον ψεύσασθαι τὸν θεόν, ἰσχυρὰν παράκλησιν ἔχωμεν οἱ καταφυγόντες κρατῆσαι τῆς προκειμένης ἐλπίδος.

CONTEXT:

Before returning to Psalm 110 and Jesus' Melchizedekian priesthood (7:1–28), the author prepares for this discussion by explaining why God takes oaths like the one found at the beginning of Psalm 110:4 (6:13–20). *Hint:* It's not because he can't be trusted.

COMMENTARY:

After citing God's promise to Abraham from Genesis 22:17, the author explains why God's promise was preceded by an oath (see Gen 22:16). After all, God doesn't need to "swear" (ὀμνύω; v. 16) to be believed. He does it for our sakes—that is, for inheritors of the Abrahamic promise (τοῖς κληρονόμοις τῆς ἐπαγγελίας, v. 17b). In fact, he swears because he *really* wants (περισσότερον βουλόμενος, v. 17a) to show us just how sure his word is *so that* (ἵνα, v. 18a) we might have not just encouragement but *strong* encouragement (ἰσχυρὰν παράκλησιν, v. 18b). Don't miss the goodness and kindness of our God: he—the *never-lying God*—adds oaths to already-sure promises because he knows exactly what we frail humans need to anchor our hope in things to come, and he very much wants to give it to us.

ὀμνύουσιν > 3PPAI, they swear an oath ‖ ἀντιλογίας > disputes, hostilities ‖ πέρας > end ‖ βεβαίωσιν > confirmation ‖ ὅρκος > oath ‖ περισσότερον > even more, more excessive ‖ βουλόμενος > PMPMSN, desiring, intending ‖ ἐπιδεῖξαι > AAN, to show, demonstrate ‖ κληρονόμοις > heirs ‖ ἀμετάθετον > unchangeableness ‖ βουλῆς > resolve, purpose ‖ ἐμεσίτευσεν > 3SAAI, guaranteed ‖ πραγμάτων > matters, things ‖ ἀδύνατον > impossible ‖ ψεύσασθαι > AMN, to lie ‖ ἔχωμεν > 1PPAS, we might have ‖ καταφυγόντες > AAPMPN, those who have taken refuge ‖ κρατῆσαι > AAN, to hold fast ‖ προκειμένης > PPPFSG, set before

Further Reading: Hebrews 6:13–20
Jared Compton

HEBREWS 7:1–3

¹ οὗτος γὰρ ὁ Μελχισέδεκ, βασιλεὺς Σαλήμ, ἱερεὺς τοῦ θεοῦ τοῦ ὑψίστου, ὁ συναντήσας Ἀβραὰμ ὑποστρέφοντι ἀπὸ τῆς κοπῆς τῶν βασιλέων καὶ εὐλογήσας αὐτόν, ² ᾧ καὶ δεκάτην ἀπὸ πάντων ἐμέρισεν Ἀβραάμ, πρῶτον μὲν ἑρμηνευόμενος βασιλεὺς δικαιοσύνης ἔπειτα δὲ καὶ βασιλεὺς Σαλήμ, ὅ ἐστιν βασιλεὺς εἰρήνης, ³ ἀπάτωρ ἀμήτωρ ἀγενεαλόγητος, μήτε ἀρχὴν ἡμερῶν μήτε ζωῆς τέλος ἔχων, ἀφωμοιωμένος δὲ τῷ υἱῷ τοῦ θεοῦ, μένει ἱερεὺς εἰς τὸ διηνεκές.

CONTEXT:

After an extended exhortation (5:11–6:20), the author returns to the argument he began in 5:1–10. The messianic son Jesus (5:5–10; 7:1–3) is the long-anticipated Melchizedekian priest-king of Psalm 110 (7:1–28).

COMMENTARY:

Hebrews 7:1–3 comprises one long sentence whose subject—Οὗτος ... ὁ *Μελχισέδεκ* (v. 1a)—is separated from its predicate—μένει (v. 3b)—by a *fifty-six-word* description of Melchizedek (vv. 1b –3a) that is drawn from the only other place in the OT that mentions his name outside of Psalm 110:4—Genesis 14:17–20. The delayed verb makes sure we see the point of the author's extended allusion. Jesus, the psalmist's forever priest (see 5:6), comes from a non- and, indeed, *pre*-Levitical order of priests (see 7:10), whose eponymous exemplar (i.e., Melchizedek), at least according to the Genesis narrative, *remained* a priest forever.

Μελχισέδεκ > Melchizedek ǁ **Σαλήμ** > Salem ǁ **ὑψίστου** > most high ǁ **συναντήσας** > AAPMSN, who met ǁ **ὑποστρέφοντι** > PAPMSD, returning ǁ **κοπῆς** > slaughter ǁ **εὐλογήσας** > AAPMSN, blessed ǁ **δεκάτην** > a tenth ǁ **ἐμέρισεν** > 3SAAI, apportioned ǁ **ἑρμηνευόμενος** > PPPMSN, being translated ǁ **ἔπειτα** > then, next ǁ **ἔστιν** > 3SPAI, he is ǁ **ἀπάτωρ** > without father ǁ **ἀμήτωρ** > without mother ǁ **ἀγενεαλόγητος** > without genealogy ǁ **ἔχων** > PAPMSN, having ǁ **ἀφωμοιωμένος** > RPPMSN, resembling ǁ **μένει** > 3SPAI, he remains ǁ **διηνεκές** > continuously, without interruption, for all time

Further Reading: Hebrews 7:1–10
Jared Compton

²³ καὶ οἱ μὲν πλείονές εἰσιν γεγονότες ἱερεῖς διὰ τὸ θανάτῳ κωλύεσθαι παραμένειν· ²⁴ ὁ δὲ διὰ τὸ μένειν αὐτὸν εἰς τὸν αἰῶνα ἀπαράβατον ἔχει τὴν ἱερωσύνην· ²⁵ ὅθεν καὶ σῴζειν εἰς τὸ παντελὲς δύναται τοὺς προσερχομένους δι' αὐτοῦ τῷ θεῷ, πάντοτε ζῶν εἰς τὸ ἐντυγχάνειν ὑπὲρ αὐτῶν.

CONTEXT:

The author continues to draw out the significance of Jesus' Melchizedekian priesthood. He's already said it replaces the Levitical priesthood (7:11–19). Now he'll tell us why (7:20–25).

COMMENTARY:

What makes Jesus' priesthood permanent and, therefore, allows God to say, "You are a priest *forever*" (Ps 110:4, see 7:16) is the quality of his life. Notice: "*Because he remains forever* (διὰ τὸ μένειν αὐτὸν εἰς τὸν αἰῶνα), he has a permanent priesthood" (v. 24). Thus, the psalmist's promise of a Melchizedekian priest at once signaled the transience and insufficiency of the Levitical priesthood and, at the same time, signaled the new quality of the anticipated priest: he would be a priest who *remained* (cf. 7:1–3) or, conversely, who was not by death prevented from remaining (διὰ τὸ θανάτῳ κωλύεσθαι παραμένειν, v. 23). Earlier the author hinted that what gave Jesus this type of life—allowing him to be resurrected from the dead by the Father (7:16)—had everything to do with his godly character (see 5:7; cf. 1:9; also 9:14) formed by hard-fought obedience (5:8).

εἰσιν > 3PPAI, they are || γεγονότες > RAPMPN, having become || κωλύεσθαι > PPN, to be prevented || παραμένειν > PAN, to continue, stay on || μένειν > PAN, to remain || ἀπαράβατον > permanently || ἔχει > 3SPAI, he has || ἱερωσύνην > priesthood || ὅθεν > from which, for which reason || σῴζειν > PAN, to save || παντελές > completely || δύναται > 3SPMI, he is able || προσερχομένους > PMPMPA, those who draw near || ζῶν > PAPMSN, living || ἐντυγχάνειν > PAN, to intercede

Further Reading: Hebrews 7:20–25
Jared Compton

³ πᾶς γὰρ ἀρχιερεὺς εἰς τὸ προσφέρειν δῶρά τε καὶ θυσίας καθίσταται· ὅθεν ἀναγκαῖον ἔχειν τι καὶ τοῦτον ὃ προσενέγκῃ. ⁴ εἰ μὲν οὖν ἦν ἐπὶ γῆς, οὐδ᾽ ἂν ἦν ἱερεύς, ὄντων τῶν προσφερόντων κατὰ νόμον τὰ δῶρα· ⁵ οἵτινες ὑποδείγματι καὶ σκιᾷ λατρεύουσιν τῶν ἐπουρανίων, καθὼς κεχρημάτισται Μωϋσῆς μέλλων ἐπιτελεῖν τὴν σκηνήν· ὅρα γάρ φησιν, ποιήσεις πάντα κατὰ τὸν τύπον τὸν δειχθέντα σοι ἐν τῷ ὄρει.

CONTEXT:

Having established that Jesus is the long-anticipated Melchizedekian priest-king, the author of Hebrews now turns to his main point (8:1–10:18; see κεφάλαιον in 8:1). Jesus serves in heaven in the true tabernacle, the tabernacle that was the pattern for God's instructions to Moses in Exodus. As the author will now show, the location of Jesus' service implies something about the nature of his priestly sacrifices.

COMMENTARY:

If every high priest sacrifices, then so must Jesus (5:1–10). However, if Jesus is seated at God's right hand (see 8:1, alluding to Ps 110:1), then what might this suggest about the nature of his sacrifices? That is, priests on earth offer sacrifices in a tabernacle that is a "copy" (ὑποδείγματι, v. 5a) and "shadow" (σκιᾷ, v. 5a) of the heavenly tabernacle where Jesus serves, something the author proves (v. 5b) by citing Exodus 25:9, 40. Moses was to make everything according to a very specific pattern: τὸν τύπον τὸν δειχθέντα σοι ἐν τῷ ὄρει. The participle phrase, standing in the second attributive position, specifies the pattern Moses was to follow. Sacrifices offered in the *real* tent, the author implies, are surely superior (see 8:6a) to those offered in the *copy* tent.

προσφέρειν > PAN, to offer ‖ δῶρα > gifts ‖ καθίσταται > 3SPPI, he is appointed ‖ ὅθεν > from which, for which reason ‖ ἀναγκαῖον > necessary ‖ ἔχειν > PAN, to have ‖ προσενέγκῃ > 3SAAS, he might offer ‖ ὄντων > PAPMPG, being ‖ προσφερόντων > PAPMPG, those who offer ‖ ὑποδείγματι > example, pattern, sketch ‖ σκιᾷ > shadow ‖ λατρεύουσιν > 3PPAI, they serve ‖ ἐπουρανίων > heavenly (things) ‖ κεχρημάτισται > 3SRPI, he had been warned ‖ μέλλων > PAPMSN, being about to ‖ ἐπιτελεῖν > PAN, to complete ‖ σκηνήν > tabernacle ‖ ὅρα > 3SPAM, see to it ‖ φησιν > 3SPAI, he says ‖ ποιήσεις > 2SFAI, you shall make ‖ τύπον > type, pattern ‖ δειχθέντα > APPMSA, was shown

Further Reading: Hebrews 9:11–28
Jared Compton

¹⁰ ὅτι αὕτη ἡ διαθήκη, ἣν διαθήσομαι τῷ οἴκῳ Ἰσραὴλ μετὰ τὰς ἡμέρας ἐκείνας, λέγει κύριος· διδοὺς νόμους μου εἰς τὴν διάνοιαν αὐτῶν καὶ ἐπὶ καρδίας αὐτῶν ἐπιγράψω αὐτούς, καὶ ἔσομαι αὐτοῖς εἰς θεόν, καὶ αὐτοὶ ἔσονταί μοι εἰς λαόν· ¹¹ καὶ οὐ μὴ διδάξωσιν ἕκαστος τὸν πολίτην αὐτοῦ καὶ ἕκαστος τὸν ἀδελφὸν αὐτοῦ λέγων· γνῶθι τὸν κύριον, ὅτι πάντες εἰδήσουσίν με ἀπὸ μικροῦ ἕως μεγάλου αὐτῶν, ¹² ὅτι ἵλεως ἔσομαι ταῖς ἀδικίαις αὐτῶν καὶ τῶν ἁμαρτιῶν αὐτῶν οὐ μὴ μνησθῶ ἔτι.

CONTEXT:

Jesus is a heavenly priest, serving in the superior heavenly tabernacle and, by implication, serving with better sacrifices (8:1–6a). Before talking about those sacrifices, however, the author turns to say something about the covenant Jesus mediates. It too is better because it contains better promises, promises that are fulfilled only because of an extraordinary act of God himself (8:6b–13).

COMMENTARY:

In these verses the author tells us not only what the better promises of the new covenant are but also how they will be fulfilled. Everything turns on the final ὅτι-clause in v. 12, which provides the ground or basis for bringing about all the better promises of vv. 10–11. In the anticipated new covenant, *every* (πάντες, v. 11) covenant member will have a life-giving, saving knowledge of God. And all this will be possible only because (ὅτι) God will fully and finally take away all their sins (v. 12a). The text, citing Jeremiah 31:31–34, says he'll once-and-for-all *forget* about their sins! How sin can be so fully expunged is an open question at this point in the author's argument. But we anticipate it will have something to do with Jesus' heavenly priesthood, carried out in the true heavenly tent, where different and indeed *better* sacrifices are offered than those offered by priests serving in the copy tent on earth.

διαθήσομαι > 1SFMI, I will decree, ordain ǁ λέγει > 3SPAI, he says ǁ διδούς > PAPMSN, giving ǁ διάνοιαν > mind ǁ ἐπιγράψω > 1SFAI, I will write upon ǁ ἔσομαι > 1SFMI, I will be ǁ ἔσονται > 3PFMI, they will be ǁ διδάξωσιν > 3PAAS, they shall teach ǁ πολίτην > fellow citizen, neighbor ǁ λέγων > PAPMSN, saying ǁ γνῶθι > 2SAAM, know ǁ εἰδήσουσιν > 3PFAI, they will know ǁ ἵλεως > merciful ǁ ἀδικίαις > unrighteousness, wrongdoings ǁ μνησθῶ > 1SAPS, I will remember

Further Reading: Hebrews 8:6b–13
Jared Compton

¹³ εἰ γὰρ τὸ αἷμα τράγων καὶ ταύρων καὶ σποδὸς δαμάλεως ῥαντίζουσα τοὺς κεκοινωμένους ἁγιάζει πρὸς τὴν τῆς σαρκὸς καθαρότητα, ¹⁴ πόσῳ μᾶλλον τὸ αἷμα τοῦ Χριστοῦ, ὃς διὰ πνεύματος αἰωνίου ἑαυτὸν προσήνεγκεν ἄμωμον τῷ θεῷ, καθαριεῖ τὴν συνείδησιν ἡμῶν ἀπὸ νεκρῶν ἔργων εἰς τὸ λατρεύειν θεῷ ζῶντι.

CONTEXT:

Even on the old covenant's highest day—the Day of Atonement (see Lev 16)—only one person could enter, and only for a short time, into God's presence. All this, the author tells us, was meant to highlight the inability of Levitical sacrifices to take away sin and provide full access to God (9:1–10).

COMMENTARY:

Here the author says that Messiah's blood (τὸ αἷμα τοῦ Χριστοῦ, v. 14a) is able to do what animal—Levitical—blood could never do. It can cleanse. And, more than that, it can cleanse sufficiently to allow humans to serve the living God. That, we're told, was the very purpose (εἰς τὸ λατρεύειν, v. 14b) of Jesus' sacrifice. That long-anticipated cleansing announced in Jeremiah's promised new covenant (see 8:12) is finally available through the surprising but necessary death of Israel's long-awaited Messiah.

τράγων > of goats || **ταύρων** > of bulls || **σποδός** > ashes || **δαμάλεως** > heifer || **ῥαντίζουσα** > PAPFSN, sprinkling || **κεκοινωμένους** > RPPMPA, those who are defiled || **ἁγιάζει** > 3SPAI, sanctifies || **καθαρότητα** > purity, ritual cleanness || **προσήνεγκεν** > 3SAAI, he offered || **ἄμωμον** > without blemish || **καθαριεῖ** > 3SFAI, will cleanse || **λατρεύειν** > PAN, to serve, worship; **ζῶντι** > PAPMSD, living

Further Reading: Hebrews 9:11–28
Jared Compton

HEBREWS 11:1-2

¹ ἔστιν δὲ πίστις ἐλπιζομένων ὑπόστασις, πραγμάτων ἔλεγχος οὐ βλεπομένων. ² ἐν ταύτῃ γὰρ ἐμαρτυρήθησαν οἱ πρεσβύτεροι.

CONTEXT:

If Jesus' death fulfills what the OT anticipated, and if he'll soon return to fully and finally save those who are his (10:37; cf. 9:28), then believers must hold fast to him while they wait. Despite what the wilderness generation implied (see 3:7–4:13), such patient waiting, such persevering *faith*, is possible. To prove it, the author gives his friends *thirty-eight examples* of persevering faith drawn from Israel's past (11:2–40). His point: if these "ancients" (οἱ πρεσβύτεροι, v. 2) could persevere, so too could his audience.

COMMENTARY:

Before cataloging his list of faithful heroes, the author clarifies what their faith entailed. His description is found in v. 1. And v. 2—and its mirror in v. 39—tell us faith's effect. The description involves a double-predicate—two predicate nouns (ὑπόστασις and ἔλεγχος)—and each is restricted by a plural genitive substantive (ἐλπιζομένων and πραγμάτων). Faith might not yet be sight, but it's nevertheless grounded in objective realities. As the author puts it, it's the "substance" or "reality" (ὑπόστασις) of hoped-for things (see ὑπόστασις in 1:3). That is, faith allows one right now to experience its object *at least in a preliminary way*. And it's this experience, this ὑπόστασις, that provides the faithful with sufficient "convicting evidence" (ἔλεγχος) for what remains, at least for the time being, unseen (οὐ βλεπομένων). This is why the author will later say that the audience's faith gives them real, if preliminary, access to the "heavenly" city (12:22), even while their full experience of that city is still "to come" (13:14).

ἔστιν > 3SPAI, it is ‖ ἐλπιζομένων > PPPNPG, of things being hoped for ‖ ὑπόστασις > essence, substance ‖ πραγμάτων > matters, things ‖ ἔλεγχος > proof ‖ βλεπομένων > PPPNPG, of things being seen ‖ ἐμαρτυρήθησαν > 3PAPI, they were commended

Further Reading: Hebrews 11:6, 13–16, 39–40
Jared Compton

³² καὶ τί ἔτι λέγω; ἐπιλείψει με γὰρ διηγούμενον ὁ χρόνος περὶ Γεδεών, Βαράκ, Σαμψών, Ἰεφθάε, Δαυίδ τε καὶ Σαμουὴλ καὶ τῶν προφητῶν.

CONTEXT:

The author's catalogue of faithful heroes (and heroines!) includes two lists. The first is found in vv. 3–31; the second in vv. 32–38. In the first, each entry is prefaced by the dative noun πίστει (see, e.g., vv. 3, 4, 5, 7). In the second, the entire list is introduced by the prepositional phrase διὰ πίστεως (see v. 33). What also distinguishes the lists is the non-canonical ordering of the author's rapid-fire list in v. 32b and especially his first-person editorial comment in v. 32a.

COMMENTARY:

Hebrews 11:32 designates the beginning of the author's second list of heroes (vv. 32–38). But it also gives us one of the few autobiographical details we have about the letter's author. It tells us his gender. "I do not have time *to tell* (διηγούμενον) about" every faithful hero from Israel's past. Speculation, of course, abounds about the author's identity. But, with this participle, we can at least affirm one thing: he was *male*. It's unlikely the reference is pseudonymous—i.e., a female author assuming a male identity—simply because so much of the letter's success depends upon the author's intimate knowledge of his audience and their intimate knowledge of him (see, e.g., 13:22).

λέγω > 1SPAS, shall I say ǁ ἐπιλείψει > 3SFAI, it will fail ǁ διηγούμενον > PMPMSA, telling ǁ Γεδεών > Gideon ǁ Βαράκ > Barak ǁ Σαμψών > Samson ǁ Ἰεφθάε > Jephthah ǁ Σαμουήλ > Samuel

Further Reading: Hebrews 2:1–4
Jared Compton

²⁰ ὁ δὲ θεὸς τῆς εἰρήνης, ὁ ἀναγαγὼν ἐκ νεκρῶν τὸν ποιμένα τῶν προβάτων τὸν μέγαν ἐν αἵματι διαθήκης αἰωνίου, τὸν κύριον ἡμῶν Ἰησοῦν, ²¹ καταρτίσαι ὑμᾶς ἐν παντὶ ἀγαθῷ εἰς τὸ ποιῆσαι τὸ θέλημα αὐτοῦ, ποιῶν ἐν ἡμῖν τὸ εὐάρεστον ἐνώπιον αὐτοῦ διὰ Ἰησοῦ Χριστοῦ, ᾧ ἡ δόξα εἰς τοὺς αἰῶνας τῶν αἰώνων, ἀμήν.

CONTEXT:

After a final chapter full of exhortations (13:1-19), the author closes his "brief word of exhortation" (13:22-25), but not before issuing a timely and encouraging benediction (13:20-21).

COMMENTARY:

Hold on to Jesus! It's a big task, considering the audience's circumstances. And the author—a wise and seasoned pastor—knows this. Thus, he concludes his letter asking God to do what only God can do. "May ... *God*... equip you with everything good (ἐν παντὶ ἀγαθῷ) for doing his will, and may *he* work in us what is pleasing to him." Don't miss this: God does all this "through" (διά) his son, Jesus Christ, both for his own pleasure (τὸ εὐάρεστον ἐνώπιον αὐτοῦ, v. 21) and his son's glory (ᾧ ἡ δόξα). That is, God's commitment to our perseverance is grounded in his commitment to his own pleasure and Jesus' glory.

ἀναγαγών > AAPMSN, who brought up || ποιμένα > shepherd || καταρτίσαι > 3SAAO, put in order, restore || ποιῆσαι > AAN, to do || ποιῶν > PAPMSN, making || εὐάρεστον > pleasing, acceptable

Further Reading: Hebrews 13:22-25
Jared Compton

⁹ καὶ ταῦτα εἰπὼν βλεπόντων αὐτῶν ἐπήρθη καὶ νεφέλη ὑπέλαβεν αὐτὸν ἀπὸ τῶν ὀφθαλμῶν αὐτῶν. ¹⁰ καὶ ὡς ἀτενίζοντες ἦσαν εἰς τὸν οὐρανὸν πορευομένου αὐτοῦ, καὶ ἰδοὺ ἄνδρες δύο παρειστήκεισαν αὐτοῖς ἐν ἐσθήσεσιν λευκαῖς.

CONTEXT:

In this opening chapter of Acts, the resurrected Jesus just instructed His disciples that the Holy Spirit would come upon them and that they would be His witnesses throughout the entire world (Acts 1:8).

COMMENTARY:

There are two genitive absolutes in these verses: βλεπόντων αὐτῶν (1:9) and πορευομένου αὐτοῦ (1:10). Genitive absolutes always include an anarthrous genitive participle, occur more frequently in narrative texts, and are adverbial (usually temporal) though grammatically independent. The first genitive absolute, βλεπόντων αὐτῶν, reveals that *while they were looking* Jesus ascended into heaven. This is made more emphatic by the prepositional phrase ἀπὸ τῶν ὀφθαλμῶν αὐτῶν. The second genitive absolute πορευομένου αὐτοῦ echoes the same event but focuses on Jesus' ascension: the apostles gazed intently *while He was going*. The apostles would soon be testifying about this eye-witness event of Jesus' ascension (see Acts 2:32).

εἰπών > AAPMSN, had said || βλεπόντων > PAPMPG, seeing || ἐπήρθη > 3SAPI, was taken up || ὑπέλαβεν > 3SAAI, took up || ἀτενίζοντες > PAPMPN, gazing intently || πορευομένου > PMPMSG, departing, leaving || ἐσθήσεσιν > clothing

Further Reading: Acts 1:1–11
Douglas Brown

²² ἄνδρες Ἰσραηλῖται, ἀκούσατε τοὺς λόγους τούτους· Ἰησοῦν τὸν Ναζωραῖον, ἄνδρα ἀποδεδειγμένον ἀπὸ τοῦ θεοῦ εἰς ὑμᾶς δυνάμεσιν καὶ τέρασιν καὶ σημείοις οἷς ἐποίησεν δι' αὐτοῦ ὁ θεὸς ἐν μέσῳ ὑμῶν καθὼς αὐτοὶ οἴδατε, ²³ τοῦτον τῇ ὡρισμένῃ βουλῇ καὶ προγνώσει τοῦ θεοῦ ἔκδοτον διὰ χειρὸς ἀνόμων προσπήξαντες ἀνείλατε, ²⁴ ὃν ὁ θεὸς ἀνέστησεν λύσας τὰς ὠδῖνας τοῦ θανάτου, καθότι οὐκ ἦν δυνατὸν κρατεῖσθαι αὐτὸν ὑπ' αὐτοῦ.

CONTEXT:
This passage develops Peter's argument about Jesus in his sermon on the day of Pentecost.

COMMENTARY:
These three verses form one complex sentence that describes Jesus through a list of accusative modifiers. The main clause is found in verse 23: τοῦτον ... ἀνείλατε, *you executed this one.* Several accusatives point to τοῦτον, all of which refer to Jesus. The first accusative is Ἰησοῦν (2:22), which serves as the antecedent of τοῦτον. Second, Ναζωραῖον (2:22) stands in apposition to Ἰησοῦν. Third, ἄνδρα (2:22) stands in apposition to Ναζωραῖον and is further modified by the accusative adjectival participle ἀποδεδειγμένον. Fourth, the adjective ἔκδοτον (2:23) directly modifies τοῦτον. Fifth, the accusative relative pronoun ὅν (2:24) refers to τοῦτον and introduces a relative clause that further describes Jesus.

ἀκούσατε > 2PAAM, listen, hear || ἀποδεδειγμένον > RPPMSA, attested || ὡρισμένῃ > RPPFSD, defined, determined || ἔκδοτον > delivered up, given up || προσπήξαντες > AAPMPN, nailed to (a cross) || ἀνείλατε > 2PAAI, executed, put to death || ἀνέστησεν > 3SAAI, raised || ὠδῖνας > birth pangs || κρατεῖσθαι > PPN, to be held

Further Reading: Acts 2:14–36
Douglas Brown

⁴¹ οἱ μὲν οὖν ἀποδεξάμενοι τὸν λόγον αὐτοῦ ἐβαπτίσθησαν καὶ προσετέθησαν ἐν τῇ ἡμέρᾳ ἐκείνῃ ψυχαὶ ὡσεὶ τρισχίλιαι. ⁴² ἦσαν δὲ προσκαρτεροῦντες τῇ διδαχῇ τῶν ἀποστόλων καὶ τῇ κοινωνίᾳ, τῇ κλάσει τοῦ ἄρτου καὶ ταῖς προσευχαῖς.

CONTEXT:

This passage recounts the beginning of the church and the conversion of nearly 3,000 Jews after Peter's sermon on the day of Pentecost in Jerusalem.

COMMENTARY:

Consider the participle προσκαρτεροῦντες in verse 42. This is a periphrastic participle used with the being verb ἦσαν. Periphrastic participles are anarthrous verbal participles used with a being verb to form one unified verbal idea. Together ἦσαν προσκαρτεροῦντες forms the main verb of the clause: *they were devoting*. The imperfect tense of ἦσαν and the present tense of προσκαρτεροῦντες combine to form the equivalent of the imperfect tense. Thus, Luke emphasizes the ongoing nature of the believer's devotion to the apostles' doctrine and Christian fellowship.

ἀποδεξάμενοι > AMPMPN, received ‖ ἐβαπτίσθησαν > 3PAPI, were baptized ‖ προσετέθησαν > 3PAPI, were added ‖ ὡσεί > about ‖ προσκαρτεροῦντες > PAPMPN, devoting ‖ κλάσει > breaking ‖ προσευχαῖς > prayers

Further Reading: Acts 2:37–47
Douglas Brown

SEPTEMBER 26
ACTS 3:8-9

⁸ καὶ ἐξαλλόμενος ἔστη καὶ περιεπάτει καὶ εἰσῆλθεν σὺν αὐτοῖς εἰς τὸ ἱερὸν περιπατῶν καὶ ἁλλόμενος καὶ αἰνῶν τὸν θεόν. ⁹ καὶ εἶδεν πᾶς ὁ λαὸς αὐτὸν περιπατοῦντα καὶ αἰνοῦντα τὸν θεόν.

CONTEXT:
In the wake of Pentecost (Acts 2), Peter and John heal a well-known lame man who was begging at the Beautiful Gate to the temple.

COMMENTARY:
In verse 8, Luke uses four participles of manner: ἐξαλλόμενος, περιπατῶν, ἁλλόμενος, and αἰνῶν. These participles are adverbial and modify the finite verbs ἔστη καὶ περιεπάτει καὶ εἰσῆλθεν. Manner answers the question "how" but is different from means. Means explains or defines the action of the main verb, whereas manner explains the attitude of the main action or indicates the mode in which the main action is performed. Wallace says that manner is "the participle of style" and adds "extra color" to the action of the main verb (*GGBB*, 627). In this case, the healed lame man *entered the temple in the manner of walking, leaping, and praising God.*

ἐξαλλόμενος > PMPMSN, leaping up || ἔστη > 3SAAI, stood || ἁλλόμενος > PMPMSN, leaping || αἰνῶν > PAPMSN, praising || εἶδεν > 3SAAI, saw || αἰνοῦντα > PAPMSA, praising

Further Reading: Acts 3:1–10
Douglas Brown

269

¹⁹ μετανοήσατε οὖν καὶ ἐπιστρέψατε εἰς τὸ ἐξαλειφθῆναι ὑμῶν τὰς ἁμαρτίας, ²⁰ ὅπως ἂν ἔλθωσιν καιροὶ ἀναψύξεως ἀπὸ προσώπου τοῦ κυρίου καὶ ἀποστείλῃ τὸν προκεχειρισμένον ὑμῖν Χριστὸν Ἰησοῦν.

CONTEXT:
Immediately after the lame man was healed, Peter preached in Solomon's portico in the Temple.

COMMENTARY:
At the turning point of his sermon, Peter exhorts his fellow countrymen to *repent* and *turn back* (μετανοήσατε καὶ ἐπιστρέψατε). Next, he expresses three purposes. Authors can articulate purpose in many ways in Greek. The first purpose is found in the articular infinitive τὸ ἐξαλειφθῆναι. When an articular infinitive is governed by εἰς it usually conveys purpose or result. The second and third purposes are introduced by the subordinate conjunction ὅπως followed by two subjunctive verbs: *so that the times of refreshing might come* and *so that God might send the appointed Christ*. These three purposes adverbially modify Peter's imperatives; they provide motivation to *repent* and *turn back* and ultimately show God's sovereign plan of salvation.

μετανοήσατε > 2PAAM, repent ‖ ἐπιστρέψατε > 2PAAM, turn back ‖ ἐξαλειφθῆναι > APN, to be blotted out, to be wiped away ‖ ὅπως > so that, in order that ‖ ἔλθωσιν > 3PAAS, may come ‖ ἀναψύξεως > refreshing ‖ ἀποστείλῃ > 3SAAS, may send ‖ προκεχειρισμένον > RPPMSA, having been appointed

Further Reading: Acts 3:11–26
Douglas Brown

270

SEPTEMBER 28

ACTS 4:19-20

¹⁹ ὁ δὲ Πέτρος καὶ Ἰωάννης ἀποκριθέντες εἶπον πρὸς αὐτούς, Εἰ δίκαιόν ἐστιν ἐνώπιον τοῦ θεοῦ ὑμῶν ἀκούειν μᾶλλον ἢ τοῦ θεοῦ, κρίνατε ²⁰ οὐ δυνάμεθα γὰρ ἡμεῖς ἃ εἴδαμεν καὶ ἠκούσαμεν μὴ λαλεῖν.

CONTEXT:
Acts 4 records the arrest of Peter and John and their hearing before the Council. Peter and John, standing with the newly healed lame man, boldly proclaim Jesus despite the Council's warnings to stop preaching Jesus.

COMMENTARY:
Peter and John respond to the Council's warning not to preach or teach in the name of Jesus with a first-class conditional sentence. The protasis is introduced with εἰ and the indicative verb ἐστιν; the apodosis is simply κρίνατε: *Whether it is right in the sight of God to listen to you rather than God, you decide.* This use of εἰ introduces an indirect question, or rhetorical question, and should be translated as *whether* in English. Peter and John's answer subtly, but firmly, rebukes the Council's prohibition from preaching Jesus and affirms their commitment to obey God rather than men and speak about what they have seen and heard (cf. 1 Jn 1:1–4).

ἀποκριθέντες > APPMPN, answering, answered ‖ εἶπον > 3PAAI, said ‖ ἀκούειν > PAN, to listen to, to obey ‖ κρίνατε > 2PAAM, decide, judge ‖ δυνάμεθα > 1PPMI, able, can ‖ εἴδαμεν > 1PAAI, saw, have seen ‖ ἠκούσαμεν > 1PAAI, heard ‖ λαλεῖν > PAN, to speak

Further Reading: Acts 4:13–22
Douglas Brown

September 29
Acts 5:14–15

[14] μᾶλλον δὲ προσετίθεντο πιστεύοντες τῷ κυρίῳ, πλήθη ἀνδρῶν τε καὶ γυναικῶν, [15] ὥστε καὶ εἰς τὰς πλατείας ἐκφέρειν τοὺς ἀσθενεῖς καὶ τιθέναι ἐπὶ κλιναρίων καὶ κραβάττων, ἵνα ἐρχομένου Πέτρου κἂν ἡ σκιὰ ἐπισκιάσῃ τινὶ αὐτῶν.

CONTEXT:

After the death of Ananias and Saphira (5:1–11), Luke explains that God was performing many signs and wonders in and around Jerusalem through the apostles.

COMMENTARY:

This sentence ends with a ἵνα clause. Ἵνα is a subordinating conjunction that usually introduces a dependent clause with a subjunctive verb, as is the case here: ἵνα ... ἐπισκιάσῃ. Wallace summarizes that ἵνα clauses with the subjunctive function in one of seven ways, but the most common are purpose clauses, result clauses, or substantival clauses (GGBB, 471–77). In Acts 5:15, Luke used an adverbial purpose ἵνα clause to express the intention of the people for the sick to come under the shadow of Peter in hopes of finding healing. The fact that healing was not certain demonstrates that this ἵνα clause is not expressing result.

προσετίθεντο > 3PIPI, were added ‖ πιστεύοντες > PAPMPN, believing ‖ πλατείας > streets ‖ ἐκφέρειν > PAN, carried ‖ ἀσθενεῖς > sick ‖ τιθέναι > PAN, to lay, place ‖ κλιναρίων > beds ‖ κραβάττων > mats, pallets ‖ ἐπισκιάσῃ > 3SAAS, might overshadow

Further Reading: Acts 5:12–16
Douglas Brown

SEPTEMBER 30
ACTS 6:2-4

² προσκαλεσάμενοι δὲ οἱ δώδεκα τὸ πλῆθος τῶν μαθητῶν εἶπαν, Οὐκ ἀρεστόν ἐστιν ἡμᾶς καταλείψαντας τὸν λόγον τοῦ θεοῦ διακονεῖν τραπέζαις. ³ ἐπισκέψασθε δέ, ἀδελφοί, ἄνδρας ἐξ ὑμῶν μαρτυρουμένους ἑπτά, πλήρεις πνεύματος καὶ σοφίας, οὓς καταστήσομεν ἐπὶ τῆς χρείας ταύτης, ⁴ ἡμεῖς δὲ τῇ προσευχῇ καὶ τῇ διακονίᾳ τοῦ λόγου προσκαρτερήσομεν.

CONTEXT:
The early church experienced growing pains as the widows of Greek-speaking Jews visiting Jerusalem were being overlooked in the daily distribution of food (6:1). To resolve the problem, the apostles led the Hellenists to nominate qualified deacons whom they would appoint to serve tables.

COMMENTARY:
Nearly all translations take the participle προσκαλεσάμενοι in 6:2 as attendant circumstance. This means that they translate this dependent verbal participle as a finite verb and add *and* to make it parallel with the main verb εἶπαν: *The twelve called the number of disciples and said ...* Wallace explains that there are usually five structural clues in identifying an attendant circumstantial participle: 1) the tense of the participle is aorist; 2) the tense of the main verb is aorist; 3) the mood of the main verb is indicative or imperative; 4) the participle precedes the main verb in order; and 5) these usually occur in narrative texts (*GGBB*, 642). Attendant circumstance participles pick up the mood of the main verb as a coordinate action. In Acts 6:2, the apostles first *summoned* the disciples and then *spoke* to them.

προσκαλεσάμενοι > AMPMPN, called, summoned || εἶπαν > 3PAAI, said || ἀρεστόν > pleasing, desirable || καταλείψαντας > AAPMPA, having neglected || διακονεῖν > PAN, to serve || τραπέζαις > tables || ἐπισκέψασθε > 2PAMM, select || μαρτυρουμένους > PPPMPA, of good repute || καταστήσομεν > 1PFAI, we will appoint || χρείας > need || προσκαρτερήσομεν > 1PFAI, will devote

Further Reading: Acts 6:1-7
Douglas Brown

³² ἐγὼ ὁ θεὸς τῶν πατέρων σου, ὁ θεὸς Ἀβραὰμ καὶ Ἰσαὰκ καὶ Ἰακώβ. ἔντρομος δὲ γενόμενος Μωϋσῆς οὐκ ἐτόλμα κατανοῆσαι. ³³ εἶπεν δὲ αὐτῷ ὁ κύριος, Λῦσον τὸ ὑπόδημα τῶν ποδῶν σου, ὁ γὰρ τόπος ἐφ' ᾧ ἕστηκας γῆ ἁγία ἐστίν.

CONTEXT:

Acts 7 recounts Stephen's speech before the Jewish leadership in Jerusalem. In this section, he recounts Yahweh's encounter with Moses at the burning bush (Exod 3:5, 6).

COMMENTARY:

Consider the relative clause at the end of verse 33: ἐφ' ᾧ ἕστηκας. Relative pronouns are "hinge" pronouns because they relate two clauses to each other. Regular relative pronouns refer to an antecedent in the previous context but function as a substantive in the new relative clause. In this instance, the relative pronoun ᾧ refers to τόπος. Notice that while ᾧ and τόπος agree in gender and number (masculine, singular), their cases are different: τόπος is nominative, ᾧ is dative. Why? Because *the relative pronoun (RP) agrees with its antecedent in gender and number, but its case is determined by the function it has in its own clause."* (*GGBB*, 336). Τόπος is the subject of the main clause; ᾧ is the object of the preposition ἐφ'.

ἔντρομος > trembling || γενόμενος > AMPMSN, having become || ἐτόλμα > 3SIAI, dare, show boldness || κατανοῆσαι > AAN, to look || εἶπεν > 3SAAI, said || λῦσον > 2SAAM, untie, loose || ἕστηκας > 2SRAI, are standing

Further Reading: Acts 7:30–34
Douglas Brown

¹⁸ ἰδὼν δὲ ὁ Σίμων ὅτι διὰ τῆς ἐπιθέσεως τῶν χειρῶν τῶν ἀποστόλων διδοται τὸ πνεῦμα, προσήνεγκεν αὐτοῖς χρήματα ¹⁹ λέγων, Δότε κἀμοὶ τὴν ἐξουσίαν ταύτην ἵνα ᾧ ἐὰν ἐπιθῶ τὰς χεῖρας λαμβάνῃ πνεῦμα ἅγιον. ²⁰ Πέτρος δὲ εἶπεν πρὸς αὐτόν, Τὸ ἀργύριόν σου σὺν σοὶ εἴη εἰς ἀπώλειαν ὅτι τὴν δωρεὰν τοῦ θεοῦ ἐνόμισας διὰ χρημάτων κτᾶσθαι.

CONTEXT:

In Acts 8, Philip evangelized the Samaritans, and many believed and were baptized. These verses reveal part of Peter's verbal exchange with Simon the Magician.

COMMENTARY:

One of the NT's most frequently used subordinating conjunctions is ὅτι (used nearly 1,300 times). In these three verses, Luke used it two times in two different ways. The first use is substantive in verse 18: the ὅτι introduces the indirect discourse (i.e., specialized object) of what Simon the magician *saw* (ἰδών) and should be translated *that*. It explains the content after a verb of perception. The second use of ὅτι in verse 20 is causal and should be translated *because*. It introduces an adverbial subordinate clause that provides the ground or basis for why Peter desired Simon's silver to perish with him.

ἰδών > AAPMSN, having seen || ἐπιθέσεως > laying on || δίδοται > 3SPPI, was given || προσήνεγκεν > 3SAAI, offered || δότε > 2PAAM, give || κἀμοί > me also || ἐπιθῶ > 1SAAS, lay || εἶπεν > 3SAAI, said || ἀργύριον > silver || εἴη > 3SPAO, may [it be] || ἀπώλειαν > destruction, ruin || κτᾶσθαι > PMN, obtain

Further Reading: Acts 8:14-24
Douglas Brown

² πᾶσαν χαρὰν ἡγήσασθε, ἀδελφοί μου, ὅταν πειρασμοῖς περιπέσητε ποικίλοις, ³ γινώσκοντες ὅτι τὸ δοκίμιον ὑμῶν τῆς πίστεως κατεργάζεται ὑπομονήν.

CONTEXT:

In his epistle, James, the half-brother of Jesus, writes to believers that are scattered throughout the region.

COMMENTARY:

James begins his letter with a command regarding Christian thinking: ἡγήσασθε. While imperatives normally precede their direct object, James places πᾶσαν χαράν first to emphasize the mindset Christians should have concerning the various difficult circumstances in which they live. The adjective πᾶσαν with the anarthrous noun could indicate either joy which is exclusive, or the quality of joy meaning "pure," "sheer," or "utter," joy. Considering that 1 Peter 1:6 indicates that grieving while rejoicing during trials is not sinful, it is best to take πᾶσαν as intensifying joy. The word περιπέσητε ("fall into") indicates that the trials are unexpected and unwanted. The participle γινώσκοντες could be taken generically, bearing the force of the imperative, or as causal. Since the NT frequently grounds ethical commands in current knowledge, this is best understood as the cause for regarding trials as an occasion for joy.

ἡγήσασθε > 2PAMM, consider ‖ πειρασμοῖς > trials ‖ περιπέσητε > 2PAAS, fall into ‖ ποικίλοις > diverse ‖ γινώσκοντες > PAPMPN, knowing ‖ δοκίμιον > testing ‖ κατεργάζεται > 3SAPM, produces

Further Reading: James 1:1-4
Wayne Cornett

JAMES 1:9–10

⁹ καυχάσθω δὲ ὁ ἀδελφὸς ὁ ταπεινὸς ἐν τῷ ὕψει αὐτοῦ· ¹⁰ ὁ δὲ πλούσιος ἐν τῇ ταπεινώσει αὐτοῦ· ὅτι ὡς ἄνθος χόρτου παρελεύσεται.

CONTEXT:

James has been instructing his readers to travel with joy through the various difficult circumstances of life. They may do this because they know the journey is making them mature and they can call on God who will give them the wisdom needed to navigate through the troubles. James now turns to specific trials of want and wealth.

COMMENTARY:

Because of James's denunciation of the wicked rich in 5:1–6, readers of English translations often assume that the rich individual in v. 10 is an unbeliever. The grammatical structure of the Greek, however, indicates that the rich one in this instance is also a brother. The article in v. 10 is in the substantive position without a noun to modify, making it natural for the reader to supply ἀδελφός from v. 9, especially since the syntax requires that the imperative from v. 9 governs v. 10 and the two verses are structurally parallel. The poor believer can rejoice in his high position in Christ and the wealthy believer may rejoice not his transitory wealth which elevates him in the eyes of the world, but in his identification with Christ and His people who are looked down on in the world.

καυχάσθω > 3SPMM, boast ‖ ταπεινός > lowly ‖ ὕψει > high position / exaltation ‖ ταπεινώσει > humiliation ‖ ἄνθος > flower ‖ χόρτος > grass ‖ παρελεύσεται > 3SFMI, will pass away

Further Reading: James 1:9–12
Wayne Cornett

OCTOBER 5
JAMES 1:12

[12] μακάριος ἀνὴρ ὃς ὑπομένει πειρασμόν· ὅτι δόκιμος γενόμενος λήψεται τὸν στέφανον τῆς ζωῆς, ὃν ἐπηγγείλατο ὁ Κύριος τοῖς ἀγαπῶσιν αὐτόν.

CONTEXT:

Verse twelve both concludes the section started in v. 9 and introduces the section on temptation that carries through v. 18. James contrasts the transitory nature of both trials and material wealth with the eternal nature of blessedness enjoyed by those who endure trials. So the trials are actually good gifts from God, not temptations to commit evil.

COMMENTARY:

While the aorist participle γενόμενος could be causal, it is more likely temporal, indicating that the enduring precedes the reception of the crown but does not cause it. The genitive ζωῆς could be of quality contrasting the crown with those that fade away, a genitive of definition indicating that the crown belongs to the future life, or an epexegetical genitive meaning crown which is life. The latter fits best here and in Revelation 2:10 where the phrase is also found. Eternal life is what the Lord has promised to those who love Him. His promise is the reason they will receive the crown. Although the crown serves as an extra incentive for enduring, enduring is the fruit of their love for Him.

ὑπομένει > 3SPAI, endures || πειρασμόν > trial || δόκιμος > approved || γενόμενος > AMPMSN, having been || λήψεται > 3SFAI, will receive || στέφανον > crown || ἐπηγγείλατο > 3SAMI, has promised || ἀγαπῶσιν > PAPMPD, those who love

Further Reading: James 1:12–18
Wayne Cornett

JAMES 1:21

²¹ διὸ ἀποθέμενοι πᾶσαν ῥυπαρίαν καὶ περισσείαν κακίας, ἐν πραΰτητι δέξασθε τὸν ἔμφυτον λόγον, τὸν δυνάμενον σῶσαι τὰς ψυχὰς ὑμῶν.

CONTEXT:

James is addressing Christ followers. He has reminded them that the unchanging God who only gives good gifts has given them the new birth by the word of truth (1:16–18). Therefore, they should be quick to listen to the word and slow to become angry (1:19–20).

COMMENTARY:

Although some take the participle ἀποθέμενοι as one of attendant circumstance having imperatival force, it could also be a temporal participle. The former appears unlikely since (1) participles of attendant circumstance rarely occur outside of narratives and (2) it would imply that believers can have not only all *kinds* of "moral filthiness" but can also live a life of "abundant wickedness." James is indicating that his readers have or ought to have put off the old conduct of life. Having done this, instead of becoming angry when hearing God's word, they should welcome God's word by willingly submitting to it. The aspect of the aorist infinitive σῶσαι views the action as a whole, including not only eschatological deliverance but also the process of sanctification.

ἀποθέμενοι > AMPMPN, having put off || ῥυπαρίαν > fleshliness, moral turpitude || περισσεία > abundance || κακία > wickedness || πραΰτης > meekness || δέξασθε > 2PAMM, receive || ἔμφυτος > implanted || σῶσαι > AAN, to save

Further Reading: James 1:18–27
Wayne Cornett

OCTOBER 7

JAMES 2:1

¹ ἀδελφοί μου, μὴ ἐν προσωπολημψίαις ἔχετε τὴν πίστιν τοῦ Κυρίου ἡμῶν Ἰησοῦ Χριστοῦ τῆς δόξης.

CONTEXT:

After James encourages his readers to be people who obey the word and not merely listen (1:22–25), he informs them that not all who appear to be of the Christian religion actually have something that is pure and pleasing to God (1:26–27). The Father, who gives good gifts with simplicity regardless of the standing of the recipient, expects those who claim to worship Him to do the same.

COMMENTARY:

The genitive τῆς δόξης could be appositional, epexegetical, or descriptive. Seeing that glory is not used as a title in the OT or elsewhere in the NT, an epexegetical use is unlikely. Using it as merely descriptive seems too weak considering the theological import that glory often has in the Bible. "Lord of Glory" appears to be the best understanding (cf. Ps 24:8 LXX, 1 Cor 2:8). Τοῦ Κυρίου is most likely an objective genitive, though some modern commentators argue for it being subjective. James is saying that having faith in Christ is not consistent with showing preferential treatment to some. It is foolish to reject someone based on outward appearance while claiming to trust in the Lord of Glory who became poor for man's sake, concealing His glory with flesh.

προσωπολημψίαις > partiality ‖ ἔχετε > 3SPAM, hold

Further Reading: James 2:1–13
Wayne Cornett

JAMES 2:14

¹⁴ τί τὸ ὄφελος, ἀδελφοί μου, ἐὰν πίστιν λέγῃ τις ἔχειν, ἔργα δὲ μὴ ἔχῃ; μὴ δύναται ἡ πίστις σῶσαι αὐτόν;

CONTEXT:

James has demonstrated that merely listening to God's word does not mean one has "pure religion." Rather, it is only when one hears and does that word that it becomes clear that he has the real deal. James illustrates this point by addressing the sin of partiality, which he points out is a violation of loving one's neighbor as oneself. Therefore, he concludes that some will be judged by the "law of liberty" without mercy because they did not show mercy. James endeavors now to clarify what type of faith results in receiving salvation from that judgment. He begins with a rhetorical question indicating a faith void of good deeds is unable to save (2:14). He justifies this with a practical illustration (2:15–18) and then with a theological one (2:19–20). He concludes with two OT examples of the type of faith that receives mercy and is delivered from judgment.

COMMENTARY:

Τί introduces James's rhetorical question. Straying from the most common use of the aorist in third-class conditions, James opts for ἐάν plus the present subjunctives λέγῃ and ἔχῃ to indicate repeated claims habitually unaccompanied by good works. The article with πίστις is anaphoric specifying "that faith" which is void of deeds. The aorist tense of the infinitive σῶσαι is best understood as consummative. James says ultimately this kind of faith cannot save anyone at the final judgment.

ὄφελος > benefit || λέγῃ > 3SPAS, [someone] says || ἔχειν > PAN, to have || ἔχῃ > 3SPAS, might have || δύναται > 3SPPI, is able || σῶσαι > AAN, to save

Further Reading: James 2:14–26
Wayne Cornett

OCTOBER 9
JAMES 3:7-8

⁷ πᾶσα γὰρ φύσις θηρίων τε καὶ πετεινῶν, ἑρπετῶν τε καὶ ἐναλίων, δαμάζεται καὶ δεδάμασται τῇ φύσει τῇ ἀνθρωπίνῃ· ⁸ τὴν δὲ γλῶσσαν οὐδεὶς δύναται ἀνθρώπων δαμάσαι· ἀκατάσχετον κακόν, μεστὴ ἰοῦ θανατηφόρου.

CONTEXT:
Verses 7-8 are in the middle of one unit of thought found in 3:1-12. James has returned to the topic of speech that he introduced back in 1:26.

COMMENTARY:
James uses four partitive genitives to indicate every kind of animal out of the four groups of living things, reminiscent of Genesis 1:26. Both pairs of the conjunctives τε καί show the correspondence between the genitives, so "both ... and" is the best translation. The present δαμάζεται, like many verbs in this section, is omnitemporal (gnomic present) expressing timeless action that is generally true. Following the two passive verbs, ἀνθρωπίνῃ is probably a dative of agency. The adversative δέ marks a strong contrast between man's ability to subdue animals and his inability to subdue his own tongue, which can be more destructive than any animal.

φύσις > kind || πετεινῶν > birds || ἑρπετῶν > creeping things/reptiles || ἐναλίων > of the sea || δαμάζεται > 3SPPI, is subdued || δεδάμασται > 3SRPI, has been subdued || δαμάσαι > AAN, to subdue || ἀκατάσχετον > uncontrollable || μεστή > full || ἰοῦ > poison || θανατηφόρου > deadly

Further Reading: James 3:1-12
Wayne Cornett

JAMES 3:13

¹³ τίς σοφὸς καὶ ἐπιστήμων ἐν ὑμῖν; δειξάτω ἐκ τῆς καλῆς ἀναστροφῆς τὰ ἔργα αὐτοῦ ἐν πραΰτητι σοφίας.

CONTEXT:

James has been expressing his concern for inconsistency between one's profession and practice, most recently in the area of speech (3:1–12). He now identifies the source of such contradictions: earthly wisdom. The connection of wisdom with speech is clear to anyone familiar with Proverbs. Further, this discussion of earthly wisdom provides a smooth transition to his next topic, friendship with the world (4:1–12).

COMMENTARY:

Third-person singular imperatives like δειξάτω are difficult to translate into English, as the English language only has a second-person imperative. As such, δειξάτω is often translated as "let him," but "he must" perhaps better conveys the force of the imperative. The genitive σοφίας could be a genitive of source, indicating that heavenly wisdom is the source of meekness. One could also take it as an attributive genitive making meekness modify wisdom. The former appears to fit the overall context better. While the phrase ἐν πραΰτητι σοφίας could be modifying the verb δειξάτω, indicating the means by which one must prove his wisdom, since the noun ἔργα is closer it appears more likely that this phrase describes the kind of works that are expected.

ἐπιστήμων > understanding || δειξάτω > 3SAAM, must show || ἀναστροφῆς > conduct || πραΰτητι > meekness

Further Reading: James 3:13–18
Wayne Cornett

OCTOBER 11
JAMES 4:7–8

⁷ ὑποτάγητε οὖν τῷ θεῷ, ἀντίστητε τῷ διαβόλῳ, καὶ φεύξεται ἀφ' ὑμῶν.
⁸ ἐγγίσατε τῷ θεῷ, καὶ ἐγγιεῖ ὑμῖν· καθαρίσατε χεῖρας, ἁμαρτωλοί, καὶ ἁγνίσατε καρδίας, δίψυχοι.

CONTEXT:
This unit, 4:7–10, follows a hard denunciation of spiritual adultery that concludes with the reminder that pride places one in opposition to God, while humility places one under God's grace.

COMMENTARY:
James uses οὖν as an inferential conjunction to introduce this section packed with ten imperatives indicating the required actions that are the appropriate response to Proverbs 3:34 quoted in James 4:6. The imperative ὑποτάγητε is likely reflexive ("submit yourself"), although a permissive sense of the passive is possible ("allow yourself to be subjected"). Submission is a sign of humility. As with all the imperatives in this section, ὑποτάγητε is aorist and views the action as a whole. The two future indicatives, φεύξεται and ἐγγιεῖ, are both predictive. These two future verbs are conditional where the preceding imperatives joined with καί stand in place of the protasis. Satan will flee if we resist him. God will draw near to us if we draw near. The next two imperatives (καθαρίσατε and ἁγνίσατε) explain how one draws near to God. The necessity of true repentance is highlighted by pairing these imperatives with two harsh vocatives (ἁμαρτωλοί and δίψυχοι).

ὑποτάγητε > 2PAPM, submit || ἀντίστητε > 2PAAM, resist || φεύξεται > 3SFMI, will flee || ἐγγίσατε > 2PAAM, draw near || ἐγγιεῖ > 3SFAI, he will draw near || καθαρίσατε > 2PAAM, cleanse || ἁγνίσατε > 2PAAM, purify || δίψυχοι > double-minded

Further Reading: James 4:1–10
Wayne Cornett

JAMES 5:7

⁷ μακροθυμήσατε οὖν, ἀδελφοί, ἕως τῆς παρουσίας τοῦ Κυρίου. ἰδοὺ, ὁ γεωργὸς ἐκδέχεται τὸν τίμιον καρπὸν τῆς γῆς, μακροθυμῶν ἐπ' αὐτῷ, ἕως λάβῃ ὑετὸν πρώϊμον καὶ ὄψιμον.

CONTEXT:
James has just issued a strong denouncement of the non-Christian rich who have amassed their wealth by oppressing believers (5:1–6). The oppressed are powerless to do anything other than cry out, but the Lord has heard their cry.

COMMENTARY:
The vocative ἀδελφοί indicates a shift in topics while οὖν signals that what follows flows logically from the previous topic. The plight of the poor believers at the hands of the unsaved rich of 5:1–6 will not continue forever because the Lord has heard the cry of the oppressed brothers and is going to judge their oppressors. The aorist imperative μακροθυμήσατε views the action as a whole. Paired with a genitive, the first ἕως functions as a preposition denoting the action's terminus. The first article is monadic denoting the uniqueness of the Lord's coming and τῆς γῆς is a genitive of origin.

μακροθυμήσατε > 2PAAM, be patient ‖ παρουσίας > coming ‖ γεωργός > farmer ‖ ἐκδέχεται > 3SPPI, waits ‖ τίμιον > precious ‖ μακροθυμῶν > PAPMSN, being patient ‖ λάβῃ > 3SAAS, receives ‖ ὑετόν > rain ‖ πρώϊμον > early rain ‖ ὄψιμον > late rain

Further Reading: James 5:7–11
Wayne Cornett

¹³ διὸ ἀναζωσάμενοι τὰς ὀσφύας τῆς διανοίας ὑμῶν νήφοντες τελείως ἐλπίσατε ἐπὶ τὴν φερομένην ὑμῖν χάριν ἐν ἀποκαλύψει Ἰησοῦ Χριστοῦ.

CONTEXT:

Peter began the body of his letter by praising God for the believer's new birth and ultimate, future salvation when Christ returns (1:3–12). Faith in this promise provides the basis for joy and an expectant hope in the midst of suffering and trials.

COMMENTARY:

In 1 Peter 1:13, Peter commands his readers to *set their hope upon* the salvation presented in the preceding verses. Notice that Peter often places modifiers of a noun between the noun and its article, as in τὴν φερομένην ὑμῖν χάριν. The participle phrase φερομένην ὑμῖν modifies the noun phrase τὴν χάριν, *the grace being brought to you*. The time when the grace is brought is expressed with the preposition ἐν, *at the revelation of Jesus Christ*. The word order may seem strange, since the preposition is separated from the participle it modifies, but the meaning is clear. The two participles at the beginning of the verse give the means by which to carry out the command. *By preparing their minds for action and by being self-controlled,* the readers must fully set their hope on the gracious salvation Christ will bring to them when he is revealed.

ἀναζωσάμενοι > AMPMPN, binding up || ὀσφύας > loins || διανοίας > mind || νήφοντες > PAPMPN, being self-controlled || τελείως > fully || ἐλπίσατε > 2PAAM, set your hope || φερομένην > PPPFSA, being brought || ἀποκαλύψει > revelation

Further Reading: 1 Peter 1:3–13
Mark A. Mills

286

¹⁸ οἱ οἰκέται ὑποτασσόμενοι ἐν παντὶ φόβῳ τοῖς δεσπόταις, οὐ μόνον τοῖς ἀγαθοῖς καὶ ἐπιεικέσιν ἀλλὰ καὶ τοῖς σκολιοῖς. ¹⁹ τοῦτο γὰρ χάρις εἰ διὰ συνείδησιν θεοῦ ὑποφέρει τις λύπας πάσχων ἀδίκως.

CONTEXT:

In 1 Peter 2:11, Peter shifts his focus from his readers' identity in Christ to how they should maintain good works with respect to various authorities, the antagonistic ones in particular. General commands begin this section, followed by instructions for the citizen-government, slave-master, and wife-husband relationships.

COMMENTARY:

Peter begins this instruction with a direct address to the οἰκέται. Notice that no finite verb appears in verse 18—only a participle. Many commentaries treat ὑποτασσόμενοι like an independent imperative verb because no *grammatical* connection between this participle and a verb exists in the sentence. However, by using a participle, Peter *logically* subordinates these instructions to the preceding general instruction to "honor everyone" (2:17). He uses the same direct address-participle pattern with the instructions to wives (3:1), husbands (3:7), and everyone (3:8). How, then, should slaves show honor to everyone, even their masters who are harsh or unjust? *By respectfully submitting* to that earthly authority, *enduring the sorrow of unjust suffering*, because they are *keeping in mind what God* expects of them.

οἰκέται > household slaves ‖ ὑποτασσόμενοι > PPPMPN, being subject ‖ δεσπόταις > masters ‖ ἐπιεικέσιν > gentle ‖ σκολιοῖς > harsh, unjust ‖ συνείδησιν > conscience, consciousness ‖ ὑποφέρει > 3SPAI, endures ‖ λύπας > sorrows ‖ πάσχων > PAPMSN, suffering ‖ ἀδίκως > unjustly

Further Reading: 1 Peter 2:13–25
Mark A. Mills

OCTOBER 15
1 PETER 3:9

⁹ μὴ ἀποδιδόντες κακὸν ἀντὶ κακοῦ ἢ λοιδορίαν ἀντὶ λοιδορίας, τοὐναντίον δὲ εὐλογοῦντες, ὅτι εἰς τοῦτο ἐκλήθητε, ἵνα εὐλογίαν κληρονομήσητε.

CONTEXT:

Peter concludes his instructions to believers who are suffering in specific relationships (2:18–3:7) by addressing them all. In 3:8 he generally exhorts the persecuted readers to have Christ-like qualities of like-mindedness, sympathy, brotherly love, a kind heart, and a humble mind.

COMMENTARY:

In verse 9, Peter commands the readers, as he did previously with specific groups, how they should "honor everyone" (2:17). These abused readers must show honor *by not repaying* the *evil* or *insults* they received, that is, by not retaliating or taking revenge. Rather, they must honor *by blessing* those who are hostile toward them, following Christ's example (2:21–24). The readers *were called* to this, namely, imitating Christ, who brought great blessing to them by suffering abuse and death. The ἵνα clause expresses the purpose of their calling, which is to *inherit* their ultimate *blessing*, securely guarded in heaven (1:3–4). Peter can make such unnatural demands because their calling accompanies the new birth, which enables them to live contrary to the impulses of sin aroused by suffering.

ἀποδιδόντες > PAPMPN, repaying ‖ ἀντί > for ‖ λοιδορίαν/-ας > insult, abuse ‖ τοὐναντίον > instead ‖ εὐλογοῦντες > PAPMPN, blessing ‖ ἐκλήθητε > 2PAPI, you were called ‖ εὐλογίαν > blessing ‖ κληρονομήσητε > 2PAAS, you might inherit

Further Reading: 1 Peter 3:1–12
Mark A. Mills

⁴ ἐν ᾧ ξενίζονται μὴ συντρεχόντων ὑμῶν εἰς τὴν αὐτὴν τῆς ἀσωτίας ἀνάχυσιν βλασφημοῦντες, ⁵ οἳ ἀποδώσουσιν λόγον τῷ ἑτοίμως ἔχοντι κρῖναι ζῶντας καὶ νεκρούς.

CONTEXT:

Peter concluded chapter 3 with Christ, the righteous one, suffering death for unrighteous sinners, and being raised and exalted with all authority. His sinless behavior and acceptance of God's will provide the pattern to follow for those he saves.

COMMENTARY:

Verse 4 consists of a relative clause referring to the Gentiles' pursuit of passions (4:2-3). Note the word order: relative pronoun phrase, main verb, genitive absolute, participle. The genitive participle συντρεχόντων and pronoun ὑμῶν give the reason why the Gentiles think the believer's "ceasing from sin" is strange: they *are surprised with reference to* their unrestrained lifestyle *when you don't run with* them *to the same flood of reckless living*. The next participle, βλασφημοῦντες, grammatically agrees with the subject of the main verb, providing the result of the Gentiles' surprise: *they revile*. Its position at the end of the clause identifies the antecedent of the following relative clause in v. 5. These revilers are *the ones who will give an account* to the exalted Christ who is *ready to judge the living and the dead*. Believers should endure suffering not only because of Christ's righteous example but also because he is the sovereign Judge.

ξενίζονται > 3PPPI, they are surprised || συντρεχόντων > PAPMPG, running with || ἀσωτίας > reckless abandon || ἀνάχυσιν > flood || βλασφημοῦντες > PAPMPN, reviling || ἀποδώσουσιν > 3PFAI, they will give || ἑτοίμως ἔχοντι > PAPMSD, being ready || κρῖναι > AAN, to judge || ζῶντας > PAPMPA, living

Further Reading: 1 Peter 4:1-11

Mark A. Mills

¹⁰ ὁ δὲ θεὸς πάσης χάριτος, ὁ καλέσας ὑμᾶς εἰς τὴν αἰώνιον αὐτοῦ δόξαν ἐν Χριστῷ ὀλίγον παθόντας αὐτὸς καταρτίσει, στηρίξει, σθενώσει, θεμελιώσει.

CONTEXT:

In this letter, Peter instructed his suffering readers to endure as Christians, while humbly submitting to God's will, keeping their behavior pure with their eyes on Christ, the one who endured unjust abuse and death for the benefit of sinners.

COMMENTARY:

As Peter concludes the body of the letter, he directs the readers' attention to *the God of all grace*. Not only is this grace given in regeneration and ultimate salvation (1:3–13), but also in the trials and humble service of the Christian life (2:19–20; 3:7; 4:10; 5:5). The readers must remember the end goal of their salvation *in Christ*, that God is *the one who called you to his eternal glory*. While it is true that they are suffering at the hands of antagonists, it will only last *a little while* from an eternal perspective. The final four verbs are strung together with no conjunctions, heightening the impact of God's actions toward the suffering readers. This gracious God who called them, *he will restore, confirm, strengthen, and establish*, righting every wrong and securing their place with him in Christ for eternity.

καλέσας > AAPMSN, called ‖ παθόντας > AAPMPA, having suffered ‖ καταρτίσει > 3SFAI, he will restore ‖ στηρίξει > 3SFAI, he will confirm ‖ σθενώσει > 3SFAI, he will strengthen ‖ θεμελιώσει > 3SFAI, he will ground, establish

Further Reading: 1 Peter 5:1–11
Mark A. Mills

⁸ ταῦτα γὰρ ὑμῖν ὑπάρχοντα καὶ πλεονάζοντα οὐκ ἀργοὺς οὐδὲ ἀκάρπους καθίστησιν εἰς τὴν τοῦ κυρίου ἡμῶν Ἰησοῦ Χριστοῦ ἐπίγνωσιν.

CONTEXT:

Peter opens this epistle affirming that God had equipped his believing readers with everything necessary to live a godly life, since they were called to share his glorious and virtuous nature. Peter then urged them to put forth effort to grow in godly virtues.

COMMENTARY:

Verse 8 explains the importance to a believer of *these things*, i.e., the faith, virtue, knowledge, self-control, endurance, godliness, brotherly affection, and love enumerated in the preceding verses. Structurally, Peter arranges the participle pair ὑπάρχοντα καὶ πλεονάζοντα as an informal condition (*if they belong to you and they are increasing*) and a negated adjective pair οὐκ ἀργοὺς οὐδὲ ἀκάρπους as the benefit of these qualities (*neither useless nor fruitless*). Each pair links a static with a dynamic idea. Notice how this possessing and growing in the seven qualities *make (you) productive in the knowledge of our Lord Jesus Christ*. Peter's desire for believers is not simply that they gain information about Christ, but that they diligently pursue knowing him by means of putting the excellence of his character into practice.

ὑπάρχοντα > PAPNPN, being present ‖ πλεονάζοντα > PAPNPN, increasing ‖ ἀργοὺς > useless ‖ ἀκάρπους > fruitless ‖ καθίστησιν > 3SPAI, they make (you) ‖ ἐπίγνωσιν > knowledge

Further Reading: 2 Peter 1:1–11
Mark A. Mills

¹⁹ καὶ ἔχομεν βεβαιότερον τὸν προφητικὸν λόγον ᾧ καλῶς ποιεῖτε προσέχοντες ὡς λύχνῳ φαίνοντι ἐν αὐχμηρῷ τόπῳ, ἕως οὗ ἡμέρα διαυγάσῃ καὶ φωσφόρος ἀνατείλῃ ἐν ταῖς καρδίαις ὑμῶν.

CONTEXT:

Beginning in verse 12, Peter stressed to his readers the importance of constantly remembering the truth they had received. He assured them that the prophecies of Christ's future return will be fulfilled, recounting the event where he became an eyewitness of the Lord's honor and glory (1:16–18).

COMMENTARY:

As Peter writes of his experience on the mountain, he describes *the prophetic word* using the comparative adjective βεβαιότερον, *more reliable*. Writers of Koine Greek sometimes used comparative forms like this with a superlative (*most reliable*) or elative (*very reliable*) sense. Whether Peter compared the prophecies of Scripture to something less reliable or described them as fully reliable, he warns his readers to *pay attention* to these writings, since they refute the heresies of the false teachers he will address in this letter. He completes this thought with three light metaphors: *a lamp*, *the day*, and *the morning star*. The foretold return of Christ, like the sunrise of the day of the Lord, will dispel the darkness of this present night. Although the lamp of prophecy will no longer be needed on that day, it is indispensable for informing and comforting believers' hearts today.

ἔχομεν > 1PPAI, we have ‖ βεβαιότερον > more reliable, firm ‖ προφητικόν > prophetic ‖ ποιεῖτε > 2PPAI, you do ‖ προσέχοντες > PAPMPN, paying attention ‖ λύχνῳ > lamp ‖ φαίνοντι > PAPMSD, shining ‖ αὐχμηρῷ > dark ‖ διαυγάσῃ > 3SAAS, dawns ‖ φωσφόρος > the morning star ‖ ἀνατείλῃ > 3SAAS, rises

Further Reading: 2 Peter 1:12–2:3
Mark A. Mills

OCTOBER 20

2 PETER 2:9–10A

⁹ οἶδεν κύριος εὐσεβεῖς ἐκ πειρασμοῦ ῥύεσθαι, ἀδίκους δὲ εἰς ἡμέραν κρίσεως κολαζομένους τηρεῖν, ¹⁰ μάλιστα δὲ τοὺς ὀπίσω σαρκὸς ἐν ἐπιθυμίᾳ μιασμοῦ πορευομένους καὶ κυριότητος καταφρονοῦντας.

CONTEXT:

In chapter 2, Peter turned his readers' attention to false teachers, who are under the Master's condemnation. He supports this claim with an extended first-class condition (2:4–10a), where he appeals to OT evidence of God's actions toward the ungodly and the righteous.

COMMENTARY:

The protasis of the condition (2:4–8) presents evidence of God's past dealings with angels, Noah, and Lot. The apodosis (2:9–10a) concludes that the Lord is able to save the godly even as he punishes the wicked. The infinitives ῥύεσθαι and τηρεῖν with οἶδεν express what the Lord knows how to do or is able to do, which is *to deliver the godly* and *to guard the unrighteous for the day of judgment*. This shift of grammatical subject from ὁ θεός (2:3) to κύριος (2:9) suggests the deity of Christ who does what only God can do. Peter then associates those facing judgment with the perverse character of the false teachers he is about to describe in detail. Believers can rest assured that their gracious Lord knows how to rescue them from temptation, and that he reserves punishment for the unrighteous and perverse.

οἶδεν > 3SRAI, knows ‖ εὐσεβεῖς > godly ‖ πειρασμοῦ > trial, temptation ‖ ῥύεσθαι > PMN, to deliver, rescue ‖ ἀδίκους > unrighteous ‖ κολαζομένους > PPPMPA, being punished ‖ τηρεῖν > PAN, to keep ‖ μάλιστα > especially ‖ μιασμοῦ > corruption ‖ πορευομένους > PMPMPA, who are following ‖ κυριότητος > lordship, dominion ‖ καταφρονοῦντας > PAPMPA, who are despising

Further Reading: 2 Peter 2:4–19
Mark A. Mills

⁸ ἐν δὲ τοῦτο μὴ λανθανέτω ὑμᾶς, ἀγαπητοί, ὅτι μία ἡμέρα παρὰ κυρίῳ ὡς χίλια ἔτη καὶ χίλια ἔτη ὡς ἡμέρα μία. ⁹ οὐ βραδύνει κύριος τῆς ἐπαγγελίας, ὥς τινες βραδύτητα ἡγοῦνται, ἀλλὰ μακροθυμεῖ εἰς ὑμᾶς μὴ βουλόμενός τινας ἀπολέσθαι ἀλλὰ πάντας εἰς μετάνοιαν χωρῆσαι.

CONTEXT:
In chapter 2 Peter warned his readers of false teachers, describing their sensuality, greed, and future destruction by God's judgment. Chapter three addresses their doctrinal heresy, in which they mock Christ's coming and future judgment.

COMMENTARY:
Peter switches from the false teachers to his readers with the negative imperative λανθανέτω, the same verb used for the mockers' ignorance of the flood by which God judged the ancient world (3:5). The reader must not be ignorant of God's relationship to time. A judgment of fire is coming (3:7) and the Lord will perform it exactly on time, whether it will come in *a day* or *a thousand years*. Peter informs the reader that what appears to be God's delay, hesitation, or slowness, is actually his mercy toward those who will come to repentance (3:8). Peter draws a strong contrast between the ungodly and believers (*you*, see 1:1) with ἀπολέσθαι. This verb and its noun form denote the destruction of the ungodly on the day of judgment (2:1, 3; 3:6, 7, 16). But believers, though they may experience physical death, will never experience destruction (3:9).

λανθανέτω > 3SPAM, let (it) escape notice, be hidden from || χίλια > one thousand || βραδύνει > 3SPAI, he hesitates, delays || βραδύτητα > slowness, delay || ἡγοῦνται > 3PPMI, they regard, consider || μακροθυμεῖ > 3SPAI, he is patient || βουλόμενος > PMPMSN, desiring, wishing || ἀπολέσθαι > AMN, to perish, be destroyed || μετάνοιαν > repentance || χωρῆσαι > AAN, to come to, to reach

Further Reading: 2 Peter 2:20-3:9
Mark A. Mills

[17] ὑμεῖς οὖν, ἀγαπητοί, προγινώσκοντες φυλάσσεσθε, ἵνα μὴ τῇ τῶν ἀθέσμων πλάνῃ συναπαχθέντες ἐκπέσητε τοῦ ἰδίου στηριγμοῦ, [18] αὐξάνετε δὲ ἐν χάριτι καὶ γνώσει τοῦ κυρίου ἡμῶν καὶ σωτῆρος Ἰησοῦ Χριστοῦ. αὐτῷ ἡ δόξα καὶ νῦν καὶ εἰς ἡμέραν αἰῶνος.

CONTEXT:

Having refuted the mockers who deny future fiery judgment (3:3-7), Peter reassured believers of their exemption from that destruction and anticipation of a recreated heavens and earth (3:8-13). The OT and NT Scriptures guarantee these future events (3:14-16).

COMMENTARY:

Peter closes his letter with two imperative verbs: φυλάσσεσθε and αὐξάνετε. The conjunction δέ coordinates αὐξάνετε with another verb. It cannot be coupled with ἐκπέσητε in the ἵνα purpose clause, because that would require the subjunctive form αὐξάνητε. The other option is φυλάσσεσθε. Although these 2P forms could be indicative or imperative, commands to *be on guard* against error and to *grow in the knowledge* of the Lord best fit the context. Peter's aim in this letter was to remind these believers of the truth in which they were established (1:12-15; 3:1-2), and knowledge of the Lord is a major theme in this letter (1:2-3, 5-8; 2:20). When believers devote themselves diligently to knowing their Lord and Savior Jesus Christ, they can stand firm in God's truth against heresy and licentiousness, bringing eternal glory to their God.

προγινώσκοντες > PAPMPN, knowing in advance || φυλάσσεσθε > 2PPMM, be on your guard || ἀθέσμων > lawless, unprincipled || πλάνη > error || συναπαχθέντες > APPMPN, being led away by || ἐκπέσητε > 2PAAS, (lest) you fall from, lose || στηριγμοῦ > steadfastness || αὐξάνετε > 2PPAM, you grow || γνώσει > knowledge || σωτῆρος > Savior

Further Reading: 2 Peter 3:10-18
Mark A. Mills

¹⁵ εἶπεν δὲ πρὸς αὐτὸν ὁ κύριος· πορεύου, ὅτι σκεῦος ἐκλογῆς ἐστίν μοι
οὗτος τοῦ βαστάσαι τὸ ὄνομά μου ἐνώπιον ἐθνῶν τε καὶ βασιλέων υἱῶν τε
Ἰσραήλ· ¹⁶ ἐγὼ γὰρ ὑποδείξω αὐτῷ ὅσα δεῖ αὐτὸν ὑπὲρ τοῦ ὀνόματός μου
παθεῖν.

CONTEXT:

Saul's conversion was met with significant suspicion due to his active role in
persecuting the saints in Jerusalem. Not only did the Lord appear to Saul, but he
also appeared to Ananias to command him to minister to Saul (9:10), in spite of
Ananias' objections.

COMMENTARY:

The Lord explains that Saul is a *chosen vessel* (σκεῦος ἐκλογῆς), an attributive
genitive construction. As a *chosen vessel*, Saul's new purpose in life was *to carry*
(τοῦ βαστάσαι—purpose infinitive) the Lord's name to *Gentiles*, *kings*, and *the
children of Israel*. His ministry would be marked by suffering (9:16). God
emphasized that *he himself would show him* (ἐγὼ γὰρ ὑποδείξω αὐτῷ) *how much it
was necessary for him to suffer for the sake of his name*. Note that the persecutor has
become the persecuted, a characteristic of all those who bear the name of Jesus
(cf. 9:14).

ἐκλογῆς > elect, chosen one ‖ βαστάσαι > AAN, to carry ‖ ὑποδείξω > 1SFAI,
I will show ‖ παθεῖν > AAN, to suffer

Further Reading: Acts 9:10–22
Neal Cushman

³⁴ ἀνοίξας δὲ Πέτρος τὸ στόμα εἶπεν· ἐπ᾽ ἀληθείας καταλαμβάνομαι ὅτι οὐκ ἔστιν προσωπολήμπτης ὁ θεός, ³⁵ ἀλλ᾽ ἐν παντὶ ἔθνει ὁ φοβούμενος αὐτὸν καὶ ἐργαζόμενος δικαιοσύνην δεκτὸς αὐτῷ ἐστιν.

CONTEXT:

Peter's vision of the unclean creatures resulted in a new and difficult understanding for the apostle. Not only was Peter's diet to be expanded through this three-fold vision but also his fellowship with Gentiles, a fact that he did not quite grasp at first. Thus, it would be accurate to say that Peter does not entirely understand why God was asking him to visit the house of Cornelius.

COMMENTARY:

Although the theological statement, "God is not one who shows partiality" (οὐκ ἔστιν προσωπολήμπτης ὁ θεός) is not a new idea (see Dt 10:17; 2 Ch 19:7), its application in this context is. The door of salvation had been thrown wide open to Gentiles upon the death and resurrection of Jesus Christ, and now Peter was grasping this for the first time. Later, Paul picks up on this theme in Romans 2:2 and Ephesians 6:9. Peter's statement in verse 35 cannot indicate anything other than one's spiritual condition before God: "but in every nation (or *people*) the one who fears God and works righteousness is acceptable to him." Since Peter follows up on this statement with a clear gospel message, culminating with the necessity of personal faith (10:43), "acceptable" (δεκτὸς, 10:35) can only indicate the imputation of Jesus' righteousness, and not some type of moral ethic achieved by human effort.

καταλαμβάνομαι > 1SPMI, comprehend || προσωπολήμπτης > one who shows partiality || δεκτός > acceptable

Further Reading: Acts 10:23–33
Neal Cushman

OCTOBER 25
ACTS 11:16–17

¹⁶ ἐμνήσθην δὲ τοῦ ῥήματος τοῦ κυρίου ὡς ἔλεγεν· Ἰωάννης μὲν ἐβάπτισεν ὕδατι, ὑμεῖς δὲ βαπτισθήσεσθε ἐν πνεύματι ἁγίῳ. ¹⁷ εἰ οὖν τὴν ἴσην δωρεὰν ἔδωκεν αὐτοῖς ὁ θεὸς ὡς καὶ ἡμῖν πιστεύσασιν ἐπὶ τὸν κύριον Ἰησοῦν Χριστόν, ἐγὼ τίς ἤμην δυνατὸς κωλῦσαι τὸν θεόν;

CONTEXT:

Following Cornelius's conversion in Acts 10, it was manifestly clear to Peter that God was extending salvation to Gentiles without their adhering to requirements of the Mosaic covenant. God revealed this change in salvation history through three visions given to Peter (Acts 10:9–16), confirming it by giving Gentiles the Holy Spirit when they believed the gospel.

COMMENTARY:

Peter continues to defend God's approval of Gentile salvation by recounting Jesus' words on the significance of Spirit baptism (Acts 1:5). If we assume that these Gentile converts truly received the Holy Spirit at the time of their believing in Jesus (first-class conditional construction), then any obstacle placed in their pathway to salvation would be in opposition to God (see also Acts 10:47): "who was I to hinder God" (ἐγὼ τίς ἤμην δυνατὸς κωλῦσαι τὸν θεόν)? Therefore, we may conclude that if we were to hinder anyone from coming to Christ by adding requirements, we are acting in opposition to God himself.

ἐμνήσθην > 1SAPI, recalled ‖ ἴσην > equal, same ‖ δωρεά > gift ‖ κωλῦσαι > AAN, to hinder

Further Reading: Acts 11:1–18
Neal Cushman

¹³ κρούσαντος δὲ αὐτοῦ τὴν θύραν τοῦ πυλῶνος προσῆλθεν παιδίσκη ὑπακοῦσαι ὀνόματι Ῥόδη, ¹⁴ καὶ ἐπιγνοῦσα τὴν φωνὴν τοῦ Πέτρου ἀπὸ τῆς χαρᾶς οὐκ ἤνοιξεν τὸν πυλῶνα, εἰσδραμοῦσα δὲ ἀπήγγειλεν ἑστάναι τὸν Πέτρον πρὸ τοῦ πυλῶνος.

CONTEXT:

In addition to the famine that Agabus predicted would come upon the world (11:27–30), the church at Jerusalem experienced a further trial. Herod (Agrippa) began targeting the pastors of the church in Jerusalem because it pleased the Jews. After executing James, the brother of John, he arrested Peter, intending to execute him after Passover. However, God intervened because the church prayed (12:5, 12).

COMMENTARY:

When Peter arrived at the prayer meeting, he knocked (κρούσαντος) on the door of the gate (τὴν θύραν τοῦ πυλῶνος), evidently an outer gate that led into the vestibule of the house. This clause, a genitive absolute, separates two different actors (Peter knocking; Rhoda coming to answer) in one grammatical sentence. Rhoda recognizes the voice of Peter but fails to open the gate. Out of sheer joy (ἀπὸ τῆς χαρᾶς; cf. Luke 24:41 where the disciples experience such joy at the resurrection of Christ), she runs to tell the others. Peter keeps knocking (11:16) until the others finally open the gate. It is humorous that Peter has no trouble getting through two maximum security checkpoints and the city gate (12:10) but is not able to get past the residential gate of a house that he knows so well. I am quite sure that Luke was smiling when he wrote this account.

κρούσαντος > AAPMSG, having knocked ‖ πυλῶνος > gate ‖ παιδίσκη > maid servant ‖ ὑπακοῦσαι > AAN, to hear, obey, answer (the door) ‖ ἐπιγνοῦσα > AAPFSN, having recognized ‖ ἤνοιξεν > 3SAAI, opened ‖ εἰσδραμοῦσα > AAPFSN, having ran in

Further Reading: Acts 12:6–19
Neal Cushman

²⁷ οἱ γὰρ κατοικοῦντες ἐν Ἰερουσαλὴμ καὶ οἱ ἄρχοντες αὐτῶν τοῦτον ἀγνοήσαντες καὶ τὰς φωνὰς τῶν προφητῶν τὰς κατὰ πᾶν σάββατον ἀναγινωσκομένας κρίναντες ἐπλήρωσαν, ²⁸ καὶ μηδεμίαν αἰτίαν θανάτου εὑρόντες ᾐτήσαντο Πιλᾶτον ἀναιρεθῆναι αὐτόν.

CONTEXT:

When invited to give a word of exhortation at the synagogue in Pisidian Antioch, Paul explains how Jewish history culminates in the coming of the heir of David, Jesus, who died and rose again for the sins of the people.

COMMENTARY:

The participle, ἀγνοήσαντες, is causal, modifying the main verb, ἐπλήρωσαν (to fulfill), having two objects: τοῦτον ("this one" = "him") and τὰς φωνὰς τῶν προφητῶν. Because the Jewish religious leaders disregarded both Jesus and the voices of the prophets, they actually fulfilled the scriptures in their condemnation of Jesus. God always fulfills his Word, even when it is through evil entities like Pharoah, Nebuchadnezzar, Judas Iscariot, or the Jewish Sanhedrin.

οἱ ... κατοικοῦντες > PAPMPN, ones dwelling, inhabiting ‖ ἀγνοήσαντες > AAPMPN, not knowing, disregarding ‖ ἀναγινωσκομένας > PPPFPA, being read aloud ‖ ἐπλήρωσαν > 3PAAI, fulfilled ‖ ᾐτήσαντο > 3PAMI, asked ‖ ἀναιρεθῆναι > APN, to be taken away, killed

Further Reading: Acts 13:26–35
Neal Cushman

OCTOBER 28

ACTS 14:21-22

²¹ εὐαγγελισάμενοί τε τὴν πόλιν ἐκείνην καὶ μαθητεύσαντες ἱκανοὺς ὑπέστρεψαν εἰς τὴν Λύστραν καὶ εἰς Ἰκόνιον καὶ εἰς Ἀντιόχειαν ²² ἐπιστηρίζοντες τὰς ψυχὰς τῶν μαθητῶν, παρακαλοῦντες ἐμμένειν τῇ πίστει καὶ ὅτι διὰ πολλῶν θλίψεων δεῖ ἡμᾶς εἰσελθεῖν εἰς τὴν βασιλείαν τοῦ θεοῦ.

CONTEXT:

Following Paul and Barnabas' initial ministry in the cities of Galatia, with Derbe as the last of these, they return to each church to build up the believers and appoint elders.

COMMENTARY:

The enclitic particle, τε, often acts as a conjunction to tightly join two things or actions together. Therefore, the participles εὐαγγελισάμενοι and μαθητεύσαντες are linked in this manner as "time" participles. The next adverbial participle (ἐπιστηρίζοντες) follows a verb of coming or going (ὑπέστρεψαν), thereby indicating in this clause the *purpose* of the verb ὑπέστρεψαν. Finally, we are told the *means* whereby this "strengthening" occurs. Therefore, Paul and Barnabas return to these churches for the purpose of strengthening the souls of the disciples *by means of* exhorting them to persevere in the faith. To summarize, Paul and Barnabas, having faced persecution in each of these Galatian cities, return to the churches to prepare them for further afflictions.

μαθητεύσαντες > AAPMPN, having made disciples ‖ ὑπέστρεψαν > 3PAAI, returned ‖ ἐπιστηρίζοντες > PAPMPN, strengthening ‖ ἐμμένειν > PAN, to persevere

Further Reading: Acts 14:21-28
Neal Cushman

OCTOBER 29
ACTS 14:27–28

²⁷ παραγενόμενοι δὲ καὶ συναγαγόντες τὴν ἐκκλησίαν ἀνήγγελλον ὅσα ἐποίησεν ὁ θεὸς μετ' αὐτῶν καὶ ὅτι ἤνοιξεν τοῖς ἔθνεσιν θύραν πίστεως. ²⁸ διέτριβον δὲ χρόνον οὐκ ὀλίγον σὺν τοῖς μαθηταῖς.

CONTEXT:
Following their first missionary trip, Paul and Barnabas returned to the church at Antioch to report that God had opened a door of faith to the Gentiles.

COMMENTARY:
Paul and Barnabas could have gone to Jerusalem to report to the apostles about their ministry to the Gentiles, but their primary obligation was to the church that sent them—the church at Antioch. After gathering the church for an impromptu report, Paul and Barnabas give all the credit to God for what was accomplished in this first missionary trip: "They reported what God did with them." In particular, in the next clause ὅτι introduces indirect discourse (ὅτι following a verb of speaking, thinking, or sensing), focusing not so much on *how* God opened a door of faith to the Gentiles, but *that he did it*. This statement provides the perfect introduction to chapter 15, where Gentile faith and Jewish practice are debated.

παραγενόμενοι > AMPMPN, having arrived, come ‖ συναγαγόντες > AAPMPN, having gathered ‖ ἀνήγγελλον > 3PIAI, reported ‖ ἤνοιξεν > 3SAAI, opened ‖ διέτριβον > 3PIAI, remained, stayed, tarried

Further Reading: Acts 15:1–4
Neal Cushman

302

³⁹ ἐγένετο δὲ παροξυσμὸς ὥστε ἀποχωρισθῆναι αὐτοὺς ἀπ' ἀλλήλων, τόν τε Βαρναβᾶν παραλαβόντα τὸν Μᾶρκον ἐκπλεῦσαι εἰς Κύπρον, ⁴⁰ Παῦλος δὲ ἐπιλεξάμενος Σιλᾶν ἐξῆλθεν παραδοθεὶς τῇ χάριτι τοῦ κυρίου ὑπὸ τῶν ἀδελφῶν.

CONTEXT:

After their trip to Jerusalem, Paul and Barnabas returned to their sending church at Antioch to report the results of the first theological council of the church. After a time of ministry in Antioch, Paul and Barnabas prepared to head out on another missionary journey. However, a controversy arose between them when Barnabas wanted John Mark to accompany them. Two teams resulted, with Barnabas choosing John Mark as his partner in the work, and Paul choosing Silas.

COMMENTARY:

For today's readers of this account, it is typical for people to take sides: some side with Barnabas and his compassionate approach to ministry; others argue that Paul's position on the importance of faithfulness in ministry is paramount; Paul apparently argued that it was too risky to give Mark another chance. Others say that from the perspective of God's providence, two teams were now being sent out, so twice the work was taking place. In other words, win, win! Although each of these views has merit, the text appears to suggest that the church may have sided with Paul. This is significant because Luke uses the same language here as when the church originally commended Paul and Barnabas to begin their first missionary journey (cf. Acts 14:26). The final clause in verse 40 can only modify the actions of Paul and not Barnabas, irrespective of the favorable results that occurred through Mark's ministry later (see 2 Tim 4:11). Did Barnabas and Mark proceed without the clear blessing of the church at Antioch?

παροξυσμός > provocation, controversy || ἀποχωρισθῆναι > APN, separated || ἐκπλεῦσαι > AAN, sailed away || ἐπιλεξάμενος > AMPMSN, having chosen || παραδοθείς > APPMSN, being committed, commended, handed over

Further Reading: Acts 15:35–40

Neal Cushman

OCTOBER 31
ACTS 17:17

¹⁷ διελέγετο μὲν οὖν ἐν τῇ συναγωγῇ τοῖς Ἰουδαίοις καὶ τοῖς σεβομένοις καὶ ἐν τῇ ἀγορᾷ κατὰ πᾶσαν ἡμέραν πρὸς τοὺς παρατυγχάνοντας.

CONTEXT:
While Paul waited for Silas and Timothy to rejoin him at Athens, his spirit was stirred as he observed idol worship taking place throughout this great city of the Roman Empire.

COMMENTARY:
While in Athens, Paul worked at reaching two distinct groups with the gospel: the Jews and "God-fearers" (τοῖς σεβομένοις) who gathered at the synagogue, and the Greeks who happened to be in the marketplace (τῇ ἀγορᾷ) when he was there. This is clear from the placement of ἐν before both phrases in the sentence. That he did this repeatedly is indicated from Luke's use of the phrase, "every day" (κατὰ πᾶσαν ἡμέραν), an expression which indicates daily repetition (see Luke 9:23; 11:3; 22:53; Acts 2:46, et al. for uses of κατά with ἡμέρα). Therefore, Paul's ministry in Athens was consistent with what he had done in other cities. He reached out both to Jews and Greeks repeatedly, declaring the gospel where people gathered. The encounter with the Epicureans and Stoics was merely an example of the evangelistic work that Paul was doing every day. We should ask ourselves if our pattern for living includes persistent and repetitious speaking the gospel.

διελέγετο > 3SIMI, contended, argued, discussed || τοῖς σεβομένοις > PMPMPD, ones worshipping || ἀγορᾷ > marketplace || τοὺς παρατυγχάνοντας > PAPMPA, who happened to be near, chancing by

Further Reading: Acts 17:16–34
Neal Cushman

304

¹ ἐγένετο δὲ ἐν τῷ τὸν Ἀπολλῶ εἶναι ἐν Κορίνθῳ Παῦλον διελθόντα τὰ ἀνωτερικὰ μέρη κατελθεῖν εἰς Ἔφεσον καὶ εὑρεῖν τινας μαθητὰς ² εἶπέν τε πρὸς αὐτούς· εἰ πνεῦμα ἅγιον ἐλάβετε πιστεύσαντες; οἱ δὲ πρὸς αὐτόν· ἀλλ᾽ οὐδ᾽ εἰ πνεῦμα ἅγιον ἔστιν ἠκούσαμεν.

CONTEXT:
Upon arriving in Ephesus, Paul encountered some disciples who had repented under the preaching of John the Baptist, but who had not yet believed in Jesus. When they heard Paul's message about Jesus, they believed in him and were baptized; when Paul laid hands upon them, they received the Holy Spirit and spoke in tongues.

COMMENTARY:
Although the term "disciple" (μαθητής) in the NT typically indicates that a person has put his faith in Jesus Christ, this is not the case in this passage (cf. Matt 9:14; Luke 5:33; 7:18). These individuals had a deficient understanding of the work of Christ in salvation and had not yet received Christian baptism. To discern their spiritual condition, Paul asks a simple question, and they provide an answer. The conditional particle εἰ often appears in sentences with other particles or conjunctions, but in this sentence it occurs alone and therefore introduces a question. As with some other Greek particles like ἄν, it is best left untranslated: "Did you receive the Holy Spirit when you believed?" The answer to Paul's question is surprising: these disciples of John seem to be ignorant of the existence of the Holy Spirit. Although their understanding of pneumatology could be as deficient as this answer seems to indicate, I would suggest that they knew about the Holy Spirit through the preaching of their mentor (see Mark 1:7-8), but they lacked knowledge about the death and resurrection of Christ, and the giving of the Spirit at Pentecost. So why does their answer omit the term "giving" here (perhaps a form of δίδωμι)? It is likely assumed in this sentence through "ellipsis." Interestingly, John 7:39 contains a similar grammatical construction with the Holy Spirit as the topic and the omission of δεδομένον.

διελθόντα > AAPMSA, passing through ‖ ἀνωτερικά > upper ‖ κατελθεῖν > AAN, came, went down ‖ εὑρεῖν > AAN, found

Further Reading: Acts 19:3-7
Neal Cushman

¹ ὃ ἦν ἀπ᾽ ἀρχῆς, ὃ ἀκηκόαμεν, ὃ ἑωράκαμεν τοῖς ὀφθαλμοῖς ἡμῶν, ὃ ἐθεασάμεθα καὶ αἱ χεῖρες ἡμῶν ἐψηλάφησαν περὶ τοῦ λόγου τῆς ζωῆς— ² καὶ ἡ ζωὴ ἐφανερώθη, καὶ ἑωράκαμεν καὶ μαρτυροῦμεν καὶ ἀπαγγέλλομεν ὑμῖν τὴν ζωὴν τὴν αἰώνιον ἥτις ἦν πρὸς τὸν πατέρα καὶ ἐφανερώθη ἡμῖν— ³ ὃ ἑωράκαμεν καὶ ἀκηκόαμεν, ἀπαγγέλλομεν καὶ ὑμῖν, ἵνα καὶ ὑμεῖς κοινωνίαν ἔχητε μεθ᾽ ἡμῶν. καὶ ἡ κοινωνία δὲ ἡ ἡμετέρα μετὰ τοῦ πατρὸς καὶ μετὰ τοῦ υἱοῦ αὐτοῦ Ἰησοῦ Χριστοῦ.

CONTEXT:

As the opening verses of the letter, verses 1-3, along with verse 4, set the direction for what follows and thus serve a critical role in determining the overall message of 1 John.

COMMENTARY:

The most striking feature of these verses is the extensive use of what we might call "experiential" verbs to support multiple verbs of communication. The Apostle John wants to make it infinitely clear that he is testifying about (μαρτυροῦμεν) and announcing (ἀπαγγέλλομεν, *twice*) what he and the other apostles have heard (ἀκηκόαμεν, *twice*), seen (ἑωράκαμεν, *twice*), carefully examined (ἐθεασάμεθα), and even touched with their hands (αἱ χεῖρες ἡμῶν ἐψηλάφησαν). He is thus a credible eyewitness of the truths he is about to present from the ministry of Jesus that he witnessed ἀπ᾽ ἀρχῆς (the very beginning of Jesus' earthly ministry). So, what is John about to tell us about? He is writing concerning the message of life (περὶ τοῦ λόγου τῆς ζωῆς). And that message of life is about the Life that has appeared (ἡ ζωὴ ἐφανερώθη). The indirect references to Jesus and his message using ἡ ζωή and the relative pronoun ὃ without an antecedent ("that which") force readers to pause and consider the significance of what John is saying. Jesus is life! In fact, Jesus is *eternal* life. He is both the source and substance of the life that the Father gives to all those who put their faith in him. This is why John can go on to say that he is announcing this Life to his readers in order that they might have fellowship with him and his companions. That fellowship, however, is not the ultimate focus. God through John is inviting those who read this letter to join in the fellowship that the apostles had with the Father and the Son. How do we do that? The rest of the letter tells us how!

ἀκηκόαμεν > 1PRAI, we have heard ‖ ἑωράκαμεν > 1PRAI, we have seen ‖ ἐθεασάμεθα > 1PAMI, we observed ‖ ἐψηλάφησαν > 3PAAI, they touched ‖ ἐφανερώθη > 3SAPI, it appeared

Further Reading: John 1:1-18; 3:16

Martin M. Culy

⁴ καὶ ταῦτα γράφομεν ἡμεῖς, ἵνα ἡ χαρὰ ἡμῶν ᾖ πεπληρωμένη.

CONTEXT:

John has introduced himself not only as an eyewitness of Jesus, but as a *reliable* eyewitness who is announcing to his readers the word of life (1:1–2), a message that will bring fellowship both with him and with the Father and the Son (1:3) to all those who embrace it. Now we learn in 1:4 another purpose for John's letter.

COMMENTARY:

The conjunction καί marks thematic continuity with what precedes, suggesting that readers' experience of the full measure of joy is linked to experiencing the full benefit of their κοινωνία with the Father and the Son (1:3). John introduces the overarching reason for his letter using a purpose clause introduced by ἵνα, which then requires a subjunctive main verb (ᾖ). In this case, the present tense ᾖ is used with a perfect participle to form a perfect periphrastic construction (ᾖ πεπληρωμένη), which is equivalent in force to a finite perfect verb. The demonstrative pronoun ταῦτα likely refers to the entire letter. It is unclear from the textual tradition whether John wrote ἡμῶν or ὑμῶν. Both have good textual support, but since the two terms likely would have been pronounced the same way, faulty hearing could have led to unintentional changes in either direction. If John wrote ἡμῶν, he may well have been speaking inclusively: "our joy *as Christians.*" If this is the case, the meaning, whether we read ἡμῶν or ὑμῶν, is essentially the same. This is a letter designed to promote fullness of joy among the people of God.

ᾖ > 3SPAS, it might be ‖ πεπληρωμένη > RPPFSN, made full

Further Reading: John 15:11; 16:24; 10:10
Martin M. Culy

⁵ καὶ ἔστιν αὕτη ἡ ἀγγελία ἣν ἀκηκόαμεν ἀπ' αὐτοῦ καὶ ἀναγγέλλομεν ὑμῖν, ὅτι ὁ θεὸς φῶς ἐστιν καὶ σκοτία ἐν αὐτῷ οὐκ ἔστιν οὐδεμία. ⁶ Ἐὰν εἴπωμεν ὅτι κοινωνίαν ἔχομεν μετ' αὐτοῦ καὶ ἐν τῷ σκότει περιπατῶμεν, ψευδόμεθα καὶ οὐ ποιοῦμεν τὴν ἀλήθειαν.

CONTEXT:

In the previous verse, we learned that at least one of John's primary purposes in writing his letter was to bring about fullness of joy. Part of this joy would flow out of sharing in the fellowship that the apostles enjoyed with the Father and the Son (1:3).

COMMENTARY:

The ὅτι in v. 5 is epexegetical, picking up the cataphoric demonstrative pronoun αὕτη: *"This* is the message, *namely."* As is typical in an equative clause (X = Y), the subject has an article (ὁ θεός) and the predicate does not (φῶς). "Light" was commonly used in the ancient world as a metaphor for moral purity, while "darkness" was a natural metaphor for moral impurity. The metaphorical description of God's character continues in the second half of the ὅτι clause, this time using an emphatic negative statement (οὐκ ... οὐδεμία): "there is *no* darkness *at all."* This emphatic language drives home the point that God is absolutely free of moral corruption. And by connecting verse 5 to what precedes with a καί, we are reminded that all that is good in life—eternal life (1:2), fellowship with God and other believers (1:3), and fullness of joy (1:4)—flows out of a right understanding of who God is. Right understanding, though, is not enough. None of these blessings are possible without choosing to live in light of the fact that the God with whom we are now in covenant relationship is holy, holy, holy. The thematic unity with what precedes is enhanced by the repetition of κοινωνία (vv. 3, 6), here pointing to a relationship of intimacy between the Father and Son and followers of Jesus, a relationship that depends on avoiding walking in darkness (ἐν τῷ σκότει περιπατῶμεν). To think that a genuine Christian can live in sin is to live a lie (ψευδόμεθα) and reject the truth of a gospel that transforms the lives of those who embrace it. Indeed, John's choice of language in verse 6 reminds us that the truth is not simply something to be believed, it is something to be practiced (ποιοῦμεν τὴν ἀλήθειαν).

ἀγγελία > message || ἀκηκόαμεν > 1PRAI, we have heard || ψευδόμεθα > 1PPMI, we lie

Further Reading: 1 Peter 1:15–16

Martin M. Culy

1 JOHN 2:1

¹ τεκνία μου, ταῦτα γράφω ὑμῖν ἵνα μὴ ἁμάρτητε. καὶ ἐάν τις ἁμάρτῃ, παράκλητον ἔχομεν πρὸς τὸν πατέρα Ἰησοῦν Χριστὸν δίκαιον.

CONTEXT:

In the preceding verses (1:5–10), John has begun to address common misconceptions about sin.

COMMENTARY:

The term of endearment, τεκνία (the diminutive form of τέκνον), is used here and six other times in the letter to convey John's fatherly concern. We have already learned that he was writing so that "our" joy, as Christians, might be full. Now we see a second purpose for the letter: ἵνα μὴ ἁμάρτητε. Christians who have been conditioned to expect that their lives will be filled with sin tend to read 1 John 2:1 this way: "My little children, I am writing these things to you so that you may not sin. But *whenever* anyone does sin ..." This, however, is not what John wrote, nor is it what he meant. John uses the aorist tense ἁμάρτητε to portray the sin in view as an act rather than a process (present tense). The abnormality of sin for Christians is reinforced through the use of a third-class condition in the next clause (καὶ ἐάν τις ἁμάρτῃ), which we might translate: "and if anyone *should happen* to sin." Rhetorically, then, John's language here (and throughout the letter) forces us to re-examine our view of sin and its power over us as believers. He presents sin not as something that is common in the Christian life, but as something that might happen at times and thus needs to be dealt with. John has already given part of the solution to sin in 1:9. Now, he fleshes out what happens when we confess sin that we happen to commit: Jesus Christ, the Righteous One, serves as our advocate before the Father. In Jesus Christ, the Righteous One (δίκαιον stands in apposition to Ἰησοῦν Χριστόν), we have the best possible person to take up our case (παράκλητον ἔχομεν) before the Father (πρὸς τὸν πατέρα). When Jesus speaks, the Father listens. When he reminds the Father that his blood has covered our sins and that we have been adopted as his children, there is no chance that our sins will be held against us. God is faithful and just to forgive our sins and cleanse us from all unrighteousness because Jesus stands before him as our advocate testifying that our sins have been dealt with through his death.

ἁμάρτητε > 2PAAS, you might sin || ἁμάρτῃ > 3SAAS, he should sin || παράκλητον > advocate

Further Reading: Hebrews 7:25
Martin M. Culy

³ καὶ ἐν τούτῳ γινώσκομεν ὅτι ἐγνώκαμεν αὐτόν, ἐὰν τὰς ἐντολὰς αὐτοῦ τηρῶμεν.

CONTEXT:

In 2:1–2, we were told that this letter has what for many is a startling purpose: "that you do not sin." The Apostle John acknowledges that Christians sometimes sin, and when we do sin, we have a remedy (1:9) and an advocate (2:1). His language, though, makes it clear that sin is not supposed to be a *normal* part of a Christian's experience.

COMMENTARY:

The use of καί again signals continuity in the argument that John has been developing. The phrase ἐν τούτῳ ("by this") points forward to the conditional clause ἐὰν τὰς ἐντολὰς αὐτοῦ τηρῶμεν, which uses the so-called "third-class condition" because it is pointing to a future possibility. By placing the direct object τὰς ἐντολὰς αὐτοῦ before the verb τηρῶμεν, John puts emphasis on God's commands. Whether or not a professing Christian keeps God's commands is presented as a ready test of whether or not that person truly knows God. When we look at our lives and find ourselves living in conformity to God's will (walking in the light), we have great confidence that we genuinely know him and belong to him, with the perfect ἐγνώκαμεν pointing to someone who has already entered into a relationship with God.

ἐγνώκαμεν > 1PRAI, we have come to know ‖ τηρῶμεν > 1PPAS, we keep

Further Reading: Matthew 28:19–20

Martin M. Culy

³ καὶ πᾶς ὁ ἔχων τὴν ἐλπίδα ταύτην ἐπ᾽ αὐτῷ ἁγνίζει ἑαυτόν, καθὼς ἐκεῖνος ἁγνός ἐστιν.

CONTEXT:

John has just spoken about the return of Jesus and what is going to happen to Jesus' followers when he returns: ὅμοιοι αὐτῷ ἐσόμεθα ("we will be like him!").

COMMENTARY:

The demonstrative ταύτην is anaphoric, pointing back to the hope of Jesus' Second Coming (3:2). The hope that Christians have is hope "in him," with ἐπ᾽ αὐτῷ most likely pointing to Jesus. As is typical, John uses emphatic language: "Every" (πᾶς) person who is anticipating Jesus' return behaves in a particular way: he purifies himself. And to drive home the importance of this action, John emphatically reminds us of Jesus' pure character by placing both ἐκεῖνος and ἁγνός before the verb ἐστιν. By using the comparative conjunction καθὼς ("just as"), John reminds us that those who believe that Jesus is coming again take steps to prepare themselves to meet the pure bridegroom as a pure bride. To do anything else would be like going to your own wedding in a mud-covered swimsuit, utterly inappropriate and inconceivable. God through John makes it clear that meeting Jesus at his return is not simply about having the imputed righteousness of Jesus. The Bride of Christ is called to *make herself ready*. The verb ἁγνίζει is active, not passive. Christians who have been washed in the blood of the Lamb intentionally purify themselves day-by-day in this life in anticipation of meeting their utterly pure Master when he returns.

πᾶς ὁ ἔχων > everyone who has ‖ ἐπ᾽ αὐτῷ > (directed) toward him ‖ ἁγνίζει > 3SPAI, he purifies ‖ ἁγνός > pure

Further Reading: Hebrews 12:14; Revelation 19:7–8
Martin M. Culy

November 8
1 John 3:11

¹¹ ὅτι αὕτη ἐστὶν ἡ ἀγγελία ἣν ἠκούσατε ἀπ' ἀρχῆς, ἵνα ἀγαπῶμεν ἀλλήλους.

CONTEXT:

John has just reminded us that both those who do not practice righteousness and those who do not love believers show that they are not truly children of God.

COMMENTARY:

Although the vast majority of English versions begin a new sentence and a new sub-section here, with most implying that John used γάρ here, the use of ὅτι marks a stronger connection between the first clause in verse 11 and the sentence that began in verse 10. Once again, John uses a demonstrative pronoun (αὕτη) that points forward (cataphoric) and is here picked up with an epexegetical ἵνα: "*This* is the message ... *namely.*" The ὅτι at the beginning of the verse indicates that the reason that John can claim that someone who does not love his brother is not a child of God (3:10) is because that claim is consistent with what they had been taught from the beginning. Jesus requires those who belong to him to love other Christians. The repetition of the love command throughout 1 John, the stark statement that those who fail to love Christians do not belong to God (3:10), and the reminder that the love command is one of the first things they had learned as followers of Jesus (ἀπ' ἀρχῆς) all serve to emphasize the non-negotiable nature of loving one another. When we embrace the gospel, we are made part of the *family* of God. Those who acknowledge Jesus as their Lord will focus their lives on obeying the command he had given to his followers from the very beginning. This is why no one can genuinely be a Christian and refuse to love their brother or sister in Christ. Doing so would show that they have not surrendered to the lordship of Jesus.

ἡ ἀγγελία > the message

Further Reading: John 13:34–35; James 2:14–17;
1 Peter 1:22; 3:8; 1 Corinthians 13:1–7
Martin M. Culy

¹² θεὸν οὐδεὶς πώποτε τεθέαται. ἐὰν ἀγαπῶμεν ἀλλήλους, ὁ θεὸς ἐν ἡμῖν μένει καὶ ἡ ἀγάπη αὐτοῦ ἐν ἡμῖν τετελειωμένη ἐστίν. ¹³ Ἐν τούτῳ γινώσκομεν ὅτι ἐν αὐτῷ μένομεν καὶ αὐτὸς ἐν ἡμῖν, ὅτι ἐκ τοῦ πνεύματος αὐτοῦ δέδωκεν ἡμῖν.

CONTEXT:

John has just reminded us that loving one another is an obvious response to God's love for us.

COMMENTARY:

By putting the direct object, subject, and adverb before the verb in 4:12, John reminds his readers emphatically that no one has ever had a good look at God. Why does John say this in this context? Notice what comes next. Our love for one another shows that God remains in us. More than that, it represents the culmination (τετελειωμένη) of his love for us. In other words, although no one has seen God directly, when they see his transforming power at work within us through our love for one another, they get a glimpse of what God is like. Our love for one another, though, does not just testify to *others* that we belong to God; it is also the evidence that proves to us (ἐν τούτῳ γινώσκομεν) that we are in a right relationship with him (we remain in him and he remains in us). In 4:13, the first ὅτι introduces the content of what we know, modifying γινώσκομεν, while the second ὅτι is epexegetical, picking up the thought introduced by the cataphoric demonstrative τούτῳ ("By *this* we know that ... *namely* from his Spirit"). Why does John suddenly refer to the Holy Spirit? He does so because our love for one another proves that we are indwelt by the Holy Spirit, which in turn gives us great confidence that we know God. The use of ἐκ with τοῦ πνεύματος likely points to the Spirit's activity, prompting our love for one another, as the source of our knowledge that we are in right relationship with God.

πώποτε > ever ‖ τεθέαται > 3SRMI, he has observed ‖ τετελειωμένη > RPPFSN, having been made complete ‖ δέδωκεν > 3SRAI, he has given

Further Reading: John 1:18; Romans 8:9–11; 1 John 3:6; 2 Peter 1:3
Martin M. Culy

³ αὕτη γάρ ἐστιν ἡ ἀγάπη τοῦ θεοῦ, ἵνα τὰς ἐντολὰς αὐτοῦ τηρῶμεν, καὶ αἱ ἐντολαὶ αὐτοῦ βαρεῖαι οὐκ εἰσίν.

CONTEXT:

The preceding verses remind us that belief in Jesus, the Christ, brings about new birth, which results in people who love both God and God's children. And to truly love other believers, with right motives and genuinely loving actions, we first have to love God by keeping his commands.

COMMENTARY:

John once again introduces the point he wants to make with a (cataphoric) demonstrative pronoun (αὕτη) that points forward to an epexegetical ἵνα. In the ἵνα clause, the direct object τὰς ἐντολὰς is fronted for emphasis. The context makes it clear that the genitive τοῦ θεοῦ introduces the conceptual object of ἡ ἀγάπη. The fact that 5:3 reinforces the point expressed in 5:2 makes it even more striking. Contrary to much modern thinking, love for God is defined, first and foremost, in terms of keeping his commands. This goes against the common mantra that "Christianity is not about rules." For many today, even a slight emphasis on the commands of Scripture is viewed as oppressive, burdensome, or legalistic. First John repeatedly rejects this myth and here reminds us that just the opposite is true. God's commands are *not* heavy or burdensome. Notice again the placement of both the subject (αἱ ἐντολαὶ αὐτοῦ) and predicate (βαρεῖαι) before the verb in the final clause to make the statement more forceful. Claiming that Jesus calls his followers to a "yoke-free" existence, despite the fact that he explicitly states just the opposite, may sound pious and grace-focused, but it plays into the modern notion that rules are inherently evil or oppressive. Just as Jesus made clear elsewhere, his yoke (everything he commands) is light. And in 1 John we learn that obedience to his commands not only represents an act of love toward God, but is also the path to fullness of joy, the very purpose for which John wrote his letter (1:4).

τηρῶμεν > 1PPAS, we keep ‖ βαρεῖαι > burdensome, heavy

Further Reading: John 14:15, 21, 23; Matthew 11:28–30

Martin M. Culy

¹⁸ οἴδαμεν ὅτι πᾶς ὁ γεγεννημένος ἐκ τοῦ θεοῦ οὐχ ἁμαρτάνει, ἀλλ' ὁ γεννηθεὶς ἐκ τοῦ θεοῦ τηρεῖ αὐτὸν καὶ ὁ πονηρὸς οὐχ ἅπτεται αὐτοῦ.

CONTEXT:

John has just talked about sin and the seriousness of sin. Now he turns to the nature of those who have been born again and the intentional approach they take to combat sin.

COMMENTARY:

Once again, John speaks in very black-and-white language. "*Everyone* who has been born of God (πᾶς ὁ γεγεννημένος ἐκ τοῦ θεοῦ) *does not sin* (οὐχ ἁμαρτάνει)." As in 3:6, there is no basis for claiming that John's focus with the present tense ἁμαρτάνει is on "continual" or repetitive sin. Rather, he is again highlighting the fundamental contradiction between sin and genuine new birth. And this is something every Christian knows or should know (Οἴδαμεν). Here, though, he goes on to clarify *how* the born-again person avoids sin using ἀλλ' to introduce a clause that contrasts sharply with the idea of a life of sin. The meaning of this clause has been debated, with many assuming that ὁ γεννηθεὶς ἐκ τοῦ θεοῦ refers to Jesus. The parallel language with the preceding clause, however, makes this very unlikely. Furthermore, in the latest edition of the Greek NT (UBS⁵/NA²⁸), the editors rightly agreed that John wrote ἑαυτόν ("himself"), rather than αὐτόν ("him"). Thus, the way that someone who has been born of God avoids sin is by "keeping" himself or herself, i.e., taking steps to avoid sin by the Spirit whom God has given us. And the result is that the evil one does not touch that person. This claim sets the stage for John's final exhortation, which concludes this letter: "Children, *guard yourselves* from idols" (5:21). The Christian life is portrayed in both 5:18 and 5:21, as well as in the rest of the letter, as an active battle against sin that can be regularly, if not perfectly (see 1:9 and 2:1), successful.

οἴδαμεν > 1PRAI, we know ‖ γεγεννημένος > RPPMSN, the one who has been born ‖ γεννηθείς > APPMSN, the one who was born ‖ ἅπτεται > 3SPMI, he touches

Further Reading: 1 Corinthians 10:13; 2 Corinthians 5:17
Martin M. Culy

¹ ὁ πρεσβύτερος ἐκλεκτῇ κυρίᾳ καὶ τοῖς τέκνοις αὐτῆς, οὓς ἐγὼ ἀγαπῶ ἐν ἀληθείᾳ, καὶ οὐκ ἐγὼ μόνος ἀλλὰ καὶ πάντες οἱ ἐγνωκότες τὴν ἀλήθειαν, ² διὰ τὴν ἀλήθειαν τὴν μένουσαν ἐν ἡμῖν καὶ μεθ' ἡμῶν ἔσται εἰς τὸν αἰῶνα.

CONTEXT:

In 2 John, John is writing to "the elect lady and her children" (likely a reference to a local church) to encourage them to continue walking in the truth (vv. 4–6) and warn them not to receive false teachers (vv. 5–11).

COMMENTARY:

Truth and love are dominant themes in John's writings. 2 John is no exception. In verse 1, John writes that he loves the church ἐν ἀληθείᾳ ("in truth"). He adds that the church is loved by πάντες οἱ ἐγνωκότες τὴν ἀλήθειαν ("all the ones that know the truth"). He then says this love is possible διὰ τὴν ἀλήθειαν ("because of the truth"). For John, truth is the basis for love. In other words, apart from the truth, love is not possible. This fact is reflected in his argument to not receive false teachers in verse 10. Straying from the truth will always short-circuit love.

ἐκλεκτῇ > chosen ‖ κυρίᾳ > lady ‖ ἐγνωκότες > RAPMPN, the ones who know

Further Reading: 2 John 1–3; cf. 9–10
Todd Bolton

⁴ ἐχάρην λίαν ὅτι εὕρηκα ἐκ τῶν τέκνων σου περιπατοῦντας ἐν ἀληθείᾳ, καθὼς ἐντολὴν ἐλάβομεν παρὰ τοῦ πατρός. ⁵ καὶ νῦν ἐρωτῶ σε, κυρία, οὐχ ὡς ἐντολὴν γράφων σοι καινὴν ἀλλ’ ἣν εἴχομεν ἀπ’ ἀρχῆς, ἵνα ἀγαπῶμεν ἀλλήλους. ⁶ καὶ αὕτη ἐστὶν ἡ ἀγάπη, ἵνα περιπατῶμεν κατὰ τὰς ἐντολὰς αὐτοῦ· αὕτη ἡ ἐντολή ἐστιν, καθὼς ἠκούσατε ἀπ’ ἀρχῆς, ἵνα ἐν αὐτῇ περιπατῆτε.

CONTEXT:

After greeting the local church (vv. 1-3), John then proceeds to encourage them to continue walking in the truth by loving one another.

COMMENTARY:

John rejoices greatly to find members of the local church περιπατοῦντας ἐν ἀληθείᾳ ("walking in truth"). In verse 6, walking in the truth is equivalent to walking κατὰ τὰς ἐντολὰς αὐτοῦ ("according to his commandments"). And the commandment John highlights in verse 5 is ἀγαπῶμεν ἀλλήλους ("love one another"). In verse 2, John showed that the truth is the basis of love. Here, John emphasizes love as the application of truth. On the one hand, love is not possible apart from truth. On the other, truth must always be expressed in love. When believers are cherishing the truth and expressing it in love, there is cause for great rejoicing.

ἐχάρην > 1SAPI, I rejoiced ‖ λίαν > very ‖ εὕρηκα > 1SRAI, I found ‖ ἐλάβομεν > 1PAAI, we received ‖ εἴχομεν > 1PIAI, we have

Further Reading: 2 John 1-6
Todd Bolton

⁸ βλέπετε ἑαυτούς, ἵνα μὴ ἀπολέσητε ἃ εἰργασάμεθα ἀλλὰ μισθὸν πλήρη ἀπολάβητε. ⁹ Πᾶς ὁ προάγων καὶ μὴ μένων ἐν τῇ διδαχῇ τοῦ Χριστοῦ θεὸν οὐκ ἔχει. ὁ μένων ἐν τῇ διδαχῇ, οὗτος καὶ τὸν πατέρα καὶ τὸν υἱὸν ἔχει. ¹⁰ εἴ τις ἔρχεται πρὸς ὑμᾶς καὶ ταύτην τὴν διδαχὴν οὐ φέρει, μὴ λαμβάνετε αὐτὸν εἰς οἰκίαν καὶ χαίρειν αὐτῷ μὴ λέγετε.

CONTEXT:

Having greeted the church (vv. 1–3) and encouraged them to continue walking in the truth by loving one another (vv. 4–6), John gets to his main purpose in the letter: warning the church not to receive those who do not teach the truth.

COMMENTARY:

John has already shown that truth is the basis of love (vv. 1–2), and love is the application of truth (v. 6). Verse 7 explains that there are many deceivers denying the truth that Jesus came in the flesh. If believed, such a denial of truth will derail love. Asyndeton (no conjunction) in verse 8 alerts John's readers to the importance of the present imperative βλέπετε ("Watch out"). In addition to their own watchfulness, the readers are exhorted to μὴ λαμβάνετε ("not receive") anyone who does not hold to the truth. John's readers must share the Apostle's zeal for truth. However, defense of the truth is not John's primary passion. Truth is a vital means to the end of knowing the Father and the Son (v. 9) and walking in love (v. 6). John's zeal for the truth is born out of a passion for the Father and the Son. Therefore, his readers are to be watchful and not receive anyone who, through false teaching, might derail their enjoyment of God.

ἀπολέσητε > 2PAAS, you lose ‖ εἰργασάμεθα > 1PAMI, we worked for ‖ μισθόν > reward ‖ πλήρη > full ‖ ἀπολάβητε > 2SAAS, you receive ‖ προάγων > PAPMSN, one who goes ahead ‖ διδαχῇ > teaching

Further Reading: 2 John 7–11
Todd Bolton

2 JOHN 12

¹² πολλὰ ἔχων ὑμῖν γράφειν οὐκ ἐβουλήθην διὰ χάρτου καὶ μέλανος, ἀλλ' ἐλπίζω γενέσθαι πρὸς ὑμᾶς καὶ στόμα πρὸς στόμα λαλῆσαι, ἵνα ἡ χαρὰ ἡμῶν ᾖ πεπληρωμένη.

CONTEXT:
John closes his warning letter by expressing his desire to see the church in person.

COMMENTARY:
The closing of John's letter masterfully achieves two purposes. First, by expressing οὐκ ἐβουλήθην διὰ χάρτου καὶ μέλανος ("I did not desire through pen and ink"), he reinforces how dire the warning is to abide in the teaching of Christ (v. 9). The seriousness of the situation made John do something he did not want to do. Second, by expressing ἐλπίζω γενέσθαι πρὸς ὑμᾶς καὶ στόμα πρὸς στόμα λαλῆσαι ("I hope to come to you to speak mouth to mouth"), John reaffirms his loving commitment to them. His desire is to see their mutual joy fulfilled through in-person fellowship. Pen and ink are no substitute for face-to-face communication. Virtual community may be necessary in dire circumstances, but every believer should hope to return to joyful personal presence with one another. Afterall, loving one another is the commandment that has been received from the beginning (v. 5).

χάρτου > paper || μέλανος > ink || γενέσθαι > AMN, to be

Further Reading: 2 John 12–13
Todd Bolton

³ ἐχάρην γὰρ λίαν ἐρχομένων ἀδελφῶν καὶ μαρτυρούντων σου τῇ ἀληθείᾳ, καθὼς σὺ ἐν ἀληθείᾳ περιπατεῖς ⁴ μειζοτέραν τούτων οὐκ ἔχω χαράν, ἵνα ἀκούω τὰ ἐμὰ τέκνα ἐν ἀληθείᾳ περιπατοῦντα.

CONTEXT:

3 John is a letter from the Apostle to his dear child in the faith, Gaius. The letter commends Gaius for his hospitality to those that have gone out for the sake of the name and condemns Diotrephes for being a hindrance to the progress of the gospel. After greeting and praying for Gaius in verses 1-2, John then rejoices over the good report he has received about him.

COMMENTARY:

John says ἐχάρην γὰρ λίαν ("For I rejoiced greatly") when he received the testimony that Gaius was ἐν ἀληθείᾳ περιπατεῖς ("walking in the truth"). In fact, he adds μειζοτέραν τούτων οὐκ ἔχω χαράν ("I have no greater joy than this") than to hear about his children walking in the truth. John's greatest joy in ministry is to see his children living in light of the truth of the gospel. For Gaius, this was demonstrated through his work of love on behalf of visiting missionaries (vv. 5-6a, 7). What a thrill it was for John to see his beloved child welcoming and caring for brothers in Christ without the Apostle's prompting. The goal and greatest joy of all leaders should likewise be their people showing Christlike love motivated by the truth.

λίαν > exceedingly || μειζοτέραν > greater

Further Reading: 3 John 1-6a
Todd Bolton

⁶ ... οὓς καλῶς ποιήσεις προπέμψας ἀξίως τοῦ θεοῦ· ⁷ ὑπὲρ γὰρ τοῦ ὀνόματος ἐξῆλθον μηδὲν λαμβάνοντες ἀπὸ τῶν ἐθνικῶν. ⁸ ἡμεῖς οὖν ὀφείλομεν ὑπολαμβάνειν τοὺς τοιούτους, ἵνα συνεργοὶ γινώμεθα τῇ ἀληθείᾳ.

CONTEXT:
John has prayed for and rejoiced over Gaius because of his warm welcome of visiting missionaries (vv. 2–6a). He then exhorts Gaius to continued faithfulness by encouraging him to send them on their way in a manner worthy of God.

COMMENTARY:
John's chief encouragement is for Gaius to προπέμψας ἀξίως τοῦ θεοῦ ("send them in a manner worthy of God"). He bolsters his encouragement with a reason indicated by γάρ in verse 7. These believers have gone out ὑπὲρ τοῦ ὀνόματος ("for the sake of the name"). They are completely dependent on God and His people as they go out for the glory of the name of Jesus Christ. As a result (οὖν), Gaius and others should support people like this. Interestingly, John's purpose clause, indicated by ἵνα, does not focus on the missionaries' need, but on the senders' participation in gospel ministry. Gaius and others should support visiting missionaries, becoming συνεργοί ("fellow workers"), so that they may share in their joyful Christ-centered ministry. Missions is a joint effort between those sending and those sent.

προπέμψας > AAPMSN, send forward ‖ ἀξίως > worthily ‖ ἐθνικῶν > Gentiles ‖ ὑπολαμβάνειν > PAN, to support ‖ συνεργοί > fellow workers

Further Reading: Acts 15:3; Titus 3:13; Acts 5:41
Todd Bolton

⁹ ἔγραψά τι τῇ ἐκκλησίᾳ· ἀλλ' ὁ φιλοπρωτεύων αὐτῶν Διοτρέφης οὐκ ἐπιδέχεται ἡμᾶς. ¹⁰ διὰ τοῦτο, ἐὰν ἔλθω, ὑπομνήσω αὐτοῦ τὰ ἔργα ἃ ποιεῖ λόγοις πονηροῖς φλυαρῶν ἡμᾶς, καὶ μὴ ἀρκούμενος ἐπὶ τούτοις οὔτε αὐτὸς ἐπιδέχεται τοὺς ἀδελφοὺς καὶ τοὺς βουλομένους κωλύει καὶ ἐκ τῆς ἐκκλησίας ἐκβάλλει.

CONTEXT:

Having exhorted Gaius to support the visiting missionaries by sending them on their way in a manner worthy of God (v. 6), John exposes Diotrephes for his divisive selfish desires.

COMMENTARY:

John has commended Gaius for walking in the truth by welcoming visiting missionaries that have gone out for the sake of the name (vv. 3–7a). He desires that Gaius send them on their way in a manner worthy of God (v. 6) so that he and others might be fellow workers in gospel ministry (v. 8). For John, two vital components of gospel ministry are a desire to see Christ exalted and a cooperative spirit between those sending and those sent. Diotrephes fails on both counts. Instead of Christ's glory, Diotrephes is ὁ φιλοπρωτεύων αὐτῶν ("the one who loves being first"). Instead of cooperation, Diotrephes οὐκ ἐπιδέχεται ἡμᾶς ("does not acknowledge us"), λόγοις πονηροῖς φλυαρῶν ἡμᾶς ("speaks evil words against us"), οὔτε ἐπιδέχεται τοὺς ἀδελφούς ("does not receive the brothers"), τοὺς βουλομένους κωλύει ("prevents those that want to [receive them]"), and ἐκ τῆς ἐκκλησίας ἐκβάλλει ("casts them out of the church")! Ministry has become all about him, not Christ and His sent ones. What a stinging indictment on a supposed minister of the gospel.

φιλοπρωτεύων > PAPMSN, one loving to be first || Διοτρέφης > Diotrephes || ἐπιδέχεται > 3SPMI, receive, acknowledge || ὑπομνήσω > 1SFAI, I will call attention to || φλυαρῶν > PAPMSN, speaking maliciously about || ἀρκούμενος > PPPMSN, being content

Further Reading: 3 John 6–10
Todd Bolton

³ ἀγαπητοί, πᾶσαν σπουδὴν ποιούμενος γράφειν ὑμῖν περὶ τῆς κοινῆς ἡμῶν σωτηρίας ἀνάγκην ἔσχον γράψαι ὑμῖν παρακαλῶν ἐπαγωνίζεσθαι τῇ ἅπαξ παραδοθείσῃ τοῖς ἁγίοις πίστει. ⁴ παρεισέδυσαν γάρ τινες ἄνθρωποι, οἱ πάλαι προγεγραμμένοι εἰς τοῦτο τὸ κρίμα, ἀσεβεῖς, τὴν τοῦ θεοῦ ἡμῶν χάριτα μετατιθέντες εἰς ἀσέλγειαν καὶ τὸν μόνον δεσπότην καὶ κύριον ἡμῶν Ἰησοῦν Χριστὸν ἀρνούμενοι.

CONTEXT:

Jude opens and closes his letter by reminding his readers of their beloved and protected status in God the Father through Jesus Christ (vv. 1, 24). His readers need this encouragement because they are being called to contend for the faith amidst ungodly opposition.

COMMENTARY:

Jude alerts his readers to the importance of his letter with the use of the vocative ἀγαπητοί in verse 3. The concessive phrase πᾶσαν σπουδὴν ποιούμενος γράφειν ὑμῖν περὶ τῆς κοινῆς ἡμῶν σωτηρίας ("although I was very eager to write to you about our common salvation") further stresses the importance. Jude wanted to write another letter entirely, but the urgency of the situation demanded something different. Jude urges his readers ἐπαγωνίζεσθαι τῇ ἅπαξ παραδοθείσῃ τοῖς ἁγίοις πίστει ("to contend for the once-delivered-to-the-saints faith"). The word order and description of faith is striking. First, the description "once delivered" assumes that the essential message of the gospel and its implications was largely complete at the time of Jude's writing. Second, the participle παραδοθείσῃ connotes something valuable that has been entrusted to someone else. The faith is a sacred trust given to the saints. The saints must therefore contend for this precious asset because of mounting ungodly opposition in verse 4 indicated by γάρ. Two essential elements of the faith are under attack: τὴν τοῦ θεοῦ ἡμῶν χάριτα ("the grace of our God") and τὸν μόνον δεσπότην καὶ κύριον ἡμῶν Ἰησοῦν Χριστόν ("our only Master and Lord, Jesus Christ"). The grace of God and lordship of Christ are being undermined, calling for Jude's urgent letter.

σπουδήν > eagerness, diligence ‖ κοινῆς > common ‖ ἀνάγκην > necessity ‖ ἐπαγωνίζεσθαι > PMN, to contend ‖ ἅπαξ > once ‖ παρεισέδυσαν > 3PAAI, snuck in ‖ πάλαι > long ago ‖ προγεγραμμένοι > RPPMPN, ones having been written about ‖ ἀσεβεῖς > ungodly ‖ μετατιθέντες > PAPMPN, changing, perverting ‖ ἀσέλγειαν > licentiousness ‖ δεσπότην > master

Further Reading: Jude 1–4, 20–23
Todd Bolton

JUDE 5

⁵ ὑπομνῆσαι δὲ ὑμᾶς βούλομαι, εἰδότας ὑμᾶς ἅπαξ πάντα ὅτι Ἰησοῦς λαὸν ἐκ γῆς Αἰγύπτου σώσας τὸ δεύτερον τοὺς μὴ πιστεύσαντας ἀπώλεσεν.

CONTEXT:

After greeting his readers with their special status (vv. 1–2) and instructing them to contend for the faith amidst opposition (vv. 3–4), Jude spends the bulk of his letter reminding his readers of a necessary mindset while contending for the faith.

COMMENTARY:

In verses 5–19, Jude has one objective: Ὑπομνῆσαι δὲ ὑμᾶς βούλομαι ("Now I want to remind you"). The content of his reminder is two-fold and stated with the ὅτι clause in verse 5: Ἰησοῦς λαὸν ἐκ γῆς Αἰγύπτου σώσας τὸ δεύτερον τοὺς μὴ πιστεύσαντας ἀπώλεσεν ("Jesus, having saved a people out of Egypt, later destroyed those who did not believe"). Setting aside the startling notion that it was Jesus who saved a people out of Egypt (!), Jude's point in all the verses that follow is that God knows how to save the godly and punish the ungodly (cf. 2 Pt 2:9). He alternates between OT examples and contemporary illustrations. Notice the use of the demonstrative οὗτοι in verses 8, 10, 12, 14 (τούτοις), and 16 to shift the focus from OT examples to the readers' contemporaries. The situation Jude's readers find themselves in has been experienced throughout biblical history with the same result: God will judge the ungodly and keep His people. This truth frees God's people from concern with self-preservation and allows them to leave judgment with God (v. 9) and have mercy and seek to save others (vv. 20–23).

ὑπομνῆσαι > AAN, to remind ‖ ἅπαξ > once ‖ Αἰγύπτου > Egypt

Further Reading: Jude 5–19; 2 Peter 2:9
Todd Bolton

²⁰ ὑμεῖς δέ, ἀγαπητοί, ἐποικοδομοῦντες ἑαυτοὺς τῇ ἁγιωτάτῃ ὑμῶν πίστει, ἐν πνεύματι ἁγίῳ προσευχόμενοι, ²¹ ἑαυτοὺς ἐν ἀγάπῃ θεοῦ τηρήσατε προσδεχόμενοι τὸ ἔλεος τοῦ κυρίου ἡμῶν Ἰησοῦ Χριστοῦ εἰς ζωὴν αἰώνιον. ²² καὶ οὓς μὲν ἐλεᾶτε διακρινομένους, ²³ οὓς δὲ σῴζετε ἐκ πυρὸς ἁρπάζοντες, οὓς δὲ ἐλεᾶτε ἐν φόβῳ μισοῦντες καὶ τὸν ἀπὸ τῆς σαρκὸς ἐσπιλωμένον χιτῶνα.

CONTEXT:

Jude exhorts his readers to contend for the faith (v. 3) and gives them stabilizing reminders of God's track record of saving the godly and punishing the ungodly (vv. 5–19). He closes the main body of his letter with a final exhortation to his readers.

COMMENTARY:

Similar to his opening exhortation in verse 3, Jude draws his readers' attention with the use of the personal pronoun ὑμεῖς and the vocative ἀγαπητοί. He gives them four final commands: τηρήσατε (v. 21), ἐλεᾶτε (2x: vv. 22 & 23), and σῴζετε (v. 23). Several commentators have commented on the chiastic structure of Jude. Verses 20–23 correspond to verse 3 and spell out what Jude envisions when he tells his readers to contend for the faith. For Jude, contending for the faith entails keeping oneself in the love of God, showing mercy (to believers in verse 22 and likely unbelievers in verse 23), and seeking to save others out of the fire. Contending for the faith is primarily a battle for the souls of men and women. Doctrine plays a key role in keeping oneself in the love of God, expressed in the participial phrase ἐποικοδομοῦντες ἑαυτοὺς τῇ ἁγιωτάτῃ ὑμῶν πίστει ("building yourselves up in the most holy faith"). Doctrine fortifies by reminding the believer of their beloved and protected status (v. 2), the grace of God and lordship of Christ (v. 4), and God's ability to save and judge (vv. 5–19). This fortifying teaching then enables the believer to show mercy and seek to save. Like the Apostle John's teaching, truth is a vital means to walking in love.

ἐποικοδομοῦντες > PAPMPN, building up ‖ προσδεχόμενοι > PMPMPN, waiting for ‖ διακρινομένους > PMPMPA, wavering, doubting ‖ ἁρπάζοντες > PAPMPN, snatching away ‖ ἐσπιλωμένον > RPPMSA, stained ‖ χιτῶνα > garment

Further Reading: Jude 2–3

Todd Bolton

²² καὶ νῦν ἰδοὺ δεδεμένος ἐγὼ τῷ πνεύματι πορεύομαι εἰς Ἰερουσαλήμ, τὰ ἐν αὐτῇ συναντήσοντά μοι μὴ εἰδώς, ²³ πλὴν ὅτι τὸ πνεῦμα τὸ ἅγιον κατὰ πόλιν διαμαρτύρεταί μοι λέγον ὅτι δεσμὰ καὶ θλίψεις με μένουσιν· ²⁴ ἀλλ᾽ οὐδενὸς λόγου ποιοῦμαι τὴν ψυχὴν τιμίαν ἐμαυτῷ ὡς τελειῶσαι τὸν δρόμον μου καὶ τὴν διακονίαν ἣν ἔλαβον παρὰ τοῦ κυρίου Ἰησοῦ, διαμαρτύρασθαι τὸ εὐαγγέλιον τῆς χάριτος τοῦ θεοῦ.

CONTEXT:

Paul ministered in Ephesus for three years (Acts 19:1–10; 20:31). Stopping in Miletus on his way to Jerusalem, he called the elders of the Ephesian church to himself to offer parting words (Acts 20:17).

COMMENTARY:

Paul feels a deep sense of purpose in his trip to Jerusalem. He is going on account of his being *bound* by the Spirit. He is compelled even though he doesn't know what exactly the Lord has waiting for him, apart from chains and afflictions. Anticipating death, he reminds these Ephesian pastors that faithfulness to Jesus is more valuable than life itself. In this passage, ὡς with the infinitive denotes purpose, which is qualified by another infinitive. Paul has one goal in mind for the rest of his life: testify solemnly the gospel of the grace of God.

συναντήσοντα > FAPNPA, they will meet, encounter ‖ δεσμά > bonds ‖ τιμίαν > price, value ‖ τελειῶσαι > AAN, to complete, finish ‖ δρόμον > race

Further Reading: Acts 20:17-38
Jonathan D. Zavodney

²⁸ προσέχετε ἑαυτοῖς καὶ παντὶ τῷ ποιμνίῳ, ἐν ᾧ ὑμᾶς τὸ πνεῦμα τὸ ἅγιον ἔθετο ἐπισκόπους, ποιμαίνειν τὴν ἐκκλησίαν τοῦ θεοῦ, ἣν περιεποιήσατο διὰ τοῦ αἵματος τοῦ ἰδίου. ²⁹ ἐγὼ οἶδα ὅτι εἰσελεύσονται μετὰ τὴν ἄφιξίν μου λύκοι βαρεῖς εἰς ὑμᾶς μὴ φειδόμενοι τοῦ ποιμνίου, ³⁰ καὶ ἐξ ὑμῶν αὐτῶν ἀναστήσονται ἄνδρες λαλοῦντες διεστραμμένα τοῦ ἀποσπᾶν τοὺς μαθητὰς ὀπίσω ἑαυτῶν.

CONTEXT:

Paul offers parting words to the elders of the Ephesian church, which began in Acts 20:18.

COMMENTARY:

Paul's exhortation reveals the solemn heart of pastoral ministry. Pastors have been appointed ultimately *by the Holy Spirit* as shepherds of souls. Significant weight is added with Paul's relative clause ἣν περιεποιήσατο διὰ τοῦ αἵματος τοῦ ἰδίου. This group of people (i.e., the church) is unlike any other group. Paul supports his exhortation in verses 29–30. Pastors take great care because savage wolves are coming, and are already present in some sense, with corrupting doctrine. The solution, then, for pastors is to teach sound doctrine, being always on guard. If a pastor fails to shepherd, spurning the Spirit whose call appointed and spurring Christ whose blood purchased, the sheep will be devoured, and the shepherd will stand guilty.

ποιμνίῳ > flock || ἐπισκόπους > overseer || ποιμαίνειν > PAN, to shepherd || περιεποιήσατο > 3SAMI, purchased || ἄφιξιν > departure || λύκοι > wolves || βαρεῖς > savage, fierce || φειδόμενοι > PMPMPN, sparing || διεστραμμένα > PPPNPA, "things that have been corrupted" || ἀποσπᾶν > PAN, wrench, drag away

Further Reading: Acts 20:17–38
Jonathan D. Zavodney

NOVEMBER 24
ACTS 21:19–20

¹⁹ καὶ ἀσπασάμενος αὐτοὺς ἐξηγεῖτο καθ' ἓν ἕκαστον ὧν ἐποίησεν ὁ θεὸς
ἐν τοῖς ἔθνεσιν διὰ τῆς διακονίας αὐτοῦ. ²⁰ οἱ δὲ ἀκούσαντες ἐδόξαζον τὸν
θεόν, εἶπόν τε αὐτῷ· Θεωρεῖς, ἀδελφέ, πόσαι μυριάδες εἰσὶν ἐν τοῖς
Ἰουδαίοις τῶν πεπιστευκότων, καὶ πάντες ζηλωταὶ τοῦ νόμου
ὑπάρχουσιν.

CONTEXT:
Paul arrived in Jerusalem and met with Christians who received him gladly
(Acts 21:17).

COMMENTARY:
Paul's priority is to relay the great work God had done among the Gentiles.
Notice that he is explaining καθ' ἓν ἕκαστον, emphasizing the meticulousness
and perhaps enthusiasm with which he is sharing. The iterative imperfect verbs
(ἐξηγεῖτο and ἐδόξαζον) convey a continuous exchange as if to say *as Paul was
continually sharing one by one what God had done, the Jerusalem Christians were
continually glorifying God for each account*. Their response results in the recorded
words of verse 20 and following as they marvel at God's work. They then inform
Paul of the "tens of thousands" (μυριάδες) of Jews who had believed and were
zealous about keeping the law—not to earn their salvation, but as an expression
of their love and gratitude to God for saving them.

ἐξηγεῖτο > 3SIMI, he was explaining ‖ μυριάδες > tens of thousands ‖ ζηλωταί
> zealous

Further Reading: Acts 21:15–26
Jonathan D. Zavodney

328

⁶ ἐγένετο δέ μοι πορευομένῳ καὶ ἐγγίζοντι τῇ Δαμασκῷ περὶ μεσημβρίαν ἐξαίφνης ἐκ τοῦ οὐρανοῦ περιαστράψαι φῶς ἱκανὸν περὶ ἐμέ, ⁷ ἔπεσά τε εἰς τὸ ἔδαφος καὶ ἤκουσα φωνῆς λεγούσης μοι· Σαοὺλ Σαούλ, τί με διώκεις; ⁸ ἐγὼ δὲ ἀπεκρίθην· Τίς εἶ, κύριε; εἶπέν τε πρὸς ἐμέ· Ἐγώ εἰμι Ἰησοῦς ὁ Ναζωραῖος ὃν σὺ διώκεις.

CONTEXT:

Jews from Asia provoked the crowd to seize Paul, throw him out of the temple, and beat him (Acts 21:27–32). The Roman commander who intervened gave Paul permission to address the mob, which began with Paul's pre-Christian resumé (21:37–22:5).

COMMENTARY:

Paul starts with the contrastive conjunction δέ as he transitions to his supernatural conversion experience. His physical (Δαμασκῷ) and temporal (περὶ μεσημβρίαν) descriptions situate this occasion in history. The infinitive clause (ἐκ τοῦ οὐρανοῦ περιαστράψαι φῶς ἱκανὸν περὶ ἐμέ) serves as the subject of ἐγένετο. Paul describes his reaction first to the light and then to the voice. These eight words with which Jesus identified Himself, as the reader of Acts knows by now, are the eight words that radically changed Paul's life and work. It was an encounter with the risen Christ that transformed this man.

μεσημβρίαν > noon ‖ ἐξαίφνης > suddenly ‖ περιαστράψαι > AAN, shone around ‖ ἔδαφος > ground ‖ διώκεις > 2SPAI, persecute

Further Reading: Acts 21:37–22:21; 9:1–9; 26:9–18
Jonathan D. Zavodney

¹⁴ ὁμολογῶ δὲ τοῦτό σοι ὅτι κατὰ τὴν ὁδὸν ἣν λέγουσιν αἵρεσιν οὕτως λατρεύω τῷ πατρῴῳ θεῷ, πιστεύων πᾶσι τοῖς κατὰ τὸν νόμον καὶ τοῖς ἐν τοῖς προφήταις γεγραμμένοις, ¹⁵ ἐλπίδα ἔχων εἰς τὸν θεόν, ἣν καὶ αὐτοὶ οὗτοι προσδέχονται, ἀνάστασιν μέλλειν ἔσεσθαι δικαίων τε καὶ ἀδίκων ... ²¹ ἢ περὶ μιᾶς ταύτης φωνῆς ἧς ἐκέκραξα ἐν αὐτοῖς ἑστὼς ὅτι Περὶ ἀναστάσεως νεκρῶν ἐγὼ κρίνομαι σήμερον ἐφ' ὑμῶν.

CONTEXT:

The high priest Ananias and some other Jewish elders accused Paul before Tertullus, a Roman attorney (24:1–9). Paul then began his defense with an explanation that the Jews had no grounds for their accusations (vv. 11–13).

COMMENTARY:

After explaining the groundlessness of the Jewish accusations, Paul confesses that Judaism and Christianity are not entirely diverse religions. Christians believe in the God of Abraham, Isaac, and Jacob, that God disclosed in the law and the prophets (a synecdoche for the OT). Going further, Paul explains that both groups, Christians and Orthodox Jews, hope in a resurrection at the end of history. The difference between the two surfaces in verse 21: It is the belief that there was a resurrection *in the middle of history*, namely of Jesus Christ, the *first*born from the dead, that sets the two religions apart.

ὁμολογῶ > 1SPAI, confess ‖ αἵρεσιν > sect ‖ λατρεύω > 1SPAI, worship ‖ πατρῴῳ > of our fathers ‖ προσδέχονται > 3PPMI, they accept ‖ κρίνομαι > 1SPPI, I am on trial

Further Reading: Acts 24:10–21
Jonathan D. Zavodney

¹⁶ ἀλλὰ ἀνάστηθι καὶ στῆθι ἐπὶ τοὺς πόδας σου· εἰς τοῦτο γὰρ ὤφθην σοι, προχειρίσασθαί σε ὑπηρέτην καὶ μάρτυρα ὧν τε εἶδές με ὧν τε ὀφθήσομαί σοι, ¹⁷ ἐξαιρούμενός σε ἐκ τοῦ λαοῦ καὶ ἐκ τῶν ἐθνῶν, εἰς οὓς ἐγὼ ἀποστέλλω σε ¹⁸ ἀνοῖξαι ὀφθαλμοὺς αὐτῶν, τοῦ ἐπιστρέψαι ἀπὸ σκότους εἰς φῶς καὶ τῆς ἐξουσίας τοῦ Σατανᾶ ἐπὶ τὸν θεόν, τοῦ λαβεῖν αὐτοὺς ἄφεσιν ἁμαρτιῶν καὶ κλῆρον ἐν τοῖς ἡγιασμένοις πίστει τῇ εἰς ἐμέ.

CONTEXT:
Paul stood before King Agrippa to make his defense (Acts 26:1).

COMMENTARY:
In this description of his conversion experience compared to those earlier in Acts, Paul adds some detail about Jesus' unique commission to the Gentiles. Notice that in verse 16 he emphasizes sight (ὁράω, 3x). It is no coincidence, then, that the primary purpose for which God delivered and sent Paul is precisely ἀνοῖξαι ὀφθαλμούς. This restoration of sight results in the following τοῦ + infinitive clauses. Therefore, just as Paul saw the risen Jesus, so he is to show the risen Jesus to Jews and Gentiles in his preaching. The effect of his preaching will be that some, having their eyes open, will turn from Satan to God and will receive forgiveness and an inheritance.

ἀνάστηθι > 2SAAM, rise || στῆθι > 2SAAM, stand || ὤφθην > 1SAPI, appeared || προχειρίσασθαι > AMN, to appoint || ὑπηρέτην > servant || ὀφθήσομαι > 1SFPI, will appear || ἐξαιρούμενος > PMPMSN, delivering || ἄφεσιν > forgiveness || κλῆρον > portion || ἡγιασμένοις > RPPMPD, sanctified

Further Reading: Acts 26:1–23
Jonathan D. Zavodney

²² ἐπικουρίας οὖν τυχὼν τῆς ἀπὸ τοῦ θεοῦ ἄχρι τῆς ἡμέρας ταύτης ἔστηκα μαρτυρόμενος μικρῷ τε καὶ μεγάλῳ, οὐδὲν ἐκτὸς λέγων ὧν τε οἱ προφῆται ἐλάλησαν μελλόντων γίνεσθαι καὶ Μωϋσῆς, ²³ εἰ παθητὸς ὁ χριστός, εἰ πρῶτος ἐξ ἀναστάσεως νεκρῶν φῶς μέλλει καταγγέλλειν τῷ τε λαῷ καὶ τοῖς ἔθνεσιν.

CONTEXT:

Paul stood before King Agrippa to make his defense (Acts 26:1).

COMMENTARY:

In his defense, Paul makes abundantly clear that from the beginning he has stood firm with one message, doing so with God's help. This message, unlike spontaneous cult religions, has strong historical roots. Notice that Paul, in this case, does not simply state that Jesus must suffer and be raised. Rather, he poses it with two concise conditional clauses. The rhetorical effect is that he raises the level of urgency and also implies that Christ Himself is the One preaching through Paul: "*If* Christ was destined to suffer, *if* He was the first from the resurrection, *then* He would certainly declare openly the light both to the Jewish people and the Gentiles."

ἐπικουρίας > help ‖ τυχών > AAPMSN, attained ‖ ἐκτός > except ‖ παθητός > destined to suffer ‖ καταγγέλλειν > PAN, to proclaim

Further Reading: Acts 26:1–23
Jonathan D. Zavodney

²³ ταξάμενοι δὲ αὐτῷ ἡμέραν ἧκον πρὸς αὐτὸν εἰς τὴν ξενίαν πλείονες, οἷς ἐξετίθετο διαμαρτυρόμενος τὴν βασιλείαν τοῦ θεοῦ πείθων τε αὐτοὺς περὶ τοῦ Ἰησοῦ ἀπό τε τοῦ νόμου Μωϋσέως καὶ τῶν προφητῶν ἀπὸ πρωῒ ἕως ἑσπέρας. ²⁴ καὶ οἱ μὲν ἐπείθοντο τοῖς λεγομένοις οἱ δὲ ἠπίστουν.

CONTEXT:
Paul finally arrived in Rome (Acts 28:14)—the "ends of the earth" for Luke (1:8)—and the Jewish leaders said that they wanted to hear Paul's views (28:22).

COMMENTARY:
From the beginning of his conversion to the end of Luke's record, Paul has indeed been faithful to proclaim the kingdom of God. This comparative form of πολύς conveys the sense that these Jews were coming in great numbers. Paul's solemn testimony came particularly in his attempts to persuade these Jews from their own religious texts. Like most presentations of the gospel, the response is split between the believing and the unbelieving. Nevertheless, Paul persisted, urging from morning until evening.

ταξάμενοι > AMPMPN, set || ξενίαν > lodging place || ἐξετίθετο > 3SIMI, he was explaining || διαμαρτυρόμενος > PMPMSN, testifying || πρωῒ ἕως ἑσπέρας > morning until evening || ἐπείθοντο > 3PIPI, were convinced || ἠπίστουν > 3PIAI, disbelieved

Further Reading: Acts 28:23–31
Jonathan D. Zavodney

NOVEMBER 30
ACTS 28:25–27

²⁵ ἀσύμφωνοι δὲ ὄντες πρὸς ἀλλήλους ἀπελύοντο, εἰπόντος τοῦ Παύλου ῥῆμα ἓν ὅτι Καλῶς τὸ πνεῦμα τὸ ἅγιον ἐλάλησεν διὰ Ἠσαΐου τοῦ προφήτου πρὸς τοὺς πατέρας ὑμῶν ²⁶ λέγων· Πορεύθητι πρὸς τὸν λαὸν τοῦτον καὶ εἰπόν· Ἀκοῇ ἀκούσετε καὶ οὐ μὴ συνῆτε, καὶ βλέποντες βλέψετε καὶ οὐ μὴ ἴδητε· ²⁷ ἐπαχύνθη γὰρ ἡ καρδία τοῦ λαοῦ τούτου, καὶ τοῖς ὠσὶν βαρέως ἤκουσαν, καὶ τοὺς ὀφθαλμοὺς αὐτῶν ἐκάμμυσαν· μήποτε ἴδωσιν τοῖς ὀφθαλμοῖς καὶ τοῖς ὠσὶν ἀκούσωσιν καὶ τῇ καρδίᾳ συνῶσιν καὶ ἐπιστρέψωσιν, καὶ ἰάσομαι αὐτούς.

CONTEXT:

Paul testified solemnly about the kingdom of God to many Jews (Acts 28:23). Some believed, and some did not (v. 24).

COMMENTARY:

In response to certain Jews' unbelieving response, Paul quotes the famous words of the prophet Isaiah. He attributes the origin of the prophecy to the Holy Spirit and follows the Hebrew practice of placing a redundant participle to introduce the quotation. These unbelieving Jews are children of their unbelieving fathers who also possessed totally defective senses. The conjunction γάρ indicates the center of the problem: a defective heart. This unbelief stemming from a dull heart led to salvation being sent to the Gentiles (v. 28), the story which Luke has been detailing over the course of his two books.

ἀσύμφωνοι > in disagreement ‖ ἀπελύοντο > 3PIMI, departed ‖ εἰπόντος > AAPMSG, said ‖ πορεύθητι > 2SAPM, go ‖ ἀκοῇ > listening ‖ συνῆτε > 2SAAS, [not] understand ‖ ἐπαχύνθη > 3SAPI, became dull ‖ βαρέως > with difficulty ‖ ἐκάμμυσαν > 3PAAI, they closed ‖ μήποτε > lest

Further Reading: Acts 28:23–31
Jonathan D. Zavodney

ACTS 28:30-31

³⁰ ἐνέμεινεν δὲ διετίαν ὅλην ἐν ἰδίῳ μισθώματι, καὶ ἀπεδέχετο πάντας τοὺς εἰσπορευομένους πρὸς αὐτόν, ³¹ κηρύσσων τὴν βασιλείαν τοῦ θεοῦ καὶ διδάσκων τὰ περὶ τοῦ κυρίου Ἰησοῦ Χριστοῦ μετὰ πάσης παρρησίας ἀκωλύτως.

CONTEXT:

Paul arrived in Rome (Acts 28:14) and was testifying solemnly about the kingdom of God (v. 23).

COMMENTARY:

Paul stayed in Rome for at least two years in his own home, and he did not waste this time. Rather, he used his home (and time!) to welcome *all* those who were coming to him (substantive participle). In verse 31, the two active participles indicate the *way* he received them: he preached (κηρύσσων), and he taught (διδάσκων), and he did so with all boldness. Notice, moreover, that the great narrative of Luke-Acts ends with such a *hapax legomenon* as ἀκωλύτως. The powerful effect is that the message of God's kingdom and of Jesus Christ did not stop at the close of Acts but is still today traveling unhindered through the earth.

ἐνέμεινεν > 3SAAI, he stayed || διετίαν > two years || μισθώματι > rented home || ἀπεδέχετο > 3SIMI, welcomed || ἀκωλύτως > without hindrance

Further Reading: Acts 28:23–31
Jonathan D. Zavodney

DECEMBER 2
REVELATION 1:4 (PART 1)

⁴ Ἰωάννης ταῖς ἑπτὰ ἐκκλησίαις ταῖς ἐν τῇ Ἀσίᾳ· χάρις ὑμῖν καὶ εἰρήνη ἀπὸ ὁ ὢν καὶ ὁ ἦν καὶ ὁ ἐρχόμενος, καὶ ἀπὸ τῶν ἑπτὰ πνευμάτων ἃ ἐνώπιον τοῦ θρόνου αὐτοῦ.

CONTEXT:

John, a pastor to seven churches, begins a circular letter to them with the familiar greeting χάρις ὑμῖν καὶ εἰρήνη ("Grace to you and peace," 1:4), a common greeting in Christian letters of this era, which shows in the word χάρις both kindness and the grace found in the free gift Christ extends to us, giving his unmerited favor (or even "credit" or "benefit," cf. Luke 6:32–34), to which the only possible response is humble thankfulness. God is so concerned for these churches that he gives the "revelation of Jesus Christ" which "God gave him to show to his servants" (1:1) in the very "word of God and … the testimony of Jesus Christ" (1:2). We who read, hear, and keep the words of the prophecy are "blessed."

COMMENTARY:

Do I worship the God who is? ἀπὸ [θεοῦ] ὁ ὢν … ("from him who is …"). John by custom respects the holy and worthy God (cf. 4:8, 11) by not even daring to name him, instead referring to God by his *being* and *presence*. This God who is cares so much for his churches that he greets them with this concern, that they may be visited by grace and have peace with Him and with each other. "From him who is" alludes to Yʜᴡʜ, "I am who I am" (Ex 3:14). John's circumlocution gives us pause; we reflect on this extraordinary, high view of God, whom John and his faithful, enduring churches worship as the mighty (κράτος 1:6; cf. 1:8, 4:8, 11:17, "O Lord God the Almighty— κύριε, ὁ θεός, ὁ παντοκράτωρ" 15:3), whom we praise today not as one among many but as transcendent being. Do I serve the god I want, or the eternal, Almighty God who is?

ὢν > PAPMSN, being ‖ ἦν > 3SIAI, was ‖ ἐρχόμενος > PMPMSN, coming

Further Reading: Revelation 4; Hebrews 13:7–16
Ralph Slater

⁴ Ἰωάννης ταῖς ἑπτὰ ἐκκλησίαις ταῖς ἐν τῇ Ἀσίᾳ· χάρις ὑμῖν καὶ εἰρήνη ἀπὸ ὁ ὢν καὶ ὁ ἦν καὶ ὁ ἐρχόμενος, καὶ ἀπὸ τῶν ἑπτὰ πνευμάτων ἃ ἐνώπιον τοῦ θρόνου αὐτοῦ.

CONTEXT:

John witnesses to the seven churches *"from him who is ..."* God's presence in the historic church suggests the Francis Schaeffer title *The God Who is There*, which details our culture's roots and contrasts the ever-changing to God's eternal being as the source and sustainer of all that is and ever has been or will be. The "I am that I am" is our maker and is LORD, YHWH over all.

COMMENTARY:

Do I worship the God of history? The title (*"from him* who is and *who was ..."*) reveres God as eternal; from the beginning, God is consistent, himself testifying: "'I am the Alpha and the Omega,' says the Lord God" (1:8). At the new creation, God, seated on the throne, says the same, adding "the beginning and the end" (21:6). Jesus in Trinitarian unity echoes, "I am the Alpha and the Omega, the first and the last, the beginning and the end" (22:13). Jesus testifies to Laodicea, ἡ ἀρχὴ τῆς κτίσεως τοῦ θεοῦ (3:14). The Book of Life of the Lamb who was slain was written "before the foundation of the world" (13:8). In John 1:1-2, John as in his letter emphasizes ὁ λόγος ἦν πρὸς τὸν θεόν, καὶ θεὸς ἦν ὁ λόγος. οὗτος ἦν ἐν ἀρχῇ πρὸς τὸν θεόν (cf. 1 John 1:1). God is the source of history. Do we trust Christ as Lord who made all things?

Further Reading: 1 John 1:1-5, 2:13-14; John 17:24 (Jesus prays to the Father "you loved me before the foundation of the world"); Colossians 1:15-20
Ralph Slater

⁴ Ἰωάννης ταῖς ἑπτὰ ἐκκλησίαις ταῖς ἐν τῇ Ἀσίᾳ· χάρις ὑμῖν καὶ εἰρήνη ἀπὸ ὁ ὢν καὶ ὁ ἦν καὶ ὁ ἐρχόμενος, καὶ ἀπὸ τῶν ἑπτὰ πνευμάτων ἃ ἐνώπιον τοῦ θρόνου αὐτοῦ.

CONTEXT:

John witnesses to God's eternal and most real "being," not some static idea opposed to "becoming" as a form of progress. Indeed, "the LORD ... plans for [your] welfare and not for evil, to give you a future and a hope" (Jer 29:11). Our future is with God who eternally is, was from the beginning, and awaits us at the end (τέλος), when he is to come (1:8), a true end in eternal salvation (7:10).

COMMENTARY:

Do I anticipate the God who is to come? καὶ ὁ ἐρχόμενος is the third way John describes God; him "who is to come," a participle John's Gospel uses eight times. John here exhibits his faith in the incarnate Deity coming into the world! If God once came into the world as Jesus, God will again abide with us, coming to dwell with us (Rev 21:3). The "resurrection and the life" (Jn 11:25) is "coming soon" (22:7) to the persecuted, martyrs such as Antipas (2:13), and for those "about to suffer" (2:10, who exercise "love and faith and service and patient endurance," 2:19). Jesus promises, "I will keep you from the hour of trial that is coming on the whole world, to try those who dwell on the earth. I am coming soon" (3:10–11). The eternal God, who came to rescue his little ones, "is to come," revealing his grace. Do I believe in God as my future?

Further Reading: Revelation 1:1–8
Ralph Slater

⁵ τῷ ἀγαπῶντι ἡμᾶς καὶ λύσαντι ἡμᾶς ἐκ τῶν ἁμαρτιῶν ἡμῶν ἐν τῷ αἵματι αὐτοῦ— ⁶ καὶ ἐποίησεν ἡμᾶς βασιλείαν, ἱερεῖς τῷ θεῷ καὶ πατρὶ αὐτοῦ— αὐτῷ ἡ δόξα καὶ τὸ κράτος εἰς τοὺς αἰῶνας τῶν αἰώνων· ἀμήν.

CONTEXT:

Greetings, sent to the churches *from the faithful witness, the firstborn of the dead and ruler of the kings of the earth,* now honor Christ, the one who has freed us from sin by his blood. Being from God and the faithful, testifying Christ, gives the book its theme: the Lamb worthy because he shed his blood (cf. 5:6, the first "Lamb" reference) is with "him who sits on the throne" (5:13).

COMMENTARY:

Do I recognize my part in God's kingdom? John does *not* here show us that God made "all things" (as he will in Rev 14:7), but rather now reveals that Jesus has made *us* into *a kingdom, priests to his God and Father!* Here the Holy Spirit reveals through John the LORD saying that God's children "shall be to me a kingdom of priests and a holy nation" (Ex 19:4). Christ's kingdom comprises the historic "priesthood of believers" that John mentions several times as intimately connected to the Lamb's shed blood that ransoms people for God. In what way do you personally serve other Christians who are also part of this kingdom?

ἐποίησεν > 3SAAI, made || λύσαντι > AAPMSD, freed || ἱερεῖς > priests

Further Reading: Revelation 5:9–14, 12:10–11;
1 Peter 2:5, 9; Hebrews 12:22–24
Ralph Slater

REVELATION 2:7

⁷ ὁ ἔχων οὖς ἀκουσάτω τί τὸ πνεῦμα λέγει ταῖς ἐκκλησίαις. τῷ νικῶντι δώσω αὐτῷ φαγεῖν ἐκ τοῦ ξύλου τῆς ζωῆς, ὅ ἐστιν ἐν τῷ παραδείσῳ τοῦ θεοῦ.

CONTEXT:

This statement ὁ ἔχων οὖς ἀκουσάτω τί τὸ πνεῦμα λέγει ταῖς ἐκκλησίαις occurs near the end of each part of a circular letter from "him" (Jesus) to the seven churches (cf. 1:11). John asks us to "listen in" as each is from a figure who in John's vision is "in the midst of the lampstands ... like a son of man" (1:13), who can only be Jesus Christ, since only he has died and yet is "alive forevermore," holding the "keys of Death and Hades" (1:18).

COMMENTARY:

Do I hear what the Spirit says to the churches? The Bible: God's book given to churches; what would Jesus say about yours? Some hear with a listening ear to the Spirit. But some do not, neglecting the Spirit's ministry, confused about him. What is given ταῖς ἐκκλησίαις ("to the churches") is clearly given to *all* of them since it is plural, despite specifics addressed to one church at a time (e.g., "to the angel of the church in Ephesus" [2:1]). We do not need to guess the Holy Spirit's function in this and the other letters—his work is to reveal the truth about Jesus (Jn 15:26), the resurrected Lamb whose blood was shed to free us from our sins (1:5) and to make us Christ's kingdom for each other (1:6). Jesus' letters are read profitably in our churches (and by us), because they are revealed by the very same Spirit of God who gave us all the Scriptures.

ἔχων > PAPMSN, has ‖ ἀκουσάτω > 3SAAM, let him hear ‖ νικῶντι > PAPMSD, conquers ‖ δώσω > 1SFAI, will give ‖ φαγεῖν > AAN, to eat ‖ ξύλου > tree ‖ ἐστιν > 3SPAI, is ‖ παραδείσῳ > paradise

Further Reading: On the Spirit, see Psalm 51:11; Isaiah 59:14–21; 61:1; Daniel 7:13–14; Matthew 1:20; John 14:15–17, 26; 15:26–27; 16:5–15; on "tree of life," see Genesis 2:9; 3:22, 24; Revelation 22:2, 14, 19

Ralph Slater

¹¹ ἄξιος εἶ, ὁ κύριος καὶ ὁ θεὸς ἡμῶν, ὁ ἅγιος, λαβεῖν τὴν δόξαν καὶ τὴν
τιμὴν καὶ τὴν δύναμιν, ὅτι σὺ ἔκτισας τὰ πάντα, καὶ διὰ τὸ θέλημά σου
ἦσαν καὶ ἐκτίσθησαν.

CONTEXT:

Jesus' word to the churches continues in chapter 4. *Again*, the voice is "like a
trumpet" (4:1); *again*, John is "in the Spirit" (4:2), seeing the throne in heaven
and the one seated on it. Those surrounding it *never cease* praising: Ἅγιος ἅγιος
ἅγιος κύριος, ὁ θεός, ὁ παντοκράτωρ, ὁ ἦν καὶ ὁ ὢν καὶ ὁ ἐρχόμενος (4:8,
intensifying God's holiness; cf. Isa 6:3 LXX and 1:4, 8).

COMMENTARY:

Do I worship the holy and worthy God? "Worthy are you ..." (ἄξιος εἶ ...) states the
Lord's superlative worth; God is worthy to receive (λαβεῖν) glory, honor, and
power, for (ὅτι) our Lord (YHWH) has made all, calling it into existence from a
state of non-being. We honor and worship God as the source (cf. 3:14) of all,
including us—life is from God. "Axiology" studies all sorts of value judgments,
covering in ethics what is good and right and the meaning of beautiful in
aesthetics. But we do not assign God value, which is inherent in him as the most
real Being, "in the beginning," and now, and forever; nor do we worship God
because we judge him to be among a pantheon of valued beings. Instead, God is
worthy because the Divine Will made us a fact (διὰ τὸ θέλημά σου ἦσαν καὶ
ἐκτίσθησαν) long before the Divine Power gave us expression.

λαβεῖν > AAN, to receive ‖ εἶ > 2SPAI, are ‖ ἔκτισας > 2SAAI, created ‖
ἐκτίσθησαν > 3PAPI, are created

Further Reading: Genesis 1–3; Exodus 20:13; Psalm 139; Acts 17:28–29;
Revelation 7:9–12; 9:20–21; 10:6; 14:3–7
Ralph Slater

¹² ἄξιόν ἐστιν τὸ ἀρνίον τὸ ἐσφαγμένον λαβεῖν τὴν δύναμιν καὶ πλοῦτον καὶ σοφίαν καὶ ἰσχὺν καὶ τιμὴν καὶ δόξαν καὶ εὐλογίαν.

CONTEXT:

John takes us to a scene of the worthy Messiah's willful obedience—the Lamb standing "slain" three times underlines this (5:6, 9, 12), once with "the blood" by which he ransomed people for God "from every tribe and language and people and nation" (5:9). Why? So a diverse people form the "kingdom and priests to our God, and they shall reign on the earth" (5:10), a heritage (5:5) shared with no one else (5:4).

COMMENTARY:

Do I obey our incomparable Lamb? Earlier (cf. 4:11), God the Father received praise and the Spirit sent Jesus' messages to the churches. Here, the work of the Lamb is unique, yet he hears praise similar to the Father, to receive (λαβεῖν, as here) power (δύναμιν, in 5:12 and in 4:11) and wealth and wisdom and might and honor (τιμήν in both) and glory and blessing (δόξαν in both). In similarity there is both a Trinitarian, high Christology of the Lamb and a unique agency—only the Incarnate One of the line of Judah and the root of David can by obedience give himself up to death for the people of God's kingdom. God prepared the Lamb for a death and resurrection that uniquely suited Jesus, who modeled worthy obedience!

ἐστιν > 3SPAI, is || ἀρνίον > lamb || ἐσφαγμένον > RPPNSN, slain || λαβεῖν > AAN, to receive || εὐλογίαν > blessing

Further Reading: Revelation 6:1–17
Ralph Slater

REVELATION 6:10

¹⁰ καὶ ἔκραξαν φωνῇ μεγάλῃ λέγοντες· Ἕως πότε, ὁ δεσπότης ὁ ἅγιος καὶ ἀληθινός, οὐ κρίνεις καὶ ἐκδικεῖς τὸ αἷμα ἡμῶν ἐκ τῶν κατοικούντων ἐπὶ τῆς γῆς;

CONTEXT:
Opening the seals, the Lamb who was slain for us began to summon the various consequences of disobedience, such as partial famine (6:8), political (6:2) and social (6:4) division, and pestilent or violent death. The Lamb opens the fifth seal to show, at the heavenly altar, the souls of those slain for the word of God and for their witness (cf. 1:2, 9; 12:11, 17; 20:4).

COMMENTARY:
What consequence divine obedience? The souls of the martyrs, remarkably, do not appeal to stop the bloodshed; in these last days (cf. Acts 2:17, Heb 1:2) their number is yet incomplete (6:11). Rather, they appeal to the "Sovereign Lord, holy and true" (ὁ δεσπότης ὁ ἅγιος καὶ ἀληθινός) to judge and to avenge their blood. The emphasis on time (ἕως πότε ...; ἔτι χρόνον μικρόν, ἕως ... in 6:11) points to a delay in carrying out justice that nevertheless will be fulfilled despite divine patience. John strongly contrasts the divine obedience of the Lamb and his witnesses—and their *expectation* of God's sovereign justice for its holiness and truth (cf. 15:3-4, 16:5-6)—against the cowardly fear of the disobedient, who, no matter their social standing, expect the worst, not from us, but from him "who is seated on the throne, and from the wrath of the Lamb" (6:16). Do I obey the King?

ἔκραξαν > 3PAAI, cried out ‖ λέγοντες > PAPMPN, saying ‖ δεσπότης > Sovereign Lord ‖ κρίνεις > 2SPAI, judge ‖ ἐκδικεῖς > 2SPAI, avenge ‖ κατοικούντων > PAPMPG, dwelling

Further Reading: Zechariah 1:12; Deuteronomy 32:43; 2 Kings 9:7; Hosea 4:1-3; Genesis 9:5-7; Psalm 9; 79:9-10; Jeremiah 19
Ralph Slater

DECEMBER 10
REVELATION 7:9–10

⁹ μετὰ ταῦτα εἶδον, καὶ ἰδοὺ ὄχλος πολύς, ὃν ἀριθμῆσαι αὐτὸν οὐδεὶς ἐδύνατο, ἐκ παντὸς ἔθνους καὶ φυλῶν καὶ λαῶν καὶ γλωσσῶν, ἑστῶτες ἐνώπιον τοῦ θρόνου καὶ ἐνώπιον τοῦ ἀρνίου, περιβεβλημένους στολὰς λευκάς, καὶ φοίνικες ἐν ταῖς χερσὶν αὐτῶν· ¹⁰ καὶ κράζουσι φωνῇ μεγάλῃ λέγοντες· Ἡ σωτηρία τῷ θεῷ ἡμῶν τῷ καθημένῳ ἐπὶ τῷ θρόνῳ καὶ τῷ ἀρνίῳ.

CONTEXT:

John continues to contrast the wide diversity of every nation (ἔθνους), tribe (φυλῶν), people (λαῶν), and language (γλωσσῶν) he sees in heaven (cf. 5:9), among the great multitude who stand "before the throne and before the Lamb," as against all the fearful, who call to mountains and rocks to fall on them and hide them from God's face (6:16).

COMMENTARY:

Do I testify to the God who saves? The "white robes" (στολὰς λευκάς) of the faithful who stand before the throne and before the Lamb are, we later learn, washed and made white "in the blood of the Lamb" (7:14). Thus, it is by no means their own "great tribulation" (as in 7:14, ἐκ τῆς θλίψεως τῆς μεγάλης, "great tribulation"; the book's only other use, in 2:22, is due to unrepentant "adultery") that saves the cleansed multitude. Rather, in loud voice they cry out, identifying God, for the first time in the book, as the source not only of their being but of their final victory over death: "Salvation belongs to our God." In so doing the multitude again identifies the Lamb and God the Father sitting on the throne. John extends the datives—including the participle καθημένῳ—to show divine ownership of the whole plan of salvation (cf. Rev 19:1)! Do I likewise testify?

ἀριθμῆσαι > AAN, to count ‖ δύνατο > 3SIMI, was able ‖ ἑστῶτες > RAPMPN, standing ‖ περιβεβλημένους > RPPMPA, clothed ‖ στολάς > robes ‖ φοίνικες > palm branches ‖ κράζουσι > 3PPAI, cry out ‖ σωτηρία > deliverance, salvation ‖ καθημένῳ > PMPMSD, seated

Further Reading: Jonah 2:9; Deuteronomy 32:4–15; Zechariah 9:9, 12:7; Acts 4:12, 13:26, 47, 16:31; Romans 1:16; Revelation 3:4–5, 6:11
Ralph Slater

¹⁶ οὐ πεινάσουσιν ἔτι οὐδὲ διψήσουσιν ἔτι, οὐδὲ μὴ πέσῃ ἐπ' αὐτοὺς ὁ ἥλιος οὐδὲ πᾶν καῦμα, ¹⁷ ὅτι τὸ ἀρνίον τὸ ἀνὰ μέσον τοῦ θρόνου ποιμανεῖ αὐτούς, καὶ ὁδηγήσει αὐτοὺς ἐπὶ ζωῆς πηγὰς ὑδάτων· καὶ ἐξαλείψει ὁ θεὸς πᾶν δάκρυον ἐκ τῶν ὀφθαλμῶν αὐτῶν.

CONTEXT:

The final triptych of an interlude clearly meant to comfort faithful believers under the stress of persecution and threat of death, John receives verses voiced by a heavenly elder. Although unprotected from cultural pressure around them (cf. 7:14), those justified by the Lamb's blood will serve at God's throne, sheltered by the grace of YHWH.

COMMENTARY:

Am I grateful for my shepherding LORD? If "the LORD is my shepherd ... [and] he makes me lie down in green pastures" (Ps 23:1–2), then we shall indeed, as the "blessed ... dead who die in the Lord from now on, [find] rest from [our] labors" (Rev 14:13), "though I walk through the valley of the shadow of death" (Ps 23:4a). The second part of John's triptych (a three-fold panel of verse) comforts the sufferer with torments that will no longer need be endured: hunger, thirst, the sun or its scorching heat; both literal and metaphorical (cf. Matt 5:6, 11), e.g., the intense heat of persecution. The panel's third verse replaces tribulation's torment with the fruitful picture of the shepherd's guidance. Here the Lamb, seen "in the midst/middle of the throne," will properly guide those saved from persecution to springs of living water, when God will wipe away every tear from their eyes.

πεινάσουσιν > 3PFAI, will hunger || διψήσουσιν > 3PFAI, will thirst || πέσῃ > 3SAAS, will fall || ἥλιος > sun || καῦμα > burning heat || ἀρνίον > lamb || ποιμανεῖ > 3SFAI, will shepherd, lead || τὸ ἀνὰ μέσον τοῦ θρόνου > in the midst/middle of the throne || ὁδηγήσει > 3SFAI, will guide || πηγάς > springs || ἐξαλείψει > 3SFAI, will wipe || δάκρυον > tear

Further Reading: Psalm 2:9; Revelation 2:27, 12:5, 19:15; 21:4–6
Ralph Slater

³ καὶ ἄλλος ἄγγελος ἦλθεν καὶ ἐστάθη ἐπὶ τοῦ θυσιαστηρίου ἔχων λιβανωτὸν χρυσοῦν, καὶ ἐδόθη αὐτῷ θυμιάματα πολλὰ ἵνα δώσει ταῖς προσευχαῖς τῶν ἁγίων πάντων ἐπὶ τὸ χρυσοῦν τὸ ἐνώπιον τοῦ θρόνου.

CONTEXT:

The Apocalypse contains three sets of divine judgments against evil. Each set contains seven specific acts of judgment. The seventh judgment in each of the first two sets unleashes the following set. The first seven are referred to as the seal judgments.

COMMENTARY:

OT imagery is dominant in this section. The large altar was a place of judgment where animals were substituted to pay the price of sin. The small altar in the Holy Place was sprinkled with incense over the coals from the large altar, placing a sweet smell in the Holy Place. These coals, covered in the blood of the Lamb, were then sprinkled with the prayers of the saints and thrown upon a sinful world as a powerful judgment (v. 5).

ἦλθεν > 3SAAI, came || ἐστάθη > 3SAPI, stood || θυσιαστηρίου > altar || ἔχων > PAPMSN, having || λιβανωτόν > censer || χρυσοῦν > golden || ἐδόθη > 3SAPI, was given || θυμιάματα > incense || δώσει > 3SFAI, will offer || προσευχαῖς > prayers

Further Reading: Revelation 8:1–5

Thomas Hatley

²⁰ καὶ οἱ λοιποὶ τῶν ἀνθρώπων, οἳ οὐκ ἀπεκτάνθησαν ἐν ταῖς πληγαῖς ταύταις, οὐδὲ μετενόησαν ἐκ τῶν ἔργων τῶν χειρῶν αὐτῶν, ἵνα μὴ προσκυνήσουσιν τὰ δαιμόνια καὶ τὰ εἴδωλα τὰ χρυσᾶ καὶ τὰ ἀργυρᾶ καὶ τὰ χαλκᾶ καὶ τὰ λίθινα καὶ τὰ ξύλινα, ἃ οὔτε βλέπειν δύνανται οὔτε ἀκούειν οὔτε περιπατεῖν, ²¹ καὶ οὐ μετενόησαν ἐκ τῶν φόνων αὐτῶν οὔτε ἐκ τῶν φαρμάκων αὐτῶν οὔτε ἐκ τῆς πορνείας αὐτῶν οὔτε ἐκ τῶν κλεμμάτων αὐτῶν.

CONTEXT:

Even after the seal judgments (6:1–17; 8:1–5) and trumpet judgments (8:6–9:19) come upon those who remain on earth, there is still no repentance. As we will see, even as more judgments and conflicts follow in the coming chapters, no repentance is found.

COMMENTARY:

After multiple judgments, those left alive—literally, "the rest of mankind" (οἱ λοιποὶ τῶν ἀνθρώπων)—refuse to repent. Their preference over an acceptance of God's grace is to worship "the works of their hands." Ironically, it is not that these individuals refuse "to worship," but simply that they refuse to worship the one true God, the Creator of all things. Instead, they choose to worship demons (τὰ δαιμόνια) and idols (τὰ εἴδωλα) that cannot see or hear or walk.

ἀπεκτάνθησαν > 3PAPI, were [not] killed || πληγαῖς > plagues || μετενόησαν > 3PAAI, did [not] repent || προσκυνήσουσιν > 3PFAI, will [not] worship || χρυσᾶ > of gold || ἀργυρᾶ > of silver || χαλκᾶ > of bronze || λίθινα > of stone || ξύλινα > of wood || βλέπειν > PAN, to see || δύνανται > 3PPMI, are [not] able || ἀκούειν > PAN, to hear || περιπατεῖν > PAN, to walk || φόνων > murders || φαρμάκων > sorceries || πορνείας > sexual immoralities || κλεμμάτων > thefts

Further Reading: Revelation 9:1–21
Thomas Hatley

⁷ ἀλλ' ἐν ταῖς ἡμέραις τῆς φωνῆς τοῦ ἑβδόμου ἀγγέλου, ὅταν μέλλῃ σαλπίζειν, καὶ ἐτελέσθη τὸ μυστήριον τοῦ θεοῦ, ὡς εὐηγγέλισεν τοὺς ἑαυτοῦ δούλους τοὺς προφήτας.

CONTEXT:

In this passage, a "mighty angel" (10:1) sounds the seventh trumpet. With his right foot on land and his left foot on the sea, he speaks like a roaring lion (10:2, 3). This angel raises his hand and swears by Him who lives forever and ever, who created heaven and earth and the sea (10:4-6), that there would be no more delay.

COMMENTARY:

This verse articulates the reality that the Bible is one story—told by the Creator-Redeemer Himself—that anticipates a climactic conclusion with the second coming of Christ. The predicted plan of God is coming to an end, a reality that we will see developed further in the next few chapters of Revelation. This plan is referred to as a "mystery" (μυστήριον) because although it was promised initially in the OT, it has now been revealed in far greater detail in the NT. This plan will be fulfilled (or completed, ἐτελέσθη) as it was taught by God's prophets. As Christians, what a great hope we have!

ἑβδόμου > seventh || μέλλῃ > 3SPAS, is about to [blow his trumpet] || σαλπίζειν > PAN, to blow [his trumpet] || ἐτελέσθη > 3SAPI, fulfilled || μυστήριον > mystery || εὐηγγέλισεν > 3SAAI, proclaimed [as good news]

Further Reading: Revelation 10:1–11
Thomas Hatley

¹⁵ καὶ ὁ ἕβδομος ἄγγελος ἐσάλπισεν· καὶ ἐγένοντο φωναὶ μεγάλαι ἐν τῷ οὐρανῷ λέγοντες· Ἐγένετο ἡ βασιλεία τοῦ κόσμου τοῦ κυρίου ἡμῶν καὶ τοῦ χριστοῦ αὐτοῦ, καὶ βασιλεύσει εἰς τοὺς αἰῶνας τῶν αἰώνων.

CONTEXT:

Revelation 11:15 takes place after the two witnesses appear, die, are raised from the dead, and a great earthquake shakes the city (11:1-13). This verse introduces the "third woe" (11:14).

COMMENTARY:

God's response to the rejection of His witnesses and their message (11:1-13) is to demonstrate his power by raising these witnesses back to life (11:11). In 11:15, great voices (φωναὶ μεγάλαι) proclaim in heaven that the earthly kingdom—assumed to refer to the kingdom forfeited by Adam to the Serpent (cf. Gen 1-3)—will now be aligned under God's rule as part of His eternal kingdom. Notice in this verse, "He will reign (βασιλεύσει) ..." Is the antecedent "our Lord" (τοῦ κυρίου ἡμῶν) or "His Christ" (τοῦ χριστοῦ αὐτοῦ)? In other words, will *our Lord* reign forever, or will *His Christ* reign forever? Perhaps 1 Corinthians 15:24-28 provides some assistance in our understanding of this passage, where the Son turns the kingdom over to the Father. Following this announcement in Revelation 11:15, the twenty-four elders fall on their faces and worship the Lord God who is initiating His right to take possession of the earth and all the nations therein (11:16-19).

ἕβδομος > seventh ‖ ἐσάλπισεν > 3SAAI, sounded [his trumpet] ‖ ἐγένοντο > 3PAMI, there were ‖ λέγοντες > PAPMPN, saying ‖ ἐγένετο > 3SAMI, has become ‖ βασιλεύσει > 3SFAI, will reign ‖ εἰς τοὺς αἰῶνας τῶν αἰώνων > forever and ever

Further Reading: Revelation 11:15-19
Thomas Hatley

DECEMBER 16
REVELATION 12:11

¹¹ καὶ αὐτοὶ ἐνίκησαν αὐτὸν διὰ τὸ αἷμα τοῦ ἀρνίου καὶ διὰ τὸν λόγον τῆς μαρτυρίας αὐτῶν, καὶ οὐκ ἠγάπησαν τὴν ψυχὴν αὐτῶν ἄχρι θανάτου.

CONTEXT:

After the announced victory in 12:11, the earth is warned of a vindictive devil (v. 12) who has now been vanquished from heaven (v. 13) and seeks to wound the woman (likely Israel) and her children (vv. 15–17).

COMMENTARY:

In this passage, the woman with twelve stars appears to be the nation Israel (12:1–2). The "great red dragon" (12:3) or "that ancient serpent, who is called the devil and Satan" is certainly a reference to the deceiving serpent of Genesis 3:15. He seeks to devour the woman and her Child, the promised Offspring, the Christ. Revelation 12:11 provides a glimpse into the victory accessible by followers of Christ. How do these saints conquer (ἐνίκησαν)? Notice the repeated use of the preposition διά (by) that links the two concepts that provide victory: They conquered διά "the blood of the lamb" and διά "the word of his testimony." This victory is a result of Christ's accomplishment. It is ultimately because of the lamb's sacrifice that these saints "loved not their lives unto death." Why? Because they rejoiced in the greater reward yet to come.

ἐνίκησαν > 3PAAI, have conquered ‖ ἀρνίου > lamb ‖ μαρτυρίας > testimony ‖ ἠγάπησαν > 3PAAI, loved [not]

Further Reading: Revelation 12:1–17
Thomas Hatley

DECEMBER 17
REVELATION 13:9-10

⁹ εἴ τις ἔχει οὖς ἀκουσάτω. ¹⁰ εἴ τις εἰς αἰχμαλωσίαν, εἰς αἰχμαλωσίαν ὑπάγει· εἴ τις ἐν μαχαίρῃ ἀποκτανθῆναι αὐτὸν ἐν μαχαίρῃ ἀποκτανθῆναι. ὧδέ ἐστιν ἡ ὑπομονὴ καὶ ἡ πίστις τῶν ἁγίων.

CONTEXT:

The imagery of Revelation chapter 13 (specifically, the "beast") is similar to certain events in the book of Daniel—in particular, Daniel chapter 4. This beast speaks blasphemy and rules the nations. We are informed that all nations worship this beast and that he is powerful enough to make war with the saints and overcome them (Rev 13:7). A second beast is featured in 13:11-18. This beast has power to control almost every aspect of the lives of the people remaining on earth.

COMMENTARY:

In the fierce warfare of this battle against our Lord and his people, there is a principle given: God's saints will be rewarded for their patience, endurance, and faith. Notice the series of first-class conditional statements (protasis = εἰ + indicative), all of which make a logical connection and demonstrate a certain inevitability about God's plans:

> If anyone has an ear, let him hear.
> If anyone is to go to captivity, to captivity he goes.
> If anyone is to be slain by a sword, he must be slain by the sword.

Ultimately, this reality serves as a call for the ὑπομονή (endurance) and πίστις (faith) of the saints despite trials that might come. May we be characterized as those who stand firm in our faith, no matter the consequences!

ἔχει > 3SPAI, has || οὖς > ear || ἀκουσάτω > 3SAAM, let him hear || αἰχμαλωσίαν > captivity || ὑπάγει > 3SPAI, goes || μαχαίρῃ > sword || ἀποκτανθῆναι > APN, to be slain || ἐστιν > 3SPAI, is || ὑπομονή > endurance

Further Reading: Revelation 13:1-18
Thomas Hatley

¹³ καὶ ἤκουσα φωνῆς ἐκ τοῦ οὐρανοῦ λεγούσης· γράψον· μακάριοι οἱ νεκροὶ οἱ ἐν κυρίῳ ἀποθνήσκοντες ἀπ' ἄρτι. ναί, λέγει τὸ πνεῦμα, ἵνα ἀναπαήσονται ἐκ τῶν κόπων αὐτῶν, τὰ γὰρ ἔργα αὐτῶν ἀκολουθεῖ μετ' αὐτῶν.

CONTEXT:

This chapter begins with the Lamb of God standing with the 144,000 witnesses of the Lord who have taken the gospel to every part of the earth (14:1-5). Following this, several angels make proclamations regarding the Lord's divine judgment (14:6-7), the fall of Babylon (14:8), and those who worship the beast or take his mark (14:9-11). Finally, a voice from heaven announces blessings on those who die in the Lord.

COMMENTARY:

Those in the last days who die in the Lord are blessed and rewarded. Notice the specific language that is used in this passage: μακάριοι οἱ νεκροὶ οἱ ἐν κυρίῳ ἀποθνήσκοντες ἀπ' ἄρτι. This language of blessing (μακάριοι) appears at various places throughout Revelation (e.g., 1:3; 16:15; 19:9; 20:6; 22:7, 14). Additionally, it is reminiscent of Jesus' language in the Sermon on the Mount in Matthew 5:3-11. For example, "Blessed (μακάριοι) are the poor in spirit, for theirs is the kingdom of heaven" (5:3). Surely, this passage is a call to stand firm and faithful unto the Lord as we contemplate the reality that our deeds are never forgotten but follow us even beyond the grave (τὰ γὰρ ἔργα αὐτῶν ἀκολουθεῖ μετ' αὐτῶν).

ἤκουσα > 1SAAI, heard || λεγούσης > PAPFSG, saying || γράψον > 2SAAM, write || ἀποθνήσκοντες > PAPMPN, die || ἀπ' ἄρτι > from now on || ναί > indeed || λέγει > 3SPAI, says || ἀναπαήσονται > 3PFPI, may rest || κόπων > labors || ἀκολουθεῖ > 3SPAI, follow

Further Reading: Revelation 14:12-20
Thomas Hatley

⁵ καὶ μετὰ ταῦτα εἶδον, καὶ ἠνοίγη ὁ ναὸς τῆς σκηνῆς τοῦ μαρτυρίου ἐν τῷ οὐρανῷ.

CONTEXT:

We find in chapter 15 an example of how God's judgments begin with activity in heaven. The action is led by seven angels with seven final plagues. Standing on a sea of glass is a multitude of martyrs who play harps and sing the Song of Moses and of the Lamb. These are those believers who did not take the name or number of the Beast.

COMMENTARY:

Notice how the imagery in Revelation 15 is from the OT tabernacle and temple system of worship which included the teaching of God's acceptance through sacrifice and the disposition of his wrath through judgment. The word for temple or sanctuary (ναός) is sometimes used to describe the holy of holies in the tabernacle. That would fit this reference with its imagery of the tabernacle or "the tent" (τῆς σκηνῆς) of Moses. Notice how these last judgments come from the holy of holies and are carried by angels. Angels were part of the adornment of the holy of holies while only one man—the high priest—could enter the holy of holies with only one acceptable sacrifice.

εἶδον > 1SAAI, looked || ἠνοίγη > 3SAPI, was opened || ναός > sanctuary || σκηνῆς > tent || μαρτυρίου > witness

Further Reading: Revelation 15:1–5
Thomas Hatley

⁸ καὶ ἐγεμίσθη ὁ ναὸς καπνοῦ ἐκ τῆς δόξης τοῦ θεοῦ καὶ ἐκ τῆς δυνάμεως αὐτοῦ, καὶ οὐδεὶς ἐδύνατο εἰσελθεῖν εἰς τὸν ναὸν ἄχρι τελεσθῶσιν αἱ ἑπτὰ πληγαὶ τῶν ἑπτὰ ἀγγέλων.

CONTEXT:

In the context of this passage, the last set of seven judgments is about to begin. The seven angels have been given golden bowls full of the wrath of God to be poured out on the unbelieving and rebellious people still on the earth.

COMMENTARY:

God's glory and holiness are offended by rebellion. His stored wrath will be poured out. This passage gives us some understanding as to how and why He must destroy rebellion. Notice the specific word choice here: "The sanctuary was filled with smoke from the glory of God and from His *power* (δυνάμεως)." However, "No one *had the power* (ἐδύνατο; or 'was able') to enter the sanctuary ..." Here were find a contrast between the *power* (δυνάμεως) of God in the sanctuary (ναός) and the *power*—or lack thereof—(ἐδύνατο) of man in the sanctuary (ναός).

ἐγεμίσθη > 3SAPI, was filled ‖ ναός > sanctuary ‖ καπνοῦ > smoke ‖ ἐδύνατο > 3SIMI, was able, had the power ‖ εἰσελθεῖν > AAN, to enter ‖ τελεσθῶσιν > 3PAPS, were finished ‖ ἑπτά > seven ‖ πληγαί > plagues

Further Reading: Revelation 15:6–8
Thomas Hatley

¹⁵ ἰδοὺ ἔρχομαι ὡς κλέπτης. μακάριος ὁ γρηγορῶν καὶ τηρῶν τὰ ἱμάτια αὐτοῦ, ἵνα μὴ γυμνὸς περιπατῇ καὶ βλέπωσιν τὴν ἀσχημοσύνην αὐτοῦ.

CONTEXT:
This last set of judgments is similar to the plagues visited through Moses upon Pharaoh and Egypt. In this outpouring, the systems of Babylon are finally destroyed.

COMMENTARY:
In 16:15, the Lord anticipates His return, declaring that it will be sudden and without warning. Therefore, those who anticipate His coming must remain vigilant and pure. Notice the two present active participles describing this preparation: γρηγορῶν (staying awake) and τηρῶν (keeping or guarding). The point of this passage is that those who "stay awake" and "keep their garments" will never be put to shame. In this way, this passage is a call and a reminder to always be ready for Christ's return.

ἔρχομαι > 1SPMI, I am coming || κλέπτης > thief || γρηγορῶν > PAPMSN, stays awake || τηρῶν > keeping || ἱμάτια > garments || γυμνός > naked || περιπατῇ > 3SPAS, might [not] walk || βλέπωσιν > 3PPAS, might see || ἀσχημοσύνην > shamefulness (perhaps in this context a euphemism for genitals)

Further Reading: Revelation 16:1–16
Thomas Hatley

¹⁴ οὗτοι μετὰ τοῦ ἀρνίου πολεμήσουσιν καὶ τὸ ἀρνίον νικήσει αὐτούς, ὅτι κύριος κυρίων ἐστὶν καὶ βασιλεὺς βασιλέων καὶ οἱ μετ' αὐτοῦ κλητοὶ καὶ ἐκλεκτοὶ καὶ πιστοί.

CONTEXT:

Chapters 17 & 18 in the Apocalypse describe the judgment upon Babylon, the end-time rebellious city destined for doom. In contrast to that devastating destruction, Revelation 17:14 provides encouragement by noting that Christ will defeat those who oppose him.

COMMENTARY:

The term οὗτοι refers back to the earthly kings of verse 12 who give their power and authority to the beast (Antichrist figure) in verse 13. The two verbs, πολεμήσουσιν and νικήσει are in the future tense. At this time during the coming tribulation period the Antichrist and his underlings will make war against the Lamb (Christ). However, Christ will fully defeat them, a victory described graphically later in Revelation 19:11–21. Such destruction is the opposite of what believers will face. They are described with the three terms κλητοί, ἐκλεκτοί, and πιστοί and will be present with Christ as he wins the day, a strong encouragement for those whose hope is in Jesus.

ἀρνίον > lamb || πολεμήσουσιν > 3PFAI, will wage war || νικήσει > 3SFAI, will conquer || ἐστίν > 3SPAI, is || βασιλεύς > king || κλητοί > called || ἐκλεκτοί > chosen || πιστοί > faithful

Further Reading: Revelation 17:1–18
Mike Stallard

356

December 23
Revelation 18:20

²⁰ εὐφραίνου ἐπ᾽ αὐτῇ, οὐρανὲ καὶ οἱ ἅγιοι καὶ οἱ ἀπόστολοι καὶ οἱ προφῆται, ὅτι ἔκρινεν ὁ θεὸς τὸ κρίμα ὑμῶν ἐξ αὐτῆς.

CONTEXT:
At the destruction of Babylon, merchants are mourning the great loss (18:15–19). In contrast, those in heaven, the saints, apostles, and prophets, are commanded to rejoice over Babylon's downfall. This is in harmony with the four hallelujahs beginning the next chapter (19:1–6).

COMMENTARY:
Looking back upon Babylon, the text uses the verb form ἔκρινεν, which in this context suggests an accomplished judgment (in the tribulation period). God's perspective is different from most humans. He wants all who belong to him to adopt His posture toward the judgment. The use of all three terms—ἅγιοι, ἀπόστολοι, and προφῆται—forces the conclusion that no believer is to refuse the request. Notice the use of the imperative εὐφραίνου. In addition, the reason that believers are to rejoice is ὅτι (because) God has indeed judged. Two exceptional applications for believers emerge. First, it is possible at times in God's providence to celebrate the hurting of others, when it is tied to direct judgment from God. Second, God's ultimate judgments are not merely for his glory, although they lead to his praise (19:5). In 18:20, the judgment against Babylon is noted as ὑμῶν, implying that it has a direct purpose for believers. God in his judgment is doing something for those who believe, namely, avenging the blood of his people (cf. 18:24, 19:2).

εὐφραίνου > 2SPPM, rejoice ‖ οὐρανέ > heaven ‖ ἅγιοι > saint ‖ ἔκρινεν > 3SAAI, has judged ‖ κρίμα > judgment

Further Reading: Revelation 18:15–19:6
Mike Stallard

² ὅτι ἀληθιναὶ καὶ δίκαιαι αἱ κρίσεις αὐτοῦ· ὅτι ἔκρινεν τὴν πόρνην τὴν μεγάλην ἥτις ἔφθειρεν τὴν γῆν ἐν τῇ πορνείᾳ αὐτῆς, καὶ ἐξεδίκησεν τὸ αἷμα τῶν δούλων αὐτοῦ ἐκ χειρὸς αὐτῆς.

CONTEXT:

This causal statement is given right after the first of four "hallelujah statements" in 19:1–6. These statements send praise to the Lord for his judgments just stated upon Babylon in chapters 17–18. Such praise can only be proclaimed because God's ways are true and just.

COMMENTARY:

This remarkable declaration asserts that praise for God's judgments upon Babylon is possible because God's judgments can be described in two ways using the words ἀληθιναί (true) and δίκαιαι (just). Simply put, God is right when he appropriately judges the harlot of Babylon who destroyed so many lives with her immorality and killed many saints. God is the one who can righteously avenge the saints. In this light, passages such as these answer the question, "What gives God the right to pour out His wrath upon the earth?" Besides the themes of *Creator* (chapter 4) and *Redeemer* (chapter 5), the answer lies in the fact that those who undergo the end-time judgments of God deserve their fate. Christians can rejoice that God always does right.

ἀληθιναί > true || δίκαιαι > righteous, just || κρίσεις > judgments || ἔκρινεν > 3SAAI, has judged || πόρνην > harlot || μεγάλην > great || ἔφθειρεν > 3SIAI, was corrupting || πορνείᾳ > immorality, fornication || ἐξεδίκησεν > 3SAAI, has avenged or vindicated || αἷμα > blood || χειρός > hand

Further Reading: Revelation 15:1–4, 16:4–7, 19:1–6
Mike Stallard

⁶ μακάριος καὶ ἅγιος ὁ ἔχων μέρος ἐν τῇ ἀναστάσει τῇ πρώτῃ· ἐπὶ τούτων ὁ δεύτερος θάνατος οὐκ ἔχει ἐξουσίαν, ἀλλ᾽ ἔσονται ἱερεῖς τοῦ θεοῦ καὶ τοῦ Χριστοῦ καὶ βασιλεύσουσιν μετ᾽ αὐτοῦ τὰ χίλια ἔτη.

CONTEXT:

This verse is part of the section presenting the thousand-year reign of Christ (20:4–6) which follows the Second Advent with its attendant judgments (19:11–21). Prior to this statement, which affirms the happiness of those who reign with Christ, is the binding of Satan during this thousand-year time period (Rev 20:2–3).

COMMENTARY:

Those who are resurrected before the millennium constitute the first resurrection (v. 5). In verse 6, several descriptions are given for those who enjoy this first resurrection: (1) they are blessed, happy, or favored (μακάριος); (2) they are holy (ἅγιος) or separated unto God and away from sin; (3) they will never face the second death which has no power over them (cf. Rev 20:14–15); (4) they will be priests (ἱερεῖς) to God and Christ, which highlights their direct communion with the Lord; (5) they will reign with Christ for one thousand years, which focuses on their administrative rule on earth during that time. This group of favored or saved souls includes those martyrs of verse 4 but also encompasses all of the saved who have been glorified either through the rapture or by resurrection.

μακάριος > blessed || ἔχων > PAPMSN, having || μέρος > part || ἀναστάσει > resurrection || πρώτῃ > first || δεύτερος > second || ἔχει > 3SPAI, has || ἐξουσίαν > power, authority || ἔσονται > 3PFMI, will be || ἱερεῖς > priests || βασιλεύσουσιν > 3PFAI, will reign || χίλια > thousand || ἔτη > years

Further Reading: Revelation 20:1–10
Mike Stallard

DECEMBER 26
REVELATION 20:14–15

¹⁴ καὶ ὁ θάνατος καὶ ὁ ᾅδης ἐβλήθησαν εἰς τὴν λίμνην τοῦ πυρός. οὗτος ὁ θάνατος ὁ δεύτερός ἐστιν, ἡ λίμνη τοῦ πυρός. ¹⁵ καὶ εἴ τις οὐχ εὑρέθη ἐν τῇ βίβλῳ τῆς ζωῆς γεγραμμένος, ἐβλήθη εἰς τὴν λίμνην τοῦ πυρός.

CONTEXT:

In Revelation 20:10, the devil is justly thrown into the lake of fire for a final judgment that is endless. Revelation 20:11–15 follows with the sad truth that those who are unsaved and stand before God in their own insufficient righteousness will in the end join Satan in the lake of fire.

COMMENTARY:

In 20:14, death (θάνατος) may refer to the dead bodies of those who have been resuscitated to face this fateful Great White Throne judgment. If so, Hades (ᾅδης) would refer to the spirits of the unsaved which have been rejoined to their bodies. Thus, the entire person is cast into the lake of fire. Others see the reference to death and Hades as simple personification. At any rate, this is the portrayal of the end of death, the great enemy of the human race which God promises to eliminate for his people (Rev 21:4). The expression "lake of fire" stands in apposition to the "second death" so that the two expressions are equivalent. The Book of Life gives the list of those who know the Lord. The destiny of those without Christ, whose names are not in the book, is the lake of fire. Sadly, many Christians today do not take this passage seriously as motivation to share their faith with those whose future is utter darkness.

ᾅδης > Hades || ἐβλήθησαν > 3PAPI, they were thrown || λίμνην > lake || πυρός > fire || δεύτερος > second || ἐστιν > 3SPAI, is || εὑρέθη > 3SAPI, was found || βίβλῳ > book || γεγραμμένος > RPPMSN, having been written || ἐβλήθη > 3SAPI, was thrown

Further Reading: Revelation 20:11–15
Mike Stallard

⁴ καὶ ἐξαλείψει πᾶν δάκρυον ἐκ τῶν ὀφθαλμῶν αὐτῶν, καὶ ὁ θάνατος οὐκ ἔσται ἔτι οὔτε πένθος οὔτε κραυγὴ οὔτε πόνος οὐκ ἔσται ἔτι, ὅτι τὰ πρῶτα ἀπῆλθαν.

CONTEXT:

This verse is part of the marvelous and beautiful description of the New Heaven, New Earth and New Jerusalem (the eternal state) given in Revelation 21:1–22:5. The full presence of the Triune God (21:3) leads to the removal of death and the curse (21:4–5). This takes place after the millennium of Revelation 20. Believers from every dispensation will enter into this ultimate time of kingdom reality where all things are made right.

COMMENTARY:

The opening clause of this verse is a partial quote from Isaiah 25:8 and repeats the words from Revelation 7:17. The future verb "he (God) will wipe away" (ἐξαλείψει) launches this precious promise. All tears are removed. There are no unhappy tears on anyone's face. Part of the reason this can be so is that there will be (ἔσται) no more death. The great enemy will be removed. Further, a series of other negatives (mourning, crying, and pain) will also be taken away. These negatives are joined together by a series of conjunctions (οὔτε = nor) highlighting the completion of God's promise essentially to remove the curse. The verse finishes with an all-encompassing and summarizing promise: "the first things (τὰ πρῶτα) have passed away (ἀπῆλθαν)." This last verb (an aorist) looks at all the things in the verse from the vantage point of accomplishment—the viewpoint of a believer standing in the eternal state without all the shackles of a life under the curse. The earlier verbs in 21:4 are future pointing to the hope of those who live now under the curse as did the original readers of the Apocalypse. It is important for believers to live now with confidence and hope in light of the greatest promise that God has given.

ἐξαλείψει > 3SFAI, will wipe away ‖ δάκρυον > tear ‖ ὀφθαλμῶν > eyes ‖ ἔσται > 3SFMI, will be ‖ πένθος > mourning ‖ κραυγή > crying ‖ πόνος > pain ‖ πρῶτα > first things ‖ ἀπῆλθαν > 3PAAI, have passed away

Further Reading: Revelation 21:1–27
Mike Stallard

DECEMBER 28
REVELATION 21:22

²² καὶ ναὸν οὐκ εἶδον ἐν αὐτῇ, ὁ γὰρ κύριος ὁ θεὸς ὁ παντοκράτωρ ναὸς αὐτῆς ἐστιν καὶ τὸ ἀρνίον.

CONTEXT:

This verse continues to give the description of the beautiful New Jerusalem that began in 21:9 and ends in 22:5. The statement alerts the reader to what may be a surprising fact about this city—no temple can be seen.

COMMENTARY:

It is quite appropriate that the text uses the word ναός for temple instead of ἱερόν, the latter being the term for the entire temple mount compound. But ναός refers to the inner sanctum of the temple proper—the edifice that contained the Holy of Holies where the Ark of the Covenant was placed. In this context, Revelation 21:22 highlights that term to emphasize the ultimate purpose of the temple to be a place where the presence of God could be localized and expressed (as it was on the Day of Atonement). In place of an earthly edifice, God's presence in the New Jerusalem is represented by an absolute fullness never before experienced by believers (see Rev 21:3). Our experience of God will be direct, not indirect, as we stand face to face with our Creator. Another feature of this text is that the Lamb (ἀρνίον) who is Christ, is also the temple. This implies Christ's equality with the Lord God Almighty (ὁ ... κύριος ὁ θεὸς ὁ παντοκράτωρ). Believers will also enjoy forever the presence of God through Christ the Savior.

ναόν > temple || εἶδον > 1SAAI, saw || παντοκράτωρ > Almighty || ἐστιν > 3SPAI, is || ἀρνίον > lamb

Further Reading: Revelation 21:22–22:5
Mike Stallard

⁵ καὶ νὺξ οὐκ ἔσται ἔτι καὶ οὐκ ἔχουσιν χρείαν φωτὸς λύχνου καὶ φωτὸς ἡλίου, ὅτι κύριος ὁ θεὸς φωτίσει ἐπ᾽ αὐτούς, καὶ βασιλεύσουσιν εἰς τοὺς αἰῶνας τῶν αἰώνων.

CONTEXT:

This verse is the last one in the description of the New Jerusalem that began in 21:9. What follows 22:5 is the epilogue to the Apocalypse. The preceding verses (22:3-4) restate the earlier verses (Rev 21:3-4) which highlight the end of the curse and the presence of God.

COMMENTARY:

There are two main thoughts in this verse. First, there will be no night (νύξ) in the New Jerusalem. The explanation for this is that the saints at that time will possess no need (χρείαν) for light either from a lamp or from the sun. The reason is because (ὅτι) the Lord God illumines (φωτίσει) them. Second, the verse teaches that the saints will reign forever. The term *forever* is the Greek expression εἰς τοὺς αἰῶνας τῶν αἰώνων (literally—"unto the ages of the ages"), a common way to speak of forever. This means that the saints do not just reign for the thousand years of the millennium but throughout the eternal state as well. The ultimate destiny of the saints is both an activity (reigning) and enjoyment (the light of the Lord). Again, this truth gives another reason to live confidently in the here and now in spite of all circumstances.

νύξ > night || ἔσται > 3SFMI, will be || ἔχουσιν > 3PPAI, will have || χρείαν > need || φωτός > light || λύχνου > lamp || ἡλίου > sun || φωτίσει > 3SFAI, will illumine || βασιλεύσουσιν > 3PFAI, will reign || εἰς τοὺς αἰῶνας τῶν αἰώνων > forever and ever

Further Reading: Revelation 22:1-5
Mike Stallard

¹⁷ καὶ τὸ πνεῦμα καὶ ἡ νύμφη λέγουσιν· ἔρχου. καὶ ὁ ἀκούων εἰπάτω·
ἔρχου. καὶ ὁ διψῶν ἐρχέσθω, ὁ θέλων λαβέτω ὕδωρ ζωῆς δωρεάν.

CONTEXT:

This verse is part of the epilogue of Revelation (22:6–21) giving the "last of the
last things." This invitation to come to Jesus is followed by a warning to those
who would tamper with the biblical text (22:18–19), a promise from Jesus that
he is returning quickly (22:20), a prayer for Jesus to return (22:20), and a
benediction of grace (22:21).

COMMENTARY:

This passage can rightly be called the last invitation in the Bible. In the first
clause, the Spirit (πνεῦμα) is the Holy Spirit (no other option fits) and the bride
(νύμφη) appears to be the Church. Both the Holy Spirit and the Church issue an
imperative—"Come!" While some scholars see this as an imploring for Christ to
come (see the prayer "Come, Lord Jesus" later in Rev 22:20), it is best, in light of
the two later clauses in the verse, to see the imperative as inviting people to
come to faith in Christ, the one who can deliver the soul. Although the chapter
is written to believers, the appeal is broader. The second clause appeals to those
hearing the words, challenging them to come. The last clause notes the freeness
of the gospel invitation in two ways. First, the appeal is made to those who are
willing (ὁ θέλων) to take (λαβέτω) salvation. Second, this salvation is described
as the "water of life" (ὕδωρ ζωῆς) which is to be taken "without cost" (δωρεάν).
Thus, the last gospel invitation in the Bible emphasizes the grace (note 22:21) of
God and not salvation by works.

νύμφη > bride || λέγουσιν > 3PPAI, say || ἔρχου > 2SPMM, come || ἀκούων >
PAPMSN, the one who hears || εἰπάτω > 3SAAM, let [the one who hears] say ||
διψῶν > PAPMSN, the one who is thirsty || ἐρχέσθω > 3SPMM, let [the one who
is thirsty] come || θέλων > PAPMSN, the one who wishes || λαβέτω > 3SAAM, let
[the one who wishes] take || ὕδωρ > water || δωρεάν > freely, without cost

Further Reading: Revelation 22:17–21
Mike Stallard

²⁰ λέγει ὁ μαρτυρῶν ταῦτα· ναί, ἔρχομαι ταχύ. Ἀμήν, ἔρχου κύριε Ἰησοῦ.

CONTEXT:

It is highly significant that, apart from the closing benediction of Revelation 22:21, the last statement of the Bible is a prayer for the Lord Jesus to return to earth. The Apocalypse starts with a portrait of Christ (chapter 1) followed by instruction for the seven churches to live in the light of what is to come (chapters 2–3) and a horrific earthly tribulation that precedes the coming of Christ (chapters 4–19). Everything points to Christ's return (chapter 19) and the establishment of his millennial kingdom and the eternal state (chapters 20–22).

COMMENTARY:

The one who testifies (ὁ μαρτυρῶν) is clearly the Lord Jesus as the prayer at the end of the verse reveals. Christ gives witness to "these things" (ταῦτα) which, in light of the focus on the entire book of Revelation given in 22:18–19, must refer to the entire vision of the Apocalypse. Of course, the book draws the reader continually to the Second Coming of Christ and beyond as he establishes his forever kingdom (millennium plus eternal state). Jesus affirms the promise to return in the second clause which reminds of the earlier promise in the Upper Room Discourse (Jn 14:3). The granted assurance is not just that he is coming back to earth but that he is coming *quickly* (ταχύ). This thought should be interpreted in terms of an open-ended nearness to the eschaton, although a good case can be made for the idea of suddenness of the events when the eschaton begins. The final clause gives the prayer of John for the Lord Jesus to come which is a valid prayer for any believer. This should silence those Christians who say that any focus on Christ's return detracts from the believer's living for today (cf. 1 Pt 1:13).

λέγει > 3SPAI, says || μαρτυρῶν > PAPMSN, the one who testifies || ναί > yes || ἔρχομαι > 1SPMI, I am coming || ταχύ > quickly || ἔρχου > 2SPMM, come

Further Reading: Revelation 19:11–16
Mike Stallard

CONTRIBUTOR BIOGRAPHIES

David L. Allen (PhD, University of Texas) is the founder of Preaching Coach, a ministry for pastors and Bible teachers to sharpen preaching and teaching skills. He is also the Distinguished Visiting Professor of Practical Theology and Dean of the Adrian Rogers Center for Biblical Preaching at Mid-America Baptist Theological Seminary in Cordova, TN. **Hebrews 1–5.**

Jared M. August (PhD, Baptist Bible Seminary) is Associate Professor of New Testament & Greek at Northeastern Baptist College in Bennington, VT. He has published articles in journals such as *Bibliotheca Sacra, Bulletin for Biblical Research, Themelios,* and *Tyndale Bulletin.* **Editor, Matthew 1–7; 17–28.**

Mark H. Ballard (PhD, Southeastern Baptist Theological Seminary) is Founding President and Professor of Applied Theology & Church Planting at Northeastern Baptist College in Bennington, VT. **2 Timothy.**

Todd Bolton (MDiv, The Cornerstone Seminary) serves as Associate Pastor of Valley Bible Church in Hercules, CA. He is also Professor of Biblical Languages at The Cornerstone Bible College and Seminary in Vallejo, CA. **2 John, 3 John, Jude.**

Douglas Brown (PhD, Trinity Evangelical Divinity School) is Seminary Dean and Director of the Master of Divinity Program at Faith Baptist Bible College and Theological Seminary in Ankeny, Iowa. **Acts 1–8.**

Jared Compton (PhD, Trinity Evangelical Divinity School) is Assistant Professor of New Testament and Greek at Bethlehem College and Seminary in Minneapolis, MN, and the author of *Psalm 110 and the Logic of Hebrews* (T&T Clark, 2015). **Hebrews 6–13.**

Aaron Contino (MA, Baptist Bible Seminary) ministers through preaching and teaching at The Blue Church, a healthy small church in the suburbs of Philadelphia, PA. He is currently a Doctor of Ministry student at Baptist Bible Seminary (Biblical Exposition). **John 1–12.**

Wayne Cornett (PhD, Mid-America Baptist Theological Seminary) is Associate Dean of Graduate Programs and Chairman of the Department of New Testament and Greek at Mid-America Baptist Theological Seminary in Cordova, TN. **James.**

Martin M. Culy (PhD, Baylor University) has served as Bible translator, college and seminary professor, pastor, and church planter. He is the founding editor of the Baylor Handbook on the Greek New Testament commentary series and has authored numerous books. **1 John.**

Neal Cushman (PhD, Baptist Bible Seminary) is Dean of Bob Jones University Seminary in Greenville, SC. **Acts 9–19.**

Thomas K. Dailey (PhD, Baptist Bible Seminary) is Professor of New Testament at Virginia Beach Theological Seminary in Virginia Beach, VA. **1 Timothy.**

Roger G. DePriest (PhD, Baptist Bible Seminary) is Faculty Associate at Virginia Beach Theological Seminary in Virginia Beach, VA, and Executive Director at Grace Biblical Counseling Ministry. **John 13–21.**

Joseph D. Fantin (PhD, Dallas Theological Seminary; PhD, University of Sheffield) teaches New Testament at Dallas Theological Seminary. His research interests include the Gospel of John, Hebrews, Greek language and linguistics, exegetical method, and the first-century world as it contributes to understanding the New Testament. **Romans 12–16.**

Candi Finch (PhD, Southwestern Baptist Theological Seminary) is Associate Dean of the College at Mid-America, Dean of Women, and Associate Professor of Women's Studies in Theology at Mid-America Baptist Theological Seminary in Cordova, TN. **Galatians.**

Russell Fuller (PhD, Hebrew Union College), Director of Theology Classroom, teaches online the core of the theological curriculum: Theology, Old Testament, New Testament, Hebrew, Greek, and Pastoral Ministries. You can reach him at www.russelltfuller.com. **1 Thessalonians.**

Paul A. Hartog (PhD, Loyola University Chicago) is Professor of Theology at Faith Baptist Theological Seminary in Ankeny, Iowa. He is the author of *Polycarp and the New Testament* (Mohr Siebeck), *Polycarp's Epistle to the Philippians and the Martyrdom of Polycarp* (Oxford University Press), and *Calvin on the Death of Christ* (James Clarke). **2 Corinthians 7–13.**

Thomas Hatley (DMin, Liberty Baptist Theological Seminary) has served as pastor at Immanuel Baptist Church in Rogers, Arkansas since 1992. **Revelation 8–16.**

Jeff Kimble (BA, State University of New York) is a retired Christian and public school educator who serves as a layperson in the Conservative Congregational Christian Conference (4Cs). He earned his A.S. in Business and English (1994) and B.A. in History with a concentration in the history of the Christian tradition (2015) from the State University of New York Empire State College. **Colossians.**

Markus T. Klausli (PhD, Dallas Theological Seminary) is Professor for New Testament and Greek at Columbia Biblical Seminary in Columbia, SC where he also serves as the mentor for the BA-MDiv program. He is a member of the Evangelical Theological Society and has research interests in the General Epistles. **Titus, Philemon.**

Randy A. Leedy (PhD, Bob Jones University) was for many years the lead Greek professor at Bob Jones University Seminary, Greenville SC. His work in creating the Greek New Testament sentence diagrams for BibleWorks® software has led to his current service promoting sentence diagramming as a valuable tool for Greek exegesis and pedagogy (www.NTGreekGuy.com). **2 Corinthians 1–6.**

J. James Mancuso (MALS, Syracuse University) has been active in the field of librarianship since 1977, serving as a theological librarian at Christian colleges since 2000. He holds a bachelor's degree in Linguistics, and a master's degree in Library Science, and studied New Testament Greek at Mid-America Baptist Seminary. **Matthew 8–16.**

Eric M. McConnell (MA, Piedmont International University) is the Lead Pastor of Suncoast Baptist Church in Port Charlotte, Florida, and an adjunct professor at Trinity Baptist College in Jacksonville, Florida. Additionally, Eric is a PhD candidate at Baptist Bible Seminary at Clarks Summit University. **Luke 1–13.**

Donald C. McIntyre (MAR, Liberty University) is a Southern Baptist minister who has served multiple rural churches in interim pastor roles and has most recently served as a pastor in central PA. He is a PhD candidate at Liberty University and concurrently a PhD student at Baptist Bible Seminary. **2 Thessalonians.**

Tim Miller (PhD, Westminster Theological Seminary; PhD Midwestern Baptist Theological Seminary) serves as Associate Professor of New Testament at Detroit Baptist Theological Seminary. With previous experience as an assistant pastor in Philadelphia, he is actively involved in pulpit supply with churches in the Detroit area. **Luke 14–24.**

Mark A. Mills (PhD, Baptist Bible Seminary) serves as an adjunct professor of intermediate and advanced Greek at Chafer Theological Seminary, a group leader of men at the G3 Expository Workshops, and an elder and teacher at First Baptist Church of Lindale, Texas. **1 Peter, 2 Peter.**

Evan P. Pietsch (EdD, The Southern Baptist Theological Seminary) is an enterprise business leader, an adjunct instructor of business for Boyce College, and Garrett Fellow for systematic theology and leadership courses at The Southern Baptist Theological Seminary. He has delivered conference sessions for the *Society of Professors in Christian Education* (SPCE). **1 Corinthians 13–16.**

R. Vivian Pietsch (EdD, The Southern Baptist Theological Seminary) is a church ministry leader, Garrett Fellow for systematic theology, discipleship, and leadership, and a teacher of women's Bible studies who seeks to teach deep theological truths in an accessible and engaging format. She has delivered conference sessions for the *Society of Professors in Christian Education* (SPCE). **1 Corinthians 9–12.**

Nicholas G. Piotrowski (PhD, Wheaton College) serves as the President and Academic Dean of Indianapolis Theological Seminary where he also teaches New Testament. He has been married to Cheryl for over 15 years and is the father of Silas and Andreas. **Romans 1–5.**

Charlie Ray III (PhD, New Orleans Baptist Theological Seminary) is Assistant Professor of New Testament and Greek and Associate Dean of Biblical Studies at New Orleans Baptist Theological Seminary. Charlie's research has focused on the use of the OT in the NT, particularly how the use of the OT in the NT informs the preaching of the NT today. He currently serves as one of the pastors at Immanuel Community Church. **Romans 6–11.**

Jonathan Rinker (PhD, Baptist Bible Seminary) is Associate Professor and Chair of the Bible/Theology Department at Appalachian Bible College, and a pastor of a local church. He is writing the Gospel of Mark volume for the *New Testament Exposition Commentary* (RBP). **Mark 11–16.**

Trent A. Rogers (PhD, Loyola University Chicago) is Assistant Professor of New Testament and Greek and Dean of the School of Biblical and Theological Studies at Cedarville University. His teaching and publication interests include New Testament, Greek, and Biblical Theology. **1 Corinthians 1–8.**

Ralph Slater (M.A., University of Rhode Island) is Associate Editor at Northeastern Baptist Press. Ralph enjoys mentoring, writing, editing, and teaching various classes. **Revelation 1–7.**

Wayne T. Slusser (PhD, Baptist Bible Seminary) is Dean and Professor of New Testament and Greek at Baptist Bible Seminary in Clarks Summit, Pennsylvania. Dr. Slusser produces a weekly blog, "Greek for a Week," at www.NTresources.com that offers exegetical insights and strategies to learn, retain or grow one's knowledge of New Testament Greek. **Mark 1–10.**

Mike Stallard (PhD, Dallas Theological Seminary) is Vice President of International Ministries at Friends of Israel. He previously served as Dean and Director of PhD Studies at Baptist Bible Seminary. **Revelation 17–22.**

William C. Varner (EdD, Temple University) is Professor of Biblical Studies & Greek at The Master's University. He has authored more than a dozen books, including an exegetical commentary on Philippians, and over a hundred journal and magazine articles. **Philippians.**

John Vo (PhD, Baptist Bible Seminary) is Lead Pastor at Truth Baptist Church, South Windsor, CT, and adjunct professor at Baptist Bible Seminary. **Ephesians.**

Jonathan D. Zavodney (MDiv, Indianapolis Theological Seminary) serves as the assistant to the president at Indianapolis Theological Seminary. He has a passion to provide theological education to local churches around the world, especially the training of pastors. **Acts 20–28.**

www.ingramcontent.com/pod-product-compliance
Lightning Source LLC
Chambersburg PA
CBHW021700120626
46545CB00004B/1335